BIOLEXICON
A Guide to the Language of Biology

BIOLEXICON
A Guide to the Language of Biology

By

CHARLES BLINDERMAN

Clark University
Worcester, Massachusetts

Chiropteran, a Bat
from Greek *chiro-,* hand + *pteran,* wing

CHARLES C THOMAS • PUBLISHER
Springfield • Illinois • U.S.A.

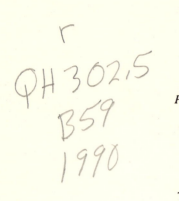

Published and Distributed Throughout the World by

CHARLES C THOMAS • PUBLISHER
2600 South First Street
Springfield, Illinois 62794-9265

© *1990 by* CHARLES C THOMAS • PUBLISHER

ISBN 0-398-05671-4

Library of Congress Catalog Card Number: 90-10765

With THOMAS BOOKS *careful attention is given to all details of manufacturing
and design. It is the Publisher's desire to present books that are satisfactory as to their
physical qualities and artistic possibilities and appropriate for their particular use.*
THOMAS BOOKS *will be true to those laws of quality that assure a good name
and good will.*

Printed in the United States of America
SC-R-3

Library of Congress Cataloging-in-Publication Data

Blinderman, Charles, 1931–
    Biolexicon : a guide to the language of biology / by Charles
Blinderman.
        p. cm.
    Includes bibliographical references.
    ISBN 0-398-05671-4
    1. Biology—Terminology. 2. English language—Etymology.
I. Title.
    [DNLM: 1. Biology—terminology. 2. Nomenclature. QH 83.5 B648b]
QH302.5.B59 1990
574′.014—dc20
DNLM/DLC
for Library of Congress   90-10765
                                                            CIP

PREFACE

Biolexicon is a guide for students and others who need or want to learn the meanings of words in the vocabulary of biology, especially in the vocabulary of medicine. The first principle of the book is that learning this vocabulary is made easier through knowing the meanings of elements that make up whole words. Its second principle is that knowing this history will contribute to a comprehensive and interdisciplinary liberal education.

The reader should anticipate incursions into philosophy, religion, history, mythology, theories of evolution, Renaissance anatomy, spooky obsessions that frighten people. I hope that *Biolexicon* will provide an economical way to decipher the words of a very large biological vocabulary. I hope the book will be not only informative and useful, but also at least sometimes, enjoyable.

Long lists of words can be intimidating. Though it's necessary to have these lists as examples of how elements join to make up words, it is not necessary to memorize the words themselves. We are pursuing the elements given in **bold** at their fullest presentation and listed alphabetically in the index. Fortunately, there's a finite number of these elements.

Tracking elements will often lead us to prehistoric ancestral sources that have themselves gone extinct while their desendants live on in various linguistic sites. The process is like reconstructing an extinct animal ancestor from its modern descendants. The geneologies of these elements are given in boxes which are not parenthetical comments but very much at the heart of the process of learning the meanings of biological words. One box will reveal, for example, that *Oedipus* is a sibling to *platypus* and that these words are cousins to *fetch, moped, podiatrist,* and *pajamas.*

The elements are called prefixes, suffixes, and bases; for the central part of a word, the term *base* has been chosen in preference to *stem* and *root. Stem* as a noun is not used at all, and *root* is used for an original prehistoric hypothesized term from which the elements evolved.

v

Like an element in chemistry, the base joins with other parts to form compounds.

As in the past, English continues to adopt words from foreign languages and to build its vocabulary by the more generative process of inventing new words from old elements. Close to 500 words enter English every year, most of them inventions that reside in technical vocabularies. Knowing what the elements mean will prepare the pre-medical or medical student, the aspiring biologist, the practitioner of any biological science, and anyone else to decipher these new words that might name a newly discovered microbe or mastodon, a disease, or a surgical procedure.

As in the past, English continues to give new meanings to old words. Greek *thorax*, which once meant breastplate underwent metaphoric transference in referring to the body area that used to be covered by that shield. Latin *acetabulum*, which once meant vinegar cup, underwent such transference in referring to the cup of the pelvis that embraces the knob of the femur. *Culture* is used metaphorically in describing a planned growth of micro-organisms. Recently, *lawn* became a metaphor for surface growth on a culture. A particular kind of transference is someone's name being generalized to some thing or event. *Iris* was once the goddess of the rainbow; *morphine* comes from the name of the god of sleep; and *arachnid*, from the name of a precocious spinster, now refers to spiders. Transferences of old words and names provide many intriguing stories.

Other observations on how the biological vocabulary has been constructed will be given in appropriate places in the text, and at times illustrated. For now, I hope that the exploration will be as pleasurable for the reader as it has been for the writer.

Abbreviations:
- <   stemming or derived from
- >   producing or giving rise to

cp.	compare	adj.	adjective
syn.	synonym	orig.	originally
ant.	antonym	pert.	pertaining to
lit.	literally	etym.	etymological
pl.	plural		

IE	Indo-European	L.	Latin
OE	Old English	Fr.	French
E.	English	Gk.	Greek

ACKNOWLEDGMENTS

I would like to thank Mary Hartman and Irene Walsh of the Clark University Goddard Library for the imaginative detective work they did in locating sources for text and illustrations. Several readers gave me useful advice on parts of the developing manuscript—Professor Paul Burke, Dr. Paul Erikson, Dr. Linda Lorenzani, Dr. James Riggs, Laura Blinderman, and Ford Mathis, who drew many of the illustrations as well. Special thanks to Irma Blinderman for her editing and proofreading. I would also like to thank the etymologists, biologists, and other scientists on whose research this book is based.

CONTENTS

Page

Preface v

Part I: Introduction

Chapter 1. The Biolexicon 3
     2. History of English 17

Part II: Sources

Chapter 3. From Echoes to Eponyms 27
     4. Greek Mythology 37
     5. Metaphors 62
     6. More Metaphors 95

Part III: Affixes

Chapter 7. Prefixes 105
     8. Direction and Location 116
     9. Colors and Numbers 127
    10. Suffixes 139

Part IV: Natural History

Chapter 11. Evolution 145
    12. Geology 157
    13. Taxonomy 166
    14. Metazoa 174

Part V: Birth and Growth

Chapter 15. Gen 187
    16. Living and Growing 200
    17. Sensing 209
    18. Thinking 223

Part VI: Anatomy

Chapter 19.   Body and Bones 233
        20.   Head, Skull, and Face 249
        21.   Torso, Muscles, and Viscera 262
        22.   Roots of Hair 279
        23.   Affliction and Repair 291

Part VII: Conclusion

Chapter 24.   Phiz 308
        25.   Love and Fear 324

Appendices 337
         A.   Grimm's Law 337
         B.   Alphabet 341
         C.   Combinations 343
Bibliography 347
Illustrations and Permissions 349
Index 353

ILLUSTRATIONS

	Page
Chiropteran, a Bat	iii
Sea cucumber	4
Stamen and pistil	10
African chameleon	12
American Indians	58
Anthropophagi preparing dinner	23
Tarantula	30
Darwin's tubercle	33
Eponymic scorpion	34
Ammonites and Ammon	35
Ceres	37
Titan Atlas and atlas first cervical vertebra	39
Goddess Aphrodite and the sea mouse	41
Venus' girdle	42
Priapulus	42
Hercules beetle	44
Aesculapius attending sick man	43
Dormatorium	45
Monster chimaera and sea cat	47
Flying dragon	48
Hercules fighting Hydra and hydra	49
Mythological Gorgon, gorgonia, and medusa	49
Satyr holding syrinx	51
Nymph and nymphon	52
Seaworm *Nereis*	53
Psyche	54
Labyrinthodont teeth and labyrinth of ear	55
Intestine	56

Sirens and mudfish 58

The blinding of Cyclops and copepod cyclops 57

Caduceus. 59

Argonaut 60

Culina, or kitchen 68

Cloaca maxima and condor cloaca 68

Clavis and ape clavicle 71

Head and proboscis of butterfly 70

Acetabula, boy holding pelvis, and acetabuklum 71

Boy holding amnium and fetal structures 73

Fascia clothing and striated muscle 76

Spinal cord neuroglia cell 75

Vascula, Mercury, and kangaroo marsupium 77

Sacculus . . . . : 79

Miter and mitral valve 80

Tunics and tunica 80

Tapeworm *Cestoda* 82

Fibulae and tibia 83

Tibiae with syrinx and trumpet salpinx 84

Greek flagellum, flagellated protozoa and flagellated person 85

Carpenter's shop 87

Smith with mallet forging metal on incus and bones of the inner ear 88

Ancient serrae 88

Sea anemone 89

Belemnites 90

Trypanosoma 89

Ivory arrow-head used by sagittarii and seaworm *Sagitta* 91

Clitellum on horse and of earthworm 92

Old yoke and zygomatic arch of gorilla 94

Cochlea 99

Membranes of brain 100

Nidus or nest 100

Sacral bone 102

Hyoid bone and chiasma 104

Leeuwenhoek's microscope 110

Pleisosaurus dolichodeirus 111

Aneurysm 112

Pleisosaurus macrocephalus 114

Amphioxus 117

Acus crinalis or hair pin and apex or cap on head 117

Dextral and sinistral openings 119

Planes 122

Peripatus 123

Prosthetic devices 126

Drosophila melanogaster 133

Trephination 136

Artiodactyla and Perissodactyla toes 138

Fossil footprint of dinosaur 141

Garden snail *Helix*, double helix, and helix of ear 146

Saltatio 152

Scheuchzer's *Homo diluvii testis* .154

Beringer's *Lugensteine* 155

Hesperopithecus haroldcookii 156

Trilobite 159

Calculi 163

Phosphatic coprolites 164

Diastole and systole 170

Coeloms 176

Coleopteran tiger beetles and ladybug 178

Crinoid 181

Marsupial skull 183

Orang-utan 185

Man and ape 186

The cell 194

Plastic surgery 197

Ichneumon wasp and larvae 202

Speculum 211

Capsa 216

Dissection 227

Autopsy 228

Cro-Magnon drawing 230

Silurian crinoid 230

Anatomical drawing 233
Skeleton 236
Spine 237
Armadillo 238
A brachiating ape 240
The arm 239
Greek woman at play with tali 243
The leg 243
Polyp 247
Oedipus and platypus 248
The skull 252
The eye 255
The ear 257
Rhinocerus 258
Lingula anatina 260
Shark's head and teeth 261
Thorax 263
Bellybuttons 264
Egyptian amulets representing the heart 266
Mastodon teeth 274
Sarcophaga carnaria and Cyprian sacrophagus 279
British nudibranches 281
Hair 284
Gymnasts 283
Two villi 284
Lemur teeth 285
Hirsutism 287
Tragus of ear 288
Pinnigrade feet 290
Plague doctor 293
Urinary discharge, from ancient Egyptian papyrus depiction 295
Dicephalic monster 301
Pagan surgical instruments 302
Hydrotherapy 303
Dr. Jenner at vaccination. 307
Physiognomic signs 310

Phrenological signs 311
Criminal faces. 312
The Humours. 314
Chaucer's Doctour 316
Endocrine glands 320
Ophiolatry 321
Mantis religiosa. 322
Hogarth's Bedlam 323
The Nightmare, by Johann Fuseli 329
Luposilopophobia 333
Gnomes and ichthyosaurus 335

BIOLEXICON
A Guide to the Language of Biology

PART I: INTRODUCTION

CHAPTER 1—THE BIOLEXICON

1.1 Adoptions
1.2 Advantages
1.3 To Be Human
1.4 Etymology

The characteristics of modern English arose from English having been remarkably, maybe uniquely, hospitable to adopting words from other languages. All of English has been enriched by this hospitality, and the scientific vocabulary has benefited particularly from Greek and Latin adoptions. These Latin and Greek adoptions sometimes seem like an impenetrable code, but they have brought advantages to the scientific vocabulary, advantages that can be seen in tracking the history of words like *human*. The study of the history of words in the general as well as in specialized scientific vocabularies is called *etymology*. Etymology is the subject of this book.

1.1 Adoptions

Starting five hundred years ago, Arabic has endowed English with dozens of words. *Assassin* is from Arabic. A medieval character with the nickname Old Man of the Mountains encouraged his gang to get high on *hashish* and then go out and murder Crusaders. From the name of the weed they ate there came the name of their profession: *assassin*. *Assassin* entered English in the early 16th century, *hashish* and the compound *assassinate* much later in that century. When a bloodsucking insect of the Reduviidae family was identified three hundred years later, it received the popular name *assassin bug*.

Less bloody histories attend other words that English adopted from Arabic:

alcohol	*alfalfa*	*amber*	*caliber*
alkali	*artichoke*	*emerald*	*average*
nitre	*syrup*	*giraffe*	*gazelle*
algebra, entered E. in 1541			

Words may enter English directly from a foreign language's own stores, as *sputnik* rocketed into English from Russian in 1957. Or they may undertake extensive journeys from one language to another, sometimes wandering across the globe. A couple of useful words that originated in Greek were transmitted through Arabic:

3

Gk. *chyma* became Arabic *alchemy* and, in 1555, E. *chemist*, in 1600 E. *chemistry*. Gk. *xeros*, dry, is the source of Arabic *elixir* as well as the name of a photocopying process. *Camphor* came to E. from Arabic at the beginning of the 14th century; it travelled into Arabic from Malay.

A Sanskrit word, *sunya*, empty, was adopted by Arabic as *sifr*, with the same meaning; this travelled into English in the mid-14th century as *cipher*. Arabic *sifr* also travelled into Italian and came into E. in the late 16th century as *zero*.

Sanskrit itself, through its descendant Hindi, has contributed *pepper, cheetah, anaconda,* and *jungle* to the vocabulary of natural history, and *sugar* and *sacchar* to the vocabulary of the kitchen and the laboratory. That story begins with Sanskrit *sarkara*, sugar. This went into Italian as *zucchero*, from which, eventually, Middle French *sucre* and E. *sugar*. *Sugar* came into E. in the second half of the 13th century. Centuries later, the Sanskrit root was revisited to produce, in 1665, *saccharine*, which orig. meant like sugar, very sweet, and in 1880, as *saccharin* became a word for a sugar substitute. The base for *sugar* and *saccharin* therefore undertook a long journey: Sanskrit > Arabic > Italian > French > English.

From German itself have come *anlage*, the initial embryological stage of organ development, *diener*, a laboratory handyman, and words originally from Greek transmitted through German into the vocabulary of psychiatry, such as *psychoanalysis, narcissism, Oedipal complex.*

Renaissance and subsequent explorations introduced Europe to the fauna and flora and exotic diseases of faraway lands. A quick inventory displays words from these languages:

African languages >	*chimpanzee, gorilla, gnu, yam, tsetse*
	banana
Persian >	*kala-azar, borax*
Hebrew >	*balsam, balm*
Tibetan >	*panda*
Chinese >	*trepang,* sea cucumber

Sea cucumber
Genus *Holothuroidea*

Japanese >	*sodoku,* fever caused by infection from a rat bite
Sinhalese >	*beri-beri*
Austronesian >	*kangaroo, koala*
	kiwi, bird and fruit
	pangolin, an anteater
	agar, seaweed nutrient
	bantam, an Indonesian bird

Samoan   > *palolo*, a worm, taxonomic name
                               Eunica viridis

The people who originally settled into North America contributed words for the plants and animals of this land,

terrapin	*sequoia*	*persimmon*	*hickory*
opossum	*squash*	*skunk*	

woodchuck, orig. Algonquian *ockqutchaun*

Those who originally settled into South America contributed, mostly through the intermediary of Spanish:

maize	*marijuna*	*jaguar*
potato	*cocaine*	*jaguarundi*
tomato	*quinine*	*coati-mundi*

ipecac, an emetic

These words for animals, plants, diseases, do not exhaust the vocabulary that English adopted from entirely unrelated languages; but the total contribution from these languages is small relative to the fragment consisting of words from native English (about 5%) and tiny relative to the great number from Greek and Latin.

Ninety-five percent of the words in the medical vocabulary comes from Greek and Latin. The abundance of Greek and Latin terms could inspire a pretentiousness by which we intimidate people by using uncommon terms instead of common ones, such as *cephalalgia* instead of *headache*, *lentigo* instead of *freckle*, *rhexis* instead of *rupture*, and *verruca* instead of *wart*.

In turning our attention to Greek and Latin, we can note first that in ancient times these adopted words from other languages. The Greek invaders who took over Crete absorbed some Cretan words:

sponge	*syrinx*	*salping*, trumpet, oviduct
turpentine	*hyacinth*	*porphyra*, purple

labyrinth, once a Cretan palace

It should be noted that some of these terms have not definitely been traced back to Cretan, and that the original sources of other words in the medical vocabulary remain uncertain: *coccyx, clitoris, abdomen.*

It has been estimated that the Latin medical vocabulary is at least half Greek. All Roman medical literature was written in Greek. Among many other words, Latin adopted Gk. *nausea, skeleton,* and *placenta.* Gk. *gangraina* became L. *gangrene,* and Gk. *dakruma,* tear, L. *lacrima.* The New Latin of the Renaissance did this too, for example, Gk. *amoibe* becoming *amoeba,* today's *ameba.* Sometimes, Latin would find an equivalence for a Greek term, as it did in substituting *spiritus* for the Greek *pneuma.*

Many words have come into English with the same form and often with the same meaning that they had in ancient Greece and Rome, such as

colon	*myopia*	*pneumonia*
apoplexy	*paralysis*	*siphon*

Arthritis, synapse, and *glaucoma* appear in Hippocrates, *synapse* orig. referring to bones rather than to nerves and *glaucoma* to an opacity of the lens (*cataract* today); *bulimia,* an insatiable hunger, and *pancreas* in Aristotle; *styloid,* for a structure resembling a pillar, in the Roman physician Galen.

Anthrax orig. meant a burning piece of coal; *aroma,* a spice; and *idiot,* a person who refused to participate in politics. Gk. *brachion,* arm, evolved into *brace,* To Aristotle, *organic* meant mechanical, as it still does in *organ,* the musical instrument; but it developed into meaning living, as in *organism* and *organic chemistry.* We will devote considerable attention in later chapters to such changes in meaning.

A change in form might be extreme. Gk. *glykyrrizo* became *glycrrhiza* in classical Latin. Vulgar Latin dropped the initial *g* and made some other changes to produce *liquiritia;* this went into Anglo-French and then into Middle English as *lycorys,* presently *licorice.* The original Gk. source has two bases that are alive today: *glyco* for sweet and *rrhiza* for root, licorice being a sweet root.

Most of the words in the biological vocabulary would have been unfamiliar to the Greeks and Romans from whose languages they have been fabricated. Though Socrates knew that *chloro* referred to green and *phyll* to leaf, he would have been stumped by *chlorophyll.* Though Marcus Aurelius knew that *dent* referred to teeth, he could not have cruised down to a neighborhood drugstore to buy a *dentifrice.*

The process of creating new words for the biological vocabulary and for the vocabularies of other sciences, is to take a base from Greek or Latin and attach to it one or more prefixes and suffixes. This process is called compounding.

1. Bases

If we wish, we could rely upon the resources of native English for the production of new words. In the 15th century, a reckless inventor of words created *not-to-be-thought-upon-able,* but this lost out to its competitor: *inconceivable.* We could on such models create *that-which-has-never-given-birth.* The actual word, which is less clumsy than this phrase and would be understood by non-English speakers, is *nulliparous.* *Nulli* means not, as in *nullify,* and **par** is a base for birth; thus, *nulliparous* means that-which-has-never-given-birth.

Knowing that **par** means birth, we have a clue to figuring out the meanings of other unfamiliar words with this base in them. Most could define *ante-* as meaning before and *-ion* as meaning act of, process of. Knowing the meanings of these two elements makes *antepartum* and *parturition* easy to understand as words meaning before birth and the process of birth. *Ovi* means egg and *vivi* means life. Therefore:

oviparous	pertains to laying eggs, as birds do
viviparous	pert. to giving birth to live young, as we do
oviviviparous	pert. to eggs that hatch within the body, the young being born alive, as some fish and reptiles do

The following words display **par** combining with less familiar parts.

gemmiparous	pert. to reproduction by budding
fissiparity	reproduction by fission
primipara	female that has had first offspring
dentiparous	giving birth to, bearing, teeth

From the same source could come two different forms of a word. One form refers to the object itself. The other form is used in combinations. For example:

object:	*pharynx*	*larynx*	*coccyx*	*phalanx*
combining base:	*pharyng*	*laryng*	*coccyg*	*phalang*
combination:	*pharyngeal*	*laryngitis*	*coccygotomy*	*phalanges*

The above words for objects do exist by themselves, *pharynx, larynx, coccyx, phalanx*, but many bases don't — they can live only in symbiosis with another element, e.g., *chondro*, cartilage, *gyn*, woman, and *kerato*, horn.

A single base may have a short form and a long form:

From noun, short form	From genitive, long form
derma, skin	*dermato*
ceno, recent	*cenato*
gyn, woman	*gyneco*
hepar, liver	*hepato*
ophthalm, vision	*ophthalmo*
pneumo, lung, gas	*pneumato*
phan, appearance	*phanero*

2. Prefixes

The same prefix will appear in terms from many biological studies. For example, the Gk. prefix **a-** (**an-** before a vowel), which means not, lack of, appears in

zoology	*anaerobic*, without air
paleontology	*Azoic*, time of no life
anatomy	*agnatha* lacking jaws
medicine	*anaesthetic*, pert. to no feeling
psychology	*anhedonia*, inability to experience pleasure
taxonomy	*Anota*, without ears, a genus of reptiles

Chapters 7–9 discuss prefixes.

3. Suffixes

The way in which a single suffix may be combined with bases in the manufacture of words in different biological studies is illustrated by Gk. **-oid**, like. A word used in science fiction for a human-like robot is *android*.

anatomy	*deltoid*, a muscle shaped like the Greek letter delta
chemistry	*colloid*, suspension of particles, lit. like glue
primatology	*anthropoid*, like a human being

Chapter 10 discusses suffixes.

The biolexicon has many synonyms, for example, E. *kidney* and words for kidney from the L. base *ren* and the Gk. base *nephr*, words for foot from the E. *foot*, L. *ped* and Gk. *pod*. The claim has been made that the L. base more often relates to the entity itself, while the Gk. base is used for disorders and repairs. We can illustrate this generalization with a sample inventory.

	Latin		Greek	
bone	*os, oss*	*ossicle*	*osteo*	*osteoporesis*
skin	*cut*	*subcutaneous*	*derm*	*dermatology*
egg	*ov*	*ovary*	*oo*	*oophorectomy*
eye	*oculu*	*ocular*	*op*	*myopic*
muscle	*muscu*	*musculus*	*myo*	*myositis*
navel	*umbili*	*umbilicus*	*omphalo*	*omphalitis*

The generalization doesn't always work. *Ossicle*, a word for a little bone, does exemplify the generalization that the Latin term describes the entity; but *ossify*, turning into bone, is also from Latin and contradicts the generalization, in that Latin words don't relate to a disorder. *Oophorectomy*, removal of the ovaries, does exemplify the generalization that the Greek term describes surgical repair; but *ootheca*, a case for the ovaries, contradicts the generalization in that this Gk. word relates to a structure itself.

Perhaps the easiest approach to this issue is to remember that the Latin terms usually were the earlier immigrants into English, and so apply to the more obvious, while the Greek terms came later and refer to the more subtle aspects of study and practice resulting from discoveries of the Renaissance and after.

1.2 Advantages

One of the advantages of having ancient Greek and Latin as the foundation languages for the scientific vocabulary is that they are permanent, far less subject to change than is living vernacular English. The lexicons of Greek and Latin are rich in parts that can be combined to produce millions of words, thousands of which will appear in the coming decade alone.

Another advantage is that this source is available for use by any language. The same animal will go under different names in the vernacular of different countries. The animal we call a *screech owl* is known as a *Pazifishe Kreischeule* in German and a *Scops de Cooper* in French. *Otus asio*, its taxonomic name, is the same everywhere. The sea cucumber goes under different names in different languages, for example, *trepang* in Chinese; but *Holothuria edulis* is its international name. The same animal can go under different names even within a single country—for example, in the

U.S., *earthworm, angleworm, night crawler,* etc. This animal has only one taxonomic name from sea to shining sea: *Lumbricus terrestris.*

Some languages like to use native sources. For example, in scientific German, we confront such curiosities as *Saurerstoff* for *oxygen, Seitenwandbein* for *parietal, Schildrüse* for *thyroid,* and *Zwölffingerdarm* for what is known more globally as *duodenum,* a section of the intestine.

The scientific term is less emotive than are available common synonyms. The poet William Wordsworth disapproved of the anti-Romantic cool scientific attitude and insulted a botanist with this;

> A primrose by the river's brim
> Was but a dicotyledon to him,
> And nothing more.

Wordsworth's botanist is so icily scientific that he will "peep and botanize on his mother's grave."

For purposes of scientific discourse, a word such as *dicotyledon* < Gk. *di-,* two + *cotyledon,* a cavity, is preferable to *primrose* because *dicotyledon* comes unadorned with the emotive associations of *primrose* < L. *prim,* first + *rosa,* rose. It might be that people from the Romantic period to today have not been more turned on by *primrose* than by *dicotyledon.*

The scientific term is thought to be more precise than its vulgar synonym, though this is often enough not the case—*kidney stone* is as precise as *nephrolite.* The scientific term is usually shorter, as *nulliparous* is shorter than *condition-of-never-having-given-birth.* And usually there is no commonplace synonym available, as there isn't for *mitochondria, stethoscope,* or *capillary.*

1.3 To Be Human

A single element appears in different biological fields, for example, the suffix *-oid* in words from anatomy, chemistry, and primatology. For this section, we will focus on Gk. **andr,** a base for male. **Andro** (the o̱ a vowel to make compounds easily pronounceable) appears in the common vocabulary in *android, Andrew* and *Alexander.* In the field of social anthropology, **andro** means husband, as in *polyandry,* the condition of a woman's having more than one spouse. Although a plant cannot decently have husbands, it can have male and female organs. **Andro** for the male organ, the stamen of flowering plants, finds employment in many botanical terms, e.g.,

anandrous	lacking stamens; cp. *triandrous*
pachysandra	a plant which has a thick stamen—*pachy,* means thick
androecium	the site that holds the stamen—*ecium* lit. means house
androphore	stalk for stamen
androspore	spore emitted by stamen

We also find **andro** in entomology, *androconium (coni,* dust) the scales on a male butterfly's wings that emit a pheromone, a sexual attractant. Some living things have both female and male features; they are *androgynous.*

Andro is in genetics: *androgenesis,* a word for the unusual case of the development of an egg that contains only paternal chromosomes, and *androcyte;* in biochemistry: *androgen, androsterone,* male hormones; and in medicine and psychiatry:

andrology	the study of diseases of the male organ
andropathy	diseases peculiar to males
andriatrics	treatment of these diseases
anandria	loss of virility
misandria (apandria)	fear of men

Philanderer is synonymous with womanizer, the behavior caught in *philandry,* though *Philander laniger* labels a wooly opossum. Plants and animals have also received taxonomic names with **andro** in them.

The terms noted with **andro** as their base illustrate the way in which knowing one base will give insight into the meaning of many words from various fields.

Andro is accompanied by its mate, Gk. **gyn(eco)**, base for woman or female.

androgyne or, less common, *gynander*	a being, human or otherwise, that has both male and female organs, a hermaphrodite

Gynecology is a familiar word, though *gynephilia* isn't. It translates into "a morbid desire in adolescent boys to be in the company of women or girls." *Dorland's Medical Dictionary,* from which this definition is taken, lists 46 words that begin with **gyn(eco)**. Many words have the base in positions other than first. The general vocabulary offers *misogyny* and *philogyny,* for hatred and love of women. The botanical vocabulary offers a number of words with this base, which, in botany, refers to the pistil, e.g.,

Amaryllis stamen

gynoecium	residence for the pistil, plant's female organ
macrogynospore	a large pistil spore

Poppy pistil

Taxonomy offers at least nine labels, e.g., *Coelogyne cristata,* an orchid.

Andro and **gyn(eco)** for man and woman are from Greek. But, as may be self-evident, *man* and *woman* are native English, < OE *mann.* Putting the prefix *wif* in front of *mann* renders *wifmann,* the female man, which changed its spelling and pronunciation to become *woman.* Although *wif* became *wife,* it retains its original sense of woman in a few words, e.g., *midwife,* who isn't necessarily a wife, or even a woman.

Male and *female* both come from Latin, though from different Latin sources. A Latin term for male was *mas,* which lives on as that in *masculine* and disguised in *macho; mas* was changed in French to *masle,* and *masle* was changed in Middle English to *male. Female,* however, traces back through French to L. *femina.*

Man and *woman, male* and *female,* the bases *andro* and *gyneco,* and almost all the words in the general and scientific vocabularies came from an ancestral language spoken five thousand years ago. At that time, somewhere between India and Europe lived a small group of people who may have called themselves the Arya, but who go under the name Indo-Europeans today.

For earth, Indo-European used the term *dhgham.* As this word moved into Greek, its form changed into Gk. *khamai,* on the ground, from which were derived a word for an on-the-ground tea, *chamomile,* and a word for a lizard, the *chameleon,* lit. earth lion.

Dhgham's original sense of earth is also retained in Latin, another descendant of Indo-European. L. *hum* is a base for earth, as in *inhume,* to put into the earth, and *exhume,* to take out of the earth. Earth or soil is often moist; hence, *hum* also is a base for moisture: *humus.*

Recognizing our connection with the earth may induce us to be *humble,* to have a sentiment of *humility* toward our existence, and maybe to feel *humiliated,* these three words from IE *dhgham.* IE *dhgham* also led to L. *humanus* which brought forth *human* and its compounds, *humane, humanitarian, humanity, humanities, humanist, humanism* (its offspring, *secular humanism*) and, an adjective for those who act beastly on dates, *sub-human.*

A poem by the naturalist writer Thomas Hardy is appropriate here because

African chameleon
Chamaeleo chamaeleon

it connects us to the earth from which our flesh came and to which it will
return.

Transformations

Portion of this yew
Is a man my grandsire knew,
Bosomed here at its foot:
This branch may be his wife,
A ruddy human life
Now turned into a green shoot.

These grasses must be made
Of her who often prayed,
Last century, for repose;
And the fair girl long ago
Whom I often tried to know
May be entering this rose.
So, they are not underground,
But as nerves and veins abound
In the growths of upper air,
And they feel the sun and rain,
And the energy again
That made them what they were!

With a change in the internal vowel, L. *hum* became *hom:* as in *Homo sapiens,*
homicide, homage, and, through Spanish, *hombre.* "Homo," observed Shakespeare in
Henry IV, "is a common name to all men." The base from L. can be **homo** or **homi:**

homi

hominid	of the human family
hominoid	like a human being
ad hominem	technique of arguing against a proposition on the basis of personality
homunculus	an embryo in the form of a human being
Anaptomorphus homunculus	an extinct lemur

A Greek word which has nothing to do with being human is just like L. **homo,** but Gk. **homo-** means same, as in *homogenize* and *homosexual.* Words that sound the same but mean different things are called *homophones,* adj. *homophonic.* Other examples are *cell* and *sell; rain, rein,* and *reign; meat, meet,* and *mete; love* (the affliction) and *love* (the score of zero).

IE *dhgham* went into another descendant, Proto-Germanic, as *(dh)ghmon,* which became *gumon,* which became Old English *goma.* The fellow marrying the bride was the bride's man, or *bridegoma.* But *guma* got confused with *grom,* an OE word for boy, specifically the boy who cleaned and tidied horses. So the bridegroom today not only espouses, but also grooms his beloved.

1.4 Etymology

The word *etymology* combines the Greek elements *etym,* for true meaning, with *-logy,* study of. In the general vocabulary, the present definition of a word often does not align with its original or etymological meaning. If we were to use words today only in their "true" meaning, the word *arrive* would be restricted to those who come in by boat: it developed from Latin *ad-,* to + *ripa* shore or bank, source also of *river, rival,* and *riparian,* an adjective pertaining to a river's banks. Etymologically, a *sophomore* is a wise fool, but most living sophomores are neither wise nor foolish. A *candidate* once wore white—the sense of whiteness still in *candle* and *candid;* but nowadays a candidate may wear a blue suit pinstriped with maroon.

We find this circumstance of a word meaning something other than the sum of its parts also in the biological vocabulary. If we dissect *autopsy,* we discover that it divides into *auto,* self + *ops,* viewing + *-y,* condition of, and therefore means the condition of viewing oneself, a ghastly picture of a real autopsy.

anemia	lit. lacking blood
	but actually, condition of lower red blood cell count
capillary	place for hair
	actually, a small blood vessel
trichinosis	condition of having hair
	actually, a parasitic disease
stethoscope	instrument for viewing chest
	actually, instrument for hearing heartbeat

Occasionally, we will come upon terms that don't mean at all what they seem to. *Cardiospasm* seems easy enough to define: a spasm of the heart. It means a disorder in the cardiac sphincter, which is not in the heart but between the esophagus and stomach, the part of the stomach near the heart (*cardiospasm* is also known as *achalasia*).

Protocol and *mitral* are two more examples of disagreement between etymological meaning and actual meaning. When papyrus was in use, the first sheet, that displaying the table of contents, was glued on to the roll. The Greek term for this was *proto-*, first + *col*, glue (as in *colloid*). The word subsequently expanded in meaning to refer to a proper way of behaving and then to mean a program for laboratory work. *Protocol* no longer means what it meant in the days of papyrus.

A constant source for biological words is the process of taking a characteristic from one thing and applying it to another as is done in metaphors. A *mitral* valve is not a hat, though *miter* means hat; and there is no longer anything sacred about the *sacral* bone. Mythology also provides bases that have been redirected, for example, *psyche*, which stems from Psyche, a nymph.

More often than is the case with words of the general vocabulary, words in the biological vocabulary do mean the sum of their parts. Learning parts, about 1000 of them, will be the key to understanding tens of thousands of words in the biolexicon, as illustrated in knowing what **andro** and **gyn(eco)** mean. Dissecting biological terms, cutting the unfamiliar word into familiar parts, will usually give its definition, or at least a clue to what it means. Three examples will suffice to illustrate this point here: *presbyopia, karyogamy,* and *pilose*.

presbyopia
Presby is a Gk. base that means old, as in *Presbyterian,* and *opia* means vision, so that the term translates into the vision of older people, the vision caused by aging of lenses.

karyogamy
Gk. *kary* means nucleus and *gam* means marriage, as in *bigamy,* so that the word translates into marriage, or union, of nuclei.

pilose
L. *pil* means hair, *-ose,* full of, therefore: hairy. The base is in *caterpillar,* lit. a hairy cat.

Treating biological terms through etymological analysis in the context of what people have thought about themselves and about the world they inhabit has advantages. This approach can provide pleasant thrills of recognition or surprise and some harmless fun. It may even be of use in guiding us to a more precise use of words. I'll illustrate this by referring to a cluster of words that have hidden bites to them, as *bite* itself does in the phrase a biting remark.

1. We all know what *sarcasm* means. The Gk. *sarc* is the same as in the word *sarcoma,* a tumor of the flesh. *Sarcasm* literally means biting of one's flesh, the flesh of the lips—it has a sense of snarling rage to it.

2. *Remorse* is related to *morsel:* both words come from Latin *mordere,* to bite, *morsel*

being a little bite or snack and *remorse* being literally a biting again, going back to a memory and tearing until it hurts. *Mordant,* pertaining to sharp and biting wit, is another relative of *morsel.*

3. Latin *mandere,* to chew, is the ancestor of *manger, mange,* a disease in which the hair is chewed away, and *mandible,* a jawbone. *Manger, mange,* and *mandible,* all coming from the same Latin source, may be considered siblings. They have cousins in Greek: *masticate,* to chew, *masseter,* a muscle used in chewing, and *mustache,* which came to English from French, and came to French from Italian, and came to Italian from Greek *mustax,* upper lip.

4. *Fret* comes from Old English *fretan,* to devour, and though it today means to worry, it has the old sense of eating away, at one's self—and in the specialized lexicon of geology, does mean to erode.

5. *Psomophagia* may deserve to be retrieved from obscurity. Gk. *psomos* means morsel and *psomophagia,* lit. the eating of morsels, has been narrowed to mean the very fast swallowing or bolting of food; one who does it while you are leisurely dining is a sub-human *psomophage.*

Learning elements that combine to make words is a more cheerful as well as more efficient way of understanding biological vocabulary than memorizing long lists of words. Imagine columns of words as though they were on the menu of a Chinese restaurant. For your dinner, you can choose an appetizer from Column A, a main course from Column B, and a dessert from Column C, or if you're dieting, just something from Column B plus an item from A or C. Each of the columns lists five items. You therefore can have a choice of at least 125 possible combinations.

Column A	Column B	Column C
a(n)-, not	*cephal,* skull, head	*-ic,* pertaining to
peri-, around	*gnath,* jaw	*-ous,* full of
en-, in	*card,* heart	*-osis,* condition of
micro-, small	*scope,* a viewing	*-logy,* study of
pro-, in front of	*gastro,* stomach	*-itis,* inflammation of

Some combinations wouldn't make much sense—*agnathology,* the study of lacking jaws, is something no normal person would specialize in. Some make sense, but don't exist—*microcarditis,* inflammation of a small heart. These combinations do exist:

acephalic	*encephalitic*	*anencephalic*	*gastrology*
pericephalous	*pericardium*	*periscope*	*microscopic*
prognathous	*cardiology*		

If we add to the columns so that there are ten elements in each, we have the clues to 1000 words.

One might choose to spend an afternoon memorizing 10,000 words, an enterprise designed to cause gastritis. Just memorizing also means that one would miss such delights as learning that *cheer* as in *cheerful* comes from Middle English *chere,* which meant mood, and that came from Old French *chiere,* which meant face. And that comes from Late Latin *cara* which comes from Gk. *kara* which comes from IE *ker,* head or horn; so that *cheer* numbers among its relatives many words having to do with head or horn, such as *cranium, unicorn,* and *horny.*

CHAPTER 2—HISTORY OF ENGLISH

2.1   Descent from Indo-European
2.2   From Old to Middle English
2.3   The Renaissance
2.4   Note on Grimm's Law

The four children of a house down the street share certain physical features: hair texture and color, eye color, stature. You might be able to reconstruct their unobserved parents from such a survey. If, for example, all the offspring are tall and sport curly brown hair, hazel eyes, a sharp nose and assertive chin, you could sensibly guess that their parents have the same features, or at least that the parents are not blue-eyed pug-nosed chinless short redheads.

Through an examination of words in modern European languages, linguists have reconstructed two thousand words used by the speakers of the original language from which English, Italian, Irish, and even Iranian and Hindi descended.

The history of biological terminology, like the history of most of the common English vocabulary, opens with a group of people who left no literature and little other evidence about who they were, just where or when they lived. But they spoke to each other. The memorials of what they spoke about remain in the descendants of the words they used to describe territory, farming instruments and products, kinship systems, horses, and parts of the body.

Like all Indo-European roots, that for salmon, *lax*, is hypothetical, a reconstruction from words alive today. Words for salmon and salmon-like are similar from New York City to Bombay. Swedish *lax* and Sanskrit *lac*, the base of *lacquer* and *shellac*, substances of a salmon color. This bit of archeological linguistics suggests that the people lived near where salmon swam.

Cognate means born together, derived from the same source; *lax* and *lac* are cognates, derived from IE *laks*.

The procedure of tracing back from extant words to the extinct roots is also exemplified by relatives of the word *mouse*. It's *mus* in many languages, Danish and German, Greek and Latin and Sanskrit; it appears as *mysz* in Polish and *mys* in Russian. A plausible hypothesis is that all these different but similar forms trace back to the same ancestor, reconstructed as IE *mus*. If similarities of this sort are found also for words referring to other animals, to plants, to people, to kinship systems, and so on, it seems reasonable to infer that the languages including these words are progeny of the same parent, that is, Indo-European.

Because descendant languages have cognates for copper and its alloy bronze, the reasonable assumption is that the original IE group lived in an area that contained copper and tin. Another less strong assumption is that the area also had deposits of gold and silver. But words for iron are different. It seems that the original IE group knew and used gold, silver, and bronze but not iron. Similar examination of thousands of other cognates sheds some light upon where and when and how the Indo-Europeans lived and who they were.

2.1 Descent from Indo-European

The tribe may have called itself Arya. *Arya* is a reconstruction from the *ar* in the old word *aryan* and from the place-names *Armenia, Iran,* and *Ireland.* The tribe is known today as Indo-European (IE). About six thousand years ago, a period called the Bronze Age, fragments of the IE population began to wander elsewhere, carrying their original language with them throughout Europe and into Asia. The original site cannot be identified with more exactness than somewhere in the temperate zone between Europe and Asia (specific sites have been identified as being on the shores of the Caspian, the Black Sea, the Danube, as far north as the Baltic and as far south as Anatolia, in Turkey).

Just as everybody's street dialect changes as he or she moves out from the home neighborhood into the larger world, dialects of original IE language also changed — into two major branches. These two branches are differentiated by what seems a small feature: how they pronounced a sound of the original IE word for hundred.

One group pronounced the sound as a hard *k*, and that is known as the *centum* group, *centum* pronounced "kentum" and meaning one hundred. After splitting off from their parents, those speaking the centum dialect bifurcated into Greek, Latin, Celtic (existent today in Irish and resurgent Welsh) and Proto-Germanic, the parent of the Scandinavian languages, of German, Dutch, and English.

The other dialect group pronounced the original sound as a soft *s,* its word for one hundred, *satem*, becoming the identifying tag. From this group came Armenian and Albanian; Balto-Slavic; and Indo-Iranian. The Balto-Slavic dialect group further split into Baltic and Slavic. From the first arose Lithuanian and Latvian, and from the second Bulgarian, Croatian, Bohemian, Polish, Slovak, Russian and Ukrainian. The Indo-Iranian dialect group further split into Indic and Iranian. From the first rose Sanskrit, the source of Hindi, Sinhalese, and many other languages; and from the second Iranian, Kurdish, Afghan, and several other languages. From the satem group also came about twenty other languages which have gone extinct (e.g., Phrygian, Lydian, Thracian, Toccharian).

What happened may be visualized as a geneology. At the top we have the living children, languages that often look very different. But if we trace back Lithuanian, Slovak, Russian, and Bulgarian, we find that they had the same parent: Baltic-Slavic. If we trace back Sanskrit and Persian, we find they had the same parent: Indo-Iranian. Baltic-Slavic and Indo-Iranian descended from the satem group, so that Russian and Hindi, a Sanskrit language, share the same grandparent, the satem group. The earliest literature from descendants consists of the Hindu sacred texts, the Vedas, and a medical text, the *Sushruta Samhita,* both compiled three thousand years ago.

Similarly, modern-day Greek, Latin descendants such as French and Italian,

Celtic descendants such as Irish and Welsh, and Proto-Germanic descendants such as Danish and English all have the same grandparent, the centum group. And, the bottom line of this geneology, the satem and centum groups descended from the original great-grandparent of almost all modern European languages and some Asian, Indo-European.

The Indo-Europeans were illiterate, but linguistic analysis of words in the modern descendants has reconstructed about 2000 words of their vocabulary. From original IE have come hundreds of thousands, an optimist would say millions, of words in common and biological English.

2.2 From Old to Middle English

The Celts were the earliest inhabitants of Great Britain whose language is known. They settled in the islands before 2500 B.C. They were conquered first by the Romans, who left Britain in the 4th century A.D., and then by Germanic tribes in the 5th century. From one of these Germanic tribes, the Angles, came the name *Angleland,* later *England.* The Proto-Germanic dialects of the Angles and Saxons merged into the dialect known as Anglo-Saxon or Old English. OE took hundreds of place names from the conquered Celts, such as *Thames* and *London,* and a few other words, among the hoard the word *bug* — maybe.

When missionaries came to Great Britain from Rome to convert the pagan Anglo-Saxons, OE accepted about 400 secular as well as religious words.

purple	*lobster*	*plant*	*sponge*	*cherry*	*aloe*
poppy	*rose*	*crutch*	*chest*	*circle*	
phoenix, E. < L. < Gk.					

Danish Vikings, cousins of the Angles and Saxons, invaded England in the 9th century. English borrowed almost 1000 words from Danish, for example, *ugly* and *egg;* three pronouns; and place-names. In 1066, William of Normandy invaded England.

The linguistic consequence of that invasion was the introduction into English of French words in government and law, such as *court, crime,* and *power;* in military affairs, such as *enemy, navy, soldier;* in religion, such as *clergy* and *damnation;* in fashion, cooking, and art. So significant was the effect of French upon English that after the 12th century the language is no longer known as Old English, but as Middle English.

Two important points emerge from this survey. The first is that English has welcomed words from other languages. The second is that few of the words reflect anything of what we would call science. Science emphasizes experimentation, the progressive accumulation of data, and the design of theories to explain what happens in the world. From the Roman through the Norman invasion, natural phenomena were rarely studied scientifically in England, in Europe, or anywhere else. That science was a matter of slight interest is seen in the kinds of words that came into English from the successive linguistic invasions, Latin (e.g., *cherry*), Danish (e.g., *rotten*), and French (e.g., *justice*).

An example of medieval interest—or disinterest—in natural history is provided by the *Bestiary,* a collection of stories about animals. But the *Bestiary* is not interested in the ways animals really behave; it's interested in how non-human behavior, real or imaginary, can be a role model for our behavior. A snake's shedding of its skin provokes the moral that Christians can also shed their sins and emerge as fresh and new as the snake. A few lines from a *Bestiary* passage on the whale will be quoted as an illustration of the thesis that natural phenomena were of interest not in themselves but as provocations for moralizing. The story on the whale begins:

> Cethegrande is a fis
> The mostest that in water is.

The whale is a fish that's the greatest in the water. Its back looks like a "neilond," source of *island* and sailors seeing it think it's great turf for a picnic. They row over, set up the Anglo-Saxon equivalent of a barbecue, warm themselves and drink— "warmen hem well and drinken." The whale, feeling the fire, submerges, the sailors going down with it—"the fir he feleth and doth hem sinkin." We learn from the behavior of the whale that sin offers an attractive surface; but when we party in sin, the devil does his dirty deed:

wo so listneth deules lore	whoso listens to devil's lore
on length, it sal him rewensore;	at length, shall regret it;
wo so festeth hope on him,	whoso fastens hope on him,
he al him folgen to helle dim.	shall follow him to dim hell.

2.3 The Renaissance

Before William of Normandy prepared to invade England, Arabic scholars had recovered manuscripts of ancient Greece and Rome. They discovered a new world of speculation on philosophy, religion, and medicine and other scientific subjects. The works of Galen went through Arabic before being translated into European languages. This exposure of Galen was not always beneficial, since Galen made many mistakes in his descriptions of anatomy. His word was taken as gospel, not to be questioned. Such authoritarianism is always an impediment to scientific progress, even when it occurs within science itself.

In the 9th century, the first medical school was founded, at Salerno. The founding of subsequent medical schools at Bologna, Padua, and Sienna testifies to the early influence of Italy in the history of medicine. By the 14th century, biological concepts, that is, words, began to find their way into the English vocabulary. During the second half of that century, words orig. Greek came into English: *arsenic, artery, hydra;* and from Latin: *cornea, cadaver, distill, digit, hyena, reptile.*

The medieval art of alchemy should be noted here. Its purpose was dual: the exoteric, or obvious, purpose was to convert base metals, such as lead, into noble metals, such as gold; the esoteric, or hidden, purpose was to transform the alchemist himself, to convert him into a noble being. From alchemical lingo came words still used in chemistry.

verbs	nouns	adjectives
distill	*gypsum, soda*	*immaterial*
dissolve	*essence*	*volatile*
sublimate	*arsenic*	

Gk. *aither* meant upper air; alchemists converted that to *ether*, which of course exists today, its adjective form, *ethereal*, meaning light as air, heavenly. *Ether* came into E. in the 14th century, *ethereal* in the early 16th.

A dividing line in the history of medicine is drawn with Andreas Vesalius, a Belgian anatomist whose works, especially his 1543 *De humani corporis fabrica*, displayed a real scientific approach, with well-drawn plates and accurate descriptions of human anatomy.

English acknowledges the Moorish influence in the Arabic words *alkali* (1325), *average* (1490), *algebra* and *alcohol* (both 1540). Arabic renovated earlier Greek or Latin words which came through Arabic into English as *zero* and *elixir*. By 1540, the Renaissance had come to England. So had science.

From the Renaissance on, English has taken in words from many of the languages of the world. Most of the relevant words from non-IE sources are in the names of living things and products from non-IE countries, examples of which were noted in the previous chapter.

Thousands of words from native English or closely related languages of the Proto-Germanic branch are, of course, used in the lexicon of biological sciences, nouns such as *kidney*, first recorded in E. in the 13th century; and *beaker* and *flask*, both 14th century; most verbs, prepositions, conjunctions, pronouns. But the more technical terms are from Latin and the most technical from Greek. The Renaissance was manifested in discoveries in outer space, the moon's terrain, the planets' orbits; and in inner space, life in a drop of pond water, the circulation of the blood. Words had to be coined to describe these phenomena.

From French, English took *rheumatism, spasm, sphere, surgeon*. From Latin and Greek through Latin, Renaissance English adopted over 10,000 terms. Further examples of these adoptions from French, Latin, and Greek follow.

1500–1550	1550–1600	1600–1650	1650–1700
panacea	*scientific*	*specimen*	*stamen*
vertigo	*hereditary*	*vertebra*	*microscope*
appendix	*nausea*	*forceps*	*organism*
cornea	*species*	*appendage*	*fossil*
	skeleton	*acid*	*geology*
	theory	*coronary*	*cell*
	energy	*ligneous*	*botany*
	virus	*antenna*	*rabies*
	larynx	*stamen*	*lens*

Importations continued. Here's a very small sample of a very large population: *zoology*, 1726; *paramecium*, 1750; *hydrogen*, 1790; *biology*, 1802; *gastropod*, 1820; *paleontology*, 1838; *bacterium*, 1847; *microtome*, 1855; *chromosome*, 1889; *mutation*, 1901; *nucleotide*, 1908; *genome*, 1925; *deoxyribonucleic* acid, 1931.

An extensive list could be drawn up of synonyms for biological referents.

OE	Latin	Greek
man-like	*hominoid*	*anthropoid*
woman	*female*	*gyn*
naught	*zero*	*cipher*
kidney	*ren*	*nephr*
foot	*ped*	*pod*
worm	*verm*	*helminth*
earth	*terr*	*geo*
life	*viv*	*bio*

The terms from native English are often more familiar, more emotive, and sometimes less decent, than those from L.

sweat < OE	*sweaten*	*perspire* < L.
chew	*caeowan*	*masticate*
spit	*spitten*	*expectorate*
shit	*scitan*	*defecate*
die	*diegan*	*expire*

Anthropo is a specimen base of how compounding becomes the source of most of the biological vocabulary. This base, for human being, is in *philanthropy, misanthrope, anthropocentric, anthropomorphism.*

primatology	*anthropoid, anthropology, anthropogenesis,* study of origin of human beings
medicine	*anthropometer,* an instrument to measure physical characteristics
epidemiology	*enanthropic,* pert. to source of disease within the body
	exanthropic, pert. to source of disease outside the body
psychology	*anthropophobia,* morbid dread of human society
	apanthropia, fear of men (cp. *apandria*)
	anthropophilic, preferring human to other animal flesh
	anthropozoophilic, adj. pert. to affection for both people and animals, e.g., of mosquitoes
other fields	*anthropophagy,* cannibalism
	anthropolatry, worship of human beings
	zoanthropia, human changing into beast
	lycanthrope, werewolf

Medieval and Renaissance students of natural history believed there existed on earth all kinds of wondrous creatures, such as dragons and people who had heads in their chests, about which Shakespeare wrote: "The anthropophagi, or men whose heads do grow beneath their shoulders." Other freaks were two-headed, dog-headed, and web-footed.

Anthropophagi preparing dinner
From Sebastian Munster, *Canibali antropophagi*, 1554

Medieval freaks: man with reversed feet, woman with single webbed foot, man whose head doth grow beneath his shoulders, and dog-headed man

2.4 Note on Grimm's Law

The Indo-Europeans might have known little about the articulation of tibia and tarsus, but they did know that they had feet and named the foot: IE *ped*. Sometimes cognates, like siblings, resemble their parents and each other: for example, Latin *ped* and Greek *pod* are obvious descendants of IE *ped*. Sometimes, however, a particular cognate, like a peculiar child, may not look like anyone else in the family: English *fetch* is also a descendant of IE *ped.*

What relates words as diverse as *podiatry, pajamas, foot,* and *fetch?* In a word, Grimm's Law. We remember Jakob Ludwig Karl Grimm as a transcriber of fairy tales. In the early 19th century, he invented a theory as grim as the fairy tale of Sneewittchen und der sieben Zwergen. This theory explains kinship between words from Germanic languages and words from Latin and Greek, the technical words of the biological vocabulary.

In a period over a thousand years, the IE group that became the Germanic peoples changed certain sounds their parents used. Though why the speakers did this is unknown—perhaps it was adolescent rebellion—a review of what was done promotes an understanding of relationships between easy words of native English and their cognates in biological Latin and Greek.

Grimm's Law shows that there's a historical relationship between the sounds *d* and *t.* IE *d* remained *d* in Greek and Latin, but changed to *t* in Proto-Germanic. *Dendrite* and *tree* are from the same source (< IE *deru*), as are *dental* and *tooth* (< IE *dent*). Similarly, IE *p* remained *p* in Greek and Latin, but changed to *f* in Proto-Germanic. *Podiatry* and *foot* are from the same source (< IE *ped*), as are *piscis* and *fish* (< IE *peisk*). Details about these and other changes are in Appendix A.

Words from the Proto-Germanic source came into English earlier than their cognates from Latin or Greek. *Fish* < Old Norse is recorded as having first appeared in English in 900; and *fisherman* at the beginning of the 15th century. *Piscatory,* pertaining to fishing, entered E. from L. about 1625; *piscine,* fish-like, in the late 18th century, and *pisciculture,* the cultivation of fish, in the middle of the 19th. The commonality between *fish* and *piscis* is understood by knowing that the orig. IE *p* sound is rendered *f* in Proto-Germanic descendants and that in Old English the word was *fisc.*

English is very rich in synonyms because it has adopted cognates from cousin IE languages and words from non-IE languages to complement its native resources in the expression of new ideas.

INDO–EUROPEAN GENEOLOGY

The geneology begins toward the end of the Neolithic Age, about 4000 BC. During the subsequent 2500 years, some of the original IE population dispersed to settle throughout Europe and into the Middle East and the Indian sub-continent. The chart omits extinct IE languages and identifies representative modern descendants.

4000–1500 BC	1000–500	0	500–1000 AD	1500	Present
SATEM					Armenian
					Albanian
Balto-Slavic	Baltic				Lithuanian
	Slavic West				Polish Slovak
	East		Old		Russian
Indo-Iranian	Indic Sanskrit				Hindi Sinhalese
	Iranian		New		Iranian Afghan
CENTUM Celtic	Gaelic		Old		Irish Scottish
	Brittanic				Welsh
Italic	Classical Latin 300 BC–100 AD				Latin
			Popular Latin Old-1200 Old-1300		French Italian
Greek	Classical 400–300 BC				Greek
Proto-Germanic	North		Old Norse		Norwegian Swedish Danish
	West				German English
	Consonant Shift		Old 700–1100 Middle 1200–1500		

PART III: SOURCES

CHAPTER 3—FROM ECHOES TO EPONYMS

3.1 Echoism
3.2 Toponyms
3.3 Eponyms: From People
3.4 Eponyms: From Mythologies

*E*tiology, base **etio**, means the study of sources. In medicine, the word has a narrowed meaning: study of the causes or origins of diseases, adj. *etiological.* The etiology of the word *biolexicon* is to be found in two roots from Indo-European, the ancient ancestor of English: IE *gwei* > *bio*, life, and IE *leg* > *lex*, word. *Lexicon* came into E. in 1600, *biology* two hundred years later, and *biolexicon* was born as the title for this book on May 4, 1988.

Sometimes, a word is formed from the initials of a longer word, as *radar* was formed from *radio detecting and ranging.* The new word may be pronounceable as a word, in which case it's an acronym, e.g., *radar, dopa* for *dioxyphenylalanine,* and *PABA* for para-aminobenzoic acid.

Another way by which a fraction of words enters the general vocabulary is by being clipped from longer words, as *van* is a clipping of the Persian *caravan,* and *cab* of the French *cabriolet.* The medical vocabulary has *flu* < *influenza* and *dropsy,* a swelling, < *hydropsis.*

3.1 Echoism

Words coming from attempts to echo sounds constitute a larger fraction of words in the biological vocabulary. Animals, especially birds, receive their names from echoes of vocalizations they make. The insect katydid, the frog kokee, and the birds bobalink, bob-white, chickadee, cuckoo, curlew, and whippoorwill received their names from their characteristic calls. Sometimes the sounds made by animals are echoed differently in different languages: the American dog barks *woof-woof,* but the Japanese dog barks *wung-wung;* the American baby cries *waw-waw,* but the Japanese baby inscrutably wails *ogya ogya.* Sometimes the echoes are alike: English *cuckoo,* German *Fasenkuckuk,* French *coucou-faisan.* Echoic names may become incorporated into the taxonomic label for an animal: cockatoos belong to the genus *Kakatoe.*

Human beings emit many noises, both healthy and disordered. In the first category, we could note happy *ha ha, ho ho, giggle,* and *hurrah.* The rasping sound made by a sore throat has echoic renditions: *cough, croup,* and *gargle.* L. *gurgulio* gave rise to *gurgle* and *gargoyle* as well as to *gargle*, and unexpectedly, to *jargon*, which entered E. from Fr. in the 14th century. English's echoic *belch* takes second place to the grander Greek *borborygmus*, a really creative word for an internal belch. E. *hickock* became *hiccup*, and also, on a mistaken parallel with *cough*, the less echoic *hiccough*. The native English *spit* is an echo of the sound of expectoration. The Greeks, who disapproved of an initial *s* before another consonant, invented *ptyal* for that sound, and this appears in *ptyalism*, excessive production of saliva, and also in *pituitary*, a cognate of *spit*.

A convenient way of charting lexical development of an Indo-European root is to set up a box which will indicate the root and then its descendants in Latin, Greek, English, and, where necessary or interesting, in other languages of the IE complex. These boxes will range from very small — the root appearing in only a few words — to very large, covering several pages. The boxes may detail not only descendants in the biological vocabulary but also in the general vocabulary of our daily talk. This chapter presents two such boxes, for IE *la* and *pneu*, both echoic.

IE *la*, talk, mutter

This source gave rise to English *lull, loon, owl* and *howl*. In Latin, it became an infinitive, *ululare*, echoic for an owl's hoot. *Ululation* means human warbling; in psychiatry, it refers more narrowly to hysterical crying. IE *la* also became, through Latin, the word *lament; lamentation* has a sense of howling to it.

In Gk. it became the base **lal**, a base meaning to talk and appearing in medical terms. The most general term for kinds of speech disorders is *lalopathy*; the term for the least decent disorder is *coprolalia*, dirty talk. With prefixes, **lal** gives us:

with *a-*, not	*alalia*, no speech
with *dys*, disordered	*dyslalia*, abnormal speech caused by physical defect
with *brady*, slow	*bradylalia*, abnormally slow talking
with *tachy*, fast	*tachylalia*, abnormally fast talking
with *rhino*, nose	*rhinolalia*, nasal talking
with *pali*, back, again	*palilalia*, repetition of sounds
with *echo*	*echolalia*, imitating other people's vocalizations
with *em-*, in + *bol, throw*	*embolalia*, the condition of having strange and meaningless words in one's speech
with *para-*, beyond	*paralalia*, a speech disorder characterized by emitting a sound other than that intended

Glossalalia, from Gk. *glossa*, tongue + **lal** + *-ia*, condition of, means speaking in tongues. It refers to experiences undergone by certain religious congregations wherein the believers suddenly vocalize words and phrases of unknown languages (or perhaps just babble).

Breathing is an audible activity. It may be that the base in *emphysema, phys,* was echoic for the puffing sound made by people suffering from the disease. Indo-European *pneu,* to breathe, seems to be another echoic or onomatopoeic root for breathing. The descendants range from familiar and short words such as *sneeze* to unfamiliar and long words, in fact to the longest word in English, longer than *supercalifragilisticexpialidocious.* This longest word, a sesquepedalian prize, is indicated in the box below.

IE *pneu,* breathe

The only native E. word from this source is *sneeze,* like its ancestor *pneu* an echoic rendition. No L. descendants, but from Gk. we have over 150 words with **pneu(mono)** for gas: for example, *pneumatic.*

pneumoperitoneal	adj. re. to space where air or gas has come in
pneumohemopericardium	space where air or gas or blood has come in the sac around the heart

Pneu(mono) combines with other bases for description of the lungs and of lung disease and repair: *pneumonia, pneumopathy.*

pneumopexy	fixation of the lung
pneumotropism	tendency of an organism to inhabit lung tissue
pneumoconiosis	diseased condition of having particles in the lungs; *coni* a base for dust

pneumonoultramicroscopicsilicovolcanoconiosis

This, the longest word in English, analyzes into **pneumono** + *ultra* + *micro* + *scopic* + *silico* + *volcano* + *coni* + *-osis* = lung + beyond + small + viewing + quartz + volcano + dust + morbid condition of.

This archaic word is no longer actually used, or at least not used with grace; it refers to the condition of having very small particles, or dust, of silica in the lungs. *Coni* for dust appears also in the useful but unfamiliar *hydroconion,* a device for spraying out water droplets as fine as dust, an atomizer.

Pneu(mono) appears in taxonomic names.

Diplococcus pneumoniae	pneumococcus
Klebsiella pneumoniae	pneumobacillus

These two bacteria are responsible for different kinds of pneumonia.

Dyspnoetus dignus	a beetle

Gk. **pnea,** breathing, breath.

---

a-	+ **pnea**		*apnea,* no breath
dys-	+		*dyspnea,* disordered breathing
eu-	+		good breathing
hyper-	+		irregular high breathing
hypo-	+		irregular low or shallow breathing
tachy	+		irregular fast breathing

From a different and apparently non-echoic IE source comes Gk. **pulm(ono)** which also refers to the lungs, e.g., *pulmonary.*

Retch, scream, cricket, and *raven* have been traced back to IE echoic *ker,* one of six homophonic reconstructions *ker.* This one, imitative of a bird's cry or the vibratory sound of human vocal cords, led through Germanic to E. *retch, cricket, screech, scream,* and the birds *rook, raven,* and *shrike.* Into L. and from that straight or through French: *crevice, decrepit.* L. *corcus,* raven, endowed E. with *corvine, cormorant,* and *Corvus,* an order of birds. From Gk. *korak,* raven, came a term for a vertebrate bone, the *coracoid.*

3.2 Toponyms

Another fraction of words in the biological as well as general vocabulary comprises the names of places; these are termed *toponyms.*

peasant	< Phasis, a river in the Caucasus
canary	< Canary Islands
tarantula	< Taranto, Italy

Tarantula
Family *Theraphosidae*

Siamese	< Siam, older name for Thailand
magnesium	< Magnesia, a city of Greece

sardonic, drily witty	< a Sardinian plant which contains a toxin that contorts the face of anyone unwary enough to eat it
Mamenchiasaurus	a dinosaur < Mamenchi, a Chinese province
Lyme disease	< Lyme, Connecticut, a treponoma infection communicated by mites
Mediterranean fever	< Mediterranean; a disease causing fever in human beings, disrupting fetal development in animals; also known by an eponym from Australian physician David Bruce: *brucellosis;* and also known as *undulant fever*

3.3 Eponyms: From People

Words from names of people are called *eponyms.* Cimry, the name of a tribe of ancient Celts, > *Cambrian,* a word denoting the first stage of the Paleozoic. A minority of nomenclators approve of eponyms in taxonomy and anatomy, arguing that honoring someone by using his or her name recognizes good service to biology and also incites an interest in biography and history.

Most nomenclators condemn eponyms as distractions that don't indicate anything useful about the plant, animal, or anatomical structure or function, but do excite conflicts about who really should be credited with having first discovered the referent. In the late 19th century, an international congress on anatomical nomenclature hid eponyms in brackets; by 1955, a similar congress decided to delete anatomical eponyms entirely.

Thousands of eponyms exist in the biolexicon, several for people who designed theories, others for those who designed procedures or instruments, more for those who first discovered or publicized an anatomical part or function, most for those who identified a disease, plant or animal, or whose names are linked to such for some reason other than discovery. The roster of eponyms include Italian, French, German, English, American, and people from many other countries.

Mendelism	theory of inheritance of discrete units from parents < *German monk Gregor Mendel*
Lamarckianism	theory that living things will themselves to change and that these changes are inherited by offspring < French naturalist Jean Baptiste Pierre Antoine Monet de Lamarck
Darwinism	natural selection or network of biological, philosophical, political ideas < English naturalist Charles Darwin (< OE *deor,* dear + *win,* friend; dear friend).
Corrigan's cautery	an instrument that destroys tissue with a hot iron disk < Irish physician John Corrigan
roentgenology	study of x-rays < German physicist who discovered x-rays, Wilhelm Konrad Roentgen
curie	unit of radioactivity < French physicist Marie Curie

condom	perhaps from an 18th century physician who developed this prophylactic
gram	a method of staining < 19th cen. Danish physician Hans Gram (no relation to the unit of measurement)

A list of people of importance in the history of medicine would include the Greek Hippocrates, the Roman Galen, the 16th century Flemish Andreas Vesalius, and several Renaissance and post-Renaissance Italians—Mondino de Luzzi (14th century), Bartolomeo Eustachius and Gabriello Fallopio (both 16th century), Marcello Malpighi (17th century).

Hippocrates, a 5th century B.C. Greek physician, is faintly remembered in the *tendon of Hippocrates*, better known as the *Achilles tendon*, also *tendo calcaneus* and *chorda magna*, and better remembered as the founder of western medicine.

Galen, physician to Marcus Aurelius and the author of over 500 works, was critically influential upon the 16th century revival of learning called the Renaissance. Two veins and a nerve were named after him.

The *bone of Vesalius* is located in the foot, the *glands of Vesalius* in lymphatic glands, and the *foramen of Vesalius* in the ear.

A hundred years after Vesalius's *Fabrica*, Marcello Malpighi revealed capillary circulation. *Malpighi's layer* of the epidermis reflects his interest in cutaneous anatomy; also named after him were corpuscles and a capsule of the spleen.

Johann Wolfgang Goethe was an 18th century poet and novelist. *Faust* and *Sorrows of Werther* are often included in great books courses. His interest in biology is reflected in his studies emphasizing a continuity from non-human to human animals. *Goethe's bone* is a term for the premaxillary. A suture fusing the maxillary and premaxillary is called either the *sutura incisiva* (it's close to the incisor teeth) or *suture of Goethe*. A mineral, *goethite*, was also named after him. Very few poets have been admitted into the biolexicon.

Baer's membrana serosa is a term for the chorionic membrane. Karl Ernst von Baer, a 19th century German embryologist, is famous or infamous for his formulation of the biogenetic law, that the human embryo in its development repeats stages of the development of precursors, for example, in having gills, a "law" caught in the phrase "ontogeny recapitulates phylogeny."

Cuvier's duct and *Cuvier's canal* relate to veins. Georges Cuvier, born in 1769, was an eminent paleontologist as well as comparative anatomist, talented at reconstructing an entire animal from fossil fragments.

Darwin's tubercle is called that because the one who first observed this small protruberance which sometimes appears on the helix of the ear honored Charles Darwin in naming it. Charles Darwin is better known as the inventor of natural selection.

Thomas Henry Huxley, Darwin's friend and collaborator, who called himself "Darwin's bulldog," when he was a 19-year-old medical student, discovered a layer of the hair follicle: *Huxley's layer*.

Bowman's capsule	around the kidney's glomerulus < William Bowman, 19th century English surgeon,

Darwin's Tubercle

his name also in *Bowman's membrane,* of the cornea, and *Bowman's muscle,* for fibers of the ciliary muscle

Broca's convolution   for the speech area of the brain
< Pierre Paul Broca, 19th century French anatomist

Organ of Corti   a structure of the cochlea
< Alfonso Corti, 19th century Italian anatomist

Eustacian tube   also the *tuba auditiva,* a duct from ear to mouth
< *Bartoloeo Eustachi,* 16th century Italian physician

Fallopian tube   also the *tubae uterinae* and *oviduct*
< 16th century Italian anatomist Gabrielle Fallopia

loop of Henle   for uriniferous tubules of kidney
< 19th century German anatomist Friedrich Henle; also named after him were *Henle's layer* (of hair follicle), *Henle's spine* (of temporal bone), and *Henley's ampulla* (of uterine tube)

Jacobson's organ   area of the palate flicked by snake's tongue for reception of odor, the *vomeronasal organ*
< 19th century Swedish anatomist and physician Ludwig Levin Jacobson, also eponymous in ear structures (a nerve, canal, and plexus)

Islets of Langerhans   pancreatic cells
< 19th century German pathologist Paul Langerhans

Shrapnell's membrane   of the tympani or middle ear
< 19th century English anatomist Henry Jones Shrapnell, eponym also for *shrapnel*

Wilde's cords   fibers on corpus callosum, also *striae transversae corporis*
< 19th century Irish physician William Wilde, his name appearing also in *Wilde's incision,* surgical technique for remedying mastoiditis, and as the surname of his son Oscar

Discoverers' names are also eponymous for diseases, e.g.,

Escherichia coli	a bacterium of the human intestine
	< German physician Theodor Escherich
Marfan's syndrome	arachnodactyly, spider-leg fingers
Colley's syndrome	thalassemia, a blood disease, affliction of Mediterranean people
Tay-Sachs disease	blindness, paralysis, affliction primarily of Jewish people
Kaposi's sarcoma	a cancer, especially destructive of people with injured immune systems
	< Hungarian dermatologist M. Kaposi
Down's syndrome	< British physician John Down
salmonella	caused by bacteria in spoiled meat; not from *salmon*, but from Daniel E. Salmon, who described it in 1914
rickettsia	typhus, Rocky Mountain spotted fever, transmitted by microbes of orders Rickettsiales and Chlamydiales
	< Howard T. Ricketts

Homophonic *rickets,* a bone disease, entered E. in the 17th century, from an unknown source.

The last and most tempting category for eponyms is taxonomy, the giving of a person's name to an animal or plant, e.g., *Eoanthropus dawsoni,* (Charles) Dawson's dawn-man; *Clarkia,* a western North American plant < William Clark; *Australopithecus boisei* < Charles Boise; *Conacodon cophater,* an extinct mammal, the species name perhaps a sign of the namer's disapproval of an American paleontologist whose surname was Cope.

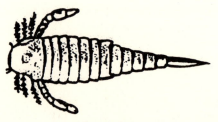

Hughmilleria
Eurypterid from the Ordovician named after Victorian geologist Hugh Miller

In his work on Eucosmine moths, the etymological entomologist Carl Heinrich named a new insect genus *Gretchen,* after his secretary. For names of its species he chose *amatana, concubitana, delicatana, deludana,* and *dulciana.* These adjectives impose upon the insects features of the secretary: love, concubinage, delicacy, delusion, and sweetness.

3.4 Eponyms: From Mythologies

The general vocabulary boasts a small but intriguing group of words that come from the names of characters in stories, such as *quixotic, pander, lilliputian.* In the medical vocabulary, naming after characters is a rare occurrence. *Syphilis* comes from a character, the hero of a 1530 poem by Giovanni Fracastoro, *Syphilis, sive morbus Gallicus,* "Syphilis, or the French Disease." *Treponema pallidium,* which entered E. 1903, is the microbe responsible for transmitting the disease.

People make up myths for many reasons, such as to narrate the birth of the universe and of their own tribes, to explain or justify the malign influences of nature, and to scare themselves.

Words in the general vocabulary that come from mythologies can be exemplified by a word which calls to mind interest in the early 19th century in ways of sparking life: *golem.* The golem in Hebrew mythology was an artificial creature created by a wise or lazy rabbi to do service for him or his people. In Mary Shelley's fiction, it became the monstrous marvel of medical science manufactured by the madman Dr. Victor Frankenstein.

The biological vocabulary has few terms that come from mythologies other than Greek or Roman, and these usually appear in taxonomic names. A very small contribution from Egyptian comes from the goddess Isis, consort of Osiris, > Egyptian *Isidium corallium,* a lichen.

Egyptian also gave us a term of broader application. This little story begins with the Egyptian god Ammon. Pilgrims who came to visit the temple of Ammon were transported there by camels. Nitrogen-containing camel droppings gave off a stink which became associated with the temple, thus: *ammonia.* The Egyptian god's name is also memorialized in the *cornu Ammonis,* the hippocampus, and in the invertebrate *ammonite.*

Hebrew
golem
Beelzebub   a devilish deity

Ammon, supreme god of the Egyptians

Ammonites
A cephalopod related to pearly nautilus

Ateles belzebuth	a spider monkey
Moloch	deity demanding sacrifice
Moloch horridus	a lizard
Satan	the adversary, or devil
Boletus satanus	a mushroom
Satanoperca	a fish
Satanellus	a mammal

Slavic or Turkish
vampire
Vampurella   an imaginary single-celled organism
Vampyrus spectrum   a bat

Hindi
brahman   the universal soul
Cremastocheilus brahma   a beetle
Buddha   Buddha
Hagiastrum buddhae   a marine protozoan
Siva   deity of destruction and preservation
Sivapithecus   a fossil ape
Rama   another deity, incarnation of Vishnu
Ramapithecus   a fossil ape (genus now includes *Sivipithecus*)

Irish
leprechaun   a forest spirit, a dwarf
leprechaunism   condition of stunted mind and body, enlarged clitoris in females, enlarged penis in males; *elfin facies, Donahue's syndrome*

A cornucopia of words for the biolexicon as well as for the general vocabulary is Greek mythology. We'll turn to this in the next chapter.

CHAPTER 4—GREEK MYTHOLOGY

4.1   Major Deities
4.2   Monsters
4.3   Nature Spirits
4.4   Homeric Epics
4.5   Other Mythical Creatures
4.6   Review of Elements

Most words in the general vocabulary that stem from mythology are from Greek sources, e.g., *panic, tantalize, cereal, martial.*

Ceres, goddess of cereal

Almost all the words in the biological vocabulary that stem from mythology are also from Greek sources. There are so many of these that even excluding some still leaves us with a large cast of characters. We'll focus on the major characters and limit taxonomic examples.

4.1 Major Deities

Greek religion and Roman after it made time of day, attitudes, processes, places, love, and so on into gods. Like poets, biologists have turned to pagan mythology for inspiration. Gk. myth itself > *Mythomantis,* a genus of insects.

According to Hebrew mythology, in the beginning there was the word. According to Greek mythology, in the beginning there was Chaos, the atmosphere, > *Chaos,* a genus of Protozoa. A Flemish chemist, J. B. van Helmont, in the 17th century changed *chaos* into *gas.*

Uranus, Heaven, appears as the name of a planet and in **uran** for the roof of the mouth, that is, the palate, as in

uranoschism	palate fissure
uranoplasty	plastic surgery of the palate
Uranichthys	a fish

Uranus, Heaven, and Gaea, Earth, had many children, the male children called Titans and the female Titanesses. The name *Titan* itself for something huge is in the adjective *titanic;* in the name of a supposedly invincible ship, the *Titanic;* and in the large extinct rhinoceros *Titantherium.*

Some of the names of the Titans have come into the biological vocabulary. Vesalius in the 16th century called the first neck vertebra the *atlas,* this name taken from Atlas or Atlantos, the titan who held up the heavens and/or the earth; also from this titan, *Atlantosaurus,* a reptile taxon.

Atlas holding up world

Of the twelve titans, Prometheus was the one especially concerned with the progress of the human species, in one account creating us, in another bringing us

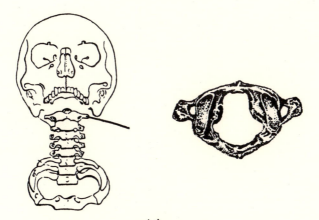

Atlas
First cervical vertebra

fire or knowledge. The memory of Prometheus is elevated in his name's entry in the subtitle of Mary Shelley's *Frankenstein: The Modern Prometheus,* and lessened in becoming the species name of a moth: *Callosamia promethea.*

From the name of the Titaness Mnemosyne come the bases *mem* and **mn.** *Mem* appears in *memory, memorial, immemorial, memento,* and *mnemonic,* a device for memorizing (the *m* is not pronounced unless it's preceded by a vowel). With negating prefix *a* + the base **mn,** we have

amnesia		loss of memory
amnesty		etym. means the same thing—a forgetting of past mischief or wisdom.
dys-	+ **mnesia**	weak memory
ec-	+	weak memory for recent events
loga	+	aphasia of senses
palin-	+	remembrance of past events
past		
para-	+	remembrance of things that didn't happen
pseudo-	+	paramnesia
Mnematidium		taxonomic name for a group of insects

The Titans fought and lost a war with new gods, the Olympians. Briareus, a mythological giant blessed with 100 arms, fought on the side of the Olympians in this war; *Briareus morbillorum* is the name of the virus that causes measles, *Briareus varicellae* of that which causes chicken pox.

As we have seen, the base for heaven is **uran.** Other Gk. deities associated with the cosmos are Helios, God of the sun (L. Sol); Eos, goddess of dawn; and Selene, goddess of the moon—these three children of the union between the Titans Hyperion and Theia. Gk. Iris was the goddess of the rainbow.

The names of these deities have been converted into bases that are in the words of several scientific disciplines:

	helio Helios, sun	**sol** Sol, sun	**iris, irid** Iris, rainbow	**eo** Eos, dawn
Chemistry	*helium*			*eosin*, a rosy dye
Anatomy		*solar plexus*	*iris* *retro-iridian*	
Medicine	*heliosis*, sunstroke	*solatus*, sun-burned *solarium*	*iridectomy*	*eopsia*, improved vision at dawn
Taxonomy	*Heliozoa*, protozoan	*Solaster*, echinoderm	*Iris*, a plant	*Eohippus*, an extinct horse
	Helianthus *tomentosus*, sunflower	*Phalaena* *solata*, a moth	*Salmo irideus*, rainbow trout	*Eoanthropus*, a fake hominid
Other	*heliophobia*, fear of sun, of sunbathing *heliocentric* *heliotropism*	*solstice*	*iridology*, predicting through analysis of iris *iridescent*	*eolith*, dawn stone *Eocene*, a geological period

The mother of Zeus, Rhea, lent her name to an ostrich-like bird, and the wife of Zeus, Hera, to a fly, *Hera mikii.* Hera gave birth to Hebe, the goddess of youth, lit. in *hebephrenia*, schizophrenic reversion to childhood; metaphoric in *hebetomy*, incision into the pubic bone. There's a homophonic *hebe* from Latin; this base means dull, as in *hebetude*, a state of lethargy, and *hebetate*, to make dull. *Hebetic* could be an adj. with happy connotations, pertaining to time of puberty, or just the opposite, pertaining to dullness.

Many of the pagan gods—the Olympians and rural spirits of stream, woodland, farm—have had their names applied to taxa of animals and plants, organs, diseases, mental conditions. Several of these gods were deifications of love, sex, marriage, as was Aphrodite, the Gk. goddess of love, base **aphrodi,** in pharmacology:

aphrodis   + *-iac*   substance or event to increase sexual desire; its ant., *anaphrodisiac*

psychology:
aphrodis   + *-ia*   increased sexual desire
                 + *mania*   *aphrodisiamania*, insane sexual hunger
hyper   + **aphrodisia**   increased sexual desire, more than mere aphrodisia

The Roman counterpart to Aphrodite was Venus, base **vene(ro).** general: *venerable, venerate, venery,* of sexual interest, *Venus's*-flytrap, a plant, and *venereal.*

anatomy:

mons veneris	pubic mount
mons, mountain	

psychology:

venero + *phobia*	morbid dread of venereal disease

medicine:

venere + *-al*	venereal (disease)
venero + *logy*	study of venereal disease

taxonomy:

Cestum veneris	Venus's girdle, a ctenophore

Aphrodite was born in Cyprus, hence *cyprian,* relating to this goddess and to those who worship her.

cypridiophobia	morbid fear of venereal disease
Cypripedium	a genus of orchids, lady's slippers

From Hermaphrodite, a Gk. androgynous god, *hermaphroditism,* which is the condition of having organs of both sexes, as in plants, earthworms, and selected people. From Eros, the son of Aphrodite and Mars, the base **eroto.**

Botticelli, The Birth of Venus, 1453

Polychaete sea mouse
Aphrodite

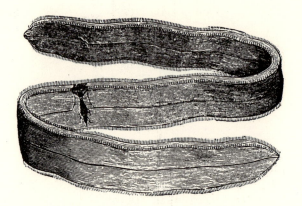

Venus' girdle, a ctenophore
Cestum veneris

eroto	+ *mania*	excessive sexual desire of male (also *satyriasis*) or female (also *nymphomania*)
	+ *path*	one who suffers from diseased eroticism (cp. *psychopath* and *sociopath*)
ero	+ *genous*	pert. to areas of the body sensitive to sexual excitement
ped	+ **erast**	one who finds children sexually attractive; cp. *pedophile*

Two deities have their names associated with the penis. From Priapus, a Gk. god of fruitfulness, come *priapism,* abnormal and perhaps embarrassing penile erection; *priapitis,* a word for inflammation of the penis; *Priapulus,* an onychophoric invertebrate. *Onychophoric,* bearing claws, refers to a phylum of small tropical forest invertebrates.

Onychophore *Priapulus*

From Phallos, a god of the male sex organ or fertility, come *phallic, phalliform, Phallos* as name for taxa of tunicates, molluscs, and reptiles,

phallo	+ *dynia*	*phallodynia,* pain in the penis
	+ *algia*	*phallalgia,* pain in the penis
	+ *oncus*	*phalloncus,* tumor of the penis
di-	+ **phallos**	*diphallos,* double penis, as of male snakes

Aesculapius tending a sick man

Hymen, Gk. god of marriage, gives us the general word *hymeneal*, pert. to marriage. **Hymen** is usually recognizable as referring to a specific membrane, the vaginal hymen, but it also applies to membranes in general:

hymeno	+ *logy*	study of membranes
	+ *ptera*	*Hymenoptera*, order of membrane-winged
	wing	insects, bees, ants, wasps
	+ *lepis*	order of parasitic worms, *hymenolepiasis*
	seizure	the disease caused by this tapeworm
	+ *plasty*	surgical repair or renovation of the hymen
	+ *-ium*	spore-bearing layer of fungi
	+ *-ectomy*	*hymenectomy*, excision of the hymen
	+ *-tomy*	incision into the hymen
Tetrahymena		ciliated protozoa genus

While Ares, or in Roman mythology Mars, has been unemployed in the biolexicon, one of his offspring is in hundreds of words: Phobos, child of Ares and Eris, goddess of discord > *phobia*.

Among the Olympians were deities who controlled the sea and the underworld. Several of them are eponyms in taxonomic terms, e.g., *Amoeba proteus* < Proteus; and *Triturus viridescens*, a common newt < Triton.

From Apollo, the god of music, art, and poetry, come the general vocabulary word *apollonian*, handsome, cultivated, and a name for an arachnid: *Apollophanes.* Apollo in his role as Paean was physician to the gods; his union with the nymph Caronis produced Asclepius, god of medicine, in Latin Aesculapius.

Thetis, hoping to insure her son's invulnerability, dipped the boy into the river Styx, but she had to hold him by his heel to do that. Those who suffer from *Achilles heel*, a.k.a. *bursa tendinis calcanei* (*achilles*); Achilles tendon, *tendo carcaneus* (*achilles*); from *achillobursitis* and *achillodynia* owe the names of their afflictions to Thetis's holding her son by the heel. As a boy, Achilles was educated by the centaur Chiron; later, fighting in the Trojan War, he was struck in the heel and limped to hell.

The river of forgetfulness was called Lethe. Lethe is the toponym for **leth**, forgetfulness, and in its L. adaptation, for terminal forgetfulness, or death.

Hercules beetle,
a coleopteran

lethe			amnesia
leth	+ *-al*		fatal
	+ *argy*		drowsiness
	+ *argus*		sleeping sickness
	+ *argo* + *genic*		productive of drowsiness
	+ *iferous*		bearing drowsiness or death, as of lethal medication
	+ *mania*		*lethomania,* narcotic addition
a-	+ **leth** + *-ia*		*alethia,* inability to forget
anti-	+ **leth** + *argic*		pert. to overcoming drowsiness
Lethacea			family of viruses causing plant disease

The L. base *morph* refers to sleep and form; its deification is *Morpheus,* god of sleep and of form.

morpho	+ *logy*		the study of structure
	+ *lysis*		dissolution of form
a-	+ **morph** + *-ous*		no form or shape, as of amoeba
mono-	+ **morph** + *-ic*		one form
pleo-	+		a few forms
poly-	+		many forms
meta-	+		change in form
ecto-	+		of an outer, skinny type
meso-	+		of a middle, muscular type
endo-	+		of an inner, heavy type

anthropo +		in the form of a human being
rhizo +		form of a root
histo	+ **morpho** + *logy*	study of tissue structure
gero	+ **morph** + *-ism*	aged form
morphine		to E. from French

Somnus, a Roman god for sleep, parallels the base **somn** for sleep:

somno + *-lent*	sleepy
+ *-arium*	place for sleep; cp. *dormitory*
somni + *ferous*	producing sleep; cp. *soporific*
somn + *ambulism*	sleepwalking; at night: *noctambulism*
para- + **somnia**	condition of responding only by reflex

The two other bases for sleep alluded to have not been personified: L. **dorm** as in *dormitory, dormant, dormouse;* and L. **sopor** as in *soporific* and *soporiferous.*

Dormitorium, a bed chamber

The Gk. god of sleep, Hypno > **hypno,** *as in* hypnosis.

hypno + *lepsy*	seizure by sleep
+ *genic*	causing sleep, cp. *soporific, somniferous*
+ *an-* +	
aesthesia	using hypnosis an as anaesthetic
+ *dont* + *-ics*	hypnoanesthesia in dentistry
+ *gogue*	*hypnagogue,* leading to sleep; cp. *synagogue;* the reason for *a* instead of *o* as the combining vowel is that *gogue* < Gk. *agogus,* leading
Hypnoticus	a crustacean

Morphine, soporific, somnolent, hypnogenic are terms applicable to taking and experiencing the effects of taking drugs. The base for drug, **narco,** is not an eponym but may find a place for examination here. About a dozen words, including the most recent coinage, *narcoterrorism,* have the base **narco:**

| **narco** + *-osis* | *narcosis,* condition of being drugged |
| + *lepsy* | seizure by sleep, inability to ward off or excessive desire for sleep |

narco + *-tic*	adj., *narcotic;* noun, *narcotics*
+ *-ine*	opium-derived drug
+ *-ism*	drugged state, addiction
osmo + **narco** + *-tic*	*osmonarcotic,* narcosis delivered through odors
smell	odors
acro +	sharp, acrid and narcotic
electro + **narco** + *-osis*	narcosis delivered through electric current
Narcomedusae	a coelenterate

Thanatos, the Gk. god of death, lives on in *Thanatos,* Freud's personification of self-destructiveness; in *Thanatophilus,* an insect genus. *Thanatophilus* refers to venomous snakes.

thanato + *phobia*	morbid dread of dying
+ *opsia*	*Thanatopsia,* title of poem by William Bryant; lit., view of death
+ *-osis*	gangrene, the decay of tissues
+ *mania*	suicidal impulse
+ *meter*	used to ascertain time of death
+ *gnomic*	adj., pert. to approaching signs of death
eu- + **thanasia**	mercy-killing

The Roman counterpart of Thanatos was Mors, the base **mort** in *mortal, mortician, mortuary,* and many other compounds. *Mortinatality,* and in a reversal of the bases, *natimortality,* calculates the percentage of stillbirths to live births. *Mortisemblant* means resembling death.

Gk. **necro,** dead, death, corpse, dead body or tissue, is used in biological, especially medical, terminology more often than the synonymous L. **mort.**

necro + *-tic*	*necrotic,* adj. pert. to dead tissue
+ *-osis*	morbid condition of dead tissue
+ *-tomy*	dissection of corpse
+ *opsy*	syn., *autopsy*
+ *polis*	city of the dead, elegant cemetary
+ *logy*	syn., *obituary*
rhino + **necro** + *-osis*	*rhinonecrosis,* condition of having dead tissue in nose
oto + **necro** + *-osis*	condition of having dead tissue in ear
steato + +	dead fatty tissue
Necrodasypus	lit. dead hairy foot, a mammal

We'll return to **necro** in the terminal chapter.

The gods insured their immortality by drinking nectar or eating ambrosia; these converted their blood into ichor. *Nectar,* in the sense the word now has and in its derivative, *nectarine,* has had an elegant etymological history. *Ambrosia* has had a more varied history, elegant enough in meaning a particularly tasty food (one expression, a dish of marshmallows, coconut, oranges, pineapple is to be recommended), less elegant in becoming the name of a beetle that eats fungus and the taxonomic name of a species of ragweed, *Ambrosia trifida. Ichor* has fared less well—it still refers to a divine flow in the blood, but it also refers to pus, to the discharge from an ulcer, a sore, or wound; *ichoremia* is another term for *septicemia. Sic transit gloria mundi,* So passes the glory of the world.

4.2 Monsters

In the pristine Chaos of Greek mythology, limbs, torsos, heads, and other anatomical debris tumbled about and attached to each other to produce creatures half-this and half-that. One such contraption was Chimaera, composed of a lion's head, a goat's body, and a dragon's tail. The general vocabulary offers *chimerical,* adj. for an insanely fanciful idea, like peace on earth. Taxonomy turned to the Chimaera for the name of a fish. A wider use is that of **chimera** as descriptive of a plant or animal made up of tissues from a species or gender other than its own, for example, a human being with an organ transplanted from an ape or a human male with surgically implanted female organs.

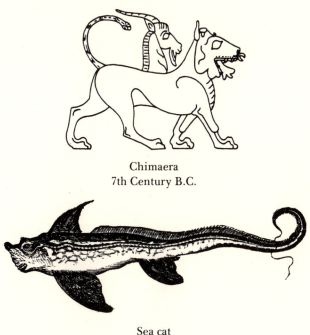

Chimaera
7th Century B.C.

Sea cat
Chimaera monstrosa

The name of the *cecropia* moth comes from Cecrops, half-man and half-dragon. From Gk. *drakon* to L. *draco* come words for dragons, such as the constellation that looks like a dragon, *Draco;* the tapeworm superfamily *Dracunculoidea;* the nematode *Dracunculus;* a genus of flying lizards, or dragons, *Draco;* and an aristocratic vampire, *Dracula.*

Among the menagerie of many other mythological monsters is the viperish *Echidna.* The name exists as that for Australian egg-laying mammalian anteaters, and as the

Flying dragon
Genus *Draco*

base **echin** for spiny: *echinate, echinococcus, Echinodermata,* a phylum that includes starfish and other *echinoids.* Echidna gave birth to the multiheaded *Hydra* > **hydra,** now a genus of freshwater polyps and, capitalized, a constellation. Gk. **demon,** a spirit > *demonology,* the pre-scientific and contemporary belief (not just study of) that these supernatural creatures infest the world and, at times, those who sermonize against them.

The hanging tentacles of a jellyfish reminded a taxonomist of the snake-like hair of Medusa, one of three monstrous sisters, the Gorgons. The pattern of veins around a newborn baby's belly button or omphalos and the similar pattern decorating that area of someone suffering from cirrhosis of the liver resembles the untidy hairdo of Medusa, hence: *caput* (for head) *medusae,* also called *cirsomphalos.*

The toxicity of a jellyfish's sting might have aided the comparison between the coelenterate and the mythological monster whose appearance petrified people. **Medusa** and **medusoid** refer to jellyfish; and the surname, *Gorgon,* is in the order of corals, *Gorgonacea,* and also in taxa of reptiles, echinoderms, and platyhelminths. *Gorgon* also means a remarkably ugly woman.

Hercules fighting Hydra

Hydrozoan
Hydra viridis

Gorgon
6th Century B.C. Temple of Artemis

Gorgonia nobilis

Jellyfish *Medusa*

4.3 Nature Spirits

Brown's *Composition of Scientific Words* lists 63 terms for spirit, including a few already presented (e.g., *Beelzebub, lemur, Satan*). Pagan water and woodland spirits cavort throughout the biological vocabulary.

From Flora, the Roman goddess of flowers: **flor** > *florist, flower,* etc.

flora	population of plants
ex- + **flor** + *esce*	*effloresce,* to bloom
	note that *ex-,* out of, can become *ef-*
Florisuga mellivora	a hummingbird

From Fauna, Roman goddess of animals:

fauna	population of animals; adj., *faunal*
avi, bird + **fauna**	*avifauna,* population of birds in a district

And from Faunus, Flora's brother, god of animals:

faun	a half-goat, half-man
Phanaeus faunus	a beetle

Faun should not be confused with homophonic *fawn*, a young deer < Fr. < L. *fetus*, offspring; and *fawn*, to show excessive affection or deference, < OE.

Fauns are the Roman counterparts of Gk. satyrs. **Satyr** is the general name for a family of goatish woodland spirits. *Satyr* was an 18th century generic name for apes, though today it is the name of an insect genus. **Satyr** appears in *satyriasis* and *satyromania*, both words for male sexual obsession.

Satyr holding syrinx

Pan, a satyr with the characteristic head and torso of a man, the ears, horns, and legs of a goat > the word *panic*, anxiety caused by the apparition of Pan frolicking naked among the trees. *Pan* gives us, among other taxonomic names, that of the chimpanzee: *Pan troglodytes*. *Chimpanzee* comes from an African language, Bantu; apparently it's a coincidence that the word for this ape includes a *pan*. *Troglodytes*, a Gk. word for cave dweller, is applied by Robert Louis Stevenson to his character Mr. Hyde.

The homophonic **pan** means all. This base has been useful in words of the general vocabulary, such as *panorama* and *panchromatic*, and in the biological vocabulary:

pan + *hygrous* humid	humid in all its parts
+ *demic* people	pandemic, general epidemic
+ *ptosis* drooping	*panoptosis*, drooping of all abdominal organs
+ *som* + *-ous*	*pansomous*, pert. to whole body
+ *opthalm* + *-itis*	*panopthalmitis*, inflammation of all of the eye
+ *cyto* + *penia*	*pancytopenia*, condition of deficiency in all blood cells
+ *acos*, cure	*panacea*, a cure-all

Syn. *nostrum,* a quack cure-all < L. *noster,* our—the
connection is that the makers of "our" medicine kept
its recipe to themselves

Still another homophonic *pan* < L. *panis,* bread, as in *panivorous,* bread-eating;
companion; and *pantry.*

The nymphs were female nature spirits. **Nymph** came to mean bride and that sense
came to be used metaphorically for the premature stage of an insect or young maiden.

nympho	middle stage in insect metamorphosis; *nymphette,* pre-pubescent girl
+ *mania*	*nymphomania,* female excessive sexual desire
+ *lepsy*	*nympholepsy,* obsession, as with coins, books, ideas, art, writing, automobiles
+ *-ae*	*nymphae,* the labia minora
+ *-tomy*	*nymphotomy,* surgical incision of nymphae
Nymphon gracile	a sea spider

Theodore Chassériau, *Nymphe endormie,* 1850

Nymphon

Taxonomy of nymphs:

naiads   nymphs of springs and fountains
                        larval water stage of mayfly and other insects
  Lympha   nymph of rainwater, now **lymph** in *lymphatic, lympho-*
                        cyte, lymphoma, etc.
nereids   nymphs of the ocean

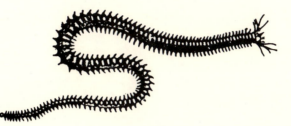

Seaworm *Nereis*

                        > nereis, a marine worm
dryads   wood- and tree- nymphs
  Mintho   Persephone, the goddess of Hades, changed the nymph
                        Mintho into a plant; hence, the word *mint* and the
                        plant genus *Mentha.*
  Arethusa   *arethusa,* north American orchid
oreads   mountain-nymphs
  Echo   *echo, echoencephalograph, echolalia,* etc.
                        echopraxia, repeating someone's actions

Echo had the misfortune of falling in love with the egocentric Narcissus, from whom the name of a plant, the *narcissus;* a psychological condition of self-love, *narcissism;* and a coelenterate taxon, *Narcissasterea. Sylvestris nympha* is a nymph of the forest, < *sylph,* a slender woman; *paranymph,* an archaic word for brides-maid.

An abundance of words comes from the nymph Psyche, Eros's girlfriend, who is associated with breath, mind, mentality, and a kind of therapy. To **psycho** can be added suffixes: *-logy,* study of; *-ic,* pertaining to, *psychic; -osis,* morbid condition of, *psychosis;* and *-ia* state of, *psychia,* loss of consciousness. *Para,* a prefix which here has the meaning of beyond combines with **psycho** in *parapsychology,* the pseudo-science of preternatural events, such as *telepathy; clairvoyance,* seeing into the future; and *psychokinesis,* movement of objects through mental direction. Psychics derive income from practicing these talents for police and other gullible people.

Psycho combines with other parts to make up at least 80 terms in the medical dictionary. Some of these terms are familiar.

psychology	*psychiatry*	*psychosomatic*	*psychopath*
psychosis	*psychedelic*	*psychic*	*psycho*

The etymological approach, knowing the meaning of parts, helps in defining less familiar terms.

psycho + *allergy*		*psychallergy,* sensitivity to certain symbols
+ *lepsy*		lit. seizure of the mind, condition of experiencing swift changes in mood
+ *genesis*		development of the psyche, or mind
brady + **psychia**		slow mental activity
slow		
algo + **psychalia**		extremely painful psychalia
pain		

Into this long but partial inventory flit butterflies *Psyche, Psychomyidae,* and *Hydropsychidae.*

Psyche

Athena, famous as the patroness of Athens, the goddess of wisdom, was once challenged to a knitting contest by a young woman, Arachne. It is not a good idea to challenge a deity, as Arachne discovered when she was transmuted into a spider, the joke being that now she could knit forever.

Arachno combines with suffixes. If we add a suffix we've already used, *-oid,* to it, we have *arachnoid,* like a spider's web. A membrane enclosing the brain seemed weblike, and so is called the *arachnoid.* Another suffix we've already used is **-id,** family of, as in *hominid:* **arachno** + *-id,* family of, renders *arachnid,* for a class of arthropods, spiders, scorpions, mites, ticks. *-Ism* can mean diseased condition of: *arachnidism* is a term for spider poisoning.

Arachno also combines with other bases, such as *lysin,* for dissolving of: *arachnolysin* is the poison of the garden spider. **Arachno** + *dactyly,* which means finger > *arachnodactyly,* having fingers so thin they resemble spider's legs. And for this base + another base + a suffix: *arachnorhinitis,* inflammation of the nose caused by mites.

Base for mites: **acaro** < Gk. *akari,* mite

acarid	member of the family *Acarina*
acariasis, acarinosis	infestation by acarids
acarodermatitis	mite-caused infection of the skin

4.4 Homeric Epics

Most of the words above are *eponyms* derived from the names of real or imaginary people. Toponyms derived from mythology are illustrated by *lethargy* < Lethe. From Labyrinth, the maze in which the Minotaur wandered, we have *labyrinth* and the adj. form *labyrinthine; labyrinth* is more narrowly descriptive of the inner ear, infection of which is known as *labyrinthitis.* This condition might call for a *labyrinthectomy. Pyo,* a Gk. base for pus, is the first element in *pyolabyrinthitis.* A genus of extinct Carboniferous salamanders had teeth that displayed a network of grooves, and the animal took its name from this pattern on its teeth: *Labyrinthodont.*

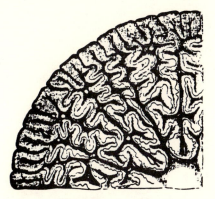

Portion of tooth of *Laybrinthodont jaegeri*

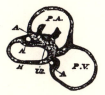

Words of the labyrinth of the ear. This drawing is twice the natural size.
Labyrinth + the cochlea constitute the inner ear.

Ut. The *utriculus* from Gk. *uter,* bag or bottle
The *sacculus* from Gk. *sac* lies behind the utriculus.
P.A. the anterior vertical semicircular canal
P.V. the posterior vertical semicircular canal
A., A., A. *ampullae* from Gk. *ampulla,* jug
H. horizontal semicircular canal

Homer's *Odyssey* > *odyssey*, an adventurous and significant journey. Ilium, the name in the *Odyssey* for the city we call Troy, was protected by a winding, twisting wall. As L. *ilium*, the word refers now to the widest of three bones comprising the lateral halves of the pelvis (as in *sacroiliac*); and as Gk. *ileum*, to the portion of the small intestine from jejunum to cecum. *Ileitis* is an inflammation of this organ, and *ileus* the term for an intestinal obstruction that causes colic and toxemia.

Continuing our odyssey from Homer to the intestines, we'll pause at *jejunum* < L. **jejune**, which means empty, boring, trite; that part of the small intestine upon autopsy is empty of food. L. *dis*, reversal + **jejune**, *disjejunare*, became French *disner*, which became Middle English *dinem* > E. *dine*, an act resulting in filling of the jejunum, often taking place in a *diner* where the conversation may range from jolly to jejune. The duodenum is a part of the small intestine emerging from the stomach. It's part of the phrase *duodenum digitorum*, which sounds like a chant in church, but means 12 fingers long, about 10 inches (*duodenum* < *duo-*, two + *denum* < *decim*, ten; *digitorum*, finger).

Cecum means blind, *cecal* referring to a part of the small intestine, and more generally to any "blind" or concluding passage. **Ceco**, the base for the cecum, has been hospitable in attaching to affixes and to a group of other bases that function like suffixes. **Ceco** attaches to *-tomy* and *-ectomy* and *-stomy*, opening into, making a mouth into; to *ptosis*, drooping; *plasty*, plastic surgery of; to *rrhaphy*, suturing of; to *pexy*, surgical fixation of; and to other bases indicating affliction and repair of an organ.

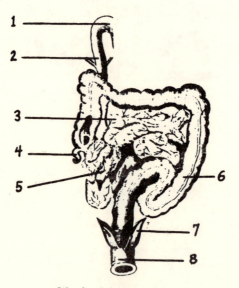

Words of the Intestine

Most of the words labelling parts of the intestine are metaphors: (1) pylorus, gate-way; (2) duodenum, 12 (finger-lengths); (3) jejunum, empty; (4) cecum, blind; also called vermiform appendix; (5) ilium, twisting; (6) colon continues its original name; (7) levator ani, the rings that raise; (8) rectum, the straight part.

caecilian	an adjective referring to blind animals, such as legless, sightless, worm-like amphibians (also: *Apoda*)

In a gruesome episode, Odysseus and his crew were imprisoned by the one-eyed giant, Cyclops, eponym of several taxa. *Cyclopia* < **cyclo** + *opia*, eye, is the word to describe a teratological, or monstrous, product in which the fetus has only one eye in the middle of its forehead. The sailors also had a dangerous episode with the witch Circe, who could convert people into pigs; *Circe* appears in a mollusc genus of that name and in *Circe* + *aster*, star, as *Circeaster*, a genus of echinoderms.

The blinding of Cyclops Polyphemus,
an Etruscan painting

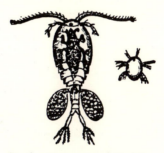

Freshwater copepod *Cyclops*,
young and mature stages

The half-woman, half-bird siren appears in Homer's *Odyssey* as an alluring mermaid whose fatally attractive song charms sailors to come visit and get killed. **Siren** is a name in taxa of insects, fish—*Lepidosiren* is a genus for lungfish, amphibians, and mammals—the order *Sirenia*, which includes mermaid-like dugongs and manatees (*dugong* is from Malayan, *manatee* from Carib).

A herald in Homer's *Iliad*, Stentor has a voice as loud as a trumpet; he cordially lent his name to the adjective *stentorian*, loud, and to *Stentor*, a genus of trumpet-shaped marine protozoa.

The Gk. god of medicine was Aesculapius, *Aesculapian* a rare word for medical healing. Through Hygeia, goddess of health, the Romans contributed a more common word: *hygiene*. Hermes, who acted as a messenger and herald for the gods, carried the *caduceus* < Gk. *karux*, herald, now the symbol for medicine. The base **med** for healing < L. *mederi*, to heal: *medicine, medical, medicate, medic.*

American Indians, including man whose head doth grow beneath his shoulders. From Père Lafitau, *Moers des Sauvages*, 1725

Odysseus and the Sirens
5th Century B.C.

4.5 Other Mythical Creatures

The salamander was mistakenly thought to be able to withstand fire. Although the actual amphibian is known not to have that ability, *salamander* (< Gk.) continues a connection with fire in being a term for a fireplace poker, a portable stove, and a clump of metal. *Salamandra maculosa* is the taxonomic label for a European salamander of glossy black and yellow patches; *gerrymander* is a blend for political redistricting that on a map looks like a salamander (< *Gerry*, a governor + *mander*).

Basileus was a Greek term for king, e.g., the title of Lysimichus, one of Alexander

Mudfish *Lepidosiren*

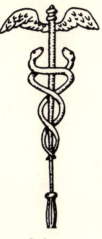

Caduceus

the Great's generals. Its diminutive, *basiliskos,* was used as the term for a serpent whose breath and looks could kill. The *basilisk* is a tropical American lizard, *Basilarchia archippus* is the name of the viceroy butterfly, and *basil* is a herb.

The *unicorn* had a horn that was pulverized into a panacea to cure all kinds of diseases. But since unicorns don't exist except in the imagination, the horns were those of other animals. The superstition that pulverized horn will cure disease contributes to the extinction of the white rhinocerous and other animals. *Unicorn < uni,* one + *corn,* horn.

A recent coinage is *mithridatism.* In the time of King Mithridates, 1st century B.C., noble people killed off their rivals by feeding them poison. To protect himself against being poisoned, the King gradually ingested poisons, thus building up an immunity and disappointing his would-be assassins. "Terence, this is stupid stuff," a poem by A. E. Housman, advises that we can build up an immunity against the serious troubles of real life by reading pessimistic poetry, such as A. E. Housman liked to write. The poem concludes with this allusion to Mithridates:

There was a king reigned in the East:
There, when kings will sit to feast,
They get their fill before they think
With poisoned meat and poisoned drink.
He gathered all that springs to birth
From the many-venomed earth;
First a little, thence to more,
He sampled all her killing store;
And easy, smiling, seasoned sound,
Sate the king when healths went round.
They put arsenic in his meat
And stared aghast to watch him eat;
They poured strychnine in his cup
And shook to see him drink it up:
They shook, they stared as white's their shirt:
Them it was their poison hurt.
—I tell the tale that I heard told.
Mithridates, he died old.

The pagan Greeks were an adventurous people. In one mythological adventure, Jason sailed off to steal a golden fleece. His ship was named *Argo*, the sailors *argonauts*. *Argonaut* became a term for the pearly or paper nautilus.

Argonaut, or pearly nautilus

4.6 Review of Elements

Some elements that have already appeared could probably be defined by anyone knowing common English. We'll conclude this chapter by noting easily defined prefixes, bases, and suffixes and then by noting those that need definition. Along with the prefix **a(n)-**, we've come upon **hypo-**, below, as in *hypopnea*, shallow breathing; **hyper-**, above, as in *hyperpnea*, overly active breathing; **anti-**, against, as in *anti-lethargic;* and **pseudo-**, false, as in *pseudoamnesia*. Similarly familiar bases are **mania**, for obsessive need, as in *erotomania* and *thanatomania;* **phobia**, as in *venerophobia* and *uranophobia;* **echo**, as in *echolalia*.

Suffixes **-tomy**, cutting, **-ectomy**, excising, and **-osis**, morbid condition of, are among the most used of all elements; e.g., *necrotomy, hymenectomy, psychosis*. Two elements are bases that function as suffixes, both familiar. **Logy** for study of is in *etymology* and *morphology*. In *lithology*, however, the **logy** doesn't mean study of, but character of (rocks). **Lepsy,** seizure, has also appeared, e.g., *narcolepsy* and *hypnolepsy;* it almost always functions as a suffix.

Additional elements that have been used often enough to warrant being put into bold now include the base **op,** eye (e.g., *cyclopia*); and seven or eight suffixes: **-ic,** pertaining to (e.g., *medic*), **-itis,** inflammation of (*ileitus*).

-ia and **-y**	condition of or state of: *cyclopia arachnodactyly, lethargy*
-iasis	morbid condition of; like *-osis satyriasis*
-id	family of: *arachnid, acarid*
-ism	usually means belief in, but in the medical vocabulary: process of— *hypnotism;* and disordered condition of: *arachnidism*
-stomy	opening: *cecostomy*

CHAPTER 5—METAPHORS

5.1   The House
5.2   The Kitchen
5.3   Other Rooms
5.4   Outdoors

A new word brings a new concept. *Science,* which came into English from French in the 14th century, was a new word and quite a new concept. What happens when a native word already relates to much the same thing is that the imported word might knock the native synonym out of the language. Had *medicine* not knocked *laechcraft* out of English, we might now be referring to physicians as *laechcrafters.* Or the imported word might take up residence alongside the native word. The resulting synonyms are not identities. *Piscator,* which came into English in the middle of the 17th century, is a synonym of, but not identical with, *fisherman. Fisherman* is the more homely word, less pompous and probably less comical.

Three points worth keeping in mind are that today's biological vocabulary comes from many sources, native and imported; that the same bases are employed in different disciplines; and that many bases are used metaphorically.

1. Medicine shares with the general vocabulary words of native English stock—such as *kidney, heart, wart, gall, wheeze.* Native English words are in the minority, occupying not more than 5% of the medical vocabulary. Latin and to an even greater extent Greek and Latinized Greek make up most of the biological vocabulary.

2. Another point of importance is that elements in the biolexicon are employable in different biological disciplines. An example of this was provided by *andro.*

botany	*androecium, androphore, androspore*
zoology	*androconium, androgynous*
biochemistry	*androgen, androsterone*
medicine	*andrology, andropathy, andriatrics andreioma, gynandromorphism*
genetics	*androcyte*
psychiatry	*polyandry*

3. Whether a word is old or new, it can, and usually does, generate meanings additional to its first meaning. Extension of meaning takes place when a feature of something old is found to be applicable to something new, as we saw with the extension of *salamander* from amphibian to furnace. The resemblance could be one of two kinds: it might be founded on appearance, an aspect of the new object or

event looking like an aspect of the old, or the resemblance might be founded on function.

As you look at your desk, you might find on it a card file, paper and paper clips, a book, a pen, a computer. The names of these objects are metaphors or have given rise to metaphors. *Desk* is a metaphor of a L. word that meant dish, L. *discus; file* of L. *filum,* thread; *pen* of L. *penna,* feather; and *clip* of OE *clyppan,* to clasp, surround. *Computer* < L. *com-* + *put* < *putare,* to think, when it came into E. in the middle of the 17th century meant to calculate—*compute* had been adopted three hundred years earlier.

Paper entered E. in the middle of the 14th century; its source, Gk. *papyrus,* probably came in later. *Book* < OE *boc,* is very old, from before 900. *Paper* and *book* are used metaphorically in *to paper over* (to conceal), and *bookmaker,* which could refer to one who actually makes books, but more usually would refer to one who takes gambling bets.

An unmarried male's state of bachelorhood relates him to a cow. The farm boy who took care of cattle (*bacca* in Latin) was called a *baccalaris;* this changed spelling and meaning and in the middle of the 13th century became *bachelor,* in the early 17th century, *baccaulaureate.* A patient receiving a flu shot is also related to a cow. An alternative of *bacca* is *vacca,* as in *vaccination* and *vaccine.*

When we turn to metaphors in biological language, we find the same processes at work. First, the terms that have undergone metaphoric ramifications come from English, Greek, and Latin. Secondly, they appear in different biological disciplines. Many of the words noted in the coming discussion will be visited again in other contexts, especially in Part V, Anatomy. And thirdly, they have become metaphors just as *desk* and *pen* have, the similarities based on either appearance or function and sometimes with equally interesting etymological evolutions from unexpected ancestors. Our specimen examples of a metaphor in the biolexicon will be *window* and its L. synonym, *fenestra.*

For an opening in a wall to let in air or light, Danish created the new word *vindauga* (Modern Danish *vindu*). This word, itself a metaphor meaning wind's eye, came into English in the late 12th century as *windoge,* and that became *window.* Eight hundred years later, computer designers picked up that word and used it metaphorically to mean an additional section on a monitor; and others used it as a metaphor for a period of time in which something can be accomplished, the launching of a spacecraft or the resolution of an agreement on nuclear disarmament. All these windows have a similar function: to let in light, literally or metaphorically.

Languages other than the Proto-Germanic also have their words for that opening in the wall. In Latin, it's **fenestra.** For someone who uses the stereotyped way of concluding a program of unwise stock investments, we might observe, if we're in a Latinized mood, that he defenestrated. If we wish to refer to a small passageway between bones, as between the middle and inner ear, we might choose *oval window,* or we might choose *fenestra ovalis.* These terms referring to an opening in the ear. *Fenestrated epithelium* refers to capillaries. *Fenestration* in architecture or anatomy relates to perforation.

Entomologists use *fenestra* as still another metaphor: the spot as translucent as a pane of glass on the wings of butterflies. Other biologists have found *fenestra* metaphorically useful for naming bryozoans and a sponge (*Protospongia fenestrata*, now extinct).

Some of the Latin and Greek elements will be used literally, as the Romans and Greeks used them, for example, L. *ren* for kidney; Gk. *card* for heart. But hundreds of terms in the biological vocabulary are metaphors formed from Latin and Greek, as happened in L. *fenestra* becoming a word for an opening between bones and for a spot on wings.

The original meaning of the terms to be treated are given along with an equal sign (=) to indicate present meaning.

To the question of what in pagan life has lent itself to metaphoric use, the answer is just about everything. Vinegar in a cup has its metaphoric use, as does the cup, and the table on which the cup sits, and the room that holds the table, the house that holds the room, the farm on which the house is located, the universe itself, as we saw with *uran* for heavens = *uran* for the hard palate (soft palate: *uvula* and base *staphvl*) because the hard palate is at the top, or heaven, of the mouth. Most of the following L. and Gk. terms were used metaphorically to name parts of the body.

5.1 The House

Indo-European families of five thousand years ago gathered into a unit like the clan, which they called *weik*.

IE *weik*

Into L. as *villa,* from which *villa* itself, *village,* and *villain,* orig. a feudal serf serving the villa. Nothing particularly disreputable about that, but words in the general vocabulary have a habit of sliding downhill, and *villain* from denoting a mere peasant took on the connotative sense of a brutal peasant, and finally settled down into its present meaning of an evil person who may or may not commit his villainy on a villa.

IE *weik* became Gk. *oikos,* house, the resultant base **eco** in *ecology* and its recent offspring, *ecocide, economy* and several other words having to do with being sited together in or as in a house. *Oecophylla smaragina* is the taxonomic name of an ant, lit. emerald leaf-house (Gk. *smaragd* is the source of the word *emerald*). *Oeceum,* house = **ecium**, site for, as in the following words.

andro	+ **ecium**	*androecium,* housing for male organs or stamens
gyno	+	site in plants for female organ, pistil
hetero different	+	of different sites
mono- one	+	one site for sex organs

dio- two	+	two, separate, sites for sex organs
syno- with	+ **ecious**	adj., pert. to male and female organs in same residence
para-	+	*paroecious,* adj. for nearness of sites of male and female organs in a plant as with mosses

For residence, the biological vocabulary also has bases from L. *colere:* **cult,** caring for, and **cole,** living in.

cult	*culture, agriculture, cultivate*
cole	
cellicolous	living in a cell
nidicolous	living in a nest
arenicolous	living in sand; also *arenaceous*

L. *arena* was transferred from meaning sand to meaning the stadium carpeted with sand that sopped up the blood of gladiators butchering each other. *Hyla arenicolor* is the taxonomic name of a frog.

The house envisioned here is a convenient fiction—the actual house pagans lived in were not so grand as a modern suburbanite two-story ranch. We proceed into this fictional house past a fence and through a gateway.

L. *septum,* fence = **septum,** a partition, of which there are 50+ kinds, e.g., *artrioventricular septum* of the heart and the *septum nasi* of the nose.

L. *porta* = **port,** e.g., *portal vein,* and Gk. *pyle,* gateway = **pyl,** passageway as between organs.

pylon	a structure, such as a tower for high-tension wires
pylorus	passage between stomach and intestine
pylethrombosis	thrombosis of the portal vein
pyloroptosis	prolapse of pyloric part of stomach
micropyle	small opening in gemmule or mass of budding cells of sponge

We are now in the courtyard, L. **atri,** which as *atrium* means any impressive, elegant, classical open central court, and metaphorically = a courtyard for the heart, the *atrium sinistrum,* left auricle; and = a siphon, the *atrial siphon,* of ascidians or tunicates.

One of the impressive features of Greek and Roman temples and palaces is their pillars. L. *styl* is used literally in architecture for pillars (as in *peristyle*). Transferring meaning from pillar to those who sat on it, *styl* became *stylites,* a term for demented people who demonstrated their disdain for worldly life by perching on the top of columns. *Styl,* pillar = **styl,** projection of temporal bone, as in *styloid process, stylomastoid* and *styloglossus.*

The house would have a roof and walls. L. *fornix,* vault or roof = *fornix,* arched structure in the brain. L. *tectum* also means roof = the roof of the midbrain. *Tectospinal* refers to nerves connecting this area to the spinal cord.

Gk. *paries*, wall = **parie**, wall-like bone. *Parietal* is an adjective in anatomy for a bone of the skull and in college life for walls enclosing or rules governing under-graduate dormitory behavior. Another base for wall comes from Gk. *diaphragma* = **diaphragm**, partition; this appears first in the Roman physician Galen. L. *claustrum*, which meant barrier, = a descriptive term for a layer dividing parts of the brain. The Gk. word for plaster was *splenion* = *splenius*, referring to a neck muscle that turns the head.

We pass through the threshold, L. *limen*, as in *subliminal*. As we stroll through the house, we're accompanied by Gk. *theraps*, attendant = **therapy**, cure. The first room we come to is the *vestibule*. The base in this word is *vest*, a L. word for clothing lit. in *vest* and metaphoric in *disinvest*. *Vestibule* (or *vestiary*) can still refer to the room in which one changes or divests himself or herself of a raincoat; in anatomy, *vestibule* = a cavity preliminary to a main cavity, as in the vestibule of sagitta, a marine worm, and the *scala vestibuli* of the human ear.

Several terms are used, like *fenestra*, for an opening: L. *hiatus*, which now has the sense of a pause; L. *lumen*, light, window = **lumen**, an opening, a space, in an anatomical tube. L. *ostium*, door = **ostium**, an orifice, pl. **ostia**. The opening or door could be at the end of an organ, such as the *ostium urethrae externum maculinae* and the *ostium vaginae* or, more often, an opening from one organ into another, such as the *ostium aortae*, the orifice between left ventricle and aorta, and *ostium pyloricum*, the orifice between stomach and duodenum. To the 50+ ostia, we can add the rare *ostiary*, a doorkeeper, esp. of a church.

100+ terms use the next base, L. *foramina*, opening = **foramen**, a passageway, esp. into a bone, allowing for the passage of nerves or blood vessels or other structures, e.g., *mastoid foramen* and *foramen magnum*, large hole, the opening at the base of the skull through which the spinal cord enters the brain. *Perforate* is a cognate of **foramen**.

The *trematode* < Gk. for a hole, is a flatworm whose body is perforated with holes; *helicotrema* refers to a spiral passageway in the ear (also called *Breschet's hiatus*). L. *meatus* is unchanged in form in **meatus**, an opening. The medical vocabulary has 100+ terms with *meatus* in them, e.g., of nose, and *urinary meatus* (this term covers both *ostium urethrae externum masculinae* and *ostium . . . feminina*).

Claus for closed, altered in Fr. *closet* and *cloister*, is in the familiar *claustrophobia*, and in another form, **clus**, in *occlusion*.

For the leaves of a door, L. used the word *valvae* = **valve**, a flap, esp. in heart. Inflam-mation of the heart valve is *valvulitis;* and cutting into this valve *valvulotomy*. For the key to open the door, L. used the word *clavis*, key = **clav**, as in *clavicle*, collarbone and *autoclave*, a self-regulating sterilizer (and also in *clavichord*, the musical instrument).

L. *limbus*, edge or border = **limb**, border of plant or brain: *limbate*, border or edge of a plant; *limbic system*, area of the brain. L. *fistula*, pipe = **fistula**, duct from abscess or passageway surgically imposed for drainage. Gk. *cloaca*, sewer, is still used (rarely) as a term for sewer and metaphorically for the **cloaca**, duct with dual function of excretion and reproduction, as in reptiles.

Clavis, a key from Ilium

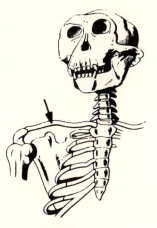

Clavicle of ape

Cloaca maxima

Cloaca of condor

Culina, or kitchen:
stove, sieve, knife, and frying pan

5.2 The Kitchen

In the kitchen, Theraps points out culinary practice and utensils that have been moved metaphorically from the kitchen to biology. Gk. *eschara*, object to hold hot coals, early came to refer to a scab formed on a burn. From *eschara*: *eschar*, a lesion or sloughing skin from a burn; adj.: *escharotic*; cognate: *scar*.

The major activity of the kitchen is cooking. The act of cooking lends itself to metaphoric treatment, as we can see in the expressions "What's cooking?," "You're really cooking (as, perhaps, with gas)," "Cooking books." The IE root *pekw*, to cook, to ripen, over the millenia gave rise to many words and is a good example of metaphoric ramification. The offspring of this family include *Pepsi-Cola, pepsin, pumpkin, cook, culinary, kiln, apricot* and *precocious*. That all these words are siblings of a single ancestor leads to a small but perhaps satisfying etymological story. What happened is indicated in this box:

IE *pekw*, to cook, ripen

Those who left the IE group and travelled east to India changed the parent language in Sanskrit. No biological terms from the Sanskrit descendant, but E. did adopt *pukka*, which means authentic, classy.

In Greek, IE *pekw* became the bases **pept** and **peps.** These relate to digestion. *Peptic* is the adjective for digestion: if it's good, it's *eupeptic,* and if it's disordered, it's *dyspeptic.* The noun form is *pepsia.* And *pekw* becomes drinkable in *Pepsi-Cola.* From the Gk. verb *peptein,* to ripen, comes *peptone,* a protein compound; *pepsin,* a digestive enzyme; and *peptide,* a synthetic pepsin.

A small story within the larger story relates how over a long time a Greek melon transformed into a Halloween prop. From Gk. *peptein* came Gk. *pepon,* a melon. This went into L. as *pepo,* which became Fr. *pompon* and this became *pumpklin.*

The adventures of IE *pekw* continue in Latin. It became L. *coquere,* to cook. This travelled from L. into OE, developing into *cook* and its compounds, e.g., *cookout,* though not *cookie,* which is from Dutch *koek,* cake. **Coct** also went into E. as *culinary, kiln* (OE *cyln* reveals a transitional spelling), *decoct(ion), concoct(ion).* The base sojourned through French to give English *cuisine* and *biscuit;* and through Italian > *ricotta,* a cheese. In the medical vocabulary, **cocto** refers to cooking and heating.

coction	boiling or digesting
coctolabile	adj. for altering some material, such as a protein, by heating it (L. *labil, perishable).*
coctostabile	adj. for maintenance of stability upon being heated

Pre-cooked or boiled first is caught in Latin *praecoquere.* This led to at least three words. It went into Greek and from Greek into Arabic: *al-birque,* fruit which ripens early. From Arabic, it went into Portuguese: *albricoque* > *apricot.* From L. *praecoquere* also *precocious,* for a child who ripens before its time, and *dementia praecox,* a youthful schizophrenia concocted by, among other traumas, etymological analysis.

Gk. *boskein* means to feed; putting the prefix *pro-* in front of the base renders *proboscis,* which became metaphorically a term for an elephant's trunk, snout of a tapir, nose of a monkey, sucking mechanism of insects, and mouth sensory organ of leeches. Mammoths and mastodons belonged to the extinct order *Proboscidea.*

For a loaf toasted on a spit, the Greeks had the word *obelias.* In 1865, it entered E. as *obelia,* name for a genus of hydrozoa. Another derivative of *obelias* is *obelisk.* Gk. *zyme,* leaven = **zyme,** enzyme.

A parasite was once one who sat near the food, a guest, perhaps one who flattered for his food. Its base, and the base of *sitology,* the study of food, is Gk. *sit,* food. Two L. bases for table are *mensa* and **tabul.** *Mensal* is in the common vocabulary, though rare, as an adjective pertaining to that which is used at the table. In biological vocabulary, *mensa* is the base of *commensalism,* a metaphor for a non-parasitic symbiosis. **Tabul** is the source of *table* (*periodic table, water table,* etc.), *tablet,* and a few

Head and proboscis of butterfly

other words. In the medical vocabulary, L. *tabula* = **tabul,** platform, e.g., *vitreous table* and *tabula externa ossis cranii. Tabellaria fenestrata* is a diatom. Gk. *tetra*, five + *peza*, foot > *trapezion*, a small quadrilateral table > *trapezius* muscle.

On the ancient table there would be what there is on the contemporary table: jars, plates, cups, perhaps a sieve. Several words which were used literally for these items have been adopted into the biological vocabulary as a result of a namer seeing some connection between the item and the anatomical part. For example, Gk. **ampulla,** a flask = a flask-like duct, sense-organ as on shark snout, part of the human ear.

The Gk. **amnion** was a plate used to hold the blood of a sacrificed lamb. In 1660 it was used as the word for the membrane enclosing the embryo of reptiles, birds, and mammals, the membrane as thin as that of a newborn lamb. The *amniotic* egg was an evolutionary advance, enabling reptiles to be free of their amphibian predecessors' need for a watery environment for eggs. *Amniocentesis* is the puncturing of this membrane to get a sample of *amniotic* fluid, *amniography* an x-ray of the sac.

L. **pat,** also a base for plate = *patina*, a plating as of metal, with metaphoric application in *patella*, kneecap, which is like a plate. *Lamina* and *lamella* < L. signify a plate in the sense of a layer. 100+ phrases have **lamina** in them, e.g., *inferior lamina* of the sphenoid bone and *submucous lamina* of the stomach. *Lamina* is the base for *laminate.* **Lamina** and **lamella,** for thin plate or membrane, are used in zoology and botany as well as in anatomy, ophthalmology, and architecture. L. *lamella* became Fr. *alemetta,* which entered E. in 1605 as *omelette.*

laminectomy	has special reference to excision of vertebral arch
laminitis	has special reference to horse's hoof
lamellirostral	adj. for a beak, such as that of ducks and flamingoes, which has lamellae for straining out food from mud
Lamellicorni	genus of beetles, e.g., scarabaeids
Lamellibrachia	bivalves

The cup is a handy object for metaphoric exploitation, since many cavities are cup-like. The Gk. cup or vinegar dish was a *cotyl* = **cotyl,** cup-like cavity in botanical and human anatomy.

cotyledon (1535)	embryonic seed leaf
cotyloid (1750)	like a cup, a cavity, such as that of vertebrae into skull, of femur into hip bone
Cotylosaur (1900)	order of dinosaurs

The Roman naturalist Pliny translated Gk. *cotyl* into *acetabulum*. L. **acetabul** also meant a cup to hold vinegar. The cup part of this reference appears in *acetabulum*, cotyloid socket of hipbone, and in *acetabula*, suckers as on trematodes; and the vinegar part in *acid*.

Two acetabula or vinegar cups on large platter

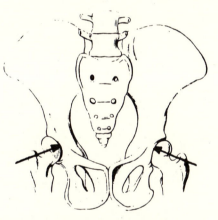

Acetabulum of ape pelvis

The Gk. drinking bowl, base *scyphi*, = *scyph*, a structure like this drinking bowl, as in *scyphus*, a part, as of a flower, and *Scyphozoan*, a jellyfish.

Gk. *kalux*, L. **calyx**, cup, is used in botany: *calyx* is the sepal covering of a flower; a small cup-like structure is a *calycle*, and *Gymnocalycium loricatum* is a cactus.

The wooden bowl on the table was the Gk. *pelyx*, which base exists in names of extinct animals. If the container were larger than a bowl, the size of a basin or tub, it would be called a *pyelos* = **pyel**, a base for the funnel-shaped part of the kidney, as in *pyelitis*, *pyelogram*, and *cystopyelonephritis*. An L. word for basin, **pelvis**, refers also to this renal structure, but more familiarly to the basin-shaped ring of bones supporting the spinal column, as in *pelvis*. *Lipodectes pelvidens* is a Paleocene mammal.

Pelvis or basin

Three utensils at the table deserve notice because the words for them became bases for anatomical parts:

Gk. *ethmo*, sieve, strainer = **ethmo**, e.g., *ethmoid*, a spongy bone in nose
Gk. *arytaina*, ladle = *arytenoid*, a cartilage
Gk. *choano*, funnel = **choan**, funnel-like structure, as in *choanocyte, choanoflagellate*

Along with figs and olives, from the pagan pantry would come a breakfast of sausages and gruel and a dish that has representatives in many cultures of past and present, pancakes. Gk. *allantois*, sausage, maintains its lit. meaning in *allantotoxicon*, sausage poisoning, but becomes metaphor in *allantoidangiopagus*, a fetal monster. The L. word for sausage, *botulus*, no longer retains any literal meaning. Spoiled sausages or other foods can cause *botulism*, food poisoning caused by *Clostridium botulinum*.

More familiar than these terms is **ather** < Gk. *athere*, gruel. **Ather** is a base for gruel-like, as in *atherosclerosis*, a condition of blockage in arteries. For the site in the heart dying because of blockage caused by a gathering of gruel, the term *infarct* is used. Its source, L. *farcire*, to stuff, is also the source of *farce*. L. **plac**, flat, appears in *placoid* and *placenta*, like a flat cake.

It's twilight. To light their homes, the pagans used candles. The Gk. *keros* retains its meaning of wax or waxy in **cer**, *ceriferous, ceromel, adipocere;* but the L. *sebum*, tallow = *sebum*, sweat, adj. *sebaceous.*

Of the terms noted, several refer to embryonic development. Identification of embryonic parts and processes started in the 15th century and is still going on today. *Embryo* came into E. in the late 16th century, *uterus* in the early 17th in Crooke's *Body of Man:* "It is called uterus properly in women." In the mid-17th century *allantois* entered the language in Thomas Browne's definition "The allantois is a thin coat seated under the chorion," a definition made more specific in the 19th century: "Known by its proximity to the shell the allantois is an important respiratory organ."

Amnion was also named in the mid-17th century, in the Royal Society's *Philosophical Transactions:* "The foetus is nourished from the amnion by the mouth." The biologist John Ray, in his 1691 *Creation*, brought *placenta* into English: "The foetus doth receive air from the maternal blood in the Placenta uterine."

Closer scrutiny permitted by the development of better instruments brought other embryological terms into E. in the late 19th century: *endoderm*, 1861, by J. R.

Boy holding amnium

Amnion surrounding twins

Greene; *gastrulation*, 1879, by T.H. Huxley; and *neurulation*, 1888 in the *American Naturalist*.

5.3 Other Rooms

L. *cella* maintains its original meaning in *cell* as a room in a prison or monastery (cp. *cellar*), but becomes metaphoric in **cell**, an anatomical unit. Gk. *thalamos*, inner room = **thalamus,** the middle part of the diencephalon. The woman's quarter was called the *gynaeceum*.

The sewing room contained a spindle, Gk. *kloster = clost*, e.g., *Clostridium tetani*, the vector for tetanus. Clotho, the Spinner, is one of the three fates. By the spindle were spools of thread. At least half a dozen bases for thread have been adapted as metaphors referring to thread-like structures—there seem 'to be no examples in English of these retaining any literal sense. The following bases all are in the modern biological vocabulary with the meaning of thread or thread-like.

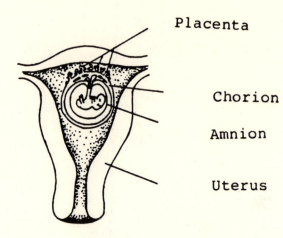

Placenta

Chorion

Amnion

Uterus

L. **fibr, fibrin,** fiber	*cystic fibrosis*
fibrin	a protein for blood clotting
fibrillation	muscular (as of heart) contraction
L. **fil**	*filament, filoform, filaceous*
Filarioidea	a genus of nematode worms
filariasis	disease caused by these worms
Gk. **mit**	
mitosis	cell division
L. **stamen**	*stamen*
Gk. **nemat**	
nematode	a worm
Gk. **chord,** string	
chordate	an animal with a backbone
notochord	structure that develops into axial skeleton
chorditis	inflammation of the vocal cord
chordectomy	surgical cutting out of the vocal cord

In the sewing room, threads might ravel into a globular mass. A single thread could be followed to unravel the mass. This single thread leading to unravelling was the orig. meaning of *clue*. *Globular* and *clue* — and *clot* and *clamp* and *glue* are all descendants of an IE root.

IE *gel*, mass

This went into Proto-Germanic to result in about two dozen words having to do with the idea of mass. A few of these are relevant to biology: *clump, clot,* perhaps *klutz* (lump-head), and, with the sense of clinging: *clutch, clam, clammy, clamp.*

IE *gel* went into L. where it became *glomus*, ball ⊃

glob	*globe, globule, globulin*
glom	*conglomerate*
glomus	a ball-like mass, as of nerves
glomerule	a clump of capillaries as in kidney nephron

L. *gluten*, glue >
glu

glue	*glutinous*	*agglutinate*
conglutinate	*deglutinate*	

gluten	a protein of wheat
gluteofemoral	pert. to buttocks and thigh

That larger bodies were identified early, smaller ones later, is shown in the dates of entrance into English of five words from Gk. bases descendants of IE *gel.* In 1675 *gluteus,* a muscle of the buttocks, and *ganglion,* a mass as of nerve tissues, were named. Much later, in 1870, the *neuroglia,* structures protective of brain and spinal cord cells, were identified, and a little after that, in 1885, the *mesoglea,* a gelatinous material in certain invertebrate cells, and *zooglea,* a bacterial mass that looks like jelly.

Spinal cord neuroglia cell

There were two homophonic roots *gel* in IE. From the *gel* that meant bright came *clean, cleanse,* and *Euglena;* from the *gel* that meant cold, freezing came OE *chill, cold, cool* and L. *gelid, gelatin, glacier, congeal, jelly.*

Latin supplies the needle, **acu,** as in *acute, acumen,* sharpness of insight, *acupuncture.*

acuclosure	using a needle to stitch hemorrhaging vessel
acusection	use of electrosurgical needle

L. **cusp,** orig. sharp, pointed, = a bump, as in *cuspid* and *bicuspid.*

Gk. *rhaptein* means to sew, = **raph,** suturing. L. **suture,** seam = a particular kind of seam, in the body. So popular are sutures, both those that occur naturally, as between bones of the skull, and those that are effected surgically, that there are well over 100 terms that have **sutura** or **suture** in them. **Sutura** is usually used for the natural seams, such as *suturae coronalis,* the seams between frontal bone and parietal bones, and *sutura internasalis,* of the nose. **Suture** may also apply to a natural seam, as in *dentate suture* (*sutura serrata*), but is more commonly used for the artificial ones, the techniques, such as *figure-of-eight suture, cobblers' suture, glovers' suture.*

Johann Wolfgang Goethe might be pleased to know that he's been immortalized not only for the romantic *Faust* and *Werther,* but also for an iron oxide, *goethite,* and a suture joining maxillary and intermaxillary bones, the *suture of Goethe,* or *sutura incisiva.*

L. also supplies the band, bandage, or ribbon or *fascia* = **fasci.** A band of tissue is a *fascia.* Related terms, all of them from Latin descendants of an original IE root *bhasko,* include a bundle of rods or *fasces* > *fascism* and the development to magical attraction uncertain, *fascinate.*

Swaddling clothes

Band for women

Fascia

Fasciculi of striated muscle

The pagans lacked baggies, but they had their containers for food and other material. About a dozen bases for containers are used in the biological vocabulary. In this category again, the literal meanings have mostly vanished, the metaphoric have been retained. A memorable example of loss of literal meaning is provided by *focus.* In Roman times, that meant hearth. The metaphoric transference came about by the hearth being the central point around which people gathered.

Words for vessels and pouches have come in without much spelling change, but with a metaphoric change from something general to something specific. For example, Gk. *kytos,* container = **cyte,** cell.

cytology	*cytoplasm*	*cytomegalovirus*	*cytosome*
cytolysis	*cytocide*	*cytotechnology*	*cytophil*

The comparable L. term for a container, a vessel, was *vas. Vas* retains its literal sense in *vase.* A *vasculum* is a fancy word for a container used by botanists to transport specimens. *Vasiform* could mean either like a vase or like a duct—the base **vaso** becoming metaphoric in referring to a duct or tube of the body.

vascular	adj. pert. to vessels that carry fluids
vas deferens	ducts that carry sperm from epididymus to penis (prefix *de-,* off, away)
vas efferens	ducts that carry sperm from testis to epididymus (cp. *efferent,* prefix *ex,* out)
vasectomy	cutting out of the vas deferens
vasospasm	sudden constriction of a blood vessel

L. *angio,* vessel = **angio,** a blood vessel, as in *angioma, angioplasty, angiograph;* and, in botany, shell, as in *angiosperm,* a flowering plant. Both *aorta* and *artery* were words in the ancient Greek lexicon, but they had considerably different meanings from what they mean today. Examining these vessels in dead bodies shows them to be bloodless. The aorta was thought to be a windpipe from which the heart hung, and the arteries were thought similarly to be windpipes. One etymology finds air, *aor,* in *aorta. Arteries* were thought to be smooth windpipes, and for the rough windpipe, the Greeks used a word for rough, *tracheia > trachea.*

L. *scrotum,* pouch = the obsolete *scrotum cordis,* the sac around the heart, now *pericardium,* and the still-used **scrotum,** pouch that holds testicles. Gk. *marsup,* also pouch = **marsup,** as in *marsupial,* where it refers to the pouch of animals such as kangaroos. *Didelphys marsupialis* is the taxonomic name of an opossum. *Marsupium* refers to the pouch of male sea horses (male sea horses bear the young) and is synonymous with *scrotum.* To structure such a sac was once called *marsupialization.*

Vascula

Three bases meaning sac also underwent specialization, from referring to a sac in general to referring to particular kinds of sacs.

L. **burs,** purse = sac

Mercury holding marsupium

Kangaroo displaying marsupium

bursitis	inflammation of a sac
Geomys bursarius	pocket-gopher
bursa copulatrix	site of clam sex organ

In the general vocabulary, **burs** underwent metaphoric extension: *disburse, reimburse, bursar;* cp. cognate *purse.*

Gk. *asco,* sac, bag

ascocarp	container for spore sac
ascites	a disease, dropsy, of fluid accumulated in chest cavity
Gymnoascus uncinatus	a fungus
ascidian	animal with notocord, e.g., tunicate

Ascar relates to nematode, roundworm, parasites of human intestine causing colic: *ascaris, ascarid.*

Gk. **sac**	*sac, sack, knapsack, satchel*
sacculus	bag-like structure of ear
Saccolabium ampullaceum	an orchid

Sacculus and nematocyte
of coelenterate *Athorybia*

Two bases for other containers:

Gk. **tars,** wicker-
basket; frame = foot-
bone, eyelid tissue

tarsus	support for foot bone or eyelid pl. *tarsi*
tarsoptosis	drooping of the eyelids
tarsier	a small, monkey-like prosimian primate

It's possible that *tarsus* for foot bone developed from a source different from that for *tarsus* as eyelid.

Gk. **theca.** case.
envelope

endothecium	lining of cavity
gonatheca	enclosure for gonads; *ootheca,* for eggs
Thecodontia	order of extinct reptiles whose teeth were housed in sockets
Trichothecium roseum	a fungus

L. *follis* means bellows. One who emits verbal air is caught in a descendant of this word: *fool.* A little bellows is a *follicul: follicle,* container for hair root, *Cephalotus follicularia,* a pitcher-plant. Gk. **cole** means sheath, as in *coleoptera,* insects with sheathed wings (beetles) and *coleocele,* hernia of the vagina, a sheathed passage.

Dressing Room

Words for clothing lend themselves to metaphoric use. The *mitral* valve, between the left atrium and left ventricle, was named because of its resemblance to the Gk. *mitra. Mitra* originally meant a headband, a device to hold a woman's hair in place. As *miter,* it later came to refer to a hat, such as that worn by a bishop, and today has application in carpentry and sailing. T.H. Huxley, who didn't like bishops, said that we can remember that the mitral valve is on the left side of the heart because a bishop is never in the right.

Ancient Semitic had a word for a gown or tunic, *kuttoneth* in Hebrew; this went into Gk. as *chiton,* tunic. In 1810, *chiton* entered E. as a word for a kind of mollusk;

Miter

Mitral valve of heart

and twenty years later re-entered as *chitin* for the cellulose-like constituent of the exoskeletons of insects and crustaceans. The base is **chit**.

A well-used base for covering is **tunic** (50+ medical terms), from L. *tunic;* in the common vocabulary, this continues without much of a change. The biolexical *tunica* means lining of an organ. *Tunicata* is a subphylum of animals whose bodies are enclosed by a tunic-like membrane; also called *Urochordata.*

Roman everyday tunic

Tunica intima or chemise

Tunicate

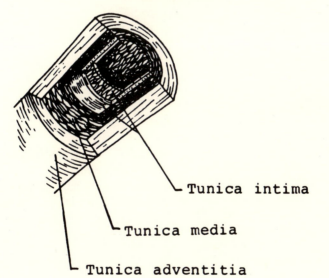

Tunica intima

Tunica media

Tunica adventitia

Gk. chlamys, tunic

Chlamydia	parasites responsible for rickettsia, psittacosis, and venereal infection
chlamydiospore	fungi and algae spore stage
chlamydate	having a mantle, e.g., mollusk, flower

Gk. *elytron,* covering
elytron　　　　　　　　　　　　part of insect's wing

L. *humerus,* cape for shoulders
humerus　　　　　　　　　　　　bone from shoulder to elbow

　　To excite affection, Venus wore a belt (or band or girdle) called a *cestum* (Gk. > L.) = *cestoda,* the name of a class of tapeworms which look like belts. Another Gk. base for band is *sphincter* = *sphincter* muscle and *sphincteralgia,* a pain in that ring-like muscle. To these bases may be added L. *zona,* belt or girdle = band in *zone* and *zonule,* a little belt or belt-like, *ciliary zonule,* ligament supporting eye lens; and L. **cingulum,** girdle = band or bundle in *cingulum,* a bundle of fibers, as of shoulder girdle, which developed into *shingles,* like a band around the throat.

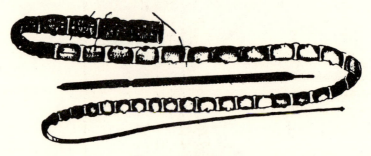

Tapeworm *Cestoda*

　　From L. *sol,* with the meaning of flat (not the *sol* meaning sun) came *sole,* a flat fish; *soleus,* a flat muscle of the calf; and *galoshes.* This surprise came about from a combination of L. *sol* with a variant of Gaul, and meant orig. the flat shoes, or sandals, worn by the Gauls.
　　The Greek or Roman would adorn herself or himself with jewelry and other accoutrements, for example, with a ring. Gk. ring is **gyr,** as in *gyrate, gyroscope,* and *gyrus,* a convolution on the surface of the brain; there are 50+ terms for various gyri. The base for L. ring is **an(n),** as in *annelid,* a worm (e.g., earthworm) and *anus.* The next adornment might be a necklace; L. *monile,* necklace, not a widely employed term, is in *Moniliales,* an order of fungi.
　　From Gk. *perone,* pin for a buckle, = **peron,** the fibula, a leg bone, adj. *peroneal; peroneus,* a muscle attached to the fibula. **Fibula** comes from L. *figere,* to fix—the resemblance being to the pin-like shape of this bone. *Fibulaster* is an Echinoderm taxon.
　　For comb, the biological vocabulary has, as it often has, a choice between a Gk. and a L. base. The Gk. base is **cten,** as in *ctenoid,* like a comb; *Ctenophora,* a phylum of comb jellies, a marine invertebrate; and *ctenodont,* having teeth like combs. The L. base is **pectin,** *pectinate* an adj. for comb-like, *pecten* a comb-like structure or process.

fibulae

Fibula and tibia
of gorilla leg

Gk. *korone*, crown > **coron**, has been widely employed, in the common vocabulary (e.g., *crown, coronet, coronation*), in physics and astronomy, and in anatomy. The seam between the frontal and parietal bones of the crown of the head is the *sutura coronalis* which entered E. in 1605, and a vessel which carries blood to the head the *coronary artery*. From **coron** came **corol**, *corolla* a term for petals, adj. *corollaceous*. In the mid-14th century, *corolla*, its botanical reference extended to mean a garland, took on an additional metaphoric meaning: monetary exchange, as paying for a garland of flowers, and from that comes the modern meaning of *corollary*; even further extension took place in the 19th century: *corollate*.

Playroom

The pagans had their musical instruments, such as the Gk. **tympan**, drum. *Tympany* is a sound made by drumming on the chest. The tympanist in a modern orchestra plays the tympani, little drums. Metaphorically, the *tympanum*, is the ear drum, adj. *tympanic*. *Tympanophorus caniculatus* is the taxonomic name of a beetle.

In the Gk. orchestra, one might also find a trumpet, or **salping**, which is a visual model for the Fallopian tubes, as in *salpingectomy*. L. *bucina*, horn, became *buccinator*, either one who plays the trumpet or muscle lining the cheek. Two flute-like instruments are the *syrinx*, a shepherd's pipe, as with base **syring**: *syringe, syringoid,* and *syringo;* and the **tibia**, a reed pipe or flute > *tibia*, shinbone.

Tibiae with syrinx

Trumpet salpinx

For a lamp, the Greeks used *lychn;* an unproductive source in the biolexicon, it appears in *Lynchnis*, genus of plants, and *lynchnoscope*, a flashlight to look into the throat.

An activity more often indulged in ancient Rome than in modern Washington, D.C., was whipping—for pleasure as well as for punishment. Four bases are used today, sometimes literally, more often metaphorically, for whip.

A widely employed term, though it does not enter into many combinations, is *stimulus*, from L. **stimul**, whip. To be stimulated is, metaphorically at least, to be whipped into excitement, < L. *stimulus*, whip.

L. **flagel** whip =	tail or appendage like a whip, e.g., *flagella, biflagellate, hemoflagellate*
Gk. **mastig**, whip =	tail, whip-like appendage, e.g., in *isomastigote, polymastigia, mastigobranchia*
Mastigophora	a class of protozoans
Mastiglas ocellata	a medusa
chilomastix	a protozoan whose flagellum is near its mouth (*chil,* lip)

Greek flagellum

Flagellate protozoan
Euglena

A Gk. base for rod or wand was *rhabdo,* as in

rhabdomancy	divining with a rod, as in locating water
rhabdomyoma	a benign tumor of muscles; when malign:
	rhabdomyosarcoma
Rhabdoviridae	virus responsible for rabies

Gk. *bak* and L. *bac* for rod, walking stick, have a couple of unexpected relatives which we'll find in the IE family of *bak.*

IE *bak*, walking stick, cane

The sense of walking stick is diminished in a Dutch word that came into E.: *peg. Bacillus* and *bacteria* are not only synonymous; they are also cognates. The Gk. descendant of the IE *bak* was *baktron,* staff, base **bac**, which became through French: *acrobat.*

bacterium	*bacteria*	*bacteriology*	*antibacterial*
corynebacterium	*gymnobacteria*	*streptobacteria*	

The Latin descendant, *baculum,* renders the same base: **bac,** as in *bacillus,* *bacillemia, bacilliform, bacillosis.* Something that falls away from the staff, is undependable, a confusion and mess is a *debacle,* and someone who allows himself or herself to get involved in a debacle is an *imbecile.*

Abactrus championi	a beetle
Bactrites elegans	an ammonite

Flagellated person
by Aubrey Beardsley

After all the activity, the Greek flagellante might have collapsed onto a mattress. Gk. *stroma,* mattress or bed covering, = *stroma,* a framework for a cell or body, *stromatolite,* a column built up by blue-green algae, and a few other words. Much more employable than this is Gk. *kline,* a bed = a place for hospital beds and care, a procedure: *clinic, clinical.*

Workroom

In the biological vocabulary, among the minority of words from native English is *stirrup,* a bone of the inner ear. OE *stigrap* meant going up with a rope, and is still used in a literal sense referring to a device for mounting a horse. The word *bridel,*

Carpenter's shop

for the harness of a horse, also is native English. *Bridel* went into French, where it received a prefix and an affix to become *debridement;* in 1835, the French word was returned to English, but now the meaning was no longer taking the bridle away: *debridement* is the taking away of tissue debris, the cleansing of a wound. *Stigrap* appears in English before 1000; the L. synonym of *stirrup*, ear bone, is *stapes,* 1660.

Pagan workshops lacked portable drills but had some basics, such as an anvil, a hammer, auger or borer, hooks, hatchets. The chart below begins with the other two earbones, the malleus and incus, and proceeds to other anatomical structures that received their names because they resemble tools in appearance or function. The major metaphoric process at work is, again, specialization—narrowing a general sense into a specialized one.

The most widely used base that comes from words used in the workshop is **organ**, from Gk. *organon*, a tool or instrument: *organ* as a musical instrument reflects the orig. sense of the word, but *organ* as a part of the body a changed sense; *organism, organic, organonomy, organography*. The sense changed in that **organ** was orig. applied to mechanism and later to that which is non-mechanical or alive.

A bone in the ear that strikes another bone might be called a *hammer*, or from L. **mall**, hammer, the *malleus*. A bony process or protuberance that looks like the head of a hammer is called a *malleolus*. The hammer strikes an object, which may be called the *anvil* or the **incus**, an earbone; its combining base is **incud** as in *incudectomy*.

That which is like a saw, such as a notched leaf, is *serrated* < L. *serra*, saw. That which rotates is like a wheel; L. *rota*, wheel = **rot**, implying rotation: *rotate; rotator*, a muscle; *roti-fer*, a microscopic water animalcule.

L. *axis*, axis = a bone	*axial*
axis	the second cervical vertebra
Gk *tryp*, borer = a protozoan	
trypanosome	microbe responsible for sleeping sickness
Gk. *pelecy*, hatchet = hatchet-like	*pelican*
Pelecypoda	a class of mollusks, e.g., clam
Pelecyosauria	order of dinosaurs with sail-like dorsal fin

Smith with mallet
forging on incus

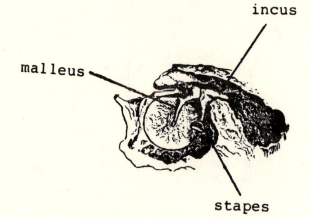

L. *actin*, ray, beam = **actin**, *actinoid, actinology, actinometer*
pert. to or associated with
rays, radiation

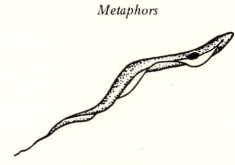

Trypanosoma

Sea anemone
Actiniaria

actinin	a protein of muscle
Actinobacillus	genus of aerobic parasitic bacteria
actinodermititis	inflammation caused by *Actinobacillus* order of sea anemones; its members: *actinians*
Actiniaria	

Gk. *belemon*, a dart = a fossil like the cuttlefish	*belemnite*
L. *uncus*, a hook or barb = **unc**	*uncus, unciform, unciferous, aduncate*
Uncinaria	genus of hookworms
L. *hama*, hook = hook-like bone	
hamate	a wrist bone

Gk. *trochl*, pulley = like a pulley	*trochlear* nerve

L. *clava*, club = like a club	*claviform*
Clavicornia	a family of beetles
Gk. *coryne*, club = like a club	*Corynebacterium*

Gk. *kauterion*, a cauter	*cautherize, cautery, thermocautery,* use of branding iron

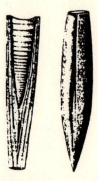

Belemnites hastatus, an extinct
cephalopod related to cuttle-fish

Restored

The Warroom

Clubs, hatchets, and darts can be used for war as well as work. Greek words for shield, sword, bow and arrow, and armed squad were used metaphorically for anatomical and other items of the biological, particularly medical, vocabulary.

Gk. *thyreus,* shield   *thyroid, thyroxin*
Gk. *xiphos,* sword
Xiphosuran order of horseshoe crabs
xiphoid process or *xiphisternum,* lower bone of sternum

L. *gladius,* sword   *gladiator*
gladiolus   a plant and same word for middle bone of sternum

Gk. **sagitta,** arrow   *sagittate, sutura sagittalis*
Gk. **tox,** bow   *toxic, toxin, antitoxin*

Ivory arrow-head used by archers,
or sagittarii

The metaphoric transference might be through the arrow being dipped in poison to
assure its lethal impact. The Gk. source is used literally in *toxophily,* an arcane word
for archery.

Gk. *phalanx,* squad
phalanx, phalang
phalanx   toe or finger bone; adj., *phalangeal*
phalanger   an Australian arboreal marsupial, family *Phalangerdidae*

5.4 Outdoors

Theraps, our guide, will lead us outside, taking a road to the fields. Gk. *hodos,*
road or way, = **od,** for distance or the way of doing something, as *exodus* is the way
out and *method* is a way of doing something systematically; **od** also appears in
episode, odometer, period, synod, cathode, anode.

exodic   leading away from, efferent, centrifugal (*exotic,* no
                                  relation, means foreign)
kinesodic   moving down the way, pert. motor impulses

On this tour of the great outdoors, we'll be protected by an umbrella. L. **umbr**
means shade or shadow, the device orig. used to provide shade, protection from the

Arrow worm
Sagitta

sun's rays. *Umbrella,* lit. little shade, was extended into *exumbrella* and *subumbrella* for parts of hydrozoans. Our horse might wear a packsaddle, in L. *clitellum;* in 1830 this was taken as a word to describe the reproductive case of earthworms, which sits on the animals like a packsaddle.

Clitellum or packsaddle on horse

Ancient words for pit became metaphors for cavities or depressions, as L. *fovea* = *fovea,* a depression in a bone, *fovea centralis* the retinal pit where image is focused. L. *fodere,* to dig > **fossa,** that which is dug up, e.g., *fossil,* and **fossa,** a cavity, as in *mandibular fossa.*

Outdoors, we find fields being plowed and furrowed by cattle yoked together. In the mid-distance, there is a cave, at the mouth of which, if we look close, we'll see a

Clitellum of the earthworm
Lumbricus terrestris

snake shedding its skin. In the far distance, there's a bridge over a stream leading to a gulf on which someone is rowing, Latin and Greek words for several of these references have been used metaphorically in the biological vocabulary. We'll sit down by an olive tree and reflect upon metaphors from Gk. and L. words for field, plowing, furrowing, yoking, caves, and other aspects of the scene.

Gk. *agros* means tilled land = **agr**, land.

agrology	*agriculture*	*agribusiness*	*agroindustry*
agrotechnician			

agronomy	the science of managing fields
agrobacteria	responsible for plant disease
agrobiology	the study of plant nutrition
agrostology	botanical study, of grasses

A farmer is tilling the field with a plowshare. L. *vomer*, once a plowshare = a nose bone. L. *stria*, furrow = **stria**, groove and more often, a layer of fibers, as in *striated*, *mallear stria of tympanic membrane, olfactory striae*. Another base for furrow appears in a curiosity: *de*, away + *lira*, furrow > *delirare*, to plow away from the furrow. It's not a far step from that to *delirious* and *delirium*.

L. *sulc* once was a base for furrow, as in a field = **sulc**, a groove or fissure. Just about any structure can have such a groove: the stomach, the heart, nerves, bones, arteries, veins. Just four will be chosen from the 300+ terms to exemplify the use of the base **sulc**: *sulcus intermedius gastricus*, a groove in the stomach near the duodenum; *arterial sulci* (also *arterial grooves*), and, from the brain, which has many of these fissures, *sulcus of corpus callosum* and *hippocampal sulcus*.

The cattle probably would be yoked—Gk. *zyg*, yoke = **zyg** for the yoking of bodies other than cattle: (1) gametes and (2) anatomical structures.

zygote	cell resulting from union of gametes
zygogenesis	birth of, formation of, a zygote
zygospore	fungi and algae gamete
Zygomycetes	class of fungi
zygoma or *zygomatic*	arch joining cheekbone and temporal bone process
zygopophysis	process that joins vertebra to another
zygodactyl	a grasping claw, such as on parrots

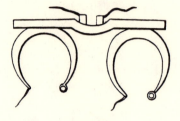

Old yoke

Zygomatic arch of gorilla

L. *alveolus,* trough, channel = **alveol,** cavity, as in *alveolus,* for air cell in a lung and cavity in a tooth socket. *alveolabial.*

Gk. *antron,* cave = **antro,** a cavity or chamber of the body, e.g., *antrodynia,* pain in a bone cavity. Gk. *ecdys* means shedding, as in *ecdysis,* shedding of skin; *ecdysone,* an insect hormone controlling molting; and H. L. Mencken's invention, *ecdysiast,* a stripteaser. L. *sinus,* hollow, curved, fold = **sin,** a certain sort of hollow, the sinus. For bridge, L. **pons** = a bridge between organs; *pontic* has a specialized use in dentistry, adj. for a denture support; cp. *pontoon.* Gk. *tons,* an oar, exists in *tonsil,* and L. *insula,* island, retains orig. meaning in *insular,* becomes metaphoric in *insulin.* Gk. *skaphe,* boat, provides the picture for *scaphoid,* anklebone, wrist bone.

Our last sight of this scene is that of a waterfall. Gk. *kataraktes,* waterfall, paints a pleasant picture in *cataract,* for a waterfall, and a less pleasant one in *cataract* for an opacity of the lens that makes the world look watery.

CHAPTER 6—MORE METAPHORS

6.1   From Plants
6.2   From Animals
6.3   From Persons
6.4   From the Greek Alphabet

We use words referring to plants, animals, persons, and their various parts extensively for metaphors in our daily speech. These metaphors refer to appearance or behavior.

couch potato	hawkish	brainless	cauliflower ears
lily-white	wolfish	gutless	cornsilk hair
wallflower	chicken	heartfelt	aquiline nose

Words may hide the plants and animals of which they're metaphors. *Sardonic,* drily sarcastic, hides a plant of Sardinia. *Risus sardonicus* is a term for an involuntary facial spasm that looks like a grin, a symptom of tetanus. A Gk. word for dog was early applied to a person such as Diogenes, who lived like a dog: *cynic. Urchin,* a street-child, comes from a word that meant hedgehog, *pavillion* from a word that meant butterfly, and *formica* from a word that meant ant.

One way of trying to foretell the future was to watch the flight of birds: L. *avis,* bird + *spic,* a base for viewing (as in *conspicuous*) + *-ous > auspicious,* an adj. meaning optimistic, boding well. A genus of goats is named *Cupra,* and the goat still performs a phantom dance in *caper* and its adj. *capricious.*

6.1 From Plants

Typical specimens are terms for beans used metaphorically for that which looks like a bean, principally the lens of the eye. One of these bases is from Gk. *phaco,* bean = **phaco,** lens.

phacitis	phacocyst	phacocystectomy	phacomalacia
phacoglaucoma	phacoid	phacolysis	phacoma

phacoscope	instrument for viewing eye lens
phacocele	hernia of lens
Phacos cristata	a trilobite

The other base is from Latin—*lens,* bean (literal in *lentil*) = **lens,** metaphoric in *lentigo,* a freckle, in *Bufo lentiginosus,* a toad, and in *lens,* e.g., the lens of the eye.

As time goes on, a particular term might lose its literal meaning entirely and exist as a metaphor that no longer carries any sense of the original meaning. This happened with Gk. *knida,* nettle, which doesn't refer anymore to a plant's nettle but to something like it: a *cnidocyst* or *nematocyst,* nettle-like or thread-like weapon discharged by coelenterates. Gk. *klon,* a sprout or twig, also seems not to be used literally any more, but is metaphoric in **clon** = a replication, e.g., *clone, cloning.*

L. *glans,* acorn, also seems not to be used literally any more, but only metaphorically for gland. The connection is that a gland early discovered, that of the lymph node, looks like an acorn. The Gk. synonym, *balanos,* still means acorn in *balanoid,* like an acorn, and *Dryoblanops aromatica,* a pleasant taxonomic name for an acorn-bearing Bornean tree that supplies camphor. This Gk. word is used metaphorically as well: the glans penis is called the *balanus* because it looks like an acorn.

The two major bases for bud are Gk. **blast** and L. **gemm.** Applied to the buds of a plant, these bases are used literally, as in *Synechoblastus nigrescens,* a budding lichen, and *gemmation, gemmiferous, gemmiparous.* These terms have been metaphorically extended to refer to the production not only of plant buds but also of bud-like structures in animals. **Blast** is commonly used in embryology for the bud-like development of cells, e.g., *blastula, blastoderm, blastomere. Gemmule* refers to the mass of cells constituting a sponge.

We can use the common (though not from native English) word *branch* literally, as for a part of a plant, or metaphorically, as in branching out. L. **furc** and **ram** have lost their literal meaning of branch, existing as metaphors in *bifurcate,* to split off, e.g., the bifurcation of the carotid artery; and *ramify,* extending, branching forth, and *ramus,* a branch of the jawbone. (Gk. homonym *branchio* means gills.)

The following charts twenty additional botanical terms from Greek and Latin that have found dual employment in being used literally and metaphorically.

Base	Literal	Metaphoric
Gk. **antho,** flower = flower-like	*anther,* part of stamen that bears pollen	*anthology* *anthozoan*
Gk. **spor,** seed = spore	*sporophyte*	*sporadic* *androspore*
Gk. **kary,** nut = nucleus	*Carya,* hickory genus *Caryota urens,* wine palm	*karyogamy* *karyolysis*
L. **nuc,** nut = nucleus	*Nucifraga,* nutcracker bird	*nucleus* *enucleate*
Gk. **rhizo,** root = root, as of tooth	*rhizophagous* *rhizogenic* *licorice*	*rhizodontropy,* crowning a tooth *rhizotomy,* cutting of spinal nerve roots
L. **cortex, cortic** bark, shell = outer layer	*cortex* of a tree	*cortex* of adrenal gland and of brain

Gk. **dendrite**, tree = tree-like	*rhododendron*	*dendrites*
L. **pin**, pine tree = like a pine tree	*pine* *pinetum*, garden of pine trees	*pineal* body
Gk. **clad**, branch = taxonomic unit	*cladophyll*, a non-leaf, such as a twig, that functions as a leaf	*clade*, a taxonomic unit
L. **spina**, thorn = thorn, backbone	*porcupine*	*spine* *spina bifida*
Gk. **acanth**, thorn	*acanthus*, thorny plant	*acanthoma*, an epidermal tumor
Gk. **amygdala**, almond = tonsil or brain section	*Prunus amygdala*, the almond plant; *amygdaloid*	*amygdala*, tonsil or cerebellum lobule *amygdalectomy* *amygdalitis* *amygdalith*
Gk. **thym**, thyme = a gland	*thyme*	*thymus*
Gk. **coccus**, berry, grain = a bacterium	*Quercus coccifera*, a berry-bearing plant	*streptococcus*
Gk. **staphylo**, grape = like cluster of grapes	genus *Staphylea*, bladdernut	*staphylococcus*
L. **uva**, grape = like cluster of grapes	*Cocccolobis uvifera*, sea grape	*uva*, a tissue layer of egg *uvula*, soft palate *Coccolobis uvifera*, sea grape
L. *morum*, mulberry berry tree = mass	*sycamore* *Acer rubrum*, red maple	*morula*, embryonic tissue mass
L. *spika*, ear of grain = spikelike	*spike*, ear of corn	*spicule*
L. *pisum*, pea = like a pea	*Pisum sativum*, a pea species	*pisiform*, like a pea; a wristbone *pisolith*,

| L. | *viscum,* mistletoe = thickness | *Viscum album* European mistletoe | *viscous, viscid* |

6.2 From Animals

Some orig. terms for animals no longer have any literal meaning in the common or biological vocabularies. An example of these terms is Gk. *echinos,* hedgehog = **echin,** thorny, in taxonomic names of beings that reminded their nomenclators of spininess. *Vacca,* L. for cow, is in taxonomic names for animals other than cows; also in *vaccine* and *vaccination,* since cows were the animals used in early experiences at inoculating people to protect them from smallpox.

The type specimen for this subsection is Gk. **coccyx, coccyg.** This meant literally cuckoo, retaining that sense in the taxonomic *Coccygomorphae,* cuckoo genus. The cuckoo's beak was taken as a metaphor to mean tailbone, the *coccyx,* combining form **coccyg,** as in *coccygodynia.* Zeus came to visit one of his girlfriends in the form of a cuckoo, hence a nickname for this deity: *Zeus coccygeal.*

To be assaulted by gadflies is enough to send one into a frenzy. Female animals in heat seemed to observers to be in that condition, and so the Gk. word for gadfly, *oistros* = **estrus,** in heat; *anestrus,* the calm period between storms of heat; and *estrogen,* the female sex hormone. It retains its literal sense in some taxonomic names, e.g., *Oestrus ovis,* sheep-botfly.

The etymology of *muscle* deserves special notice, perhaps admiration for the iron-pumpers of ancient Greece. The flexing of biceps seemed to someone like the cruising of mice under the skin, and so the Gk. and L. bases for mouse became the bases for muscle. Gk. **mys, my,** mouse is muscular in *myalgia, myoma, myocardium* and *hydromys;* also in *Myosotis,* a genus of forget-me-nots. The L. cognate **mus** mouse, is the base for *muscle* and for mouse: *Mus musculus;* **mur,** mouse, is in *Muridae,* a family of rodents, *murine* the adjective.

A depressing example of metaphoric ramification or branching conducts *tragedy* to an ear cartilage. The pagan Greeks, considerably more in tune with nature than we are, celebrated fertility by singing songs to the goat, Gk. *tragos*—the goat being a model of fertility. These songs evolved into Greek drama, into tragedy. The hairy chin of a goat metaphorized into *tragecanth,* an Asian thorny shrub and also into *tragus,* ear cartilage, a sign of old age in men being hair growth in this ear structure.

With the following twenty bases, *like* can be added to derive the metaphoric use. e.g., Gk. *kochlias,* snail = **cochl,** spiral, as in *cochlea,* the spiral tube of inner ear, and *Cochliomyia,* a genus of flies.

Base	Literal	Metaphoric
L. **musca,** fly	*Muscidae,* family of flies	*mosquito* *muscae volitantes* fly-like specks in eye
Gk. **carcin,** crab	*Carcinaspis,* crustacea	*Carcinocoris,*

Cochlea of Ear

= crab-like	taxon	insect taxon
		carcinoma
L. **cancer,** crab	*Cancricepon,* crustacea taxon	*cancroid*
chancr		*chancre,* venereal sore
canker		*canker,* mouth lesion
L. **rana,** frog	*Rana sylvatica,* wood-frog *ranarium*	*ranula,* sublingual tumor
L. **lago,** rabbit	*Lagomorpha,* order of hares and rabbits	*lagopthalmos,* incomplete closing of eyelids
L. **nid,** nest	*nidus, nidicolous* *nidify,* to build a nest *denidation,* leaving the nest	*nidus,* bacterial growth
Gk. **corac,** raven	*Corvus corx,* raven *Coraciura,* bird taxon	*coracoid,* scapula bone
L. **can,** dog	*canine*	*canine* tooth
Gk. **hipp,** horse	*Eohippus, hippodrome*	*hippus,* tremor of iris

6.3 From Persons

Biological terms may be metaphors of people, their states or functions or parts. The membranes covering the brain were given fanciful names by Arabic physicians, which accounts for the L. translations being *pia mater,* tender mother, for the inner membrane surrounding the brain, and *dura mater,* hard mother, for the outer. These two membranes, sandwiching the *arachnoid,* constitute membranes enclosing the spinal cord as well as brain.

Several of the terms for sex organs are metaphors. We have seen that *estrogen* developed from a base orig. referring to the frenzy suffered by victims bitten by flies. Gk. *hyster* meant womb and still does in *hysterectomy.* But a notion that a state of

Nidus, nest of Baltimore oriole

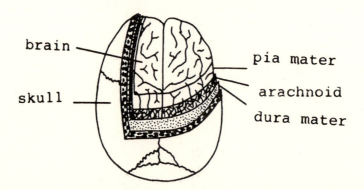

madness is peculiar to the gender that possesses a womb led to the formation, in 1650, of *hysteric* and, in 1800, of *hysteria.* The metaphoric transference is from the base's meaning a certain anatomical structure to its meaning a state of mental disturbance.

Metaphoric transference took place with Gk. *theraps,* attendant = **therap,** cure, as in *hydrotherapy, heliotherapy,* and many other terms. L. *testis,* witness. = **testis,** *testosterone.*

The metaphor might be based on a function: < L. *testis*, witness, witness of masculinity (cp. *testify, testimony*); or on appearance: L. *test*, pot, little pots.

With Gk. *orchios*, the transference went in the other direction, from **orchi** orig. meaning testes, as it still does in *orchiocele*, hernia of the testes, to its referring to an epiphytic plant, the orchid. Some orchids look like testes.

Ovary seems to have evolved directly from L. *ovum*, egg, base **ov** + suffix *-ary*, place for; but one source (Pepper) suggests that the inventor of the word *ovary* had in mind the model of L. *ovarius*, the farm slave who gathered eggs.

From words for living human beings, the biolexicon has *hebe, core, pupa,* and *sartor. Hebe*, the goddess of youth, gave her name to *hebetic*, pertaining to puberty, and *hebephrenia*, a schizophrenic regression to childhood. Another Gk. source, *kore*, girl, child, gave *core*, for pupil of the eye. The metaphoric transference here is that an image in the pupil looks like a little child or doll. The more familiar term for this comes from L.: **pupa**, literal in *pupil*, school-child, metaphoric in the *pupil* of the eye. *Pupa*, a stage in insect development, *pupivorous, puppet, puppy,* and *Buliminia pupula*, a foraminifer, also come from L. **pupa**.

L. *sartor* means tailor. *Sartorial* is an adjective for well-tailored, well-dressed. A muscle in the thigh, actually the longest muscle in the human body, received the name *sartorial* because it's employed in the work of tailoring.

We'll examine one metaphor of a body part in detail. Gk. *kondylos*, knuckle, maintains its lit. meaning in *condyloid*, like a knuckle. However, Gk. *kondylos* = **condyle**, knob-like projection so that *condyloid* can also mean like a knob. *Condyle* and its alternate form *condylus* appear in 30+ medical terms, such as *condyloma*, genital warts, *tibial condyle of femur* and *condylus humeri*. The *mandibular condyle* is the knob at the summit of the jawbone; it articulates with the fossa of the temporal bone. *Condylarthra* is a genus name of extinct ungulates, and *Condylura cristata* the name of the star-nosed mole.

L. **ocul** is a base for eye, as in *oculist* and *binocular*. It becomes metaphoric in the word *inoculate*. This word entered E. in the 15th century. It referred to the implanting of a bud or eye, as of a potato, to grafting. L. **capit** is a base for head, lit. in *decapitate*, metaphoric in *capitellum*, a knob of the lower end of the humerus, looking like a small head. L. **costa** is a base for rib, lit. in *costal*, pert. to the ribs, and *cutlet*, metaphoric in *coast* and *Costa Rica*. We'll conclude this section of words formed from bases having to do with parts of the human body with a Gk. base, **mast**, breast, lit. in *mastitis* and *mastectomy*, metaphoric in *mastodon*, an animal whose molar cusps look like nipples.

One Gk. *thym* is the base for *thyme*, a mint. Another Gk. *thym* refers to spirit or mind or emotions. There are very few terms in the medical vocabulary with *thym* in this sense—*thymoleptic* is an adj. pert. to an anti-depression drug and the strange *noothymopsychic* analyzes into mind-mind-mind, an adj. referring to the mind's emotional as well as mental processes. The most-used **thym**, in Gk. a warty outgrowth, is the base for *thymus*, an abdominal lymph gland, as in *thymolysis, thymocyte,* and *thymusectomy*.

Milk itself is a native English word. The Latin base for milk is **lac**, as is obvious in *lactate, lactation,* and *lactovegetarian*, and not so obvious in *lettuce*. Perhaps the milky juice of the plant inspired the metaphoric employment; the plant's taxonomic name is *Lactuca salvia. Lettuce* came into E. in the late 13th century; a further metaphoric extension into meaning U.S. paper currency is a contribution of the roaring twenties.

Gk. **galacto,** milk, is the base for a cluster of stars as well as for milk. For milk, **galacto** combines to form about 70 words of biochemistry and medicine: *galactometer, galactorrhea.*

galactose	an enzyme found in milk sugar
galactopoiesis	the production of milk
galactogogue	that which stimulates production of milk
galactostasis	stoppage of milk flow

The cluster of stars seemed to a viewer of 1350 to look like a stream of milk, and so it was called the *Milky Way* or, in L., *via lactea,* or, in Gk. *galaxy.*

The pagans considered the large bone at the end of the spinal column as sacred, perhaps because that bone seems to be the fulcrum for the vertebral column or because it would be more resistant than smaller bones to being disintegrated during sacrificial burning. The Greeks applied the base **hier,** sacred, to that bone, calling it the *hieron,* and the Romans translated that into **sacr.**

Base	Literal: religion	Metaphoric: vertebral
Gk. **hier,**	*hierarchy, hieroglyphics*	*hieralgia*
sacred =	*hierotherapy,* treatment by	*platyhieric,* flat
a vertebral	religious exercises	sacrum
bone	*hierophobia,* cleric's fear	*dolichohieric,* long
	of speaking in public; fear	sacrum
	of priests or hierarchy	
L. **sacr,**	*sacred, sacrosanct, sacrifice,*	*(os) sacrum*
sacred =	*desecration, consecrate*	*sacroiliac*
a vertebral		*vertebrosacral*
bone		

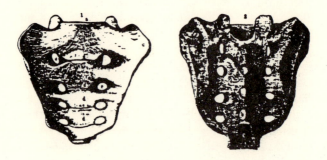

Sacrum, the sacred bone
front and rear Views

Once upon a drizzly time, an Australopithecine family strolled along the bank of a river in southern Africa. The rain mixed with carbonitite from a volcanic eruption and the bed on which the family walked fossilized. Three and a half million years later, in 1978, a team led by Mary Leakey came upon these fossilized footprints, vestiges of that Australopithecine outing.

Vestiges, orig. meaning footstep, has undergone useful semantic expansion. It has taken on the sense of anything like a footprint as a sign of past life, for example, these vestiges: the appendix, hair on the human arm. In the general vocabulary the base *vestig* combined to form a word for tracking footprints or other evidence — *investigate.*

If we human beings have a soul, after death it might be reluctant to leave this green earth and might hang around. *Ghost* is a Germanic word, but the Greeks and Romans had their words for this haunting disembodied spirit. The L. terms have lost their lit. sense. L. *lemur,* ghost, survives metaphorically in *lemur,* and L. *larva,* mask, ghost, in *larva, larvivorous.*

An Alaskan city received its name from a citation on a map: *No name > Nome.* A similarly creative process was used in labelling the bones constituting each half of the pelvis, the *ossa innominata,* or no-name bones. Dorland: "so-called from bearing no resemblance to any known objects." *Innominate* also applies to an artery leading to the common carotid, syn. *brachiocephalic.*

6.4 From the Greek Alphabet

The following chart indicates those Greek letters which have been used to designate brain waves and whose forms have been used as metaphors for anatomical structures.

alpha, beta	*alpha rhythm, beta rhythm*
gamma	*gamma globulin*

Alpha, beta, and *gamma* have recently been taken to denote types of interferon.

delta $\varDelta$	*deltoid,* triangle-shaped muscle
	subdeltoid, clavodeltoid
lambda λ	*lambdoid,* L-shaped skull suture
	lambdacism, pronouncing *r* as *l*
sigma $\varSigma$ σ	*sigmoid,* S- or C-shaped flexure
	dolichosigmoid, very long sigmoid flexure
	sigmoidotomy, colosigmoidostomy
hypsilon or **upsilon** υ	*hyoid,* U-shaped bone at base of tongue
	epihyoid, infrahyoid, hyothyroid
	Hyolithes, an extinct invertebrate
chi X	*chiasma,* intersection X as between nerves or chromosomes (syn. *decussation*)
	chiastoneural, chiastometer
omega $\varOmega$	*omega melancholicum,* melancholic frowning

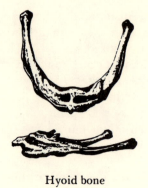

Hyoid bone

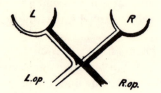

Decussation of fibers in the optic chiasma

Further details about the Greek alphabet, such as Gk. *k* to L. *c,* will be found in Appendix B.

PART III: AFFIXES

CHAPTER 7—PREFIXES

7.1 Time and Tempo
7.2 With, Together, Same, Equal
7.3 Quality
7.4 Amount and Size
7.5 Negation, Removal, Reversal
7.6 Intensifying, Thoroughly, Completely, Excessive

It must be said first of all about affixes that studying them is not the most exciting way to enjoy a weekend. But much of the biological vocabulary relies upon these elements, and so they should be learned by anyone interested in gaining control over that vocabulary. A bonus is that learning these affixes will also help in decoding words in other scientific lexicons and also in the general vocabulary. Each inventory will be introduced or followed by a short narrative about selected prefixes from the section.

As a verb, affix means to attach; as a noun, it means that which is attached. We might affix a postage stamp to an envelope or a lexical element to a base. Affixes are of two kinds: prefixes and suffixes. Pure affixes are prepositions and adverbs, but some bases function almost always as though they were affixes. Prefixes don't change the part of speech of the central base; suffixes may.

To see how these work to change or give direction to the meaning of the base, we may turn to the homely example of native English prefixes. Consider the native E. word *stand*. It exists by itself and with the prefixes *out-, under-, with-: outstand, understand, withstand,* each word carrying a different meaning because of direction given by the prefix. For negating, E. may use the prefix *mis-: misunderstand;* or *no-: nowhere, nothing;* or *un-: undo, unbend.*

Suffixes may be added to these: *understand* + *-able; misunderstand* + *-ing.* A common E. suffix is *-ness: kindness.* Note that *-ness* changes an adjective into a noun that has the quality of the adjective. *Wise,* a word that has become popular as a suffix, changes a noun into an adjective; we have the noun *street* and we affix to it *-wise* and create *streetwise.* An E. suffix may make its base into an adverb: *kind* + *-ly* = *kindly.*

The prefix, then, comes before the base and doesn't change its part of speech; the suffix comes after it and may change its part of speech. A base may be preceded by more than one prefix and followed by more than one suffix. Cognate to the E. word *stand* is the Fr. *establish,* both descendant of the IE root *sta,* which will be investigated later.

An awful example of how affixes and suffixes can be attached for compounding is provided by *antidisestablishmentarianism.* The Anglican Church in the 1830s, conceding that the Irish were Roman Catholics and not Anglicans, decided to close up Anglican churches established in Ireland, to disestablish them. A coven of Anglican professors at Oxford University disagreed with that decision. They were against the disestablishment of the churches in Ireland, and their views came to be known as *antidisestablishmentarianism.* The base *establ* preceded by two prefixes, *anti-* and *dis-,* and followed by five suffixes, *-ish, -ment, -ar, -ian,* and *-ism.*

Another awful example has already made its debut. *Pneumonoultramicroscopicsilico-volanoconiosis* consists of base + prefix + prefix + base + suffix + base + base + base + suffix.

An appropriate and shorter example of how prefixes work is seen in attaching them to the base *fix.*

ad-, to + *fix*	*affix,* lit., to attach to
pre-, before	*prefix,* lit. attached before
sub-, under	*suffix,* lit. attached under (after)

Ad- and *sub-,* as seen in the examples, change to *af-* and *suf-* before an *f.* Suffixes also attach to *fix: fixable, fixate, fixture.* L. *fix* changed into *fibula,* a clasp or buckle, which metaphorically took on use as the term for a bone of the lower leg; and through French became *fiche,* as in *microfiche.* OE cognates of the Latin are *dike* and *ditch.*

You are, probably without realizing it, familiar with many of the prefixes from Gk. and L., such as *anti-, hyper-, non-,* and the anti-Sandinista *Contras.* Most of the prefixes indicating direction (Chapter 8) will be as familiar as the *sub-* of *subway, subjugate, submarine.* The *pre-* in *pre-med* and *pre-law* obviously means before; *circum-,* around; *super-,* above; *trans-,* through, across.

In learning prefixes, keep in mind that many are already familiar or can be easily remembered by recalling their use in words you know; that half a dozen change their last letter to agree with the first letter of the base—as *sub-* does when it attaches to *fix:* not *subfix,* but *suffix;* and that while bases most often can stand by themselves, the affixes cannot; in order to live, they have to live in a symbiotic relationship with a base.

7.1 Time and Tempo

Chrono is the Gk. base for time, as in *chronology, chronometer, chronic, anachronism* and *crony,* a friend through time. *Chronodendrology* is the determination of a tree's age and growth: **chrono** + *dendro* + *-logy*). The most common L. base for time is **temp,** as in *temporary, contemporaneous, temporal.*

Terms for the day and for seasons are relevant to the biolexicon, though they are not widely used:

Gk. **hemer,** day	*ephemeral, Ephemera*
Gk. **nycto, nycti,** night	*nyctophobia, nyctitropic, nyctalopia, nyctalgia*

Nyctea nyctea	snowy owl
L. **noct**, night	*nocturnal,* its antonym *diurnal*
	noctambulist, equinox
Pyrophorus noctilucus	a firefly

Three of the four seasons have bases from L. and Gk. for employment in the biolexicon: from a Latin base for winter come *hibernate* and *hibernaculum;* from a Greek base for summer, *aestivate;* and from a Latin base for spring, *vern,* come *vernal, vernal equinox, vernal conjunctivitis, vernalize* — to accelerate a plant's growth period; and *Eubranchipus vernalis,* the taxonomic name of the delicate fairy shrimp. *Vern* carrying the sense of springtime has a pleasant connotation; however, homophonic *vern* < L. *verne,* and means domestic servant, slave, so that *vernacular* etymologically means the language of slaves.

A word formed about thirty years ago, *circadian,* has found employment in the biolexicon. It consists of *circa,* about + *di* < *dies,* day, and refers to rhythmic or periodic 24-hour biological actions.

Before and *after,* both from E., function to locate things in position relative to other things and also to locate events in a time sequence relative to other events. A similar double function is performed by *arche-, ante-, post-, pro-* and *mes-.*

Gk. **arche-**, first, primitive	*archeology, archetype*
archiblast	before the first developing cells
archebiosis	spontaneous generation
L. **ante-**, earlier than	*ante meridiem (a.m.), antecedent*
	antenatal, antemortem
ante-diluvian	before the flood
L. **post-**	*posterity, postmortem*
Gk. **pro-**, before	
pronephron	embryonic structure preceding kidney
Gk. **meso-** middle	*Mesozoic*
Gk. **brady-**, slow	
bradypnea	slow breathing
Gk. **tachy-** fast	*tachometer, tachycardia*

The sign * in the inventories below signals that the prefix changes its last letter when it attaches to bases beginning with certain consonants. To L. *fer,* to bring, to carry, may be suffixed *sub-, dis-* and *ob-,* (resultant words: *suffer, differ, offer*), *in-, pre-, trans-.* Because just what changes with what is a complicated affair, the topic has been exiled to Appendix C.

7.2 With, Together, Same, Equal

As noted earlier, Gk. **homo-** for same can be confused with L. *homo* or *homi* for human being. Of the nine prefixes in this section, half would be familiar or easy to figure out: **homo-**, same, **con-** and **syn-/sym-**, both meaning with, **equi-** and **iso-**, even.

Greek	Latin	Examples
	con- *, with	*convergent, commute*
	equi-, same	*equilibrium*
homo-, same		*homogenous*
iso-, equal		*isogamy*
		isodactylism
(h)omal-, even, level		*anomaly*
	plan-, flat, level	*planula*
		planicaudate
platy-, flat, broad		*platelet*
		platypodia
syn-, sym-, with		*synthesis*
		symphysis
tauto-, same		*tautomorphous*

7.3 Quality

Eight prefixes are in this section. Again, we will find that half or more than half of these are familiar or could easily be figured out because they exist in words of the general vocabulary, e.g., **ben-**, good, as in *benevolent* and *benefactor;* **mal**, bad, as in *malevolent,* **pseudo**, false, as in *pseudonym.* A little reflection shows that **ortho-** means straight.

A full discussion of **eu-**, good, well, true, could cover pages. It appears in the general vocabulary—*euphoria* and *euthanasia;* in religion—*Eucharist* and *evangelical;* in rhetoric—*euphemism* and *euphony;* and in biology.

eukaryote	a cell with a true nucleus
eubacteria	of the order *Eubacteriales,* genuine bacteria
eucalyptus	an Australian tree, lit. well-covered

Eu- is in concepts that have provoked much discussion and some ardent controversy: *eugenics,* coined in 1880 by Francis Galton, a cousin of Charles Darwin, and meaning the science of good birth, of how to breed good human beings and restrict the breeding of bad human beings, and a subject of more recent controversy, though the word dates back to the mid-17th century, *euthanasia.* Galton and his followers, particularly in the 1920s, argued that *eugenics* could bring about a utopia. *Utopia,* coined in the 16th century by Thomas More, doesn't etymologically mean good place: it means no place; but early utopias were good places, and so the *u-* meaning no got lost in the homophonic *eu-* meaning good.

The antonym of *utopia* is *dystopia*, lit. a bad place. H. G. Wells's *The Time Machine*, George Orwell's *1984*, and Aldous Huxley's *Brave New World* depict dystopias. **Dys-** means disordered. It exists in a long list of words, among them *dysgenics*, coined in 1915, which in the medical vocabulary means the science studying the genetic basis of disorders. It can also be used to refer to a society that encourages the birth of undesirable people. This view is offered by critics of the welfare system. It is a most controversial view.

A much tamer point is that Gk. **dys-** can be confused with L. **dis-**, also **di-** and **bis-**. Both come from an IE source that meant two. To make two of one means to break apart, this meaning seen in *dismember, disappear, diverge, disengage, divorce.* **Dys-** took on the meaning of disordered, as in *dystrophy, dysentery, dyslexia, dyspnea, dyspeptic,* and *dystopia.*

Greek	Latin	Examples
	ben-, good	*benign*
caco-, bad		*cacogenics*
dys-, disordered		*dystrophy*
eu-, good, well		*eupepsia*
	mal-, bad	*malignant*
ortho-, straight, correct		*orthodontics*
		orthopnea
para-, disordered		*paralysis*
		paracephalus
pseudo-, false		*pseudopod*

7.4 Amount and Size

Of the 23 prefixes in this section, these would be familiar: **long-**, obviously meaning long, **hyper-** (which exists as a slangy word all by itself), **hypo-**, **macro-**, **magni-**, **mega-** (as in *megabucks*), **micro-**, **multi-**, **omni-**. These and some others less immediately explicable are in familiar words. **Brev-** might not immediately indicate shortness, but it's in *brevity* and, altered, in *brief;* **lat-** might not immediately indicate wide or broad, until we think of *latitude;* and **oligo-** might not immediately indicate few or little until we get angry at an *oligarchy.*

Eu-, good, might be confused with **eury-**, wide: this little problem is resolved by knowing that if the first four letters of a word spell *eury*, then that's the prefix being used—the only exception is *eurythmics*, good rhythm. **Lat-**, wide, might be confused with *latero-*, side.

Greek	Latin	Examples
brachy-, short		*brachycephalic*
	brev-, short	*brevilingual*
dolicho-, long		*dolichosigmoid*
eury-, wide, broad		*eurypterid*

Greek	Latin	Examples
hyper-, above, excess		*hypertension*
hypo-, below, under		*hypothermy*
	lat-, dilat-	*dilator*
	wide, broad, expanded	*latissimus*
lepto-, thin, narrow		*leptodactylous*
	long-, long	*elongation, longicaudal,*
		longissimus
macro-, large		*macrocyte*
	magni-, great	*magnicaudate*
mega(lo)-, very large		*megacaryocyte*
		megalomania
mei-, mio-, less, smaller		*meiosis, Miocene*
micro-, small		*microbe*
	multi-, many	*multidentate*
oligo-, few, little		*oligogalactia*
	omni-, all	*omnivorous*
pachy-, thick		*pachyderm*
pan-, all		*panacea, pandemic*
plio-, plei-, pleo-		*Pleistocene*
more, increased		*Pliocene*
		pleomorphism
pros-, in addition to		*prosthesis*
steno-, narrow		*stenographer, stenosis,*
		stenopetalous

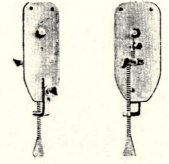

Leeuwenhoek's microscope

7.5 Negation, Removal, Reversal

Greek	Latin	Examples
a-, an-, lacking		*anaerobic*
ant-, anti-, against		*antidote, antigen*

Plesiosaurus dolichodeirus

apo-, aph-, away, off
lack of
separation
cata-, cath-, down,
complete, whole

    contra-, against
    dis-, * apart from
    separation
    in-, im- *, not

    non-, not

    ob- *, against, facing
    inversely

para-, abnormal
alongside
near
beyond
resemble

    se(d)-, apart from

apothecary
apochromatic
apostasis
catabolism
catholic
contra-indicate
dismember
divergence
immaculate, not
    stained
nonsense
nonvalent
obstacle
obliterate
paralysis > palsy
parallel
parathyroid
paranormal
paratyphoid
selection
sedition

7.6 Intensifying, Thoroughly, Completely, Excessive

Greek	Latin	Examples
ana-		*anadipsia*
hyper-		*hyperactive*
	in-, im- *	*intumescent*
	ob- *	*occlusion*
	per-, pel-	*perspiration*
		perniger, black
	red-	*redundant*

Greek	Latin	Examples
	supra-	*supravergence*
	sur-	*surexcitation*
	ultra-	*ultramicrobe*

The dissection of a word may not cut it into its proper segments. *Asterognosis* may be cut into *aster*, star, + *gnosis*, knowledge of, as though the word came from astrology. It should be dissected into *a-*, not, + *stereo*, solid, + *gnosis*, for a condition in which the patient is not able to know or recognize things, to perceive them, through handling them, a failure in sense perception.

Ana- has several meanings:

(a) upward progression	*anabolism*
(b) reversion	*anachronism*
(c) renewal	*anabiosis*
(d) intensively	*anadipsia*
(e) according to	*analogous*

Analogous structures are those that accord to a similar type, e.g., the shape of a dolphin and the shape of a shark. *Homologous* organs (Gk. *homo-*, same) are those that descended from the same source, e.g., bat's wing and the human hand.

Ana- and **an-**, not, can be confused. Suppose the prefix in a word is **an-**, but this appears before a base beginning with the letter *a*. It may then be mistaken for **ana-**. This could happen with *analgesia, anadenia, anandrous*. Since some Gk. bases begin with weird combinations of letters (e.g., *pt* in *ptosis, ct* in *ctenophore*), it might be possible that there are combinations *lg* and *nd*. But there aren't any. There isn't any base *den;* the base in *anadenia* is **aden**, gland, and the word therefore means without glands.

To complicate matters, **ana-** can lose its *a*, as in *anion* and *anode*, both really **ana-** + base. Consider *aneurysm*. This could be dissected into **an-**, not + **eury**, wide + *-ism*, condition of, so that the word would mean not wide. But the prefix is really **ana-** as in *anion*, so that the word breaks into **ana-**, intensive + **eury** + *-ism*. An *aneurysm* is a wide dilatation or bloating of a blood vessel. The word was invented by Galen.

Aneurysm

The situation is not really hopeless. First of all, there are only about a dozen words beginning with *ana* that could mean either **ana-** or **an-** + *a* of the base. And familiarity with bases will disallow making errors about which it should be.

We are now prepared to survey the ways in which attaching different prefixes to a single base results in the production of many words in the biological vocabulary. The bases selected are **bol, ceph,** and **gnath.** For the first, we provide a box.

IE *gwele*, to throw

IE *gwele* has living descendants only from Greek. A *bolus* is that which is lumped together, in veterinary medicine a large pill. The force in the universe that throws us down, according to conventional wisdom, is the down-thrower, or *diabolus*, from which *diabolic* and, greatly disguised, *devil*. Other words in the general vocabulary have the senses of things thrown together or of throwing words, the sense of throwing not altogether clear in some: e.g., *belemnite*, a dart-shaped extinct cephalopod, *symbol, problem,* and *parable*.

The base **bol,** throw, appears in biological, esp. medical, terms, one of which we've seen: *embolalia,* the condition of producing strange, incomprehensive sounds, as though having a bolus in the throat. Most of the following terms carry the metaphor of throwing pretty far; in some words, it seems to get lost altogether.

epi-	+ **bol**	+ -y	gastrulation
meta	+ **bol**	+ -ism	body processes
changing			
ana	+		building up of body
upward			
cata-	+		breaking down of body
down			
em-	+		an obstruction within a blood vessel; *embolization,* surgical insertion of such an obstruction
hyper	+ meta	+ **bolism**	excess of metabolism
glyco	+	+	excess of sugar in metabolism

A chart will conveniently illustrate how the prefixes can join with bases in the production of hundreds of words. For the bases, we turn to Gk. **cephal,** head and Gk. **gnath,** jaw. Just about any of the prefixes can combine with these bases to produce a word, though many of the combinations would not be sensible—e.g., *glycocephaly,* condition of having a sweet head. Adj. forms are given: *-ic* and *-ous.* Nouns would end in *-y, -ia,* or *-ism.* Prefixes not taken up so far are defined.

Prefixes	Cephal	Gnath
a-	*acephalic*	*agnathic*
acro-, tip	*acrocephalic*	
an- + iso-		*anisognathous*
brachy-	*brachycephalic*	*brachygnathous*
dolicho-	*dolichocephalic*	*dolichognathous*
eury-	*eurycephalic*	*eurygnathic*
iso-		*isognathous*
lepto-	*leptocephalic*	

Prefixes	Cephal	Gnath
macro-	*macrocephalic*	*macrognathous*
micro-	*microcephalic*	*micrognathous*
megalo-	*megalocephalic*	*megalognathous*
opistho-, back of		*opisthognathous*
ortho-		*orthognathous*
pachy-		*pachygnathous*
pro-		*prognathous*

Plesiosaurus macrocephalus

Bases may also be attached, e.g., *hydrocephalic, cephalgia,* headache.

In the course of embryogenesis, mistakes can happen, dozens of different warpings. These mistakes may result in the production of what are unhappily called monsters, the field studying them from the Greek word for monster, *terato* + *-logy.* A few terms will illustrate what can happen to the head:

cephalo	+ *-oma*		fetal monster lacking upper limbs and complete head
di-	+ **cephalus**		a two-headed monster
para-	+		imperfect head and maybe limbs
oto	+ **cephaly**		condition of joined ears instead of lower jaw beneath face
oxy	+		dome-shaped head
sym- +	*phyo* +		Siamese twins joined at head

Enceph means in the head, that is, the brain.

encephalitis	inflammation of the brain
encephalopsy	delusional association of colors with other events, e.g., heat, numbers
anencephaly	lacking a brain
pseudencephalon	vascular tumor instead of brain

Cephal in taxonomy:
Cephalopoda	a class of "head-foot" animals, that is, squids, octopuses
Gastropoda	a class of "belly-foot" animals, that is, snails, slugs, et al.
Cephalochordata	subphylum of vertebrates, e.g., fish-like lancelet

Agnatha has been noted as a class of jawless fish. Two terms with **gnath** have escaped from the specialized vocabulary into the more general educated vocabulary:

pro- + **gnath** + *-ous*		protruding jaw, snout as with gorilla faces
ortho- +		straight-jawed
+	+ *-ics*	science of treating malformed jaws (cp. orthodontics)

Dorland's Medical Dictionary does not list *isognathous* or *anisognathous,* but these terms are readily translatable into equal jaws and unequal jaws. If one recalls the meaning of prefixes, there should similarly be no difficulty in translating highly specialized terms.

dolichognathous	*macrognathous*	*micrognathous*
opisthognathous	*eurygnathous*	*pachygnathous*

Dynia is a base for pain and Gk. *stoma* means mouth; therefore, *gnathodynia* means pain in the jaw and *agnathostomatous* means lacking jaws and mouth.

Chaetognatha is the name of a phylum, of arrow worms. *Chaeto* means hair and **gnath,** jaw — to the person who named this animal (in 1885), the worm's mouth looked like a hairy jaw.

CHAPTER 8—DIRECTION AND LOCATION

8.1   Inventory
8.2   Close-up of Selected Prefixes
8.3   Verbs of Motion and Location

Knowing prefixes helps in understanding the difference between closely allied terms, for example, between *afferent* and *efferent. Af-* is a variant of *ad-*, which means toward, and *ef-* is a variant of *ex-*, which means out. Therefore, *afferent* pertains to nerves or vessels going toward a part, such as the central nervous system, and *efferent* to those going out from it.

Knowing the meaning of the prefix similarly helps in remembering the difference between *adductor* and *abductor* muscles. *Ad-* means toward in *adductor*, name of a muscle that draws toward the body; *ab-* means away from, and thus describes a muscle that draws away from the body. *Abducens* nerves carry impulses away from the central nervous system.

The sign * indicates that the last consonant of the prefix will change before certain other consonants. The details are noted in Appendix C. Several of the elements below are bases that function as prefixes: e.g., *acr, apic, bathy, brady*.

8.1 Inventory

Greek	Latin	Examples
	a-, ab-, abs-	*abstract, abort*
	from, away from, of	*abductor*
ac(m)-, point, tip,		*acme, acne*
extremity		*acmesthesia*
acr-, at the end, tip,		*Acropolis, Akron*
extremity		*acromegaly*
		pachyacria
	ad-, a- *	*adhesive, appendix*
	to, toward, near	*adductor*
	ambi-, both, around	*ambidexterous*
amphi-, both, around		*Amphibia*
ana-, ano-, back, reverse		*anabiosis*
upward		*anabolism*
again		*anagenesis*
intensive		*aneurysm*
	ante-, in front of	*antecubital*

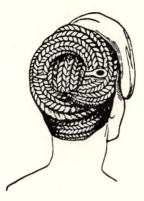

Acus crinalis, hair pin

Amphioxus

apex, apic-, summit   *apex*
tip, extremity   *apicoectomy*

Apex, cap on head

bathy-, deep, inner   *bathycardia*
                                        bathymeter

        circum-, around   *circumcorneal*
        de-, down, off   *derive*

dextro-, right   *dextropedal*
                                        ambidexterous

dia-, through   *dialysis*
                                        diathermy

        dist-, far   *distal*

ec-, ecto-, ex-, out   *ectoplasm, exodus*
from, outside

Greek	Latin	Examples
	ex- * out, off	*excision*
		efferent
en-, em-, endo-, ent-,		*endocrine*
in, within		*entomology*
epi-, upon, on, over		*epidermis*
above, after, at, near, besides		
eso-, inward, within		*esogamy, esoteric*
	fron(t)o-, forehead	*frontomalar*
hypo-, below		*hypodermic*
	in-, *, in	*inspiration*
	infra-, below, lower	*infraorder*
		infracostal
	inter-, between	*interdental*
	intra-, intro-, within	*introvert*
	intus-, within	*intussusception*
	juxta-, beside, near to	*juxtaspinal*
	lat(er)i-, side	*bilateral*
		laterigrade
	lev-, left	*levotorsion*
meso-, between		*mesomorphic*
meta-, meth-, behind		*metencephalon*
beyond		*metaphysics*
change		*metamorphosis*
		metastasis
	ob- *, back	*obstetrics*
		occiput
opistho-, behind		*opisthognathous*
para-, near		*parathyroid*
almost		*paramedic*
	per-, through	*pervasive*
peri-, near, around		*pericardium*
	post-, behind, after	*postnasal*
	pre-, in front of	*pretibial*
pro-, in front of		*proboscis*
	proxim-, nearest	*proximal*
	re-, red-, behind	*redundant*
	back, again	*respiration*
	retro-, behind, back	*retro-iridian*
	sinistr-, left	*sinister*
		sinistrodextral
	sub- *, under	*subcutaneous*
	super-, above	*superciliary,*
		pert. to eyebrows

sur-, above   *surface*

supra-, above   *supracostal*

tele-, far   *telemetry*

tra-, tran-, trans-,   *translucent*

across   *trance*

Dextral and sinistral openings of American snails
Bulimus and *Physa*

8.2 Close-up of selected prefixes

Moderately extensive discussions could be conducted with just about any of the prefixes, since each is used in many words. The following have been selected for discussion.

1. A review will indicate that some prefixes have several meanings, for example

in-	(a) intensive, (b) negative, and (c) within; thus a problem with the word *inflammable,* which could mean either not flammable or intensely flammable.
com-	(a) intensive, (b) with
L. **pro-**	for, in favor of, substituting for
Gk. **pro-**	earlier, in front of

3. Several prefixes relate both to time and space, as do **ante-** and **post-**. Others can refer to above or below, either in activity and function or location: e.g., **hyper-, hypo-**.

4. Often, a base functions like a prefix and becomes employable as a prefix: e.g., **eu, bathy, pachy, platy**. Sometimes, such a base will be followed by a dash (*bathy-*) and sometimes not.

5. **Eso-,** within, appears in *esogastritis,* inflammation of that which is within the stomach, or the mucous lining of the stomach. As a prefix for within, **eso-** appears in fewer than 20 medical words. It has a homophonic form, another *eso.* This, < Gk. *oisein,* to carry, joins with *phagus,* eating > *esophagus,* and that appears in more than 50 words.

esophagodynia   pain in the esophagus

esophagomalacia   softening of the esophagus

and, a whopper:

esophagojejunogastrostomosis

esophagus   stomach   condition of
    jejunum   opening into

Translation: condition of making an opening into esophagus and stomach, attaching them with loop from jejunum

6. a. **Tele-**, a prefix for far, is common — *telephone, telescope, telemetry.*

telediagnosis	diagnosis from a distance
	cp. *teleradiography, teletherapy, teledactyl, telecardiophone*
telangion	terminal artery
telangiitis	inflammation of capillaries
telangioma	tumor composed of capillaries
telekinesis	a talent in extrasensory perception: ability to move objects from a distance

b. The homophonic base **telo,** less common, means end, destiny, purpose, completion, as in *telencephalon. Pro-* means before; *prophase* is the first stage of mitosis. **Telo-** means end; *telophase* is the last stage of mitosis.

teleost	complete or bony fishes
teleology	a philosophical-theological term: the study of purpose in the universe
dysteleology	the theory that the universe is purposeless

Organs don't always develop toward their assigned destiny. *A-* + **telo** combines into **atelo,** which means incomplete. The umbrella word for incomplete or imperfect development is *atelia.* We can suffer from incomplete or imperfect development of any part. Some examples follow.

atelocardia	*atelocephaly*	*atelognathia*	*atelopodia*
atelostomia	*ateloprosopia*	*ateloglossia*	*atelocheiria*

bradyteleocinesis	the slowing (*brady*) of motion (*cinesis*) of a nerve communication on its way to its goal (**tele**)

7. **Epi-** appears in 300+ words in the biological vocabulary, familiar ones such as *epilepsy, epidermis, epidemic, epicenter,* and unfamiliar ones such as:

epiboly	a stage in gastrulation
epiphenomenalism	a theory that the mind is a product of an entirely physical brain
epicanthic	fold of corner of eye
epicardium	inner layer of pericardium (membranous sac enclosing the heart)
epicrisis	second crisis of a disease (**epi-,** after)
epiphyte	a plant that grows on something other than the ground; e.g., orchid

epizoic	living on animal
epigastrium	layer of stomach
epigeal	(living) on surface of earth
epigenesis	idea that embryo differentiates as it grows
epinephrine	adrenal hormone

8. **Peri-** is used extensively as a prefix for covering, as in the following medical terms.

pericardium	*perichondrium*	*pericranium*	*perimysium*
perineum	*perionychium*	*periosteum*	*peritoneum*

For covering, it also has uses in botany and zoology:

pericarp	the covering of a seed or fruit
periderm	tissue of bark
perisarc	covering of polyp colonies

Peri- does not drop its final vowel when combining with a base that begins with a vowel.

9. A satisfying discovery concerns the connection among Gk. **apo-**, away from (in Chapter 7), L. **ab-**, away from, and E. *off, of*, and *after*. They all stem from IE *apo*, which meant away from, off. If we trace descent further, we find that from this IE source also come other Proto-Germanic words: *awkward, ablaut, offal;* a Russian word: *pogrom;* L. *pos* and *pon*, as in *deposit, position, component;* and *post-*, as in *posterior, post-mortem*, and *puny*, lit. after birth.

Anatomy divides the body into several planes that distinguish between sides, between front and back, and between top and bottom.

8.3 Verbs of motion and location

Prefixes are to be found in verbs as well as in nouns and adjectives. The following verbs have been chosen for this chapter because they relate to motion and location. Many of the words in this sub-section appear both in the common and medical vocabularies, e.g., *emotion, contravention, issue*, and *succumb*.

Base	General Vocabulary		Specialized
L. mot, move	*motor, emotion*		*motoceptor*
	locomotion		*oculomotor*
			vasomotor
			ultramotivity
mov	*move, movement, remove*		
L. ven(t), come			
advent	*contravene*	*intervention*	
prevent	*supervene*	*invention*	

FRONTAL

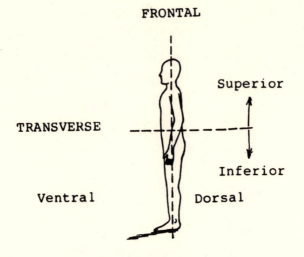

MIDSAGGITAL

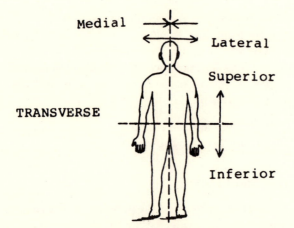

Planes are capitalized,
orientations in small letters.

L.	**i(t)**, go	*coition, issue, introitus*	
		transit, transient, transitory,	
		trance	
L.	**fug**, flee	*centrifugal*	*basifugal*
		fugitive	*febrifuge*
			nidifugous
L.	**vag**, wander	*vagrant, vague*	*vagus* nerve
L.	**ambul**, walk	*ambulance, ambulatory, perambulate*	
		nyctambulation, alley, exile	

L. *pat,* walk   *peripatetic, Peripatus*
Gk. *bet* go, walk   *diabetes*

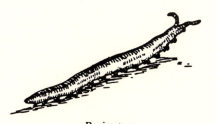

Peripatus,
an onychophore, primitive arthropod

IE deuk, to lead

One of the many native English survivors of IE *deuk* retaining the sense of leading is *team.* No Greek descendants, but hundreds of words from the L. bases **duct** and *due* and French renovations of these. They are in the biological vocabulary, e.g., *oviduct.*

levoduction	left-ward movement of an eye
adductor	a muscle that leads toward median plane
abducens	that which draws away, separates from another, e.g., *abducens* nerve

Duct and *due* often exist as pairs, the first for the noun, the second for the verb.

education	*conduct*	*adductor*	*reduction*
educe	*conduce*	*abductor*	*reduce*
		abducens	

Also: *duct, ductile,* and *douche*

L. **pos(it),** put   *posit, position*   *ovipositor*
      place   *posture, decompose*
      pon   *component*
Gk. **thesis,** put, place   *thesis, antithesis*   *diathesis*
                       synthesis   *photosyn-*
                                                     thesis
       thetic   *enthetic*
                                                       pert. to
                                                       innoculation

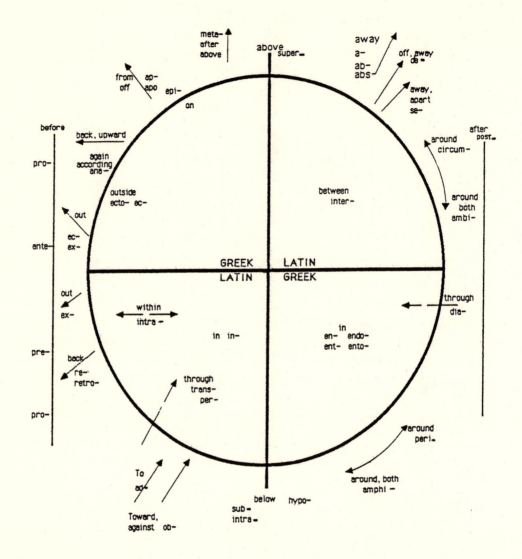

L. *cubare,* lie down

cub	*incubus, succubus, incubator*	
	concubine, cubicle	*decubitus*
cubit	*cubit*	*cubomedusae,*
		brachiocubital
		cubit, elbow
		cubitus,
		forearm
cumbe	*recumbent*	
	incumbent, succumb	*ventricumbent*

In *incubator*, the literal meaning is clear: that which (is for) lying down. But other words have the literal meaning hidden, for example, *incubus*, a male demon, lit. that which lies on (the female) and *incumbent*, one who holds an office, metaphorically and often enough literally, one who lies down.

Gk. **clin**, lie down, bend, turn	*incline, decline*	*thermocline* *patroclinous* *matroclinous*

Three Latin words with different meanings look alike and have generated bases that overlap in meaning: *cadere, cedere,* and *caedere.*

L. *cadere,* to fall, befall

cade	*cadence, cadaver*	
cid	*coincidence*	*deciduous*
	recidivism	*indeciduate*
cas	*casual, casuality*	

L. *cedere,* to go, move

cede	*precede, recede, antecedent*	
	intercede	
cess	*abscess, recession*	*retrocession*

L. *caedere,* to cut, kill

cid	*suicide, homocide*	*vermicide*
cis	*incision, decision*	

IE *sed,* to sit

The geneological surprise here is a family relationship among *soot, president, insidious, chair,* and *hostage.* IE *sed* > Germanic > OE > E. *set, settle, saddle, soot;* through other Germanic languages to E.: *ersatz, seat.* Into and out of Sanskrit as a title of a Hindu holy book: *Upanishad;* and into and out of Welsh > *stedd,* seat, as the name of an assembly, the *eisteddfod.*

To Greek and from it *hedra,* seat, chair > *hedron,* as in *polyhedron, cathedral,* and from *cathedral: chair—ex cathedra* doesn't mean from the cathedral, but from the chair.

To Latin and from it, *see,* seat of religious district.

L. *sedare,* to calm down *sedate, sedative*

L. *sedere,* to sit, and

sidere, to sit down

---

	preside	*reside*	*subside*	*dissidence*	*insidious*
	president	*residence*	*subsidence*	*assiduous*	*subsidy*
sed		*sedentary, sediment, supersede*			
sess		*session, obsess, possess, assess*			
		sessile			
		pert. to sponges			
Also:		*seance, siege, hostage*			

Prosthetic devices from Schultes,
Armamentarium chirurgicum, 1693

CHAPTER 9—COLORS AND NUMBERS

9.1 Color It Chromo
9.2 Playing the Numbers

This chapter will present bases that are used in combination with other bases to give color and number. The bases will, as usual, be uncovered in biological disciplines from anatomy to taxonomy. Taxonomy uses color bases extensively for naming living things, and a few taxonomic terms will be given to illustrate this point.

Also as usual, discussion of these elements tempts us to wander off into domains other than the one being explored. Take *litmus*. The litmus spectrum for indicating acidity or alkalinity ranges from 1–14; people interested in keeping healthy fishtanks would be concerned about the 6.0–7.6 arc of the spectrum, from chartreuse revealing acid hydrogen ion concentration to deep blue revealing base. *Litmus* came to E. from Old Norse in the early 16th century. The word is a combination of two Scandinavian bases: *lit,* dye + *mosi. Lit* appears in E. only in this word. *Mosi* tempts digression.

Our concept of dampness was expressed in IE by the root *meu,* through Proto-Germanic the origin of *mosi > moss* and *mus* — the second element of *litmus* — of *mire* and *quagmire.* Through Latin, IE *meu* gave rise to *mustard,* and through Greek, maybe, to *myso,* a base for dirt, and, also possibly, to *myriad.* An enlarged form of *meu* was *meug,* also meaning damp, but with the additional connotation of slimy. And thereby hangs a box.

IE *meug*

The sense of dampness or slipperiness led sensibly enough to *mold* and *muggy,* and, less clearly, to Proto-Germanic metaphors to *smock, schmuck, smug, smuggle,* and *meek.* Perhaps the metaphoric transference for the last of the terms is that one who is meek is not damp or slippery, but as soft and mild as moss.

Mold and *muggy* find cognates in Fr. < L. *moist, mucilage,* and *musty.* L. **muco** is the base for *mucus.* The Proto-Germanic words also find cognates in Gk. **myco** and **myxo.**

Gk. **myco** rarely means mushroom, as it does in *mycetism,* poisoning caused by eating mushrooms. More often, it means fungus.

mycology   the study of fungi

---

mycotoxin	poisoning caused by fungi
mycophagous	pert. to eating fungi
mycorrhiza	fungi on roots, a symbiotic relationship
aureomycin	medication to cure fungus infection

Gk. **myxo** means mucus and slime.

myxoid	like mucus
amyxia	condition of having insufficient mucus
myxasthenia	condition of having defective production of mucus
myxoma	a tumor which contains mucoid tissues
myxobacteria	slime mold

Myxo as a base for slime is illustrated by a word that combines this with its cognate **myco**: *Myxomycetes,* class of slime molds that cause the pathological condition of *myxomatosis.*

Litmus, which inspired this digression, will return us to color terms. The litmus solution comes from lichens such as one which received its name from its being colorful, or tinted: *Rocella tinctoria.*

9.1 Color It Chromo

The word *color* < L. appears in the taxonomic term for the mountain lion, *Felis concolor,* the kittens mottled, the adults of a uniform tawny coloration.

Some of the bases from L. and Gk. appear in words in the general vocabulary also. Most people could easily define *albino,* though few would be prepared to figure out the relationship between that word and *albumin:* both stem from *alb,* white. *Melanism* translates into the state of blackness and is applicable to populations of, for example, moths and squirrels; *melanin,* from the same source, Gk. *melan,* black, is a darkening pigmentation of skin, hair, and retina; *melancholy* is a dark mood. *Melanoma,* a malignant tumor of dark color, has recently been popularized as a threat to light-skinned people who overindulge in sunbathing.

The chromosome takes its name from the circumstance that it colors or stains easily < Gk. **chromo,** a base for color, as in *panchromatic* film. There exist in the biological vocabulary at least 210 words formed with **chromo,** the short form, or **chromato,** the long form, among them *chromesthesia,* association between another sense and that of color, for example, feeling red as hot, hearing blue as a cool sound.

chromo	+ *diagnosis*	diagnosis by change of color
	+ *genesis*	formation of a pigment
	+ *trichia*	hair coloration
chromato	+ *-in*	*chromatin,* stainable portion of nucleus
	+ *logy*	study of color
	+ *meter*	instrument to measure color or color perception

	+ *blast*	cell prior to a chromatophore
	+ *phagous*	that which "eats" or destroys color
	+ *dysopia*	complete color blindness
	+ *phore*	bearer of pigments
	+ *philia*	condition of staining easily
	+ *tropism*	orienting response to a color
psycho	+ **chrome**	association between a color and a bodily sensation
Chromocryptus albopictus		the rhyming name of a species of wasp

The words for certain afflictions, among them poliomyelitis, cirrhosis, and leukemia, also have color bases in them.

The type specimen is provided by Gk. **xanth,** yellow. Most would find it easy to define **cyte** as cell, **derm** as skin, and **odont** as tooth.

xantho	+ **cyte**	cell with yellow pigment
	+ **derm**	yellow skin
	+ **odont**	*xanthodont,* yellow tooth
	+ *ous*	*xanthous,* yellowish
	+ *opsia*	*xanthopsia,* objects appear yellow
	+ *phyll*	yellowing pigment in plants, e.g., grass
	+ *pter*	*xanthopterin,* yellow pigment of insect wings
	+ *uria*	*xanthuria,* yellowish urine
	+ *-oma*	*xanthoma,* a yellowish tumor
	+ *cyano* + *opsia*	*xanthocyanopsia,* ability to see yellow and blue in the visual field, not red and green
	+ *rrhiza*	*Xanthorrhiza,* yellow-root shrub
	root	*licorice*
Xanthomonas		genus of bacteria

Note that these terms are relevant to different fields — e.g., *Xanthorrhiza* and *xanthophyll* to botany, *xanthopterin* to zoology.

The chart that follows is not exhaustive — there are 35 bases for black alone. From hundreds of bases for different colors, the chart selects those that have given rise to the most words.

Gk. **chromo,** color	*chromosome, chromium*
Gk. **leuko,** white	*leukemia, leucorrhea*
Leucothrix barbata	a fly
L. **albi,** white	*albino, albumin, album, auburn*
Pinus albicaulis	white-bark pine
L. **argenti,** silver	*argentiferous, argentine*
argentaffin	having affinity for silver
Gk. **chrysa,** gold	*chrysanthemum*

chrysalis	cocoon stage
Penicillium chrysogenum	a mold
L. **aure**, gold	*oriole*
aurum	gold; adj., *aureate*, golden
aureole	a halo
auriasis	condition of gold deposited in tissues
	also *chrysiasis*
Aureomycin	trade name for an antibiotic
Carassius auratus	a goldfish
Ficus aurea	a fig
Marcus Aurelius	a Roman emperor
Homophonic *aur*, breath	premonition: *aura;* and *aur*, ear.
L. **lute**, yellow	
lutescence	becoming yellow
lutein	yellow pigment
Betula lutea	yellow birch
L. **flav**, yellow	
flavescence	becoming yellow
flavin	a yellow pigment
riboflavin	crystalline orange-yellow pigment (in vitamins)
	rib, a chemical affix, < *arabinose* < L. *Arabicus*, Arabian
Aurelia flavidula	a jellyfish
Gk. **xantho**, yellow	*xanthoma, xanthophyll*
Gk. **cirrho**, orange	*cirrhosis*
Cirrhosoma translucida	a moth
L. **rose**, red	*rosary, Rose*
roseola	skin rash
rosella	a species of parakeet
Erythropteryx roseotincia	a moth
L. **rube**, red	*rubric*
rubella	German measles
Picea rubens	red spruce
Gk. **erythro**, red	
erythrocyte	red blood cell
erythrophobia	fear of blushing
erythrokomos	red-haired
Melanerpes erythrocephalus	redheaded woodpecker
Gk. **rhodo**, red	*rhododendron, Rhoda, Rhodes*
Gk. **porphyr**, purple	
porphyry	a rock, e.g., feldspar
porphyrin	an organic compound
Purpura persica	a gastropod

L. **virid**, green	*verdant, Vermont*
viridian	green pigment
Bufo viridis	a toad, its poison: *viridobufagin*
Macropodus viridiauratus	paradise fish
Gk. **chloro**, green	*chlorine, chloroform, chlorophyll*
chloropicrin	tear gas
Chrysochloris trevelyani	a golden mole

An etymological analysis of *chloroform* reveals that its literal meaning is green ant < Gk. **chloro**, green + **form**, < L. *formica*, ant. Boiling green ants in water was not a popular hobby of the 17th century, but it was done. The resultant acid was called, from the L. word for the victims, *formic*. Other terms in which **form** for ant appears are *formaldehyde, Formica,* and a return to the literal meaning in the following.

Formica fusca	an ant
formiciasis	a condition caused by being poisoned by ants (e.g., by the fire ant)
formication	a sensation as of ants crawling over the skin

There is no more than a homophonic relationship between **form**, and *form* as in *formal logic,* and little more than that between *formication* and *fornication* < L. *fornix*, brothel.

Gk. **cyano**, blue	*cyanide*
cyanosis	bluish discoloration of skin
L. **glauco**, bluish-green to gray	*glaucoma*
glaucous	grayish or bluish-green
Glaucus pacificus	a sea snail
Glaucosoma hebraicum	the jewfish
Gk. **polio**, gray	*poliomyelitis*
Pteropus poliocephalus	Australian fruit bat
L. **fusc**, dark, dusky brown	*obfuscate*
Desmognathus fuscus	a salamander
Formica fusca	an ant
L. **ater, atri** black	
atribilius	black bile
Sauromalus ater	the chuckwalla lizard
L. **nigr**, black	*Negro, denigrate*
nigrosin	a dye used to stain tissue
nigrities linguae	black tongue
Solanum nigrum	black nightshade
Gk. **melan**, black	*melancholy, melanism*
Drosophila melanogaster	a fruit fly

"Hey! What's this Drosophila melanogaster doing in my soup?"

L. **macula,** spot, stain

immaculate	without spots or stain
macula, mackle	a spot or stain
macula lutea retinae	yellowish depression on retina
Ambystoma maculatum	spotted salamander

Gk. **poikil,** mottled variegated *osteopoikilosis, poikiloderma*

poikilonymy	series of various names
Platypoecilus maculatus	platyfish

Color bases combine with suffixes.

-osis	(morbid)	*cirrhosis, cyanosis*
	condition	*chlorosis,* greenish skin
-iasis	(morbid)	*formiciasis, aurantiasis,* orangish
	condition	discoloration
-escence	beginning	*albescence, flavescence, viridescence;* adj. forms: *albescent,* etc.

Color bases are employed in words for skin, blood, urine, tumors, cells, and vision — various visual defects leading to a person's imposing color upon the visual field or depriving it of color.

chroia	color of skin	*xanthochroia*
derma	skin	*leukoderma, chrysoderma, erythroderma*
emia	blood	*leukemia, erythremia, cyanemia*
uria	urine	*albumuria, melanuria, xanthinuria*
oma	tumor	*melanoma, leukoma, glaucoma, chloroma*
cyte	cell	*erythrocyte, leukocyte, rhodocyte*
		melanocyte

These conditions, forms of *chromatopsia*, invest the world with color: *cyanopia, xanthopia, chloropsia. Achloropsia* means incapacity to see green.

For ability to absorb stain, the base *phil* is used: e.g., *cyanophilous*, stainable with blue dyes. More examples of *phil* used for staining will be found in Chapter 26.

Gk. *peina*, base *pein* or more commonly **pen**, need for, or deficiency of, links to color bases.

leuko	+ **penia**	leukocyte deficiency
erythro	+	red blood cell deficiency

Pen is in words for other kinds of deficiencies as well:

glyco	+ **penia**	abnormally low blood sugar level
pan + hemato	+	*panhematopenia,* comprehensive anemia
sidero	+	deficiency in iron

Sideroderma may be noted here: skin discoloration of a bronze tint.

peinotherapy	hunger cure
peniaphobia	morbid dread of poverty
penitentiary	place for deprivation

Pen is a derivative of IE (*s*)*pen*, which counts among dozens of other descendants these words: *spider, pansy, appendix.*

Numbers are at times used as suffixes to indicate insensitivity to parts of the color spectrum.

protanopia	lit., first sightless, blindness to red
deuteranopia	blindness to green
tritanopia	blindness to blue and yellow

9.2 Playing the Numbers

Cardinal numbers indicate quantity—one, two, etc.; *cardinal* < L. *cardo*, hinge.

#	OE	Greek	example	Latin	example
1	an	*hen-*	henogenesis	**un-**	union
			hyphen		
		mono-	monothermia		
2	twa	*dy-*	dyad	*du-*	duplicate
		di-	dicephaly	**bi(n)-**	binary

		dicho	dichotomy		bifurcate
		(split)			
3	thrie	**tri-**	tripod	**tri-**	triune
4	feower	**tetra-**	tetracycline	**quadru-**	quadruped
5	fif	**penta-**	pentadactyl	**quint-**	quintuple
6	sexe	**hexa-**	hexagon	**sext-**	sextipara
7	seofon	**hepta-**	heptad	**sept-**	septigravid
8	eahta	**octo-**	octopus	**octo-**	octane
9	nigon	*enn-*	ennead	**non-**	nonagenarian
10	tyn	**deca-**	Decapoda	**deci-**	decinormal
100	hundred	**hect-**	hectogram	**cent-**	centipede
1000		**kil-**	kilowatt	**mill-**	millipede
1000000		**mega-**	megacurie		
½, partly		**hemi-**	Hemiptera	**semi-**	semipermeable

Ordinal numbers indicate order < L. **ord,** first, second, etc.

English	Greek	Example	Latin	Example
first	**prot-**	protozoa	**prim-**	primate
second	*deut(er)*	deuterium	*secund*	secundiparous
third	**trit-**	tritanopia	**terti-**	tertiary
fourth	**tetart-**	tetartanopia	**quart-**	quarter
fifth			**quint-**	quintessence

1. The Gk. *hen,* one, a unit, appears in few English words. The rare *henotheism* means belief in one god; cp. *monotheism. Hen* is disguised in *hyphen,* which consists of two prefixes, Gk. **hypo-,** under + *hen.*

henogenesis	pre-natal development of a single being; cp. *ontogeny*
Henicops maculata	a centipede

The way by which number bases combine with other bases can be illustrated by focusing on **mono-,** one, which appears in many familiar words.

monaural	*monotonous*	*monopoly*	*monogamy*	*monarch*
monotheism	*monologue*	*monocycle*	*monogram*	*monograph*
monomaniac				

A *monolith* is a large stone, e.g., of Stonehenge; in adj. form, *monolithic* refers to a temperament like a single and permanent stone, stonily stubborn, fixed on an idea. *Monk* (no etym. relation to *monkey*) also comes from **mono-,** one who lives a solitary life.

mono-	+ *phagous*	adj., pert. to a being that eats only one food, e.g., koala bear eats only eucalyptus leaves
	+ *oecius*	living in or occupying one place
	+ *gyny*	condition of having one wife

+ *petalous*	a plant with one petal
+ *treme*	an animal with one duct for evacuation and birth, e.g., platypus, echidna
Monotremata	a mammalian order: platypus
Monadopsis vampyrelloides	a protozoan

L. **un-**, one	*unify, universe, unicellular, union, onion*
Acanthrus unicornis	unicorn-fish

Gk. **proto-**, first	*protoplasm, prototype, protagonist* *protocol, protanopia*
+ *zoa*	first life
L. **prim-**, first	*prime, primary, primitive, primate* *primrose, primipara*

2. *deuce,* two in dice and cards, nickname for the devil

3.

Gk. **tri-**	*triad*
triune	three-in-one, in theology, a three-in-one god; in anatomy, three brains in one
tritanopia	lack of vision in 1/3rd of field, blue blindness

Tres < **tri-** + *phin* < L. *finiss,* end, combine to form *trephining,* an operation from primordial times for cutting into the skull, orig. to release demons clogging the noddle; instrument to do this job, a *trephine.*

4.

Gk. **tetra-**	*tetrad, tetracycline, tetradactyly*
trapezius	a muscle of the back

Tetra- + *peza,* a base for foot > *tetrapeza,* a four-footed object, such as a table > *trapezion,* a quadrilateral > *trapezium* (1545), *trapezius* (1685), *trapeze* (1860)

L. **quadru-**	
quadruped	four-footed animal
quadriceps	a thigh muscle, **quadru-** + *ceps,* head

Quadru- in the sense of square, is the source of *quarry,* stone pit. The force of the prefix is lost in *quarantine* because it has been generalized. In Italian *quarantina giorni* means forty days. The reason for choosing 40 rather than 39 or 23 days is that 40 was a magical number for the writers of scripture. Now quarantine refers to an indeterminate period of securing a plant, animal or person.

5. *Punch,* for a mildly alcoholic drink of citrus juice and alcohol, is a disguised prefix existing by itself: it comes from Sanskrit *panca,* five, because in India it consisted of five ingredients.

Trephination from Giovanni Andrea della Croce,
Chirurgiae, 1573

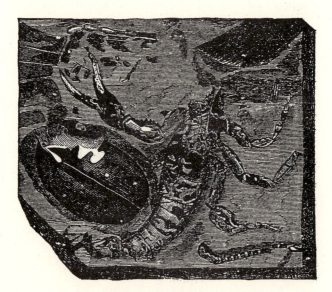

Eponymic *Cyclophthalmus bucklandi*,
a fossil scorpion

IE *penkwe*, five
    Into Sanskrit as *panca* > E. *punch*. Into Gk. as *penta* and into and out of Germanic as *fist* and *five*.

---

6. Gk. *h* is cognate to L. *s* as in hex-/sex-; also hemi-/semi-, herpes/serpent, helios/sol, hydor/sudor (sweat), hals/sal (salt)

Siesta < L. *sexta (hora)*, the sixth hour after sunrise.

7–8. L. *septuagenarian*, a person in his or her 70s < **sept** + *gen* < *ginta* 10x + *arian*; *octogenarian*, a person 80–90 years old

9.
ennead   a group of nine
noon   the ninth hour after sunrise

10. L. *decanus*, ten, has given us many words in which the number prefix is disguised, for example, *decimate; dime; dean*, orig. leader of ten people; *dicker*, to bargain, orig. for ten items; *denier*, a unit of thickness, as for silk fabric; and *doyen*, senior member of a group. Words in the biolexicon similarly disguised as descendants of *deca* are *decussate*, to cross, as with an X, and *duodenum* < **duo**, 2 + **den**, 10.

giga, billion   *gigabit*
< Gk. *gigas*, giant

nano, billionth   *nanosecond*
< Gk. *nanos*, dwarf

pico, trillionth   *picogram*
< Sp. *pico*, small amount

femto, quadrillionth   *femtometer*
< Scand. *femten*, 15

nulli, none   *nullipara*
< L. *ne* + *ullas*, any

myria, a great many   *myriad, myriapod* (e.g., *centipede*)
< Gk. *murias*, 10000

googol, a great many: 10^{10}
< echoic

artio, even (numbered)   *Artiodactyla*, an order comprising animals that have even number of toes—cattle, camel, deer, hippopotamus

perisso, odd   *Perissodactyla*, having odd number of toes—horse, rhinocerous

Ox
Artiodactyla

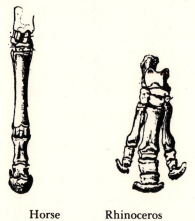

Horse   Rhinoceros
Perissodactyla

Numbering has been of obvious importance to all cultures. Incas recorded numbers by tying knots in string; others have split bamboo sticks, punched dots or etched lines on suitable surfaces, used beads in instruments such as the abacus, used fingers and toes. Roman numerals orig. indicated hand gestures.

I	an upright finger	others:	L	fifty
V	thumb and little finger		C	one hundred
X	hands crossed at wrists		D	five hundred
XVI	16		M	one thousand
MDCLVII	1657			

Today, we use Arabic symbols 1−2−3, etc., which developed from a Hindi ancestor.

CHAPTER 10—SUFFIXES

10.1   Sciences and Studies
10.2   Noun Suffixes
10.3   Adjective Suffixes
10.4   Verb and Adverb Suffixes
10.5   Miscellaneous

The prefix doesn't change the part of speech of the base. Gk. **aster** is a noun meaning star; if we precede it with *micro-*, we have *microaster*, a small star, which could be used to describe a mole's snout. The suffix need not change the part of speech of the base; if we follow the noun **aster** with *-isk*, a suffix used to denote small, the result is a noun synonymous with *microaster* but more familiar: *asterisk*, lit. small star. *-Oid*, which means like, converts the noun *aster* into the noun *asteroid*. Many of the suffixes listed below will, however, transform a noun base into an adjective. If we add *-aceous* to the noun *aster*, the result is *asteraceous*, an adjective which means pertaining to the *Asterascea* (also called *Compositae*), a family of plants which includes, unsurprisingly, the aster, and also the daisy and dandelion, the marigold and zinnia, the thistle and goldenrod and ragweed.

10.1 Sciences and Studies

Two suffixes are relevant here: Gk. **-ics** and **logy**. Gk. **-ics**, science of, attaches to a multitude of bases for the creation of words, some old and some very new.

eugenics	*orthopedics*	*pediatrics*	*aesthetics*
dysgenics	*therapeutics*	*geriatrics*	*anaesthetics*
obstetrics	*endodontics*	*systemics*	*athletics*

Gk. *logos* is versatile: as a base, it can mean word: *logos, prologue, epilogue.*

logorrhea	a flowing of words, morbid verbosity
logomania	obsessive talking
neologism	a new word

It can mean speech organs:

logoplegia	paralysis of the speech organs

It can mean reasoning and listing: *logic, illogical, logistics catalogue.*

As a suffix, **logy** (or, often, **-logy**), it means study of and is among the top ten candidates of most-used bases. Many terms ending with **logy** are so familiar as to need no definition.

biology	*zoology*	*anthropology*	*morphology*
biotechnology	*dermatology*	*embryology*	*physiology*
epidemiology		*gynecology*	*cardiology*
gerontology or *geriatrics*			

A. Studies of organs

Any base for an organ can preceed **logy** to combine into a word meaning study of that organ: e.g., *dermatology, cardiology.*

histo	+ **logy**	the study of tissue
uro	+	of the urinary system
hemato	+	of blood
hepato	+	of the liver
reno	+	of the kidneys
cyto	+	of the cell
feto	+	of fetal growth

B. Studies of living beings

phyto	+ **logy**	study of plants
phyco	+	of algae
myco	+	of fungus
arachno	+ **logy**	study of spiders, ticks, mites—specialized study of mites: *acarology*
entomo	+	insects
myreco	+	ants
malaco	+	mollusks
ichthyo	+	fish
herpeto	+	amphibians and reptiles
ophio	+	snakes
ornitho	+	birds
terato	+	monstrous births

We have seen that a particular base is usually not restricted to a particular biological study. **Arachno** is the base in taxonomy for spiders (scorpions, mites and ticks, too); it also appears in *arachnoid,* which could mean like a spider or, in morphology, web-like tissue in the brain sandwiched between the dura mater and the pia mater. **Ichthyo** is a base for fish, as in *ichthyology, ichthyophagy,* fish-eating, *ichthyolite,* a fossilized fish, *ichthyosaur,* and many taxonomic names, e.g., *Ichthyornis* (note: **ornitho,** bird), birds with fish-like vertebrae. **Ichthyo** also appears a little in the medical vocabulary, mostly for poisoning resulting from eating spoiled fish, and in about a dozen specific kinds of *ichthyosis,* the condition of having fish-like skin.

3. Other **logies:**

paleo, old

paleontology	*paleolithic*	*ornithopaleontology*
paleobotany	*paleopathology*	*anthropopaleontology*
paleozoology	*paleozoic*	

ichno, footprint

ichnology   the study of footprints
ichneumon   a wasp, a tracker of prey

Fossil footprint of dinosaur
from Connecticut Valley

copro, feces   *coprology, coprolite, coprophagy*

pharmaco, drugs

pharmacy	*pharmacology*	*pharmacotherapeutics*
pharmacopoeia	*phytopharmacology*	*zoopharmacology*

On some occasions, **logy** means character of, not study of, e.g., *lithology.*

Gk. *ethos,* custom, is the base of *ethology,* the study of animal behavior; the base *eth* for custom or character appears in *ethics.* Gk. *ethn* for people appears in *ethnic, ethnocentric, ethnography.*

10.2 Noun Suffixes

1. Diminutives

Several suffixes when added to the base act like *-isk* in making the referent smaller. **Cut** is a L. base for skin; therefore, *cuticle* is lit. a small skin. **-Cle, -cule,** and **-culus** are variants of a suffix that achieves miniaturization, as in *tentacle, molecule,* and *homunculus.*

A similar effect is achieved with L. **-il**(**la**), as in *pupil, fibril,* and *maxilla;* and with

L. **-olus** and its variants **-ole:** *nucleolus, aureole,* **-ule** and **-um:** *globule, flagellum.* From Gk. comes **-ium:** *bacterium;* pl. *bacteria.*

2. Place for, belonging to

Another category contains suffixes that indicate place for, belonging to, in the family of. **-Ium,** listed above as making the base diminutive, functions as one of these in *pericardium,* placed around the heart, and *gynoecium,* site for female organs of a plant. *Aquarium* and *auditorium* are common enough words: they show the bases combining with **-arium,** place for (also **-ary** as in *aviary*) and **-orium,** place for (also **-ory** as in *laboratory*).

For belonging to, Gk. **-id** and **-ite** are used: *hominid, arachnid, acarid; sporozoite,* microbic stage that transmits malaria. A suffix for belonging to that has dozens of uses is **-ine,** e.g., *equine, ursine, vulpine, ranine, lupine* (wolves), *anserine* (geese), *lacertine* (lizards).

3. Actor and action

A very common way of indicating the actor in English — the agent who does it — is simply to add *-er* to a word, *painter, driver, screwdriver, exerciser.* Gk. and L. also supply **-er** for actor: *cauter, scavenger,* and **-or.**

actor	*doctor*	*protractor*	*incisor*
aviator	*adductor*	*extractor*	*flexor*

From Gk.: **-ian, -ist** and **-ic.**

physician	*physicist*	*taxonomist*	*anaesthetic*
technician	*ornithologist*	*scientist*	*prophylactic*

A suffix for instrument, that which performs the action, comes from Gk.: **-bulum,** *acetabulum, mandibulum.*

For the action itself:

L. **-ence** and **-ance,** often with the sense of beginning, as in *fluorescence,* sometimes without that sense, as in *science* and *continuance.*

L. **-men(t),** *implement, instrument, ligament, foramen*
L. **-(t)ion,** *action, condition, adhesion, continuance*
L. **-tude,** with sense of means of an action, *magnitude, latitude*

Other suffixes with this sense of means of an action include *-ulum, -ula, -bulum, -bula, -brum, -trum:*

papulum	echinoderm organ performing respiration and excretion
cingulum	a belt or girdle performing action of encircling something, such as the corpus callosum of the brain
mandibulum, mandibula	jawbone

cerebrum	part of brain
claustrum	performs action of dividing brain from insula

L. **-(t)ure,** with sense of result of an action, *manufacture, fissure, ligature*

Gk. **-m(a),** with sense of result of an action: *system, spasm, aroma, stigma.*

4. Condition of, quality of

If we add *-ness* to *kind,* we transform an adjective into a noun that means having the quality of being kind. A similar transformation takes place with *gentle* into *gentleness.* The OE suffix *-ish* also means state of, condition of, quality of, though it sometimes carries a disparaging connotation: *reddish, babyish, childish.*

The most general suffixes for condition of, quality of, are Gk. and L. **-ia** and L. **-y:** *dementia, mania, encephaly.* L. **-ity** means condition of and forms abstract nouns such as *acidity, fluidity, futility, maternity.*

5. **-Ism**

A special small section should be devoted to a widely used suffix that holds several meanings: **-ism.**

condition of, state of	*melanism, cretinism*
result of action	*mesmerism, embolism*
characteristic behavior	*heroism*
doctrine, theory	*creationism, Darwinism*

10.3 Adjective suffixes

A single word in the biolexicon, like a single word in the common vocabulary, may be both adjective and noun, e.g., *anaesthetic, hyperdermic, canine, fluid.*

Gk.	**-oid,** like	*pterygoid,* like a wing
L.	**-ble,** able to	*soluble, flexible*
	-ile	*infantile, sessile*
L.	**-ose, -ous,** full of, relating to	*pilose, noxious*
L.	**-aneus**	*calcaneus*
	-lent	*corpulent, somnolent*

Changing this to **-ence** gives a noun: *corpulence, somnolence.*

Gk.	**-ic,** state of	*hypodermic, toxic*
L.	**-id**	*fluid*
	-escent	*fluorescent, opalescent*
L.	**-al,** pertaining to	*lacteal,* pert. to milk
	-ar	*ocular*
Gk.	**-ine**	*canine, leonine, volverine*

sense of made of	*opaline*
sense of located in	*uterine*
names of substances	*chlorine, peptin*
Gk. **-ive**, tendency, pertaining to	*relative, laxative*

10.4 Verb and Adverb Suffixes

L. **-ate**, perform, do	*attentuate*
Gk. **-ize**	
put into state of	*hypnotize*
impose quality of	*sterilize*
follow practice of	*pasteurize*
become, become similar to	*oxidize*
L. **-ad**, toward	*caudad*, toward the tail

10.5 Miscellaneous

Different fields in science have suffixes for specialized purposes.

In taxonomy:

-anus	*Australopithecus africanus*
-ensis	*Australopithecus afarensis*, a.k.a. Lucy
-idae	for name of animal family, e.g., *Hominidae*, or order. e.g., *Dinoflagellida*
-oidea	for class: *Crinoidea*
-aceae	for name of plant family, e.g., *Rosacea*
-ales	for name of plant order, e.g., *Fagales*

An eponymous species name might end with *-i: darwini* or *-ii: haroldcookii.*

In chemistry:

-ase, enzyme	*lactase*
-ose, sugar	*lactose, glucose*
-ate, a salt	*sulphate*
-in, a substance	*insulin, cephalin, vitamin*
-ite, a salt	*sulphite*
-id(e), a compound	*ferric oxide, cerebroside*
-ol, alcohol or phenol	*glycerol*

PART IV: NATURAL HISTORY

CHAPTER 11—EVOLUTION

11.1 Definition
11.2 Theories Explaining Evolution
11.3 Fossils
11.4 Errors and Hoaxes

Evolution, the subject of this chapter and the next, calls for a change of pace. The chapters will as usual present affixes and bases and IE roots. Evolution is the central unifying principle for all biological studies, from molecular biology and genetics to physical anthropology. It has also been a source of hot controversy for over a century. Therefore, in discussing the term and related terms, *Biolexicon* will engage in more of a historical narrative than usual.

11.1 Definition

Among many definitions of the word *evolution,* an early (17th century) meaning was unrolling, opening out. Another application of *evolution* was to the development of an individual, as illustrated in a 1670 line from the *Philosophical Transactions of the Royal Society:* "By the word Change [in insects] is nothing else to be understood but a gradual and natural Evolution and growth of the parts." Over a century later, Erasmus Darwin, moderately famous grandfather of a very famous grandson, spoke of "The gradual evolution of the young animal or plant from its egg or seed."

One of the earliest users of *evolution* in its modern sense was Charles Lyell, whose *Principles of Geology* (1830) revolutionized geological thought. In that work, Lyell wrote: "The testacea of the ocean existed first, until some of them by gradual evolution, were improved into those inhabiting the land." Charles Darwin preferred *transmutation* and *descent with modification* to *evolution.* Lyell was an early defender of the idea of *uniformitarianism,* that the dynamics of development of the earth in the past were uniform with those taking place today.

The IE root *wel* counts the word *evolution* among its many offspring.

IE *wel,* to turn, bend, twist

IE *wel* has descendants in Russian, Celtic, Proto-Germanic, Greek, and Latin. A few of these words are directly relevant to the biological vocabulary: from Celtic: *briar,* and from Proto-Germanic *worm* and *wrist.* In the common vocabulary, 25 or so other words beginning with *wr* trace back to IE *wel.* The major contributors have been Greek and Latin.

Greek **helix, helic**	*helicotrema*
helicopter	lit. winged spiral
helix	a spiral as in *double helix*
helminth	a worm, as in *platyhelminthes,* flatworm
ileus	intestinal obstruction, from a related Greek base

Garden snail *Helix*

Gk. **r(r)haphe,** to sew, to suture	*rhabdomancy*
rhapsody	lit. the sewing of song
uranorrhaphy	lit. the suturing of the heavens, of the palate
myorrhaphy	suturing of muscles
rhombus	a parallelogram of equal sides
	rhomboid, rhombic, rhrombohedron

The L. offspring of IE *wer* are bases **volv, verb, verg, verm, vert** and **vers.** The following discussion will reveal that *evolve* is etymologically related to *controversy* and that *vermin* is a close relative of the pasta *vermicelli.*

| Latin **volv** | *volvox, volume, vulva, evolve* |

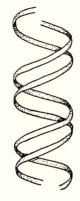

Double helix

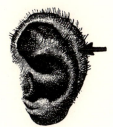

Helix of gorilla ear

devolve	to develop downward or backward
convolution	a turning
subinvolution	
L. **verb** < *verbena,*	*verbena,* a genus of showy plants
holy foliage or bough	*reverberate*
L. **verg** < *vergere,* to bend	*verge, diverge, converge*
	vergence, divergence, convergence
L. **verm** < *vermis,* worm	*vermin, vermicular, vermicelli,* etc.
vermis	part of the cerebellum

The most productive of this productive family is L. *vertere,* to turn. Inventorying the many words formed with **vert** and **vers** stimulates a respect for affixes at work.

	vert	**vers**
a-	*avert*	*aversion*
ad-	*advert*	*adverse, adversion, anniversary*
con-	*convert*	*converse, conversation, conversion*
contro-	*controvert*	*controversy*

di-	divert, divorce	diversion, diversity
	diverticulum	
	ventral diverticulum, of clam	
	diverticulosis	
	diverticulitis	
ex-	evert	eversion
extro-	extrovert	extroversion
in-	invert	inversion
	inadvertent	
intro-	introvert	
ob-	obvert	obverse
per-	pervert	perversion, perversity
re-	revert	reversion
sub-	subvert	subversion
trans-	transverse	
uni-	universe	
	vortex	verse, version, versatile, prose
	vertebra	*Megaptera versabilis*, a whale
	Zea mays everta, popcorn	*torsiversion*, abnormal rotation, as of a tooth

Other bases for to turn, bend, twist are L. *flectere, torquere, vergere, vertere,* and *mutare,* and Gk. *strephein* and *trepein.*

L. *flectere,* to turn, bend
flect   *deflect, inflect, reflect, circumflection*
flex   *flexion, flexor, retroflex*

L. *torquere,* also with the meaning of twist:
torque   *torque, torquate*
tors, tort   *torsion, contorsion, distortion*
                                             extorsion, retort, torture
                                             sinistrotorsion, torsionometer
                                             torment, torch
torsoclusion   in acupuncture, twisting shut, as of a blood vessel
nasturtium   an aromatic plant
                                             nas < nasus, nose
Heterodon contortrix   hog-nosed snake
The Proto-Germanic cognate for these words is *thwart.*

L. *mutare,* with the meaning of change:
mut   *mutate, mutation, permutation immutable,* lit. unchanging;
                                             commute, mutant, mutagenic
transmutation   an old term preferred by Darwin for evolution
Tempora mutantur, nos et mutamur in illis —The times change and we change with them.

IE *trep*, to turn

Gk.

trep, to turn

treponeme	microbe responsible for syphilis genus, *Treponema*
trepopnea	turning body to help breathing
trop	*tropic*
allotropic	pert. to a different form
entropion, ectropion	turning in and out of the eyelid

Trop combines with many other bases to designate turning toward, oriented to, guided by. For the action, the suffix *-ism* is attached, e.g., *tropism, chromatotropism* and *heliotropism;* and for the adjective, the suffix *-ic* as in *hypertropic, esotropic, stereotropic, geotropic, thermotropic,* and *neurotropic.*

hepato + **tropic**	pert. to turning toward, influencing, liver
tropo + *phyte*	a plant that lives in a changing environment
Xenopus tropicalis	a toad

Gk. *strephein*, with sense of twisting

streph

strephenopodia	heel turned inward (= *talipes varus*)

streps

arteriostrepsis	surgical twisting of an artery
Strepsiptera	order of insects

strept

Streptococcus pyogenes	a bacterium
Streptomyces	infectious fungi
streptomycin	antibiotic
Streptorhynchus vetustum	a brachiopod
stroph	*strophy, apostrophe, catastrophe*
exstrophy	turning inside out of an organ
strophocephaly	a teratological term for twisting, distortion of, the face
strobe	*strobe, stroboscope*

strabo, squinting

+ *-tomy*	cutting eye muscle tendon
+ *-smus*	*strabismus*, a visual distortion

Trop and **stroph** can be confused with *troph* < *trephein*, to nourish: *dystrophy* dissects into *dys/trophy*.

11.2 Theories Explaining Evolution

There are two general ways of understanding the origin of living things. The Book of Genesis advises that God created each species, that one species cannot give rise to another, and that all development took place in less than a week. This view is called *creationism.*

Opposed to it is evolutionary theory, which relies upon a simple principle: that all present living things developed from species no longer in existence. When paleontologists find fossils of primates going back 70 million years, and find no such fossils before then, the assumption is that the primates came from non-primates.

When anatomists reveal significant similarities among different groups of animals or plants, the assumption is that the members of the groups had a common ancestor. Guppies and tuna had a common ancestor; and so did frogs and salamanders; lizards and snakes; hummingbirds and ostriches; professors and monkeys. All the ancestors of all these animals trace back, in the evolutionary scheme, to still earlier ancestors, and they in turn, eventually, to one ancestor.

In the early years of comparative anatomy, gross anatomical features were focused upon, such as the dental apparatus of primates. The French anatomist and paleontologist Georges Cuvier, though not an evolutionist, developed a technique of recreating an entire animal from a few fossil remains. The American poet Emily Dickinson alluded to this in her poem, "With a Daisy":

> A science—so the savants say,
> "Comparative Anatomy,"
> By which a single bone
> Is made a secret to unfold
> Of some rare tenant of the mold
> Else perished in the stone.
> So to the eye prospective led
> This meekest flower of the mead,
> Upon a winter's day,
> Stands representative in gold
> Of rose and lily, marigold
> And countless butterfly!

Nineteenth century evolutionists were also impressed by vestigial organs as evidence of descent, for example, human beings' possession of a third molar, hair on the arms, an appendix; by geographical distribution; and by embryological development, which seemed to some (Darwin included) as offering the strongest evidence.

Evidence of descent today comes from molecular biology, which reveals affinities not in skulls, teeth, and toe bones but in proteins, immunological response, DNA. The scenario is that developed in a poem which concludes by drawing a moral about human equality:

> At the bottom of a chasm,
> Long before the birth of time,

Lay a piece of protoplasm
In the paleozoic slime.
The mud-flats oozed and bubbled,
And the vapors swirled and stank.
Yet his conscience was untroubled
For he neither smoked nor drank.

Very humble was his station,
He had never heard of Wells,
Yet he fathered all creation
By the splitting of his cells.

Every nation small or splendid,
Even when of Nordic blood,
Is in point of fact descended
From that little lump of mud.
                                        Ronald Lister

Evolution is a theory that has different explanations. One can be an evolutionist and still find none of the explanations satisfactory. The explanations may be grouped into two categories.

1. The process occurred randomly. This explanation is central to the explanation associated with Charles Darwin: *natural selection* or *survival of the fittest* means that nature selects, as a breeder does, from random variations. Those individuals luckily best suited to survive do so and pass their advantageous variations (somehow) onto their young until after a long time a new species arises from the old.

Natural selection has been repeatedly renovated. An early renovation is that of Robert Goldschmidt: his hypothesis of *hopeful monsters* proposes that a favorable and random mutation rapidly spreads through a population. The more recent *punctuated equilibrium* suggests that periods of stasis are interrupted or punctuated by the appearance of a descendant species.

2. The second category of explanations is that the process is not random but planned. We could hypothesize that living things wanted to change and were able to transmit their advantageous features to offspring. This idea, proposed in 1809 by the French naturalist Lamarck, is known as *Lamarckianism;* a 20th century counterpart is *Lysenkoism.* The Jesuit priest and paleontologist Teilhard de Chardin argued in his *The Phenomenon of Man* that God had planned the evolutionary sequence from inanimate matter to the human brain to ultimate, sometime in the future, merging of human beings with deity, the state of *omega.*

It is possible that an entirely radical idea holds the clue: that there is something in the essence of genes that provokes a rapid, directed, and inheritable response to non-lethal changes in the environment.

A disagreement among evolutionists concerns the rate of evolution, some agreeing with Darwin that evolution has been gradual and slow; others disagreeing a little by increasing the tempo, as punctuated equilibrium does; and others disagreeing entirely by proposing sudden and quick jumps, as the idea of hopeful monsters does. Quick jumps translates into *saltationism* < L. *salire,* to jump. This infinitive appears in four bases: *saul* (*somersault,* the *somer* < L. *supra*), *sil* (*resilient*), *sul* (*desultory, exult, insult* — lit. to jump on), and **sal,** the base with most relevance to the biological vocabulary.

sal	*saltation, saltationism, salmon*
salient	prominent
saltigrade	walking by jumping, like a kangaroo

Darwin held to the motto *Natura non facit saltum,* Nature doesn't make jumps.

Saltatio,
a leaping dance over upright swords

Evolution may be atheistic or may be compatible with theism. Atheistic evolution sees everything as being matter or energy, with no room for or even comprehensible definition of soul or spirit. This perspective, *materialism,* has a long history going back to ancient Greek philosophers; it was the philosophical support for the views of the Roman poet and philosopher Lucretius in his *On the Nature of Things. Materialism* has the base *mater* in it, and *mater,* one might be able to quickly figure out, means mother. The two words trace back to an IE root for mother, *mater,* from which come other words referring literally to motherhood or womanhood, such as *mother, maternal, matrimony,* and metaphorically to nourishing — *matriculate, metropolis* — and to the mother or base of existence — *matrix, matter, material, materialism, immaterial.* Gk. *metr,* womb, is probably related: *metritis,* inflammation of the womb, *metroscope,* instrument for examining womb.

The Gk. base **hylo** can mean both matter and wood:

methyl	wood alcohol (Gk. *methe,* strong drink)
hylomorphic	in the form of matter
hylotheism	belief that matter has divine qualities
hylophagous	eating wood

Another base for wood is **xylo,** as in a direct synonym of *hylophagous: xylophagous.*
Cp. *xylophile, xyloid, xylophone*

xylotomous	cutting into, boring into, wood
xylose	a sugar
xylem	a conduit in plants that transports water and nutrients from roots

Theistic evolution sees a deity as having started evolution going and then leaving it to work its way.

11.3 Fossils

L. *fossilus* means dug up < L. *fodere,* to dig. In 1619, it referred to any rock or mineral dug up out of the earth; in 1707 it was first used in its present restricted sense, referring to memorials of things that once lived. In 1774, the poet Oliver Goldsmith wrote that "These shells and extraneous fossils are not productions of the earth." In 1841, the American essayist Ralph Waldo Emerson used the word metaphorically: "Language is fossil poetry," the metaphor appearing also in this phrase from 1877: "The fossil impression of a dead faith." From *fossilus* also *fossa,* an anatomical term for a socket, e.g., *mandibular fossa.*

Questions about when the earth began and how it and its inhabitants developed have puzzled speculators for thousands of years. Some philosophers of ancient Greece, noting fossil shells on mountain tops, deduced that the mountains had risen out of the sea, marine animals leaving stony memorabilia of themselves high up. Others attributed fossils to the remains of cyclopean giants drowned in a great flood. The flood story also appears in Babylonian and Hebrew mythologies. Others thought that fossils were products of the stars' breathing upon the earth, or were jokes made up by nature, *lusae natura.*

11.4 Errors and Hoaxes

Six choice episodes in the history of paleontology illustrate what can happen when people, which general term includes scientists, are victims of a nympholepsy, the burning desire to force evidence into supporting theory. These six episodes tell the stories of *Homo diluvii testis* (a.k.a., *Andrias scheuchzeri*); *Lügensteine; Omphalos; Eoanthropus dawsoni; Hesperipithecus haroldcookii;* and, from the 1980s, the Paluxy footprints.

In the Renaissance, when renewed interest was directed to fossils among many other items, investigators tried to fit what they found into the scriptural story narrated in Genesis. Few had a clear notion of what fossils are. Leonardo da Vinci, who did have a clear and correct idea, was outnumbered by savants like Professors Scheuchzer and Beringer, both early 18th century naturalists who came up with imaginative but incorrect interpretations of fossils.

Professor Scheuchzer wanted to crown his career by finding a fossil of the sinners who lived before the flood drowned everybody except Noah and his family. Scheuchzer found such a fossil and named it *Homo diluvii testis,* "human witness to the flood." The French paleontologist Cuvier later correctly identified this as the fossilized skeleton of a Labyrinthodont, a prehistoric salamander.

Scheuchzer's *Homo diluvii testis*

A contemporary, and also a firm adherent of the idea that the Bible is a historical and scientific document, Professor Beringer was finding extraordinary fossils that looked like bas-reliefs, of for example spiders spinning webs, flies copulating, miniatures of the sun and the moon and comets. He later uncovered Hebrew letters and also the perpetrators of the fraud—colleagues at the University of Wurzberg who shaped the artifacts (*Lügensteine,* lying stones) from clay, baked them, and convinced depraved students to plant them where the credulous Beringer would find them.

Two years before the publication of the *Origin of Species,* that is, in 1857, a naturalist named Philip Gosse published an attempt to reconcile the biblical fact of the earth's being young with the geological appearance of old age. He proposed that dinosaurs and other prehistoric animals had never really lived, but that God had planted artificial fossils in the earth to give it the illusion of a history. God had done something similar with Adam, providing this first man with a navel—though Adam had had no mother. On that analogy, Gosse entitled his book *Omphalos,* navel. *Omphalos* did not settle the argument of whether the geological record supports or refutes the Bible.

For the fourth episode, we advance the calendar half a century, to 1911, when several English fossil-hunters found a number of fossils in an old gravel pit—cranial fragments, a jawbone, parts of prehistoric mammalian teeth, paleolithic tools, a fossilized elephant femur bone shaped into what looked like a cricket bat. They decided that the jawbone and the skull had once constituted a single head. This

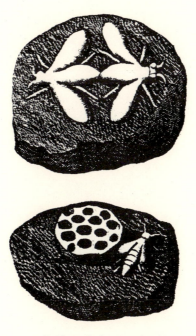

Beringer's *Lügensteine*

was an astonishing deduction, since the jawbone was that of an ape and the skull that of a human being. They named the contraption *Eoanthropus dawsoni, eo,* dawn, + *anthropo,* human being, and *dawsoni* an eponym < Charles Dawson, the major discoverer.

In 1953, evidence was presented to show that *Eoanthropus dawsoni* had never lived, that the jawbone did not belong to the skull, and that just about all the fossils found in the pit were hand-delivered there by a hoaxer. No one knows what the motive was since no one has been able to identify who did it.

Only a decade after the presentation of *Eoanthropus dawsoni,* a few American paleontologists went so far as to reconstruct a single imperfect fossil molar into an anthropoid, or even a hominid, which they named *Hesperopithecus haroldcookii, hespero,* western, + *pithecus,* of the apes, and *haroldcookii,* as one might expect, an eponym, from Harold Cook, the discover. This turned out to be a pig's tooth.

The last episode was terminated in 1987. Fossil footprints and tracks had been found in the Paluxy valley, some 40 miles south of Fort Worth, Texas. Paleontologists were content in thinking that these footprints had been impressed by dinosaurs; but creationists argued that some of them were human. And if human beings had walked the earth at the same time that dinosaurs inhabited it, then the theory of evolution would have received a serious if not a lethal blow. After fifty or so years of arguing that human beings had left their footprints along with dinosaurs in the Paluxy Valley, the creationists finally gave up that explanation.

The evolutionists who thought that *Hesperopithecus haroldcookii* was a fossil primate and the creationists who thought that some Paluxy footprints were of human beings made mistakes in interpreting real evidence. But the cases of Professor Beringer and Piltdown Man illustrate more than just mistakes: they illustrate hoaxes. The word *hoax* has a most unlikely etiology. In the religious ritual of transubstantiation, as practiced in the Roman Catholic Church, the phrase used in presenting the wafer is *Hoc est corpus meum,* Here is my body. Magicians of the 16th century changed that to a formula they used as they fooled people: *hocus-pocus.* In the late 17th century, that rhyming parody was clipped to *hocus,* which became *hoax* in 19th century England and *hokum* in the 20th century United States.

Hesperopithecus haroldcookii
(slightly enlarged)

Harold Cook's Western Ape
(greatly imagined)

CHAPTER 12—GEOLOGY

12.1   Geological Chart
12.2   Elements in the Chart
12.3   Earth

When the young Charles Darwin left on the voyage of H.M.S. *Beagle*, he accepted the date of 4004 B.C. as that of the birth of the earth. Two Anglican bishops had determined the exact time of creation: October 23rd at 9 a.m. Darwin's library on the frigate held the first volume of Lyell's recently published *Principles of Geology*. It also held Milton's *Paradise Lost*. Lyell's book made people skeptical about that date of 4000 B.C. He was among a group of geologists who proposed that the earth was much older than 6000 years and that its development had been gradual and uniform—that the processes which took place long ago were much like those which take place today: wind and water erosion, land depression and elevation, the transport of silt down rivers to form deltas, and so on. Opponents argued that the geological dynamics of the past were primarily catastrophic: volcanic eruptions, earthquakes, torrential rains, worldwide floods.

During the last decades of the 18th century and into the first decades of the 19th, geologists on both sides of the argument—uniformitarianism vs. catastrophism—contributed little by little to an understanding that as we dig down deeper into strata, we dig down into the past. As geological and paleontological evidence emerged from explorations of caves and other sites in Europe and elsewhere, a geological chart began to emerge. That chart has undergone constant change over the last two centuries as new evidence appears to ascertain what plants and animals lived when and where. New techniques have been developed to refine dates of strata and fossils.

Three terms for the general divisions of the geological chart are *era*, *period*, and *epoch*. *Era* < L. *aer*, brass, money, a counter, perhaps metaphorically meaning the beginning of a count of time. *Period* and *epoch* are of Gk. origin: < *peri-* + *hodos*, way, and < Gk. *epokhe*, pause. The major chronological divisions end in *zoic*, pert. to life.

protero-	+`zoic	first
archeo-	+	early, primitive
a-	+	lacking, no
ceno	+	recent
also *caino*		
meso	+	middle
paleo	+	old
phanero	+	appearance

157

12.1 Geological Chart

Era	Years Ago (millions)	Era	Period	Epoch	
C	0.01			*Holocene*	Gk. *holos*, whole
E	2		*Quaternary*	*Pleistocene*	L. *quartr*, fourth
N					Gk. *pleist*, most
O	13			*Pliocene*	Gk. *pleio*, more
Z	25			*Miocene*	Gk. *meio*, less
O	36			*Oligocene*	Gk. *olig-*, few
I	58			*Eocene*	Gk. *eo*, dawn
C	63		*Tertiary*	*Paleocene*	L. *terti-*, third
M	135		*Cretaceous*		L. *creta*, chalk
E	180		*Juraissic*		Fr. *Jurassique*, of the Jura Mts.
S	230		*Triassic*		L. *trias*, third
O					
Z					
O					
I					
C					
P	280		*Permian*		Russian Perm, a province
A					of eastern Russia
L			*Pennsylvanian*		(Wm.) Penn + L. *silva*, forest
E			*Mississippian*		Ojiba *missi*, big + *sippi*, river
O	345		*Carboniferous*		L. *carbon*, coal
Z	405		*Devonian*		Welsh county Devon
O	425		*Silurian*		Welsh tribe Silures
I	500		*Ordovician*		Brit. tribe Ordovices
C	600		*Cambrian*		Welsh tribe Cymrae

An inclusive term for Paleozoic, Mesozoic, and Cenozoic is PHANEROZOIC

1000	**PROTEROZOIC**
3000	**ARCHEOZOIC**
5000	**AZOIC**

In the third and fourth decades of the 19th century, geology was a popular subject for literate people. The terms *Cambrian, Silurian, Devonian, Permian, Triassic* and *Cretaceous* date from the 1830s and 1840s. **Cambrian** in the 16th century referred to Welshmen; in 1836, the geologist Adam Sedgwick first applied it to what was then known as the earliest stratum. *Silurian* was applied in 1835 to a subsequent geological period; *Devonian*, 1837; *Permian*, 1841. *Triassic* is a remnant from an older geological schedule. *Triassic, Quaternary,* and *Tertiary* are in a sense fossils of earlier classifications.

In 1832, a writer first referred to "The cretaceous rocks of southwestern England." *Ordovician* was invented in 1887.

Carboniferous dates back to 1799, a geologist named Kirwan writing at that time: "By carboniferous, I mean the various sorts of earth or stone among or under which coal is usually formed." A *Daily Telegraph* article of 1865 applied the term in a novel way: "There was a set-to between some of the speakers and the coal porters. One speaker suggested . . . the expulsion of the carboniferous brawlers."

Some terms are toponyms, that is, from the names of places chosen because the strata were first identified there: *Jurassic, Permian, Pennsylvanian, Mississipian.* Others are eponyms, words from the names of peoples or tribes: *Devonian, Silurian, Ordovician, Cambrian.*

Different forms of life characterized different periods, from Cambrian invertebrates to trilobites in the Ordovician to fish in the Silurian up to Devonian amphibians, Permian reptiles, and birds and mammals in later periods. The Cenozoic era is divided into two periods, which are further divided into epochs. These epochs are the times of the advent of primates, from insectivores to human beings. According to the evolutionary view, the lower a form appears in the geological record, the earlier it lived on earth.

Trilobite

12.2 Elements in the Chart

In the chart are elements that appear in specialized vocabularies other than that of geology.

Prefixes:

oligo-	few	*Oligochaeta,* class of earthworms
prot(er)o-	first	*protein*
paleo	old	*paleontology, paleolithic*
meso-	middle	*mesoderm*
mio-	less	*miosis*
pl(e)io-	more	*pleonotia,* extra ear

| *terti-* | third | *tertigravida,* third pregnancy |
| *qua(d)r-* | fourth | *quadrant* |

Suffixes:

-aceous	pert. to, belonging to, resembling	*pertinaceous*
-ic	pert. to	*gastric*
-ian	belonging to (place, time, etc.), follower or practitioner of	*Darwinian*
-ary	place	*library*
-ous	full of, pertaining to	*generous*

Bases:

cen	recent
cenogenesis	of recent birth
cenatophobia	fear of novelty

A homophonic **ken, cen,** Gk. empty, appears in *cenophobia,*

| *kenotoxic* | emptying of poison |
| *cenos* | an emptying as of water: *hydrocenosis* or of stones: *lithocenosis* |

eo	dawn	*eolith, eohippus, Eoanthropus*
holo	whole	*hologram, holistic, holotype, holozoic holocrine, holotrichous, Holothuria*
zo	animal	*zoology, zoophagy*

| **phan(ero)** | appearance see chart below |

IE *bha,* to shine

Words in the general vocabulary from Proto-Germanic, e.g., *beacon,* and from L. (*banner*). Five Gk. bases: **phos, phot, phen, phan, phase.**

phos, light	*phosphorus, phosphorescence*
photo	*photography, photosynthesis*
+ *tropism*	turning toward the light
Protocryptus photomorphus	a wasp
Photouris pennsylvanica	a firefly
phen, appearance	*phenomenon,* pl. *phenomena; phenotype phenology, epiphenomenalism*
phan	*epiphany, phantom* (in medicine, *phantom limb*)
phanero + *gam*	a plant that uses seeds for union
+ *zoic*	category including times when life appeared (Paleozoic, Mesozoic, Cenozoic)

chromo + **phane**	appearance, stage with color
dia- +	*diaphanous*, transparent
gastro +	*gastrodiaphany*
ophthalmodiaphanoscope	
phase	*phase, emphasis, diphrasic*
pro- + **phase**	first stage in cell reduplication

12.3 Earth

Ge is a familiar base for earth in *geology* and *geography*, less familiar in *geophagia*, *geotropism, zoogeography, phytogeography*, and *geode.*

apogee	the highest point in a circuit
perigee	the lowest point

The L. base for earth is **terra.**

terrestrial	*extraterrestrial*	*terrain*	*territory*
terrier	*subterranean*	*terrarium*	*terra firma*
terra cotta	*Mediterranean*		

terra incognita, the unexplored, unknown land

Most of the earth is covered with water, in the form of the sea, lakes, rivers. The base for water itself is the familiar **hydro**, as in *hydrogen, hydroelectric, hydrolysis, hydrocephalus,* and *hydrology. Hydrops* is a synonym for *dropsy*, accumulation of fluid (transitional form from **hydr**: ME *ydropesie; dropsy* entered E. in the late 13th century). 200 + terms in the medical vocabulary begin with **hydro** or **hydra** (not to be confused with homophonic *hydra*, the tentacled monster).

Of the three bases for the sea, one is very rarely used—Gk. *thalassa*, another is mostly restricted to the specialized vocabulary of geography and biogeography—Gk. **pelag**; and the third is an acquaintance—L. **mar**, though it has a few surprising cousins. *Thallassemia* is an anemic condition afflicting Mediterranean people; also called Cooley's anemia.

Gk. **pelag**, sea	*pelagosaur, archipelago*
pelagic	of the open sea
Phalacrocorax pelagicus	a cormorant
L. **mar**, the sea	*marine, mariculture, rosemary*
	morass
Thalarctus maritimus	polar bear
Relatives of L. **mar**	*mere, mermaid, marsh*
L. **littor**, seashore	*littoral*
Littorina littorea	a periwinkle

L. riv, stream	*river, rivulet*
Rivularia bullata	an alga
L. *ripar*, shore	*riparian*
Begonia ripicola	a begonia
Gk. *potam*, lake, stream	*hippopotamus, potamology, Mesopotamia*
Cervus mesopotamicus	a deer
Gk. *limn*, lake, pond marsh	*limnology, limnetic*
L. *lac*, lake	*lagoon, lacuna*
lacustrine	pert. to a lake
Drosophila lacicola	a fly
Gk. *pluv*, rain	*pluvial, pluviometer, pluvious*
L. *glaci*, ice	*glacier, glacial, glaciation*
Eubalaeana glacialis	a whale

IE *nau*, boat

L. descendants: *navy, navigate, navicular*, a foot bone

Gk. *naut*	*nautical, nautilus, astronaut*, etc.
	nautophone, nausea, noise
naupathia	seasickness
Naucrates ductor	pilot fish

Astonishment lit. means being turned to stone. *Stone* has a place in the biological vocabulary in reference to concretions in the body, such as kidney stones. The biolexicon and the geolexicon offer many terms for stone and/or rock.

A similar story of moderate interest concerns *unscrupulous. Scruple* retains its old sense of L. *scrup*, stone, in meaning a unit of weight in pharmacy. Its more common meaning is a conscientious objection. This happened because a stone in a sandal is a constant bother to one's foot, as a scruple in the mind is a constant bother to one's conscience. Adj., *scrupulous; Urceolaria scruposa* is the taxonomic name of a lichen.

L. **lapis**, stone	*dilapidated, lapis lazuli*
lapidary	a collector of stones
L. **calcul**, stone,	*calcium, calcification, recalcitrant*
heelbone, counting	*calculus, calculate*
hypercalcemia	too much calcium in the blood
calciphilia	a need for calcium
calcaneum	heel bone

Biliary calculus

Pancreatic calculus

Lith produces words in three categories: for large stones, for stone tools, and for concretions within the body.

1. Large stones

litho	+ *logy*	the study of stones
	+ *sphere*	the earth's rocky envelope
mega-	+ **lith**	a very large stone, e.g., at Stonehenge
mono-	+	lit. a single very large stone (up to 40 tons); adj., *monolithic*

2. Stone tools

eo	+ **lith**	dawn stone
oo	+	egg stone, small concretions
paleo	+	a tool of paleolithic times
meso-	+ **lithic**	
neo-	+	

3. Small stones within the body, for concretions or calculi: *microlith* and *macrolith, otolith* and *rhinolith* and *nephrolith.* A word for removal or emptying of these stones combines **lith** with *cenosis: lithocenosis.*

litho	+ *genesis*	formation of calculi within the body
	+ *trity*	pulverizing these calculi
	+ *clast*	implement to break calculi
	+ *pedion*	fetus mineralized

other combinations:		*lithograph, lithium*
litho	+ *phyte*	a plant that grows on rocky surface;
	plant, growth	an organism having stony structure, e.g., coral
copro	+ **lith**	fossilized feces; could also refer to calculi in bowels
Dialithus magnificus		a beetle
Heliolites porosus		an extinct coral

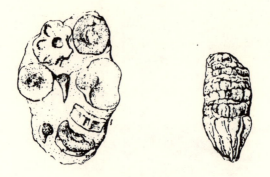

Phosphatic coprolites

Concretion in geology refers to a discrete mass of one kind of stone enclosed within another; in anatomy to lithic debris in the body. A special kind of soft concretion is a *tophus*, deposit in gout. L. *tophus* means soft stone; its sense of stone continues in *tufa*, volcanic rock.

Gk. **petri** is overt for rock or stone in several words—*petrify, petroleum;* and hidden in others. When Jesus remarked that he would build his church on Peter, he was punning, *Peter* meaning rock. **Petri** > *Peter* > *Pierrot (Pierre)* > *parrot* > *parakeet.* A herb that grows in rocks is *parsley*, and a bird that lives in rocks is a *petrel*, both these taking their names from their habitation.

petro	+ *-ous*	hard portion of temporal bone
	+ *glyph*	carving on stone
Hymenolobium petraeum		a legume
L. **sax**, rock		*sassafras*
saxicoline, -ous		growing among rocks
Saxifraga		a genus of plants that grow among rocks
		fraga < *fragus*, breaking

Sider, a Gk. base for iron, combines readily to produce *sideroderma* and *sideropenia; siderosis,* excess of iron in the blood; *siderophilous,* absorbing iron; and *siderodromophobia,* fear of trains.

Lacking necessary minerals will cause physiological problems, for example, sideropenia. Lack of iodine is responsible for goiter and cretinism; lack of zinc for dwarfism. Having too much may cause poisoning, e.g., *zincalism,* zinc poisoning, *plumbism,* lead poisoning. Inhalation of particles or dust can be lethal, as in *siderosis, asbestosis, anthracosis.* These are kinds of pneumoconiosis, **coni** base meaning dust.

Dinosaur < *dino,* terrible + **saur,** lizard was invented by Professor Richard Owen in 1841. The dinosaurs have for a century and a half provided many challenges to paleontologists and much fun to museum visitors and children. The dinosaur industry, the making of rubber floats in the form of brontosaurs and affixing tyrannosaurus decals on jelly jars, is active enough to produce now and then a poem.

The Dinosaur

Behold the mighty dinosaur
Famous in prehistoric lore,
Not only for his weight and length
But for his intellectual strength.
You will observe by these remains
The creature had two sets of brains—
One on his head (the usual place),
The other at his spinal base.
Thus he could reason "a priori"
As well as "a posteriori."
No problem bothered him a bit:
He made both head and tail of it.
So wise he was, so wise and solemn
Each thought filled just a spinal column.
If one brain found the pressure strong
It passed a few ideas along;
If something slipped his forward mind
'Twas rescued by the one behind.
And if in error he was caught
He had a saving afterthought,
As he thought twice before he spoke
He had no judgments to revoke;
For he could think without congestion,
Upon both sides of every question.

Bert Leston Taylor

CHAPTER 13—TAXONOMY

13.1 Early Taxonomies
13.2 Tax
13.3 Nom and Nom
13.4 Systematics
13.5 Taxonomic Chart

13.1 Early Taxonomies

The geological time chart reflects a way of classifying strata and the fossils within them by time. Taxonomy is also a way of classifying, of distinguishing plants from animals, insects from spiders, people from monkeys. The earliest systematic attempt to classifying living things is found in Aristotle's *Historia animalium:*

Human Beings
  Viviparous quadrupeds—mammals
    Cete: whales, porpoises
      Ovipara: fish, amphibians, reptiles, birds
        Malacia: cephalopods
          Malacostraca: crustaceans
            Entoma: other arthropods
              Ostracoderma: other mollusks

Acalephae	Tethya	Holothuria
(e.g., jellyfish)	(e.g., sea squirts)	(e.g., sea cucumbers)
	Zoophyta	Spongiae
	(higher plants)	(sponges)

I n a n i m a t e   m a t t e r

Two thousand years after Aristotle, Carl von Linne, or Linnaeus, in his 1753 *Species Plantarum,* designed the procedure of *binomial classification* still in use, that of giving the animal or plant two names, the first generic (into a genus), the second its specific (into a species); a third name, the sub-specific, may be part of the label. As the specimen is included into higher divisions, the system goes from species to genus to family to order to class to phylum to kingdom. Intermediate divisions are also used in some taxonomies, such as grade, super-family, infra-order, and tribe. *Classification, classify, classic, class* < L. **class.**

13.2 Tax

Taxonomy consists of three parts: **tax** < Gk. *tax*, order, arrangement + **nom** < Gk. *nomos*, law + *-y*, state of. The bases require investigation.

From the Gk. *taxis* comes *syntax*, the arrangement of words in a sentence, and *tactics*. In the biological vocabulary, **tax** indicates arranging, ordering, and orientation. The familiar key term is *taxidermy*, lit., reordering skin, rearrangement of animal corpse.

taxy		employed for classification
noso	+ **taxy**	inventory of disease
dys	+ **taxia**	failure in coordination to control voluntary movements
a-	+	no order, in medical use: muscular discoordination; a species of this: *alcoholic ataxia*
a-	+ **taxia** + *graph*	instrument to measure swaying from ataxia
cardi	+ **ataxia**	incoordination of heart muscles
taxis		a base referring to orientation
helio	+ **taxis**	orientation to the sun
photo	+	to light
thermo	+	to heat
chromato	+	to color
rhizo	+	to roots
aero	+	to oxygen
taxon		a level of classification, pl. *taxa*

Another *tax*, homophone of the above, is from Fr. < Latin *tangere*, to touch; this is the base in *contact* and *tactual* (and *taxes* and *taxicab*).

13.3 Nom and Nom

For **nom**, we'll start with IE. An IE root, reconstructed as *nem*, meant both to give and to take. A homophonic **nom** from a different IE root is the base for naming.

IE *nem*, to give, to take

Nem went through Proto-Germanic and Old English to become modern E. *numb*, *benumb*, and *nimble*. It may be the source of L. *numerus* > *number*, *enumerate*, and *supernumerary*, an excess of something, e.g., of nipples. In their cunning paranoia, the witch-hunters of the 16th century considered supernumerary nipples as evidence proving that the suspect was a witch.

IE *nem* > Gk. base **nom**, which has several meanings with the sense of what is customary or lawful and so can be translated as law of or management of.

One who suffers from no management experiences a sense of alienation, of loss, *anomie.*

taxo	+ **nomy**	lit. the laws governing arrangement
astro	+	lit. the laws governing stars
eco	+	lit. the management of the household
auto	+	lit. managing one's self
agro	+	scientific agriculture—*agro*, field, as in *agrarian, peregrine* falcon, *peregrinate*, to travel and from that: *pilgrim*
gastro	+	laws of good cooking and eating
binomial		pert. to law of naming by two

Homphonic with **nom**, law of or management of, is **nom**, naming.

IE *no-men*, name

Proto-Germanic	*name, naming*
Gk. **nym**	**nym** combines with affixes and other bases: *a-*, anonymous; *syno-, anto-, pseudo, acro-, tauto-, typo-, patro-, homo-*
patronym	name from father, e.g., Fitzroy, son of Roy
homonym	of same name or word
tautonym, same name	*Gorilla gorilla*
Gk. **nom**	
onomatopoeia	condition of a word's echoing a sound
L. **nom**	
nosonomy	naming, listing, of diseases
nomenclature	arrangement of names
nomenclator	orig., one who called out the names of guests; now, one who arranges names in order
innominate	lit. no name, refers to an artery and to a bone of the hip

13.4 Systematics

The classification of living things can be called just that: *classification*. It can also be called *taxonomy, nomenclature,* and *systematics.* The base of this last word, **ste**, conducts us to another IE root, one of the most impressively or depressingly productive of all: *sta*, to stand. Because so many words come from this source, an effort has been made here to focus upon those in the biolexicon.

IE *sta.* to stand

Most of the hundreds of descendants of this will be familiar, especially those from native English and close cognates, such as *stand* and *starling.* IE *sta* led to several bases from Latin and French.

sti	*institute, constitution, armistice*
ste	*obstetrics*
sist	*insist, exist*
sta	*obstacle, statue, stance, substance, stamen, stature, status, stage*
	stable (note diminutive disguised here: < L. *stabulum*)
stabile	syn. for *stable,* unmoving
frigostabile	resistant to low temperatures
coctostabile	resistant to high temperatures
staunch	pert. to stopping a flow, as of blood also: strong, obstinate
extant	existing today, at the present time, as opposed to *extinct*
distal	toward the end, the distant part

Most of the descendants from L. are in the general vocabulary, but most of the descendants from Gk. are in the specialized biological and especially medical vocabulary.

Gk. *histanai,* to cause to stand > **sta, stasis,** equilibrium, stoppage.

prostate		gland in males, lit. that which stands before (the bladder)
stasis		a consistent, unmoving stage
hypo	+ **stasis**	foundation; in genetics, refers to one gene's suppressing action of another
meta-	+	change in location of a disease, e.g., migration of cancer cells
dia-	+	separation of bones, e.g., of pubic bones
bacterio	+	arrest of bacterial growth
chole	+	arrest of bile flow
ex-	+ **stasy**	*ecstasy,* lit. a moving out of one's place, being beside oneself
iso-	+	equilibrium, equalization
ste		*system, systematics*
dia-	+ **stema**	a space, as between teeth

stal, stol < *stellein,* to send, contract

peri-	+ **stalsis**	contractions of digestive tube *hyperperistalsis, peristaltiphone*
dia-	+ **stole**	relaxation of heart as it fills with blood; *bradydiastole,* slow diastole
sys-	+	contraction of ventricles, expulsion of blood, *asystole*

Diastole and systole in dog's heart
R.V., right ventricle
L.V., left ventricle

hist, web, tissue

histo	+ *logy*	the study of tissues
	+ *zoic*	referring to animals that inhabit tissues
	+ *lysis*	dissolution of tissues
	+ *genesis*	birth of tissues

stul, pillar

styl	+ *-oid*	resembling a column, a process of the temporal bone; in *stylohyoid, styloglossus, stylosteophyte*

Gk. *stylos* led to L. *style,* which has a different meaning: writing instrument (*stylus*) or characteristic mode, as of writing. **Styl** thus means rod, either a big one, such as a column, or a small one like a stylus.

L. *stylus* >

endostyle	pharyngeal grooves in digestive passage of lower chordates, e.g., of tunicate
blastostyle	pert. to jellyfish: a structure for development of pre-medusa stage buds
stele	a root vascular system

13.5 Taxonomic Chart

There exist so many creatures great and small and so many different languages and cultures that an initial approach to taxonomy ought to stress the appropriateness of different systems of classification. Plants might be split into two groups: those that are edible and those that are not. Animals might be classified into two groups: those that do work and those that don't. Subsections could be thought up for these divisions.

Animals and plants don't classify themselves—a garter snake has no idea that it's more closely related to the turtle that's about to eat it than to the earthworm it's about to eat.

There are three major systems for classifying life. Classical taxonomy lists extinct as well as extant animals and plants, and molecular biology reveals through analysis of living tissue the times that groups split off from ancestors in the past. While these two don't always agree on relationships, they both posit models which are designed to correspond to evolutionary descent.

Cladistics is more interested in how organisms branch off than in relationship of extant organisms to extinct ones. To design taxonomies, cladistics plays down morphological features, which can fossilize, and emphasizes physiology and behavior of living beings. It produces results at variance with accepted evolutionary models, such as categorizing lung fish with mammals and crocodiles with birds. Disputes in science of these sorts are resolved eventually.

Gk. *klaein*, to break, was used in the 19th century as a source for botanical terms having to do with branches. These three terms with the base **clad** entered E. from 1855–1885.

cladocarpous	seed-bearing container at end of stem, as in mosses
cladophyll	a branch that resembles and functions as a leaf
cladoptosis	shedding of branches

1950 saw the invention of *cladogenesis*, focusing on the birth of branching of descendant groups; 1957 of *clade*, a group consisting of individuals that share homologous features; 1965, of *cladistics;* and 1965–1970, of *cladogram*, the visual representation of branching.

The following system is based upon classical taxonomy. Authoritative agencies have established rules for botanical and zoological nomenclature; nomenclators try to avoid eponyms, which are not descriptive; a name is to be appropriate to what is named; and once named, the living thing is supposed to keep the name. But many names were established before the rules were set down, and the rules aren't always followed even today. A critical conflict obtains between the gatherers, those who prefer to blur distinctions, and the splitters, those who prefer to emphasize distinctions.

The taxonomic chart has one word from English: *kingdom*, a few from Latin, most from Greek.

Kingdom		< OE *cyning* + *dom*
Division		< L. *dividere*, to separate
Grade		< L. **grad, gress** to step, walk, go
salti	+ **grade**	going by jumping
planti	+	by walking on sole of foot
cilio	+	by walking on hair
digiti	+	by walking on digits

grade	biodegradable	progress	aggression
degrade	retrograde	progressive	aggressive
gradation	ingredient	regress	digress
gradual		regression	digression

Phylum   < Gk. **phyl**, race, tribe

phylo   + *geny*   ancestral sequence
                                 phyletic, of the tribe, group, ancestral
Class   < L. *class*
Order   < L. **ord**, order, arrangement
Family   < L. *familias*
Genus   < Gk. *gen,* ancestry, tribe, pl. *genera*
Species   < L. *spec, spic,* to see

Living things are classified into four kingdoms: Monera, Fungi, Planta, and Animalia.

A. Kingdom: *Monera*   < Gk. **mono-,** one
prokaryotes   < *pro-* before, primitive + *karyo-ites*
                                 cells without true nuclei

Cyanophyceae   blue-green algae or bacteria

also called *Cyanobacteria* and *Schizophyceae*

The calcareous column produced by prokaryotic blue-green algae/bacteria is known as a *stromatolite* < Gk. *stroma,* bed covering, in L. mattress, akin to *stratum,* + *lite,* stone.

The next organisms in this and the next chapter are *eukaryotic,* that is, their cells contain a true nucleus with genetic material.

B. Kingdom: *Fungi*   < Gk. *sp(h)ongos,* sponge

Divisions Gymnomycota   < Gk. *gymn,* naked + *mycota,* fungus
          Lichens   < Gk. *leichen,* tree-moss
          Amastigomycota   < Gk. *a-* + *mastig* + *mycota*
          Mastigomycota   < Gk. *mastig,* whip + *mycota*

C. Kingdom: *Planta*   < L. *planta,* sole of the foot

Plants are *autotrophic,* which translates into being able to manufacture food, unlike animals, *heterotrophs* that have to consume their food, often after catching it.

Divisions (examples)
          Chlorophyta   < Gk. *chlor* + **phyto,** plant
          green algae
          Bryophyta   < Gk. *bry,* moss
          moss

Pteriodophyta	< Gk. *pteris,* fern
ferns	
Conifera	< L. *con,* cone + *fer,* bearing
Angiosperm	< L. *angio,* vessel + *sperm*
flowering plants	

D. Kingdom: *Animalia*	< L. *anima,* breath, life, spirit, animal
Phylum *Protozoa*	< Gk. *proto-* + *zoa*

50,000 + species. Protozoans may be free-living, like amoeba, euglena, and paramecium, or parasitic, like *Plasmodium vivax,* responsible for malaria. *Volvox* is a colonial protozoan. Phylum Protozoa is divided into four subphyla which may be further divided into superclasses, then classes, subclasses and orders.

For example, the geneology of dinoflagellates:
Subphylum *Sarcomastigophorea* Gk. *sarco,* flesh + *mastigo* + *phores,* bearing

Superclass *Mastigophora*	
Class *Phytomastigophorea*	< Gk. *phyto*
Order *Dinoflagellida*	< *Gk. dino,* whirl (homophonic *dino* as in *dinosaur* means terrible) + *flagell,* whip or tail + *ida*

Protozoans have been less favored than maidens as subjects for poetry. Sir Arthur Shipley may have been the author of this amoebic love affair:

> When we were a soft ameoba, in ages past and gone,
> 'Ere you were Queen of Sheba, or I King Solomon,
> Alone and undivided, we lived a live of sloth,
> Whatever you did, I did, one dinner served for both.
> Anon came separation, by fission and divorce,
> A lonely pseudopodium, I wandered on my course.

This is the geneology of paramecium:

Subphylum *Ciliophora*	< Gk. *cilio,* hair
Class *Ciliatea*	
Subclass *Holotrichia*	< Gk. *hol* + *trichia,* hair
Order *Hymenostomatida*	< Gk. *hymen* + stoma
Genus *Paramecium*	< Gk. *para-* + *mecium,* oval; entered E. in 1750

From these unicellular animals, we will proceed to etymologize the multicellular animals, or Metazoa.

CHAPTER 14—METAZOA

14.1   Parazoa
14.2   Radiata
14.3   Acoelomate Phyla
14.4   Pseudocoelomate Phyla
14.5   Coelomate Phyla
14.6   Hominid Classification

*M*etazoa, like *Parazoa* and *Radiata*, is a name for a group—multicellular animals. Learning these and the other terms in this chapter will be made easier by remembering that they exemplify the usual methods of word-making in the biolexicon. First of all, the words may be eponymous, Greek mythology a useful source as in *Medusa, Nereid, Arachne,* and *Cyclops*. Secondly, they may be metaphors as with *scyph*, drinking bowl = *Scyphozoa*, marine jellyfish; *cestus*, girdle, = *Cestoda*, a class of tapeworms, and = *scyphoform*, in the shape of a cup; and *cope*, handle, oar = *Copepoda*, a class of the subphylum *Crustacea*.

Thirdly, the most productive method of invention is to compound a base with affixes. Many of the bases will be familiar (e.g., *zoa, antho, homi, anthropo*). We will find many familiar prefixes, *a-, cata-, pro-, platy-, penta-, pseudo-, ex-, sub-, hemi-;* some less familiar. Familiar suffixes also appear, such as *-id* and especially *-oidea* and its alternate *-oda*, both meaning form. Unfamiliar bases and affixes are defined.

Trematoda	a fluke
Diploda	a milliped
Crinoidea	an echinoderm
Proboscoidea	an elephant
Anthropoidea	monkeys, apes and people
Hominoidea	apes and people

A warning: taxonomic suffixes have less regularity than do chemical. *-Oidea* is used for class (*Crinoidea*) and for superfamily (*Hominoidea*), *-ida* for class (*Arachnida*) and phylum (*Annelida*), *-ata* for order (*Testudinata*) and phylum (*Chordata*).

14.1 Parazoa

Phylum *Porozoa*   Gk. **por**, pore + *zoo*, animal

So relatively simple is the sponge's structure that sponges were thought to be plants, as indicated by the word *sponge* itself—Gk. *spongos* is also the source of *fungus*. In 1875, T.H. Huxley established their animal nature. Of multicellular organisms, the sponges provide a transition, *parazoa*, almost animal," between protozoa, first animal, and metazoa, higher animal. Sponges are unlike the metazoa, in that their cells enjoy a degree of independence and in lacking the more complex tissue of metazoans.

Whatever animal is taken for physical dissection, the words used to label most of its parts will come from the resources of the biolexicon. This general principle can be illustrated with turning attention to the parts of the sponge. Sponges have the following types of structures, most names of which are made up of parts that have been or will be items in *Biolexicon.*

amoebo + cyte	an amoeba-like wandering cell that has excretory as well as other functions
archeo +	an amoebocyte that develops into other cells
choano +	funnel-shaped flagellated cells in inner cavity for feeding < Gk. *choan,* funnel + *cyte*
porocyte	cell that makes up porous structure
pinacoderm	pine-like skin, outer layer of sponge wall
mesohyal	matrix of wall, holds amoebocytes < Gk. *meso-* + *hyal,* glass, middle glass
spicule	needle-like skeletal element: of silica or calcium carbonate < L. *spica,* spike
paragaster	digestive cavity < Gk. *para-,* almost + *gaster,* stomach

14.2 Radiata

Radiata refers to the radial symmetry of the three phyla that comprise this group.

Phylum *Cnidaria*   < Gk. *cnidus,* nettle, sting
        Coelenterata   < Gk. *coel,* hollow + *enter,* intestine
9500+ species

Classes:
Hydrozoa
e.g., *Hydra, Obelia*

Scyphozoa   < Gk. *skyphi,* drinking bowl
e.g., *Aurelia,* bottom-dwelling, sessile jellyfish, of order *Cubomedusae,* reclining jellyfish

Anthozoa
e.g., *Gorgonia* – jellyfish, *Corallium* – corals, sea anemones

Selected structures and forms:
nematocyst   dart-like defense mechanism

polyp	early, mobile stage in development < Gk. *poly-* + *pus*, many-footed
medusoid	adult form
exumbrella	the upper surface of a medusa's body < L. *ex-* + *umbra*, shade + -ella
subumbrella	lower surface; cp. *umbrella*, that which provides a little shade

| Phylum *Ctenophora* | < Gk. *cten*, comb + *phora*, carry, transport (*phora* as in *Porifera*) |

50+ species, comb jelly, sea gooseberry

14.3 Acoelomate Phyla

Acoelomate translates into no (true) gut tube < Gk. *a-* + **coel**, gut. Three minor phyla in this group comprise ribbon worms, some other marine worms, and endoparasites, parasites that live within the body of mollusks, echinoderms and other animals (parasites that live on the body, e.g., ticks, are exoparasites). Of the 13,000 members of the major phylum, *Platyhelminthes*, some are innocuous, such as planaria, and many are harmful endoparasites of human beings.

Gut cavity

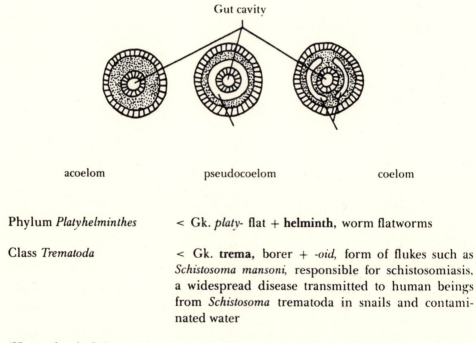

acoelom   pseudocoelom   coelom

| Phylum *Platyhelminthes* | < Gk. *platy-* flat + **helminth**, worm flatworms |
| Class *Trematoda* | < Gk. **trema,** borer + *-oid*, form of flukes such as *Schistosoma mansoni*, responsible for schistosomiasis, a widespread disease transmitted to human beings from *Schistosoma* trematoda in snails and contaminated water |

(Homophonic *fluke* meaning happy accident or coincidence, adopted from unknown source into E. in 1865.)

Class *Cestoda*   < L. *cestus*, girdle
tapeworms, such as *Taenia solium*, transmittable from infected pigs to human beings

14.4 Pseudocoelomate Phyla

Five minor phyla comprising many endoparasites and phylum *Nematoda*.

Phylum *Nematoda*   < Gk. *nemat*, thread

10,000+ species, 50 of which parasitize human beings, e.g., *Ascaris lumbricoides* and *Necator americanus*, the American hookworm, lit. American killer

14.5 Coelomate Phyla

This group begins with worms and ends with human beings.

Phylum *Annelida*   < L. *annul*, ring
Annelida includes about 20,000 species, some of which are useful as bait (*Nereis*), of great importance in cultivating soil (earthworms), and as ectoparasites (leeches). Of the three classes, one receives its name from a literal use of a Greek source: Gk. *hirudo*, leech > Class *Hirudinea*, 500 species of leeches. The other two have as their base Gk. *chaeta*, bristles: the 5500+ species of many-bristled worms, such as Nereis, are the *Polychaeta*, while the 3100+ species of worms with few bristles, such as the earthworm, belong to the *Oligochaeta*. Among other features, earthworms have a *clitellum*, packsaddle = a case or cocoon for deposition of eggs and sperm.

Phylum *Arthropoda*   < Gk. *arthr*, joint + *pod*, foot
One extinct subphylum held hundreds of families—*Trilobitomorpha;* extant subphyla hold 800,000+ species, ⅘ths of all living animals. Phylum *Arthopoda* is divided into three subphyla.

Subphylum *Chelicerata*   < Gk. **chel**, claw + **cer**, horny
e.g., Class *Arachnida*
spiders, horseshoe crabs, scorpions, ticks, mites

Subphylum *Crustacea*   < L. **crust**, shell

e.g., Class *Branchiopoda*   < Gk. **branchi**, gills + *poda*
daphnia

Class *Copepoda*   < Gk. *kope*, handle, oar
copepods—e.g., *Cyclops*

Class *Cirripedia*   < L. *cirrus*, curl + *pedia*
barnacles

Subphylum *Uniramia*   < L. *uni-* + *ramia*, branch

Class *Insecta*   < L. *in-* + *sec,* cut < *secare,* to cut

Most names for insect orders end in **pter,** winged.

Tricho	+ **ptera**	hairy-winged, e.g., caddis-flies
Di-	+	two-winged, true flies
Hemi-	+	half-winged, bugs such as aphids
Iso-	+	even-winged, termites
Hymeno	+	membrane-winged, bees, wasps, ants
Coleo	+	sheathed-winged, beetles (300,000 species)
Neuro	+	wings like nerves, lacewings

Coleopteran tiger beetles and ladybug

Ortho	+	straight-winged, grasshoppers
Strepsi	+	twisted-winged, small beetle-like insects
Lepido	+	scaly-winged, butterflies, moths
Pleco	+	twisted-winged, stoneflies
Dicty	+	net-winged, cockroaches
Ephemero	+	< Gk. *ephemer,* day; adults live a short time, only to reproduce, e.g., mayflies
Siphona	+	having a siphon, fleas
Psoco	+	living in dust, booklice and barklice
Odontata		dragonflies
Mallophaga		chewing lice
Anoplura		sucking lice
Collembola		springtails

Like protozoans, insects are rarely subjects for poetic compositions. Ogden Nash found termites and flies suitable for serious rhyme.

> Some primal termite knocked on wood,
> And tasted it and found it good,
> And that is why your cousin May
> Fell through the parlor floor today.
>
> The Lord in His wisdom made the fly,
> And then forgot to tell us why.

Other classes of Subphylum *Uniramia* are

Chilopoda	the centipedes
Symphyla	centipede-like animals
Diploda	millipedes
Pauropoda	millipede-like animals.

Phylum *Onychophora*   < Gk. *onycho*, nail + *phora*, bearing
70+ species, sometimes considered as transitional between annelids and arthropods, e.g., *Peripatus*

Phylum *Mollusca*   < Gk. **moll**, soft
100,000+ extant species; 35,000+ extinct.

Selected classes:

Bivalvia	pelycopods, mussels, clams
Cephalopoda	squids, octopuses, cuttlefish, nautilus, extinct ammonites
Gastropoda	75,000+ species, snails, slugs, limpets, whelks, nudibranchs, cowries

A taxonomic division that is sometimes favored divides the coelemates into *protostomes* < Gk. *proto-* + **stoma**, opening or mouth, and *deuterostomes* < Gk. *deutero-* second. These terms relate to features of embryonic development.

	Protostomic	Deuterostomic
sequence	mouth develops before anus	anus develops before mouth
cleavage	spiral, determinate	radial, indeterminate
coelum	from mesoderm	from primitive gut
phyla	Priapuloidea, Sipunculoidea Echiuroidea, Pogonophora, Tardigrada, Pentastomida, Bryozoa, Brachipoda, Entoprocta, Phoronida	Echinodermata, Chaetognatha, Hemichordata, Pterobranchia Chordata

Much uncertainty attends the taxonomy of the protostomic phyla, different members of which are identified as kin to pseudocoelomates, to annelids, to arthropods; some are thought of as transitions to deuterostomes. Important or interesting examples of protostomes are these:

Phylum *Pentastomida*   < Gk. *penta-* + *astomida*, of five mouths or openings
Linguatula   tongueworm, a parasite of dogs

Phylum *Brachiopoda*   < Gk. *brachio*, arm + *poda*, foot
significant as fossils—30,000 species have been identified in fossil record; fewer than 300 living species

Lingula	an extant group of brachipods like those of the Ordovician; *Lingula* from resemblance to a tongue

Invertebrate Deuterostomes

Phylum *Echinodermata* receives its name from the knobby, tubercle or spiny (Gk. *echin*, spine) condition of the skin. Echinoderms have been found as fossils in Cambrian records—20,000+ species have gone extinct, while 6,000 exist today.

Class *Crinoidea*	< Gk. *krin*, lily earliest echinoderms, 80+ species today, such as sea lilies, feather stars
Class *Asteroidea*	< Gk. **aster**, star starfish, among them the crown-of-thorns *Acanthaster* < Gk. **acanth**, spiny
Class *Ophiuroidea*	< Gk. **ophiuro**, snake brittle stars, among them *Ophiothrix*
Class *Echinoidea*	< Gk. *echin* sea urchins, sand dollars
Class *Holothuroidea*	< Gk. *holo*, whole + *thurion*, of unknown etymology sea cucumbers
Phylum *Chaetognatha*	< Gk. *chaeto*, hair + *gnatha*, jaw arrow worm sagitta
Phylum *Hemichordata*	< Gk. *hemi-* + *chordata* 100+ species, e.g., acorn worm
Phylum *Chordata*	< Gk. **chord**, cord
Sub-phyla *Cephalochordata*	< Gk. *cephalo* + *chordata* amphioxus < Gk. *amphi-* + *oxus*, sharp or *Brachiostoma;* amphioxus more familiarly known as lancet
Urochordata	< Gk. *ur*, tail + *chord* e.g., tunicate < L. *tunic*
Vertebrata Classes of Vertebrata:	
1. *Agnatha*	lack jaws and paired fins, much more abundant in fossil record than in present forms; one widespread extinct type, the *ostracoderms* < Gk. *ostrakon* shell modern representative: the lamprey

Crinoid

2. Chondrichthys	cartilaginous fish, dogfish, skates, rays and sharks < Gk. **chondr,** cartilage + *ichthy*
Subclass *Elasmobranchiomorphi*	sharks and rays < Gk. *elasmo,* beaten metal + *branchio,* gills + *morphi,* form of
3. Teleosts *Teleostomi*	complete or bony fish < Gk. *teleo,* end, complete + *ost,* bone complete mouth 30,000+ species, from guppy to eel to marlin and tarpon
4. Amphibia	< Gk. *amphi-* + *bio*
Subclass *Labyrinthodontia*	Ichthyostega, Eryops, extinct gigantic salamanders
Subclass *Lissamphibia* Order *Urodela* Order *Anura* Order *Apoda*	 tailed amphibians: newts, salamanders frogs, toads legless, blind, the caecilians

The next three classes of Subphylum *Vertebrata* are amniotes. The concept behind this word is important in understanding evolution. The sac holding the embryo received its name *amnion* in the 17th century as a metaphor based on Gk. *amnos,* lamb, this membrane being as fine as a lamb's skin (*amnion* was a Gk. term for the plate holding the sacrificial lamb). *Amniotic* means having an amnion and applies to members of the three classes that possess the membrane. The first adventurous vertebrates to leave the sea were amphibians. Anamniotic amphibians still need water or a watery site for development of eggs. The site could be a decaying log or a frog's back or even a frog's stomach.

Amniotic reptiles, birds, and mammals, not dependent upon water as an environment for eggs, could move over the earth, even inhabit deserts, which amphibians cannot do (there is a rare exception to this rule, a frog that does live in a desert — although it comes out of aestivation which could last for months, even years, only when rain provides small and ephemeral pools).

5. *Reptilia*   < L. *reptil*, creeping

Subclass *Anapsida*   < Gk. *an-* + *apsis*, loop or arch

The only surviving order of this subclass is *Testudinata* < L. *test*, shell) or *Chelonia*. Gk. *chelon* meant turtle and still does in this taxonomic name for turtles and the sub-group of terresttrial turtles, the tortoises. *Tortoise* is a toponym, from *Tartarus*, the infernal regions.

Subclass *Lepidosauria*   < Gk. *lepid*, scaly + *saur*, lizard
Order *Squamata*   < Gk. *squama*, scale
                                          lizards and snakes
Order *Rhynchocephalia*   < Gk. *rhynch*, snout + *cephal*
                                          Sphenodon, the tuatara

Subclass *Archosauria*   < Gk. *arch*, first + *saur*
Order *Crocodilia*   < L. < Gk. *krokodilos*
                                          crocodiles, alligators, caimans

6. *Aves*   < L. **avis**, bird

7. *Mammalia*   < L. **mamma**, breast

Two subclasses of mammals:

1. *Prototheria*   < Gk. *proto-* + **ther**, beast
                                          the monotremes < *mono-* + *trem*, hole) e.g., platypus
                                          < Gk. *platy-* + *pus*, foot

2. *Theria*
Infraclass *Trituberculata* early link to Mammalia

Infraclass *Metatheria*
Order *Marsupialia*
                                          < Gk. *marsip*, purse < Persian *marsu*, belly
                                          mammals with pouches, e.g., *kangaroo* < native
                                          Australian

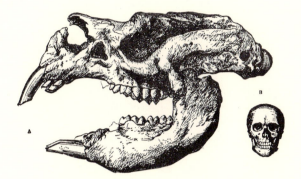

Giant Australian marsupial Diprotodon
with human skull drawn to same scale

Infraclass *Eutheria*	Gk. *eu-* + *ther* placental mammals < Gk. *plakous,* flat cake < *plax,* flat

Orders of Infraclass *Eutheria*

Insectivora	moles, shrews, hedgehogs
Carnivora	cats, dogs, etc. < Gk. *hyrakos,* shrewmouse hyrax, a
Hyracoidea	*small African mammal*
Proboscoidea	< Gk. *pro-* + *boskein,* to feed elephants
Cetacea	< Gk. **ceta,** whale
	whales, porpoises
Sirenia	sea cows, manatees, dugongs
Artiodactyl	< Gk. *arte,* even + *dactyl,* digit cattle, camels, pigs, hippopotamuses, deer, giraffes
Perissodactyla	< Gk. *periss,* odd tapirs, rhinoceroses, horses
Edentata	< L. *ex-,* lacking + *dent,* teeth anteaters, sloths, armadillos
Tubilidenta	< L. *tubus,* pipe + *denta,* teeth aardvark
Pholidota	< Gk. *pholidotos,* covered with scales pangolins = scaly anteaters
Chiroptera	< Gk. *chir,* hand + *pter* bats
Primata	< L. *prim-,* first, most important prosimians, monkeys, apes, people
Lagomorphs	< Gk. *lagos,* hare + *morph* rabbits, hares
Rodentia	< L. *rod,* gnaw rats, mice, squirrels, beavers

The following box tracks the etymology of one of the carnivores, the dog.

IE *kwon*, dog

Through Greek and Latin descendants, IE *kwon* gives the common English vocabulary about a dozen words, a few also in the medical vocabulary. Greek *kwon* > *cyn*, source of *cynic*, one who lives like a dog, and *quinsy*, a sore throat: G. *kwon* + a base from Gk. *anchein*, to strangle > *kynanchein* > L. *quinancia* > E. *quinsy*, the metaphor suitable for being throttled by a sore throat.

Latin **can** gives us *canine*, and from Romance descendants, *kennel, canary*, a bird from Canariae Insulae, the islands of dogs, and *divas canicularis*, dog days. In a Welsh word for a dwarf dog, we see *k* active again: *corgi*.

Grimm's law observes that an IE *k* sound would become a *h* sound in Proto-Germanic. A German descendant of this IE root *kwon* is *hund*, as in *dachshund*; a Dutch, *keeshond*; and an E., *hound*.

14.6 Hominid Classification

Our place in nature begins with membership in the Kingdom Animalia, our relatives all living animals. The major principle of division below the enormously wide umbrella of Animalia is whether the animals have notochords or not; those that do are in the Phylum Chordata, and true vertebrates in the Subphylum Vertebrata. Of the eight or so classes below that, we belong to the Class Mammalia. Of the three subclasses belonging to Mammalia, we assert membership in Eutheria, curiously enough the true or authentic beasts—those mammals that don't have placentas are not considered really authentic. Of the 40 or so orders of Eutheria, human beings are in Primata, along with tarsiers, monkeys, the lesser apes and the great apes, Australopithecines and Neanderthals.

Suborders of *Primata:*

Prosimii	< Gk. *pro-* + *simii*, snub-nosed tree shrews, tarsiers, lemurs
Anthropoidea	monkeys, apes, australopithecines and other hominids

Suborder Anthropoidea is divided into two infraorders, the nose emerging as the feature distinguishing the infraorders.

Infraorders of *Anthropoidea:*

Platyrrhini	< Gk. *platy-* + *rrhin*, nose
	flat-nosed monkeys of South America
Catarrhini	< Gk. *cata-*, down
	downward-pointed nosed monkeys, apes, and people

Superfamilies of Infraorder *Catarrhini:*

Cercopithecoidea	< Gk. *cerco*, tail + *pith*, ape + *-oid* baboons

Hominoidea   < L. *homi* + *-oid*
                                       apes and human beings

Families of Superfamily *Hominoidea:*

Pongidae   < Gk. *pong,* ape
                                       gibbons, siamangs, orangutans, chimpanzees, gorillas
                                       orangutan < Malay *orang,* man + *hutan,* forest

18th century depiction of
very human Orang-Utan

Hominidae   < L. *homi*

We're almost down to the lowest taxonomic level. The Family Hominidae consists of two genera, the first of which holds only extinct hominids.

Genera of Family Hominidae:

Australopithecus   < Gk. *austral,* southern + *pith* + *ecus* australopithe-
                                       cines, e.g., the species *A. africanus* < Africa; *A. afarensis*
                                       < Afar, Ethiopia; *A. robustus* < L. *robust; A. boisei,* an
                                       eponym

Homo   species *Homo habilis* < L. *habil,* work
                                       Homo erectus < L. *erect*
                                       Homo sapiens < L. *sapiens,* wise

Many hominid taxa have come and gone. When Neanderthal (or Neandertal) bones were blasted out of a limestone cliff in 1856, much uncertainty attended definition of the assemblage. It could have been entirely human, in which case it could be labelled *Homo sapiens;* or it could have been a sub-species, in which case: *Homo sapiens neanderthalensis;* or a representative of a different species entirely: *Homo neanderthalensis.* These and several other terms became taxonomic labels.

The argument about Neanderthal's status in human geneology continues more than a century after the find in the Neander valley. The latest theory is that both Neanderthal and Cro-Magnon branched off from an earlier type, the European Neanderthals dying out and the Middle Eastern living peaceably with, perhaps even mating with, Cro-Magnon.

When Eugene Dubois found the assemblage in Java, he called it *Pithecanthropus erectus,* erect ape-man, and later when paleontologists found remains similar to *Pithecanthropus erectus* in China, they named that *Sinanthropus pekinensis,* Chinese Man from Peking. These two labels lost out to a generic one: *Homo erectus.*

The family *Hominidae* consists of one genus which is extinct: *Australopithecus,* and another which has both extinct and extant members: *Homo.* All extant human beings belong to one species: *Homo sapiens.* Further division may be made on the basis of geographical site, stature, hair color, skin color, Rh factor, and number of functional molar teeth. Classification of human beings below the species level has no taxonomic value, though it has dramatic political values.

Man and ape from della Porta,
De humani Physiognomonia Libri, 1586

PART V: BIRTH AND GROWTH

CHAPTER 15—GEN

15.1 Birth
15.2 Yoke
15.3 The Cell
15.4 Semantic Shift

15.1 Birth

IE *gen(e)* is too big to be boxed. One of the most productive of all IE roots, it became the base for thousands of words descending into English from Proto-Germanic and adopted from Latin and Greek. It has been vastly productive because it designates a topic of profound concern to people—birth and descent, kin and kind. Grimm's Law anticipates that IE *g* will be English *k* and so it is in this family: *gen(e)* begat Proto-Germanic *cyn(n)*, race, and *cynn* begat *kin, kind, kindred,* and *king; gen(e)* also begat Proto-Germanic *kinth,* which begat *kindergarten* and, a seasonal joy for kindergarten lads and lassies, Kriss *Kringle.*

Many words have come into E. from this root via L. and Fr., a number of them with base **gen** tilting toward the concept of good development or birth.

general	*gender*	*generous*	*genius*
generate	*genocide*	*genial*	*ingenious*
degenerate	*gender*	*gentle*	*ingenuous*
regenerate	*gentile*	*genteel*	*gingerly*
congenital			*gendarme*

miscegenation	mating between different racial groups
progeny	offspring
progenitor	ancestor
indigenous	native, of the place originally

From a related L. source comes **nat,** to be born. Most people could easily think of a dozen words formed from *nature* and another formed from *nation. Antenatal, postnatal, native, innate,* and *naive* also come from this L. source.

nascent	born, cp. *renascent* or *renaissance,* new birth
neonate	the newborn

187

puny   < Fr. *puisne* < L. *post*, after + *ne*, birth, lit., afterbirth; in actual usage, weak

A third L. base from this complex is **germ,** which appears as *germ* itself, meaning seed literally or metaphorically—metaphoric use indicated in *germ* as microbe and *germ* as anything incipient, e.g., in Gilbert's facetious advice to writers who want to impress the world: "You must pick up all the germs of the transcendental terms and plant them everywhere"; adj., *germinal.* Cp. *germane,* relevant.

Gk. **gen** is used to form words in the scientific vocabulary relating to inheritance, birth and kind or type, the family that a person or part or substance belongs to.

generic	*gene*	*glycogen*	*zymogen*
geneology	*genome*	*hydrogen*	*halogen*
homogeneous	*genus*	*oxygen*	*antigen*
heterogeneous	*genera*	*nitrogen*	

auto- + **gen** + *-ous*		self-birth, action generated by body
ideo +		generated by mind rather than body
aero +		producing gas (e.g., as some bacteria do)
geno + *blast*		mature germ cell
+ *type*		ancestral type, that which is in the genes; ant. *phenotype,* characters appearing in the visible body

Ontogeny recapitulates phylogeny refers to the theory that the embryo in its development repeats the stages of descent—e.g., the mammalian embryo having gills and a tail.

Genic indicates opposite conditions: either productive of something, causing it, or produced by something, caused by it.

genic: producing, causing

carcino + **genic**		causing cancer; also *cancerogenic*
crino +		secretion
cryo +		low temperatures
pyo +		pus
sarco +		flesh
fibrino +		fibrin
plasmino +		blood substance that produces fibrinolysin, enzyme that breaks down fibrin TPA: tissue plasminogen activator, a dissolver of blood clots
terato +		monsters
thermo +		heat

genic: produced or caused by

psycho + **genic**		the mind (cp. *ideogenetic*)
necro +		dead matter; originating in dead matter
agno +		of unknown origin
iatro +		treatment

A syn. to *iatrogenic,* adj. pert. to an illness caused by medical treatment, is *nosocomial.* It specifically refers to that which is caused by being hospitalized. It entered E. in 1850 from L. *nosocomium,* hospital < Gk. *nosokomeian* < **noso,** disease + *kom,* care. This word underwent the etymological process called *pejoration,* moving from a good sense, being cared for, to a bad sense.

genics: science of

genetics	*cryogenics*
eugenics	*thermogenics*
dysgenics	

genesis: birth of

The base **genesis** relates to the birth of, as in the book of Genesis. This combines with other bases to produce a multitude of words. Two theories are available for the beginning of life itself. With *bio,* we have *biogenesis,* the theory that all life on earth came from an original living ancestor, perhaps supplied by extraterrestrial tourists. With *abio,* we have the opposite theory that life on earth came from inanimate matter. For the birth of the human species, or *anthropogenesis,* we also have a choice: with *poly-,* many: *polygenesis,* the theory that races stem from several different recent ancestors, and its opposite with *mon-, monogenesis,* the theory that all races stem from one recent ancestor. *Holo* means whole; therefore: *hologenesis,* the theory that the human species originated everywhere rather than in one site.

The birth of each of us starts with germ cells, the egg, **oo,** and **sperm:** *oogenesis* for the birth of egg cells and *spermatogenesis* for the birth of sperm cells.

Other words formed with **genesis:**

ceno	+ **genesis**	recent appearance of ancestral characteristics
patho	+	source of disease
ana-	+	tissue regeneration
palino	+	regeneration, as of limbs
litho	+	production of calculi in body
histo	+	production of tissues
thermo	+	production of heat in animal bodies
xeno	+	birth of offspring unlike parents, also *heterogenesis*
stranger		
partheno	+	birth without spermatic contribution
virgin		
sym- + *phyo* + **genesis**		the idea that we result from a mixture of nurture (*phyo*) and nature (*genesis*)

IE *gen(e)* begat Gk. **gon,** seed, which produces words also having to do with the birth of things. **Gon** + *-ad* > *gonad,* ovary or testes. **Gon** or the long form **gonad** may appear in the first position.

gono	+ *rrhea*	lit. a flow from the gonads; cp. *diarrhea*
	+ *cyte*	embryonic reproductive cell

gonado	+ *-ism*	*gonadism*, deficient development of gonads
	+ *pathy*	disease of the gonads
	+ *pause*	a pause or decrease in gonadal function

Or in the second position: *cosmogony*, birth of the universe; *theogony*, birth of gods.

hyper-	+ **gonad** + *-ism*	excessive gonadal function
hypo-	+ +	too little gonadal function
amphi-	+ **gony**	birth from both: sexual reproduction
oo	+	birth of egg cells; also *oogenesis*
zoo	+	birth of living things in the body

Gonium: place for birth

| *oo* | + **gonium** | cellular source of ovarian egg |
| *spermato* | + | place for birth of sperm cells |

Gk. **gn**, which also evolved from IE *gen(e)*, is the base of *pregnant, cognate, benign,* and *malign.*

Heterogenesis can come about as a result of hybridization or mutation. Hybridization comes from L. *hybrida.* L. *mutare,* to change, gives *mutate, mutation, mutagen, immutable, transmutation, permutation, commute, commutation.*

15.2 Yoke

Gk. **gam** means marriage. In the more literal sense of marriage or mating between human beings, it appears in *monogamy, bigamy, polygamy,* and *misogamy,* morbid dread of being married. *Endogamy* dissects into marriage within the group; *exogamy* into marriage by someone outside of the group; *xenogamy* into marriage with strangers. There's even a word for the morbid condition of a person's being unable to perform sexual intercourse with anyone other than his or her own true beloved: *ideo,* self + *gam* + *-ism: ideogamism.* One who suffers from this condition is an *ideogamist.* The *ideo* here is the same as in *idiot.*

Metaphorically, **gam** refers to union of germ cells, or *gametes;* birth of gametes: *gamogenesis* or longer form, *gametogenesis.*

| *microgamete* | *macrogamete* | *homogamete* | *heterogamete* |
| *isogamete* | *anisogamete* | | |

crypto	+ **gam**	plant that reproduces by spores
karyo	+	union of nuclei
gameto	+ *petal* + *-ous*	pert. to union of petals
allo	+ **gamy**	cross-fertilization

All < Gk. *allos,* other, or foreign, is the base of *parallel,* the prefix Gk. *para-,* beside, a parallel line being lit. beside another line. If we combine **all** with *erg* < Gk. *ergon,* work, we come up with a small surprise: *allergy.* If we combine the two bases **all** + *erg* with *gen*, we have *allergen*, for something that produces an allergy. And **all** + *gam* = *allogamy*.

allele	an element in genetic mutation
allocentric	ant. to *egocentric*

IE *yeug*, to join

The only native English word that survives from this through Germanic is *yoke*. Cognate to *yoke* are two words from Sanskrit: *yoga*, the exercise, the yoking to a meditative practice, and *yogi*, the one who does it.

Many of the L. descendants of IE *yeug* would not appear in the biological vocabulary (for example, *joust*, a chivalric contest), but others although familiar are also part of that vocabulary (*join, joint, juncture*).

IE *yeug* > L. *jugum*, yoke, the base **jug** as in *conjugate*, lit. to join together, *subjugate*, lit. to be under the yoke.

jugate	yoked, joined
jugum	a structure that joins two others
jugular	e.g., *jugular vein*

IE *yeug* > Gk. base **zyg**, to join or yoke. In astronomy, this > *syzygy*, a condition for the alignment of several objects, e.g., sun, moon, and earth in an eclipse. For biology, **zyg** combines into *zygote*, the cell after union of gametes.

zygo + *matic*	pert. to a skull bone
+ *dactyl*	yoked talons, e.g., claw of parrots
zygoma	cheekbone
homo- + **zygo** + *-ous*	*homozygous*, relating to same alleles
hetero +	relating to different alleles

Like *gam* and *zyg*, the base *ploid* relates to stages of embryonic development. Like them also, this base has relatives that belong both to the general and the biological lexicon. *Ploid* originated, as did its cousins *plic*, *plex*, and *fold*, from the IE root *pel*.

IE *pel*, to fold

IE *pel* begins with *p*. L. and Gk. retained the orig. *p* sound:

L. *ple* > *multiple, quadruple, triple*

L. *plicare*, to fold > *pli*, as in *duplicate, replication, pliant*

L. *plectere*, to plait > *plex*, as in *complex, apoplexy, complection,* and *plexus,* a plaiting or network of structures, e.g., *solar plexus.*

IE *pel* became Gk. **ploid,** for folding in a literal or more often figurative sense.

ha	+ **ploid**	number of germ cell chromosomes; half that of somatic cells
di-	+	double that of gamete chromosomes
eu-	+	balanced set of chromosomes
an-	+ *eu-* + **ploid**	unbalanced set of chromosomes—too few or too many
poly-	+	many sets of homologous chromosomes; e.g., *triploid, tetraploid*
hetero-	+	abnormal chromosome total

Adding *-y,* for condition or state of, converts these adjectives into nouns: *haploidy, diploidy,* etc.

Diplo, folded double, is the base in *diploma,* orig. a document folded double, and from that, one who carried the document, the *diplomat.* **Diplo** appears in anatomy: *diploe,* cranial bone tissue, and in other fields.

diplo + *osis*	*diplosis,* condition of formation of full number of chromosomes
+ *blastic*	pert. to two distinct cell layers
+ *cephalus*	monster with two heads
+ *opia*	*diplopia,* double vision
Diplococcus	schizomycetes genus—fission fungi
Diplodocus	a dinosaur

Remembering that the descendants of Proto-Germanic changed the pronunciation of *p* to *f,* we can understand that native English words for folding will begin with that *f* sound: *fold* and its combinations, *twofold, manifold.*

15.3 The Cell

With respect both to basic research and commercial activity, the burgeoning field of molecular biology stands out as one of the most active in medicine today. Laboratories in this country and abroad are assiduously pursuing work to identify the genetic location for diseases such as hemophilia, sickle-cell anemia, Fragile X syndrome, muscular dystrophy, cystic fibrosis, Tay-Sach's, Gaucher's, Parkinson's and Alzheimer's diseases.

Research into genetic constitution has advantages other than the curative. Food and fuel are two basic needs of human beings and their economies. Inventions of tomatoes that taste good, of roses that smell good, and of corn that in the conversion to methanol might replace fossil fuel are harbingers of a future in which cell biology will play a critical role.

IE *kel,* to cover, hide

From Latin and Fr., E. adopted *conceal, cell (cellar* too), *clandestine, occult, color, cilium.*

From Gk. came *kol,* sheath = **cole,** sheath or vagina.

coleus	a plant of multi-colored leaves
Coleoptera	sheath-winged insects: beetles
coleorhiza	structure of developing plant
eucalyptus	etym., a well-covered plant
coleocele	hernia of the vagina

Also from Gk.: *calyp,* conceal, covering: *apocalypse, eucalyptus* and *calyx: calyx, Gymnocalycium.*

Grimm's law anticipates that E. cognates will begin with the sound of *h,* and that's justified with many words from the Proto-Germanic source, among them *hell, hole, hollow, hide.*

The principle governing the lexicon of *cell* and words for its parts shows that the first words coming into the language refer to larger parts, later words and metaphoric application to smaller parts more difficult to see and understand.

Cell begins its career in English in 1225, maintaining its literal meaning from L. *cella,* a small storeroom, a chamber. Somewhat over four hundred years later, in the 17th century, Robert Hooke used *cell* metaphorically. His and others' work defined the cell in general as we would define it now: the material of life bounded by a membrane. *Nucleus* entered E. in 1704, meaning a nut or kernal. It also took on its present meaning centuries later.

Although *cyte* is today a synonym of *cell,* it does not trace back to the same IE source. Its prehistoric source is IE *skeu,* which also meant to cover. Other than the base **cyte,** cell, and L. **cut,** skin, IE *skeu* did not contribute words to the biological vocabulary, though it did to the general vocabulary.

The labelling of cells—plant and animal, free as in protozoa and bound as in metazoa—and their parts began in the 17th century and continues in the 20th.

1615	*membrane*
1672	*cell* in its present meaning
1705	*celia*
1800	*flagella*
1831	*nucleus* in its present meaning
1840	*protoplasm,* physical basis of life

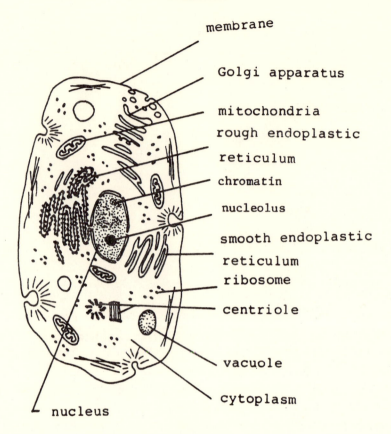

membrane

Golgi apparatus

mitochondria

rough endoplastic

reticulum

chromatin

nucleolus

smooth endoplastic

reticulum

ribosome

centriole

vacuole

cytoplasm

nucleus

The cell

1853   *vacuole,* reservoir for water
1870   *cytoplasm,* viscid and granular liquid that holds all organelles except nucleus
1875   *plastid,* an organelle of plant cells
1883   *chloroplast,* green pigment site for photosynthesis, coined by A.F.W. Schmper
1885   *chromosome,* site for genes
1895   *centrosome,* plays role in cell division
1897   *mitochondria,* agent for energy coined from *mito-* + *chondr* by Carl Benda in 1883 *Die Mitochondria*
1905   *organelle,* general term for cell organ
1908   *nucleotide,* molecules of DNA and RNA
1925   *genome,* total program of genes
1931   *dioxyribonucleic acid (DNA),* molecular component of chromosomes
1945   *ribonucleic acid (RNA),* strand complementary to DNA
1955   *lysosome,* structure holding digestive enzymes

1956   *ribosome*, organelle at which protein manufacture takes
        place; coined by R. B. Roberts in *Microsomal Particles*
        and Protein Synthesis

We'll undertake etymological examinations of two of the bases indicated in these terms: **nucl** and **plasm.**

IE *ken*, compression

Necking is, one would hope, an activity far removed from *nuclear* war, and both *necking* and *nuclear* have only, one would hope, a facetious relationship to *nutty*. Yet, these italicized words all stem ultimately from the same IE root, *ken*.

The part between the head and torso seems a compression, and hence IE *ken* went through Proto-Germanic into E. as *neck*. The sense of compression is also seen in another word from OE: *nut*, an object compressed in its shell. Germanic also produced *nook* and *nock*, a no ch. This IE *ken* (there are four other homophonic IE roots) also went into Latin as *nux*, nut, base **nuc** > *nucleus, nuclear, nuke;* and through French: *nougat*, which, as a confection with nuts, holds the original meaning.

nucleotide	an organic compound of sugar and other material
Thallasicola nucleata	a protozoan
Pinocola enucleator	pine-grosbeak

Gk. **kary,** nut or nucleus, may stem from IE *ker*, hard.

karyo	+ *type*		a profile of the chromosomes in the nucleus
	+ *gamy*		pairing of chromosomes during cell division
	+ *theca*		container for nucleus
diplo	+ **karyon**		double nucleus
pro-	+ **kary**	+ *-ote*	*prokaryote*, cell without nucleus
eu-	+	+	*eukaryote*, cell with nucleus
Caryota urens			wine-palm
Caryococcus			a bacteria parasite

A constitutent of the cell is its complex fluid or *protoplasm*, something formed. Protoplasm is composed of compounds of carbon, hydrogen, nitrogen, and oxygen. It came into English in the middle of the 19th century and was popularized by a biologist we've met several times in this text, T. H. Huxley, in his 1869 essay, "The Physical Basis of Life." Therein lies a tale in the history of popularization of scientific ideas.

Huxley was invited to give a talk to a Presbyterian congregation in Edinburgh. His friends warned him not to go, that he would be assaulted. However, he went and in his talk he claimed that there was no evidence for a spiritual basis of life, but only for the material of protoplasm and its activities. He defined protoplasm as the link that binds us and the lobsters we eat, a flower and the girl who wears it in her hair. When the talk was published, in 1869, it sent the magazine it appeared in into seven reprints. Such a sensation from a published essay had not happened in English for over a century. Huxley's perspective seemed like materialism if not atheism to its audience, and the essay provoked half a dozen rebuttals from those who believed there is a spiritual basis for life. Darwin was delighted by all the hoopla.

The prehistoric source of **plasm** is IE *pele*.

IE *pele*, flat, to spread

All the descendants in Proto-Germanic (e.g., *floor*) and Slavic (e.g., *polka*) and some of those in Greek (e.g., *planet*) and Latin (e.g., *plain*) are not relevant to the biological vocabulary.

L. *palma*	*palm*, tree and surface of hand
L. *plan*	*planaria*, a flatworm
Gk. **plasm**	*plasm, plasma, protoplasm, cytoplasm*
to mold, form	
plasmin	an enzyme that causes breakdown of fibrin
Plasmatoceras plastum	an ammonite
Plasmodium ovale	a protozoan responsible for malaria
plast	*plaster, plastic, chloroplast*
plasty	surgical repair
rhino + **plasty**	plastic surgery of the nose

Since many parts of the body can be repaired by plastic surgery, there are many words with **plasty** in them.

The 100,000 genes in the human body occupy sites on chromosomes. Each gene by itself or in collusion with other genes is responsible for instructing the manufacture of proteins. Genes line up in chromosomes consisting of DNA, ordered arrangements of four nucleotide bases. The arrangement is that of a double helix.

The word *helix* < Gk. has been employed for several different things, all of which have a spiral to them: in architecture, to a feature of columns; in mathematics, to a type of cone; in genetics, to a structure of chromosomal engagement; in natural history, to a snail; and in anatomy to the rim of the outer ear. *Helix* has been traced back to the productive IE *wel*.

Tagliacozzi, an Italian anatomist, invented plastic surgery as illustrated in this plate from his *Decurtorum chirurgia per insitionem*, 1597.

15.4 Semantic Shift

The vocabulary of cell development holds hundreds of terms, about two dozen in the sub-section identifying the development of blood cells. Most of the terms have the bases **cyte** and **blast** in them. These bases are compounded with the familiar prefixes *meta-, mega-, pro-,* and *mono-,* and with other bases. Some of these other bases are easy to define because they exist in the general vocabulary—*normo*, normal, *granulo*, grainy, or because we have come across them in other contexts: *hemo, erythro, lympho, karyo.* Only three bases may be thoroughly unfamiliar: *thrombo,* platelet; *reticulo,* reticulated, like a net; and *myelo,* marrow.

cyte **final** **form**	*erythrocyte* red blood cell	*thrombocyte* platelet	*lymphocyte* white blood cell	*granulocyte* white blood cell	*monocyte* macrophage
	reticulocyte	*megakaryocyte*		*metamyelocyte* *myelocyte*	
pro- *inter-*	*pronormo-* *blast*	*promegakaryo-* *cyte*	*prolympho-* *cyte*	*progranulo-* *cyte*	*promonocyte*

mediate
stage

blast	normoblast	megakaryo-	lymphoblast	myeloblast	monoblast
embryonic		*blast*			
stage					

hemocytoblast
stem cell

Terms in the general vocabulary have recently been exploited as metaphors having a narrowed meaning in cytology.

culture	nutrix for bacterial growth
colony	a homogeneous group of bacteria on a culture plate
splicing	hooking up pieces of DNA
	< Middle Dutch *splissen*
cloning	reproduction of DNA < Gk. *klon,* twig
ligation	attaching pieces of DNA; ligase, an enzyme, is used <
	L. *ligere,* to bind *ligere* also > *religion*
transcription	RNA replication of DNA
translation	conversion of RNA into amino acids in the cell's cytoplasm
expression	transcription of gene into RNA protein
interloping DNA	inserting a good gene into the ailing host's chromosomes
hybridization	attaching one strand of DNA to its complementary strand
packaging	a virus compounding DNA into its head

Those impressed by what biological science has achieved and is achieving daily feel confident that all diseases, including cancer, will go as extinct as smallpox. AIDS, acronym for Acquired Immune Deficiency Syndrome, at the moment of this writing, seems intractable. When—rather than if—a cure is found, that will result from investigation into what happens to cells when they are invaded by the AIDS virus. Viruses are capable of forcing the cell to form DNA necessary for viral reproduction.

In AIDS, the virus enters, debilitates, and finally kills macrophages, white blood cells that normally destroy viral invaders. The immune system being so injured, it can no longer muster defense against diseases, and the body becomes victim to them, especially to Kaposi's sarcoma and pneumocystis carinii.

Virus, technically defined as a nucleic acid that reproduces within and kills the host cell < L. *virus,* poison = **virus,** agent for infection. The word originally meant poison when it entered E. in 1590, a meaning the word *virulent* still holds: poisonous. *Virus* may have developed from IE *weis,* to flow, in which case— this is all problematic—its cognates are *ooze* (< OE *wase*); *viscous,* a thick fluid (< L.) and, even more uncertain, *weasel* (< Proto-Germanic) and *bison* (< L.).

A retrovirus, instead of making RNA from DNA as in most organisms, copies DNA from RNA.

Further research into cell biology will generate new terms produced mostly from compounding affixes and bases already in the biolexicon and new meanings of old terms, most of those from the common vocabulary. Today, *library* is used metaphorically for the total genome. Tomorrow, my daughter Laura advises me, the biolexicon might have *book* for a gene spliced out of the library. This raises the pleasant possibility of metaphoric use in genetic studies of *librarian*, *card catalogue*, and *overdue*.

CHAPTER 16—LIVING AND GROWING

16.1   Living: *viv, vit, bio, zoo, mut*
16.2   Growing: *phy, phyl, phyt, phyma, cres, cret, aux*
16.3   Bearing, Bearing Children: *fer, ferous, -fy, gest, bry, ky* or *cy, kyto* or *cyto, kyst* or *cyst*
16.4   Nourishing: *nutr, al, troph*

For origin or beginning, the general and biological vocabularies have the ubiquitous *gen,* and also Gk. *arche-* as in *archeology, archetype.* People who are for or against abortion are equally earnest in their opposed ethical orientations. *Are, abortion, earnest,* and *orientation* are cognates. What happened in this lexical tribe starts with an IE root for moving, *er.* This went into Proto-Germanic, from which issued English *are, art* (as verb), and *earnest.* The Proto-Germanic transmission is less certain than the Latin, wherein IE *er* became *oriri,* to arise, be born. Base **ori**(g) appears in *origin, aborigine,* and *orient, orientation;* base **ort** in *abort, abortion, abortifacient,* that which produces an abortion.

An economical way of listing and categorizing the many words having to do with these important events and also of appreciating cognates is to track the IE roots that relate to living, growing, giving birth, and nourishing.

16.1 Living

The bases for living, although they look very different today—*viv, vit, bio, zoo,* and even the archaic *quick* for life, as in being quick for being pregnant and the phrase the quick and the dead—are cognates, originating in a single IE source, *gwei.*

IE *gwei,* to live

   IE *gwei,* to live, became OE *cwic,* Modern English *quick,* which once held the archaic sense of alive, as in a phrase for pregnancy, quick with life. It became the L. bases **vivi** and **vita**.

vivid	*convivial*	*viviparous*	*joie de vivre*
revive	*vivacious*	*vivisect*	*vivax malaria*
survive	*vivify*	*vivarium*	*in vivo*
vital	*vitality*	*vitamin*	*arbor vitae*
vitals	*vitalism*	*vitalize*	*curriculum vitae*

A couple of terms in this inventory require a closer look. *Vitalism* is the philosophical notion that a mystical life principle imbues organic matter; Huxley specifically attacked vitalism in his essay "The Physical Basis of Life." *In vivo* means development of a being within the living body. The opposite of *in vivo* is *in vitro*, in glass, **vitr** base for glass in *vitreous*, like glass (e.g., *vitreous* humor of eyeball) and for sulphuric acid, as transparent as glass, in *vitriol*. *Vitriolic* means both pert. to sulphuric acid and in the common vocabulary to a remark that is heavily sarcastic, metaphorically acidic.

French renovation of the L. bases resulted in *viand, victual,* and *viable.*

IE *gwei* also entered Greek, where it transformed into three bases.

1. **bio** 100+ terms, including the following.

biology	*biotechnical*	*symbiosis*	*biopsy*
biochemistry	*bioelectrogenesis*	*symbiont*	*microbe*
biophysics	*bioluminescence*	*biogenesis*	*amphibian*
biodegrade	*agrobiology*	*abiogenesis*	*aerobics*
biography	*sociobiology*	*biocide*	*anaerobic*
bionics	*psychobiology*		

biota   a community of living beings in an environment
biome   the entire community and environmental conditions

These two words entered E. in the early 20th century.

2. **zoo,** meaning life rather than animal in *zoology, protozoa, zoogeography, zoophagy,* and many other terms. *Azot,* no life, is a base for nitrogen.

3. *hygies,* healthy with life, as in Hygeia, the goddess of health > *hygiene.*

Symbiosis appeared in E. in 1622, as a word for human communal living; in 1879, it expanded into a broader reference, for communal living of different species. There are three types of relationships between symbionts:

1. *mutualism* < **mut** < L. *mutare,* to change

Entered E. in 1539, but took on its present meaning in 1949: relationship in which partners contribute advantageously to each other, as with lichens. *Symbiodinium microadriaticum* consists of photosynthetic algae that synthesize fatty acids from carbon dioxide, the acids of use to an invertebrate partner that contributes waste to the algae. Tentacles of the sea anemone are poisonous to fish except for the clown fish that lives in them; payment for this protection is made by the fish's feeding the sea anemone with debris scattered from its own food. The plover performs dental hygiene on crocodile teeth, bird and reptile mutually profiting from the trade, the bird finding food and the reptile having its teeth cleaned. Many such commercial transactions occur between plants and insects.

2. *parasitism* < Gk. *para-* + *sit,* food + *-ism*

The Greek *parasitos* was a person who sat by the table with the host, careful to sit near the food. Latin adapted the word as *parasiticus* and changed the meaning a little: now the parasite flattered the host so that he could have access to leftovers from the table or elsewhere. 1727 is recorded as the year when the transference in meaning was made, parasite referring to a plant or animal that lived off another. Unlike mutualism, where both partners benefit, in parasitism one benefits and the other suffers. A convenient division is that between *endoparasites,* such as nematodes, blood flukes, *Trypanosoma brucei rhodesiensis,* a hemoflagellate that causes African sleeping sickness, the tapeworm *Taenia solium* and ectoparasites such as fleas, ticks, leeches.

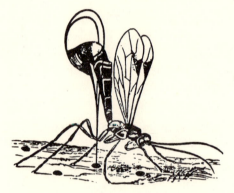

Ichneumon wasp displaying ovipositor

3. *commensalism* < L. *com-* + *mensa,* table + *-ism*

Entering E. in 1350, the word literally meant eating at the same table; in 1876, it took on its symbiotic meaning: an association in which one member or mensa-mate benefits and the other neither benefits nor suffers. An example is Remora, the shark sucker, which attaches itself to a shark and shares the disinterested shark's food.

16.2 Growing

We might anticipate that the Indo-Europeans, like other people, would be much interested in their own existence. Such an interest is reflected in the several sources for existing and growing.

IE *bheue,* to be, exist, grow

From Proto-Germanic descendants have come about twenty words (e.g., *husband,* lit. existing in the house, and the verb *be*). Not many words from

Ichneumon larvae parasitizing caterpillars

Latin: *fiat, future* and perhaps *filius,* as in *affiliate.* Gk. *phy* has generated words that exist almost exclusively in the biological vocabulary. The base means nature or growth, and as *phy* itself exists in few words, e.g., *symphyocephaly,* condition of fetal twins joining at head. The more generative bases are **phys, phyl, phyt, phyma.**

phys, nature	*physics, physicist, physician, physiology*
physic	an archaic term for medicine
metaphysics	the study of that which transcends physics or the natural world
dia- + **physis,** growth	the shaft of a long bone
sym- +	a growing together, as of chinbones
epi- +	a growth on a bone
epiphyseal plate	part which grows until pubertal hormones stop height increase
physio + *graphy*	an archaic word for study, charting of, the earth
+ *gnomy*	*physiognomy,* determination of character through features of physical body, esp. of face
phyl, ancestry	*phylum, phyla, phyletic, phylogeny*
cyto + **phyletic**	geneology of cells
homo- +	sharing same ancestry
phyte, plant	
neo- + **phyte**	*neophyte,* lit. a new growth, now a novice, an

		apprentice; > *imp*
micro-	+	a microscopic plant
epi-	+	a plant that grows on another, e.g., orchid
sapro	+	a plant that grows on rotten matter
oo	+	not growth of egg, but a stage of development of sex organs in mosses
phyto	+ *biology*	*phytobiology,* study of plants
	+ *phagous*	plant-eating
	+ *genesis*	origin and development of plants
	+ *therapy*	using plants in treatment
	+ *parasite*	plant parasite
	+ *pathy*	a disease of plants
Phytomonas		genus of flagellate protozoa
Trichophyton rosaceum		a ringworm fungus
rhino	+ **phyma,** growth	growth on nose
encephalo	+	growth in brain

Sound exists in four different homophones in English—it's a noun for a vibration of air (from L. *sonus*) and a body of water (from OE *sund,* related to *swim*), it's an adjective for health (from OE *gesund,* cp. *gesundheit*), and it's a verb, *to sound,* for measurement, ultimately < L. *subundare,* under the waves. The IE vocabulary similarly had clusters of homophones. One of these clusters was pronounced *ker;* each of the six homophonic *kers* was an ancestor of at least one word relevant to the biolexicon.

Ker 1, which is considered an echoic root, was examined in the section on echoism. From *ker* 2, to decay, came a single descendant, L. > E.: *caries.* From *ker* 3, a cherry, two descendants, L. > E.: *cornel,* a dogwood tree and, Gk. > E., *cherry.* From *ker* 4, fire, L. > E.: *carbon, carbuncle, cremate* (E. cognate, *hearth*). The descendants of *ker* 5, horn and head, will be presented in Chapter 19.

The IE *ker* we're concerned with here meant to grow.

IE *ker,* to grow

Of most direct pertinence are *create* and *procreate,* both from L. descendant *credre,* to produce. From L. also came the fertility goddess *Ceres* and the word formed from her name, *cereal.* L. bases **cres** and **cret** were modified in French so that there are some surprising cognates here.

crescent	concrete	excretion	increase
concrescence	concretion	accretion	decrease
excrescence	secretion	sincere	recruit
increment			

Gk. *auxein,* to increase, grow

aux	*auxocardia, auxometer*
heterauxesis	differential increase in growth
tachyauxesis	faster growth of one part
aug	*augment, augmentor*

For the growth or swelling of parts, several bases are available. Fr. L. *tumere,* to swell, **tum,** as in *tumor, tumid, detumescence, tumefacient.* Fr. L. *torgere,* a swelling out, **turg** as in *turgid, turgescent, turgometer.* And fr. L. *nodus,* a knot, *node, nodule,* and adjectives *nodose* and *nodulous.* Gk. gave E. *-oma,* a cancerous tumor, and **edema,** for swelling. Gk. *phys(a),* blow, inflate *emphysema*

16.3 Bearing, Bearing Children

The following box includes bases that are widely used in the biolexicon: from L: *fer* and its suffix forms *ferous* and *-fy,* and from Gk.: *pher* and *phor.*

IE *bher,* carry, bear (children)

Celtic remnant of IE *bher* is the name of a town; among the few remnants from OE are *bear* and *birth.*

L. *ferre,* to carry

fer	*fertile, transfer, transference*
	circumference, suffer
afferent	that which carries to, as a nerve
efferent	that which carries from, out to
vas deferens	tube for conduct of sperm
Apis mellifera	the honeybee; species name: carrying honey
Porifera	phylum of sponges
ferous, bearing	
carboni + **ferous**	strata bearing carbon
coni +	trees bearing cones (not *coni,* dust)
fossili +	strata bearing fossils
somni +	that which causes sleepiness
seti +	bearing bristles
costi +	bearing ribs

-fy, bearing, carrying *ramify, petrify, vivify*

L. *lat*—*lat* is the past participle form of *ferre,* to bear

ab- + *lat* + *-ion*	*ablation,* surgical removal of growth
sublation	elevation
Gk. *pherein,* to carry	*paraphernalia*

---

pher	*periphery*
pheromone	a chemical attractant
	mone clipped from *hormone*
tocopherol	a vitamin that has property of vitamin E
	Gk. *toco* is a base for childbirth: *tocology*, a rare
	word for *obstetrics*

phor

metaphor	*oophore*	*phosphorous*
euphoria	*oophorectomy*	*phosphorescent*
dysphoria	*spermatophore*	*chromatophore*

aero	+ **phore**	that which is borne by air
chaetao	+	bearing hair
xeno	+ **phoria**	act of an animal (e.g., crab)
		cementing bits of foreign matter to its shell
dia-	+ **phoresis**	profuse perspiration, lit. a carrying through
iso-	+	state of equality between both eyes
ampoule		a glass vial
ampulla		lit. jar, also sense organ as with sharks

L. *gerere*, to carry, act, do

gest	*gesture, digest, digestion, congest congestive, ingest*
gesticulate	to make gestures
gestation	pregnancy period for animal or idea, v., *gestate*

Gk. *bruein* means to grow; from the prefix *en-* + **bry** came the word for that which grows within, or *embryo*. The stage between zygote and fetus. Remembering that the way to understand biological and to a lesser degree other scientific terminology is to know the parts, words such as *embryology* and *embryonic*, and even *embryogenesis*, should be easy to translate.

Gk. *kyein*, to swell, be pregnant

cy

cyesis	pregnancy
cyesio + *-ology*	study of pregnancy
+ *gnosis*	diagnosis of pregnancy
ek- + **cyesis**	*eccyesis*, fertilized egg in wrong place, ectopic
pseudo- +	false pregnancy

cyto, cell	*cytoplasm, cytometer, oocyte*
cytaster	star-like structure in developing cell
desmocyte	early stage of fibroblast, cell that develops fibrous
	tissues
leukocytopoiesis	production of white blood cells

histiocyte	a macrophage; presence of abnormal histiocyte: *histiocytosis*
cyst, sac	*cystitis, cystoma, cysticotomy*
cystocele	protrusion of bladder

For to give birth to, one might use that E. phrase itself, the very productive Gk. base *gen,* the L. base *par(t),* or the Gk. base **toco.**

Gk. **toco,** childbirth

tocology or *tokology*	a syn. for *obstetrics*
tokodynamometer	instrument to measure uterine contractions
bradytocia	slow delivery
eutocia	ordered, good delivery
dystocia or *distocia*	difficult delivery
embryotocia	abortion
thelytocia	virgin birth of females
tocolytic	drug used to stop uterine contractions
Tocotrema lingua	a flatworm
Taeniotoca lateralis	blue perch

16.4 Nourishing

We can look forward in this section to sibling relationships between *nourish* and *nurse; elder* and *adult; alimony* and *alma mater; adolescent* and *werewolf.*

IE *(s)nau,* to flow, and in sense that milk flows: to suckle

No native English words from this source, but one offspring in Greek: *naiad,* a water nymph; and a few offspring in the medical vocabulary from L. *nutrire,* to suckle, base **nutr.**

L. nutr   *nutrition, nutrient, nurture, nutriment, nourish, nurse*

IE *al,* to grow, nourish

This is the source of the native English words *old, elder, alderman* and, surprisingly, *world. World* was once *wer-ald,* the first part meaning man (still alive in the word *werewolf*) and the second meaning age.

IE *al* became L. *alere,* to nourish, its base **al** in

aliment	that which nourishes (and a place for nourishment: *alimentary*)

alimony	lit. the state of being nourished
alma mater	lit. the nourishing mother

Also from *alere: alumni, adolescent, adult, coalesce;* and from related L. sources: *altitude, haughty, exalt, enhance, abolish, prolific* and *proletarian.*

This chapter on living and growing concludes with charting an IE root that led to viable descendants only in Greek. We might recall that it is possible to confuse the base **troph,** which relates to nourishment and development, with *trop,* which relates to turning. *Heliotrophic* means being nourished by, developed by, sunlight, while *heliotropic* means turning towards the sun.

IE *threph,* to nourish, develop

Gk. *trepso* + *logy*	study of nutrition
trophy	*atrophy, dystrophy*
ulatrophy	no nourishment to gums, shrinkage of gums
hypotrophy	failure of nourishment for tissues
tropho + *logy*	study of nutrition
+ *blast*	layer that transmits nourishment to embryo
eu- + **troph** + *-ic*	well-nourished
photo +	nourished, taking energy from light
tricho +	pert. to condition of nourishing hair

CHAPTER 17—SENSING

17.1   Seeing
17.2   Hearing
17.3   Tasting
17.4   Touching
17.5   Smelling
17.6   Other Senses
17.7   Doing and Closing

Whether we are born with any innate knowledge is a question this text makes no attempt to answer. But it is certain that much if not all of what we know comes to us through our sense organs and is transmitted into our brains where final understanding or misunderstanding takes place.

Three bases for sense, feeling, perception, are *pass (passion compassion), path; sens, sent;* and *esthes.* An immediately important point about **path** is that it can mean feeling, disease, or treatment.

Feeling	Disease	Treatment
pathos	*pathology*	*homeopathy*
pathetic	*psychopathology*	*osteopathy*
apathetic	*andropathy*	*ideopathy*
sympathy	*myopathy*	*echopathy*
antipathy	*lalopathy*	*aeropathy*
empathy	*coleopathia*	*hydropathy*
telepathy	*paleopathology*	*heliopathy*
	etiopathology	*thermopathy*
		cryopathy

L. *sent,* **sens,** feel

sentiment	*sensation*	*sensual*
sentient	*sensitive*	*sensuous*
presentiment	*sensible*	*sensilla*
resentment	*sensor*	*sensory*

sensorium   a place in the nerves registering sensation

Gk. **esthes,** feeling

aesthetics		science of an appreciation of beauty
an-	+ **aesthesia**	cond. of having no feelings; the science responsible for deletion of feeling: *anesthetics*
hemi-	+	partial lack of feeling or perception
hyper-	+	excessive sensitivity in feeling
syn-	+	describing one sense in terms of another
kin		feeling, sensation, of movement
acanth	+	perception of being pricked as by a thorn
cry	+ **anesthesia**	failure to feel cold

Synaesthesia needs examples: "warm red," "loud purple," "colorful sonata," Charles Pierre Baudelaire's describing the aroma of perfume as "soft as oboes, green as meadows." The *aesthete* is a person who really appreciates beauty, or who pretends to.

OE words often have a more concrete, familiar and even indecorous sense to them than do words from Greek and Latin. The adoptions from Romance languages may give us more subtle understanding. In any case, often the noun for a sense organ is an English word, or common French term, while the adjective < Gk. or L. as in the following examples.

Sense organ		Sense		Adjectives	
eye	ON	*see*	OE	*ocular, visual*	L.
				optical	Gk.
ear	OE	*hear*	OE	*auditory*	L.
nose	OE	*smell*	OE	*nasal*	L.
				olfactory	L.
tongue	OE	*taste*	Fr.	*gustatory*	L.
feel	OE	*touch*	Fr.	*tactile*	L.

One could propose that there is a hierachy of senses, from the more primitive—touching, tasting, feeling, smelling, discerning temperature—to the more civilized—hearing and seeing. A poem thoroughly saturated in appeals to the senses is Robert Browning's "Meeting at Night-Parting at Morning."

Meeting at Night

I

The grey sea and the long black land;
And the yellow half-moon large and low;
And the startled little waves that leap
In fiery ringlets from their sleep,
As I gain the cove with pushing prow,
And quench its speed i' the slushy sand.

II

Then a mile of warm sea-scented beach;
Three fields to cross till a farm appears;
A tap at the pane, the quick sharp scratch
And blue spurt of a lighted match,
And a voice less loud, thro' its joys and fears,
Than the two hearts beating each to each!

Parting at Morning

Round the cape of a sudden came the sea,
And the sun looked over the mountain's rim:
And straight was a path of gold for him,   him: the sun
And the need of a world of men for me.

We will proceed to examine terms, especially in the biological vocabulary, for the senses, moving, as "Meeting at Night" does, from seeing to other senses.

17.1 Seeing

The L. base **spec** gives the biolexicon *species, specimen, speculum, specific, special, specialist* among three dozen other words. Its cognates in Gk. are *skep* and **scope.**

skeptic	*microscope*	*horoscope*	*bronchoscope*
skeptical	*telescope*	*spectroscope*	*colposcope*
skepticism	*cystoscopic*	*stethoscope*	*rhinoscopy*
	fluoroscope		

skiascope   instrument for viewing a shadow

Speculum, a Roman mirror

IE *weid,* to see

This IE source has living descendants in five language families: Sanskrit, Celtic, Proto-Germanic, Greek, and Latin. Of the first three languages, the only word relevant to biological language—to natural history—is the name of a bird, *penguin* < Celtic *pen,* head + *gwyn,* white.

Gk.

eidos, form	suffix *-oid* as in *android, kaleidoscope*
idea, form	base **idea** seven kinds of ideas are listed in the psychiatry inventory (e.g., *fixed idea* or in Fr. *idee fixe*)
	base **ideo** — *ideation, ideomuscular*
	Homophone **ideo** meaning own, peculiar to one's self, in *idiot, idiosyncrasy, ideogamist*
idioglossia	one's own incoherent speech; cp. *ideologism, idiolalia, ideopathic*
histor, wise	*history, story, wise*

L. *videre,* to see
  vid and *vis*   *video, evidence, vision, view*

17.2 Hearing

L. **aud, aur,** listen to

auditory	*aural*	*auripuncture*
audible	*subural*	*preauricular*
audience	*postaural*	*auricle*

aurilave   instrument to wash out ear

Homophones **aur** gold, as in *auriferous, aurotherapy, aurococcus;* and *aur,* breath, halo, as in *aura.*

aus
ausculation   listening to sounds in body
ausculoplectrum   an instrument for such listening

Gk. acou. to hear   *acoustics*
presby + **acusia**   old age deficiency in hearing
brady- +   slow, dull hearing
diplo- + **acusis**   *diplacusis,* abnormal breaking of one sound into two
Craspedacustes sowerbyi   a medusa

L. son(at), to make a sound	*sonic, resonance, sound*
soni + ferous	that which carries sound, adj. for ear trumpet

17.3 Tasting

L. **gust** < *gustus,* to taste

gustatory	adj. pert to sense of taste
gustometry	measurement of taste thresholds

De gustibus non disputatum est — About taste, there is no disputing.

One of the unexpected etymological pairs to show up in our inventory is a family relationship between eating and pain. Words for eating, for dental structures, and a base for pain trace back to the IE root *ed,* to eat or devour. The line of descent makes relatives of an elephant's tusk, an edible snail, an obese person, and a headache.

IE *ed,* to eat, devour

   Proto-Germanic to E. *eat, tooth, tusk, fret,* which orig. meant to eat up, devour; to German to E.: *etch*

L. ed, es, eat

ed	*edible*
es	
comestible	able to be eaten
escargole	edible snail
escarole	plant for salads
obese, obesity	at first, *obese* < *ob-,* intensive + *es* was applied to a person etched away, really skinny; it changed to apply to such a person who ate all he or she could
Greek **odyne,** pain	metaphor may be that of pain gnawing at the victim
an- + **odyne**	medication or other help to kill pain
cephalo + **odynia**	headache; also *cephalgia*
glosso +	pain in the tongue
omo +	pain in the shoulder

For sharing, the Indo-Europeans had the word *bhag.* This went into Persian, from which the modern English word *baksheesh,* a tip, bribe, gratuity. In the sense of sharing one's food, IE *bhag* gave rise to Gk. *phagein,* to eat, base **phag.**

Gk. **phag,** devour, eat

Sarcophagous pertains to eating of flesh; *sarcophagus* to a tomb. Ancient tombs had corrosive substances such as lime that ate away the flesh of the corpse. *-Ous* is a suffix that makes adjectives as in these two words and also in *anthropophagous*, pert. to cannibalism.

phage, cell that eats other cells	*phagia, phagous* eating, devouring	*phagist*, one who eats, devours
phagocyte	*aphagia*	*tachyphagist*
macrophage	*dysphagia*	*geophagist*
bacteriophage	*bradyphagia*	*onychophagist*
karyophage	*tachyphagia*	*anthropophagi*
	sarcophagous	

Xylophaga dorsalis   a mollusk that eats wood

Ogden Nash, "Funebrial Reflections":

Among the anthropophagi
People's friends are people's sarcophagi.

L. **vora** < *vorare*, to eat, is a synonym of *phag*.

voracious	*carnivorous*	*lactivorous*
herbivorous	*insectivorous*	*devour*

Vermivora celata, a worm-eating warbler

What we taste can be sweet, salty, sour, or bitter. These words and many more — our taste buds respond to many sensations — have histories. We'll trace two particularly intriguing histories going back to ancient Indo-European. In Latin, the base for salt is *sal* (identical or similar forms in all the Romance and Germanic languages, e.g., Italian *sale* and Swedish *salt*); in Russian, it's *sol;* and in Irish, *salann*. Transference of IE *s* to an *h* (cp. *serpent/herpes*) is seen in Greek *halas* and Welsh *halen*. It's hypothesized that the IE person sitting at dinner used the word *sal* for the condiment. The biolexicon uses the Gk. doublet **hal** for salt: *halogen, halophyte, haloid.*

A longer, more complicated, and less certain history attends the word *sugar* and the base *sacchar*. No IE root has been identified as the source of these words. The reason for this is that the original Indo-European people did not have or know of sugar. To satisfy their sweet tooth, they used honey. But one of the migrating tribes came to a land where the sugar cane was indigenous: India, and they invented or maybe took from the original natives the word *sarkara*. Alexander the Great was delighted at his first taste of sugar. Long after Alexander's conquest, Sanskrit *sarkara* went into Italian as *zucchero*, and from there to French as *sucre* and to Middle English, in 1250, as *sugre*, which of course became our *sugar* and, not so obviously, *sucrose. Sugarcoat, sugarloaf,* and *sugar daddy* owe their existence to Sanskrit *sarkara*.

In another direction, the Indo-Iranian root developed into Greek *sakcharon*, from which **sacchar**. As early as 1665, a coiner of words turned to this Greek base for *saccharine*, very sweet, nowadays more applicable to a smile than to a sugar. A century later, other coiners invented *sacchariferous*, an adj. for a vegetable that holds sugar, *sacchariferous,* and *saccharize.* In the next hundred years, still others invented, in chronological order, *saccharic, saccharate, saccharoid, saccharify* (making starch into sugar), *saccharimeter,* and, in 1875, *saccharose* and the most familiar of all, *saccharin.* All of this illustrates again the productivity resulting from the practice of combining a base with affixes.

17.4 Touching

For bases delivering the sense of touch, we'll depart from narrative and return to inventories and boxes.

IE *tag,* to touch

    Into L. as *tangere,* to touch, from which bases

tact	*tact, tactile, intact, contact*
	tactometer, tactoreceptor
tag	*contagious;* variant of base in *contiguous*
tang	*tangible, tangent, tangoreceptor*

    The development of L. *tangere* also generated *attain, contaminate, entire, integer, taste,* and *tax* having the sense of touch, as in the revenue service's *tax* and *taxicab.* The homophonic *tax* means order, as in *taxonomy, syntax,* and *tactics,* lit. the science of ordering.

Three less well known bases are (*h*)*aph* and *ap, palp, sphygm,* and *sphinct.*

Gk. *haptein,* to touch, fasten, grasp

(h)aph, ap	*synapse*
haptic	tactile
haptometer	instrument to measure sense of touch
dysaphia	abnormal sense of touch
karyapsis	joining of nuclei
telosynapsis	union of chromosomes

L. palp, touch	*palpable*
palp	sense organs of some invertebrates
palpate	touching in diagnosis

Gk. *sphygm,* pulsation	
sphygmus	the pulse; *sphygmoid*
	sphygmograph
Gk. sphinct, tight	*sphincter*

IE *kap*, to seize

This went through Proto-Germanic into English to come out as E. *haven* and a few other words. Grimm's Law indicates that Proto-Germanic *h* finds a parallel in L. *k*: *haven* is a suitable cognate of L. *recuperate*.

IE *kap* went into L., from which four bases. The base *cap*, to seize, and its French renovations appear in dozens of words, among them *capture, capsule,* and *capacity.* The base *cup* is in *recuperate,* lit. to return from capture; and the base *cip* in *anticipate, participate, emancipate, recipe* and the abbreviation for a medical recipe: *Rx.* The fourth base is important enough to deserve bolding:

cep(t)

forceps	*inception*	*reception*	*receive*
intercept	*susceptible*	*receptor*	*amboceptor*
		perception	*perceive*
		deception	*deceive*

capsa from Pompeii

intussusception   folding of one part of intestine into another

IE *kap* became Gk. *cope*, oar, from which *copepod,* an oar-foot or small crustacean.

IE *ten*, to stretch

Many technical terms from Gk. and dozens of both technical and common from L. and Fr.

Gk.

tono	*tone, tonic, sphygmotonometer*
peritoneum	membrane that's stretched over viscera
ten	*tendon, tenotomy, tetanus < tetano,* rigid
tenomyoplasty	plastic surgery of tendon
neoteny	retention of fetal or infantile features in adult; also called *paedogenesis*

Gk. **ectasis**, stretching	*lithectasy, splenectasis* *brochiectasis*
L. *ten*, stretch	*tent, attentuate, tentorium*
tend	*distend, extend, intend, tendon*
tens	*distention, extensor, intensive, tensible*

Some sources have produced words which do not stray far from the original literal meaning. Two examples of these are L. *premere*, to press, and *pellere*, to push, drive, beat, throb.

	L. *premere* **press**	L. *pellere* **pel**	**puls**
com-	*compress*	*compel*	*compulsion, -ive*
de-	*depress*		
	decompression		
dis-		*dispel*, lit. to drive apart	
ex-	*express*	*expel*	*expulsion*
in-	*impress*	*impel*	*impulse*
inter-	*interpellant*		
re-	*repress*	*repel* *repellant*	*repulsion, repulsive*
retro-	*retropulsion*		
sub-	*suppress*		
latero-			*lateropulsion*

For itching: Gk. **psora** > *psoriasis,* a disease of skin, and L. **pruri** > *pruritis,* itching and *prurient,* that which brings on an itch, such as erotic art.

Gk. *karoun,* to stupefy, became the source for an artery which when squeezed causes stupefaction > *carotid.*

L. *mittere, mit(t)* to send, throw *intromittent*	*transmit*
miss	*remission, transmissible*
commissure	juncture of parts
Gk. *henai,* (h)e(n) to send, let go	*enema, paresis, catheter*
Gk. *stellein* to send, contract	
stal	*peristalsis, anastalsis*
stol	*diastole, systole, peristole*
bradydiastolic	abnormally slow diastole

From the L. infinitive *jacere,* to throw, comes the base *ject.* This appears in several words relevant to both vocabularies: *subject,* lit. that which is thrown under; *eject,* reject(ion), injection, dejection. Its corollary base is *jact* as in *ejaculate, adjacent, subjacent, superjacent.*

The last item relates to moving, from Gk. *kineein,* to move > base **kin** and **cin.**

kinaesthesia	*echokinesia*	*cinema*
kinetoblast	*ookinesis*	*cinemascopy*
autokinetic	*karyokinesis*	*cinesalgia*
photokinetic	*hyperkinesia*	

17.5 Smelling

Different organisms receive information about their environments from different sense organs: sharks enjoy the ampullae of Lorenzini, niches which are sensitive to electrical emissions of prey; snakes flick their tongues to carry to Jacobsen's organ in the mouth particles of odor; bats use sonar. The olfactory tissue of a dog's snout is much more extensive than the olfactory tissue of a human nose.

The ability to smell is not one of the nobler talents of human beings, as indicated in the etymology of *stink,* which has undergone pejoration, a descent in value, from its original meaning of smell. Memory of smells seems particularly intense and even dangerous, as indicated in the comparatively (compared to sound and vision) few references to smell in poetry. A zinger is provided by T. S. Eliot's "Whispers of Immortality": after treating very dry poets, such as John Donne, he turns to a courtesan named Grishkin:

> The sleek Brazilian jaguar
> Does not in its arboreal gloom
> Distill so rank a feline smell
> As Grishkin in her drawing room.

Evidence of civilized peoples'—or at least of Americans'—disdain for body odors is provided in the billions of dollars spent each year to erase odors from mouth, armpit, and elsewhere.

L. *od* < *olere,* to smell
od, ol, to emit a smell

odor	*olfactory*
malodorous	*redolent* (*red-* acts as intensive)
odoriferous	*olfactometer*

Solidago odora	goldenrod
Viola odorata	violet

Gk. **osm** < *osme,* smell	*ozone,* a gas with a strong odor
osm + *aesthesia*	*osmesthesia,* perception of odors
osmonarcotic	narcosis brought on by odors
para- +	*parosmia,* disorder in perception of odors

eu- +	normal ability to perceive odors
hyper- +	excessive sensitivity to odors
Osmanthus ulicifolius	holly-leaved olive

Another **osm,** meaning impulse, is homophonic with this **osm;** impulse **osm** appears in *osmosis, chemiosmosis,* a production of ATP, and *osmometer,* instrument to measure osmotic force.

aroma < Gk.	adj. *aromatic*
Rhus aromatica	fragrant sumac
Aromachelys odorata	musk-turtle

17.6 Other senses

Though seeing, hearing, tasting, touching, and smelling are the five senses that would come to mind in any inventory, there are other senses that animals have, for example, a sense of equilibrium, a pit viper's sense of heat in prey, a bat's radar.

Gk. *cryos,* cold > **cry** and **crym**

crystal	*cryaesthesia*	*crymopathy*	*crymophile*
cryoplankton	*cryanesthesia*	*cryophylactic*	*crymotherapy*
cryobiology	*cryogen*	*crypreservation*	*crymophyte*

cryophylactic	pert. to an organism that thrives in cold; also *psychro-philic*
Crymophilus rufus	a bird

Less often used than **cry(m)o** for cold is Gk. *psychro,* which forms synonyms with **cry(m)o:** *psychrophilic, psychrotherapy.*

Gk. *therme,* heat > **therm**

Of the scores of terms with **therm** in them, we'll list only those compounded with bases and affixes we're already met or will meet. *Thermal* and *thermic* are adj. relating to heat.

Orientation	Disorders	Treatment	Instrument
thermotaxis	*hypothermy*	*diathermy*	*thermometer*
thermotropism	*thermoplegia*	*thermotherapy*	*thermostat*
thermophile	*thermalgia*	*thermolysis*	*thermolamp*
		thermoanalysis	*thermograph*
		thermanesthesia	

Other terms

thermonuclear	*synthermal*	*thermogenesis*

thermolabile	*thermoreceptor*	*thermosiphon*
thermostabile		

thermoform	to shape by heating
thermostasis	maintenance of internal heat, as with mammals
Thermobia domestica	silverfish

L. *calere,* to be warm	*caldron, chowder, nonchalant* (not hot) *calorie, calefacient,*
	subcalorism, decalescence
L.: *siccus,* dry > **sicc**	*desiccated, siccolabile, siccostabile, siccimeter*
Gk. *xeros,* dry > **xero**	*Xerox, elixir*

xerophyte	*xerophilous*	*xerography*	*xeropthalmia*
colpoxerosis	*largyngoxerosis*	*xeroderma*	*xerophyte*

Xerus rutilans	a squirrel

17.7 Doing and Closing

Sensing is part of the larger category of doing, of acting and reacting. Two prehistoric Indo-European roots have been used for doing: *ag* and *werg*. From the first through the intermediary of Latin come the words *acting* and *reacting* and other words as much at home in the general as in the biological vocabulary. The Greek descendants, as usual, are more technical. This is the case also with descendants from *werg:* Latin offspring are more familiar than the Greek. This small section closes with a third IE box presenting bases for closing, another kind of doing.

IE *ag* to drive, do

   No survivors from this root exist in any of the languages from Proto-Germanic. But survivors do exist from L and Gk. descendants.

   The L. bases are *ag* and *act.*

agent	*act*	*reaction*
agency	*transact*	*seroreaction*

   Placing the prefix *co-* before the base *ag* renders *coagere,* to drive together, its sense that of compress. *Coagulate* means to compress into a mass. An argument that really drives to the point is *cogent.* The L. source went into Fr. as *esquatir,* to crush, and that developed into the E. *squat.*

   IE *ag* went into Gk. as the bases *ag* (*agony*) and **agog**, that which leads: *pedagogue,* one who leads children, teaches them; that which excites or leads to

---

the production of: *hvpnagogue, galactagogue, lithagogue.* The adj. suffix *-ic* can be applied, e.g., *chromagogic.*

Also from Gk.: *axiom* and **agra**, seizure, as in *pellagra* and *podagra.*

IE *werg*, to do

Proto-Germanic > English *work.* Into Greek and from there into English as bases for work. *Orgv* orig. referred to the work involved in secret religious rites, now generalized to the work involved in private sexual rites or wrongs.

org   *organ, organism, organization, etc.*
erg

| *allergv* | *energy* | *ergophobia* | *ergograph* | *ergocardiography* |
| *allergen* | *energize* | *ergomania* | *ergometer* | |

surgerv   < *chir,* hand + **erg,** working by hand
adrenergic   pert. to nerve fibers that initiate release of epinephrine, etc.

cacergasia   bad or poor work or function
ergasthenia   weakness caused by overwork
Polvergus lucidus   an ant

a- +   **erg**   *argon,* a gas that is inert, does no work
a- + *svn-* + **ergy**   not working together, lack of coordination between parts usually coordinated

---

IE *kleu*, peg, hook

From IE to Germanic to OE: *lot,* and from related Dutch: *lottery.* From IE to Greek *kleiein,* to close, sheathe, to E.

cleis. a closure
cleistothecium   case that encloses spore body
iridenclesis   surgical procedure for draining eye

One etymology of the base *clit* traces it to this Gk. source: *clitoris, clitoridectomy, Clitoria mariana,* butterfly-pea.

The form of the collarbone, hook-shaped, inspired the metaphoric use of **cleid,** hook, to **cleid,** clavicle.

cleid   *cleidagra, cleidotomy*

From L. sources: *clava,* club > *clavicorn, claviform, clavate;* and **clavi,** key > *clavichord, clavicle.*

L. *claudere,* to close
clud, clus   *include, inclusion, occlude, occlusion*

Also: *closure, enclose, claustrophobia,*
Planorbis clausulatus,   a gastropod

CHAPTER 18—THINKING

18.1 Breathing
18.2 Distinguishing
18.3 Expressing
18.4 Knowing

18.1 Breathing

We have already surveyed the echoic **pneu** and **pnea** as bases for breathing and lungs. The mind—not the brain, a subject for the chapter on anatomy—has often been associated with the breath, as with *psyche*. L. *spirare* means to breathe; its base refers not just to breathing, but to the mind or an even more elusive entity, the soul.

L. spir	*respire, inspire, spirit,* etc.
conspiracy	lit., a breathing together
spiro + *chaete*	*spirochete*, a pathogenic microorganism
spira + *-cle*	a breathing or air hole

Gk. thym, breath, spirit	
dys- + **thymia**	depression
amphi- +	manic-depressive state
lipo +	faintness
to fail	
poikilo +	state of swings in mood

Homophonic *thym* refers to the thymus gland.

Gk. no, nous, mind	*paranoia, eunoia, hypernoia, noumenon*
noo + *kleptia*	stealing of one's mind or ideas
noegenesis	the birth of new knowledge from sensing or thinking

A curious etymological specimen is *noothymopsychic,* which analyzes into mind-mind-mind and pertains to the intellectual and the affective processes of the mind.

L. mens, ment	*mental,* etc.

Homophones are **mens,** month, and **mens,** table.

18.2 Distinguishing

IE *gwhren,* to think

No survivors into English from any of the IE languages except Greek. From Gk. *phrazein,* to show, come *phrase, paraphrase, metaphrase* —a word-for-word translation. From Gk. *phren,* the mind and what the mind was thought to inhabit, the *diaphragm.* **Phren** refers to the diaphragm in *phrenoptosis, phrenospasm, phrenodynia, phrenograph, phrenectomy.* It applies to the mind in *phrenology, schizophrenia, frantic, frenzy, frenetic.*

phrenopathy		mental disorder
hyper-	+ **phrenalia**	extreme mental excitement
brady-	+ **phrenia**	slow thinking
tachy-	+	swift thinking, excessive mental activity
oligo-	+	retarded mentality
hebe	+	schizophrenia brought about by puberty
ideo	+	"morbid mental state characterized by marked perversion of ideas"
presbyo	+	mental senility
aphronesia	+	a syn. for dementia

Several terms could refer either to the diaphragm or mind: *phrenic* is an adj. which has this double reference; *phrenalgia* could be pain in the diaphragm or in the mind; *phrenoplegia* could be paralysis of the diaphragm or of mentality.

A critical component of thinking is separating or cutting off one thing from another. Gk. and L. bases for cutting often relate not only to cutting or splitting literally, but also to the discernment, metaphorically the cutting, of one idea from another. Among other etymological delights, you'll find that *science* is cousin to *schizophrenia, cadaver* to *caesarean,* and *dissection* to *sex.*

IE *skei,* to split, cut

IE *skei* > Proto-Germanic > E. *shin, sheath,* and *shit,* etymologically that which is split off from the body. The synonym *excrement,* from a different IE source, also harbors the literal meaning of that which is split off.

The Gk. descendant of IE *skei,* **schism,** is the root for *schism,* a splitting off, as of a religious sect from its parent, adj. *schismatic.*

prosoposchism		facial cleft
stomato	+ **schisis**	cleft lip, harelip
spondylo	+	vertebral arch fissure

cheilo +	cleft lip
Schistosoma	a genus of blood flukes, the disease: *schistosomiasis*

Schiz appears in words relevant over a spectrum of references, from the state of cells to the state of a disordered mind, from *schizogenesis* to *schizophrenia*. *Schizogenesis* results in a split cell, a *schizocyte*, while *schizophrenia* results in a splitting off from reality. We may suffer from various kinds of splits.

schizo + *onychia*	splitting of nails
+ *trichia*	of hair
+ *thorax*	of chest
+ *glossia*	of tongue
+ *phrasis*	of speech
+ *cephalia*	of head
+ *thyma*	a hysterical tendency to reminisce
+ *mycosis*	disease caused by bacteria

From *skei* L. developed the cousin or cognate *scire*, to cut, to know > **sci.** This appears most relevantly in *science* and its forms, such as *scientist, scientific;* and, perhaps unexpectedly, in *conscience, conscientious, omniscient, prescient,* knowing what is to happen.

L. *nescire* means not to know, to be ignorant. From this came *nescient,* ignorant, n. *nescience,* the opposite of *omniscience;* and *nice,* which once referred to an exact knowledge of something but now means something more like appropriate or pleasant.

Science is an enterprise that has well-defined principles and techniques for uncovering and explaining the facts of nature, procedures expressed in biology, geology, physics, chemistry, and other studies. In some terms, the meaning of science is ambiguous; in fact, science can mean the opposite of science.

scientology	A well-authenticated or completely false program for developing insight and health.
Christian science	A religion which professes to have methods to accomplish supernatural cures.
scientific creationism	The modern term for a philosophy-religion that goes back centuries: the idea that scientific investigation supports accounts in the Bible, for example, that geology shows that the earth is not much more than 6000 years old and that women originated from a rib.
scientism	The belief that the scientific method should be applied to all aspects of life.

L. *scindere,* to cut, split
scind   *rescind, exscind, shingle*

sciss　　　　　　　　　　　*scissors, scission, abscission*
Scissurella costata　　　　　a gastropod

IE *bheid,* to cut

L. *findere,* to split, cleave

fiss　　　　　　　　　　　*fission, fissile, fissure*
　　　　　　　　　　　　　　fissipedia, fissilingual, fissiparous
fid　　　　　　　　　　　*bifid, trifid, multifid, pinnatifid*

　　Through Germanic to OE: *bite, beetle,* and *bitter,* which might mean bitten by gadflies.

L. *caedere,* to cut, kill
cad　　　　　　　　　　　*cadaver, caduceus, caesarean* < Caesar
cid　　　　　　　　　　　*homocide, suicide, pesticide, vermicide, ecocide*
　　　　　　　　　　　　　　deciduous
cis　　　　　　　　　　　*decision, incisor, excision, scissors*
　　　　　　　　　　　　　　circumcise
Stivalius ancisus　　　　　a flea

L. *secare,* to cut
sect

sect	*dissect*	*insectivorous*	*sex*
sector	*bisect*	*vivisection*	*sickle*
section		*venesection*	

seg

| *segment* | *intersegmental* |
| *segmentary* | *intersegmental* |

Formica exsectoides　　　　an ant

Gk. *temnein,* to cut

tom, tome, ectomy

atom	*entomology*	*cardiotomy*	*hysterectomy*
anatomy	*lithotomy*	*phlebotomy*	*vasectomy*
microtome	*achillotomy*	*appendectomy*	*tonsillectomy*

Acrotomus lucidulus　　　　a wasp

First illustration of dissection from an English book,
Bartholomaeus Anglicus, *Encyclopaedia*, 1495

18.3 Expressing

We all feel and think, and some of us like to go a step further, in expressing the results of our mental activity. For that, we'll turn to IE *bha*.

IE *bha*, to speak

The terms from Proto-Germanic and Latin are not in the biological vocabulary, though they abound in the common (for example, from Proto-Germanic, *ban*, and from L. *fari*, to speak, *professor, fate, infant* (through French), and *bandit* (through Italian).

From Greek, however, have come several relevant terms important in medical diagnosis and procedure, such as *telephone*.

Gk. **phon**	*telephone, stethophone*
refers to voice	
homo- + **phone**	a word that sounds like another
nycta + **phon** + **ia**	loss of voice at night
	orthophony, tachyphonia, phonasthenia

---

xeno +			alien accent in one's normal speech
refers to speech			
phem			*tachyphemia, spasmophemia, dysphemia*
leiphemia			smooth talking
a-	+ **phem**	+ *ia*	loss of power of speech
a-	+ *taxo*	+ **phemia**	lack of coordination of speech muscles
phas			*aphasia, dactylophasia* — also *dactylology*
			sign language
a-	+ *cata*	+ **aphasia**	inability to express one's thoughts coherently

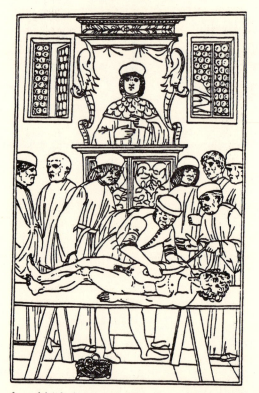

Professor from his chair (ex cathedra) supervising demonstrator
performing autopsy, from *Fasciculo di Mediani*, 1493

IE *leg,* to collect, to speak

   The history of this root shows that *leech* is a cousin of *colleague* and *sacrilege*
of *legal.* OE *laece* < IE *leg* meant physician. The physician once used as a

primary instrument the leech *Hirudo medicinalis* to bleed a patient to health or often enough to death. OE *laececraft* was replaced by a word from L.: *medicine*. No other words from Proto-Germanic descendants have survived, but several have from Latin and Greek descendants of IE.

The L. descendant *legere*, to gather, to read, exists in the bases *leg*, *lig* and *lect*. These bases are widely applied in the general vocabulary, e.g., *leg: sacrilege, legible, legal, legitimate, colleague; lig: diligent, intelligent; lect: intellect, collect, selection.*

Today's farmers and suburbanites gather firewood. So did the pagans. A L. descendant of IE *leg, lign*, underwent metaphoric ramification from referring to gathering to referring to that which was gathered. *Lign* is a base for wood: *ligneous, Limnoria lignorum,* a gribble, a small wood-boring crustacean dangerous to hulls; *grubble* might have come from *grub*.

A usual reversal here: while the L. bases are not widely employed in the biological vocabulary, the Gk. bases are. From Gk. *legein,* to gather, come the bases *lect,* as in *eclectic,* and **lex.**

lex		*lexicon, biolexicon*
a-	+ **lex** + *-ia*	*alexia,* inability to speak
dys-	+	*dyslexia*
tachy-	+	*tachylexia*
brady-	+	*bradylexia*
Gk.	*logos,* word	
	log	*logic, analogy, neologism*
auto- self	+ **logous**	own's own, as in autologous transfusion, transfusion with one's own blood
homo-	+	in comparative anatomy, pert. to a structure that stems from the same source as another, e.g., a human's hand and a bat's wing
		ant., *analogous,* a structure that resembles another but does not stem from the same source
logo	+ *agnosia*	*logagnosia,* aphasia
	+ *plegia*	paralysis of speech organs

The bases *scrib, script* from L. *scribere,* to write, draw, are central to about a dozen words in English, few of them relevant to the biological vocabulary. One word of importance to the conduct of medicine is from this source: *prescription,* which is sometimes scribbled (*scribble* is cognate to *prescription*). *Script* is in taxonomic names, such as *Arion circumscriptus,* a slug.

The Greek bases for writing and drawing are more relevant: Gk. *graphein,* to write, draw.

Cro-Magnon engraving on bone of a reindeer.
about 25,000 years ago

graph	*biography*, etc., *graphite*
chirography	handwriting
electrocardiograph	instrument to record arterial waves
	also *kymograph*
graptolite	extinct marine animals of the Paleozoic
a- + **graph** + *ia*	inability to write
logo +	failure to write down one's ideas
gram	*gram, diagram*
	electrocardiogram, cholangiogram
	engram
Grammatophyllum speciosum	an orchid
Gk. *glyph*, to carve	*petroglyph*
glyphodont	an extinct mammal
Cicada hieroglyphica	a cicada, *cicada* < L.

Silurian crinoid
Glyptocrinus decadactylus

18.4 Knowing

In 1869, the Victorian biologist Thomas Henry Huxley, whom we have met before, was invited to join a club called the Metaphysical Society. This club had as its purpose the bringing together of people representing different philosophical and religious points of view. The other members of the club had labels: Anglican, Unitarian, Positivist, Roman Catholic. Huxley's philosophical and religious point of view was inappropriate to these labels. He could have called himself an atheist, but he claimed he was not prepared to deny the existence of god, only to question it. He could have called himself a free-thinker. But he chose to invent a word.

The Gk. root for know, *gnostos,* had already been transmitted by Latin into English in 1560 as *Gnostic,* the name of an early Christian sect that professed to have mystical knowledge. By 1700, the word *gnosis* was in the vocabulary for such knowledge. Gk. *agnostos* means not known. With the Gnostics in mind as a model for those who know, Huxley coined *agnostic* for one who does not know. A decade after he coined the word, he wrote several long and controversial essays defining what *agnosticism* means. One of his definitions was that *agnosticism* means the scientific method.

IE *gno,* to know

For to know, the IE language had the form *gno.* This went into the Proto-Germanic branch, from which we have the words *know, knowledge,* and the German *Kunst,* art or skill. It went into Greek and from Gk. into L. as **gno,** which had the sense of knowing and judging.

Familiar words for seeing through and for seeing ahead, predicting, are *diagnosis* and *prognosis,* v. *prognosticate.*

a- + **gno** + *genic*	of uncertain origin
co- + **gno** + *-tion*	*cognition*
terra incognita	unknown territory
a- + **gnosia**	loss of senses
hyper +	a paranoic condition in which the patient imposes his or her own delusions upon the outside world; cp. T. S. Eliot's theory of the objective correlative
dys- +	dysfunction of intellect
dys- + *-ana* +	a dyslexic condition in which patient doesn't know or understand certain words
cyesio +	diagnosis of pregnancy
acro- + **gnostic**	knowing or feeling movement of one's limbs
auto- +	pert. to self-knowledge
ana- + **agnos** + *asthenia*	weakness brought on by reading
a- + *stereo* + **gnosis**	failure of tactile sense to identify object by its shape

gnome	
physiognomy	the derivation of character from physical, especially facial, appearance
pathognomonic	interpretation of a disease through its particular conditions.

From Latin and its descendants have come words disguised by French: *ignoramus*, one who doesn't know, *ignominious*, lit. not known, not worthy to be known, actually, shameful. From Latin *gno* may also have given rise to *normal* and *abnormal*.

We might reveal our knowledge, or keep it secret, hidden. Gk. **crypt**, hidden, is employed as itself to mean a hidden vault and, in anatomy, a pit or tube; adjective form *cryptic* refers to that which is hidden, coded, mysterious. The study of codes or secret writing is *cryptology* and *cryptography*, the interpretation of codes *cryptoanalysis* or *cryptanalysis*.

In the biological vocabulary, words formed with **crypto** fall into three categories, the first for that which is unknown, hidden, the second for structures, and the third for afflictions.

Unknown

cryptoneurous	unknown, undecipherable nervous system
cryptogenic	of unknown origin
cryptotoxic	unexpected toxicity
cryptamnesia	hidden memory
cryptozoology	investigation of unknown creatures, such as the Loch Ness monster, the Himalayan Yeti, the U.S. bigfoot
cryptesthesia	clairvoyance

Structures

cryptocarp	hidden fruiting body of a plant
cryptogam	hidden gametes, no authentic flowers
crytophyte	a plant that has hidden reproductive structures, e.g., bulbs

Afflictions

cryptitis	inflammation of a crypt
cryptorchidism	condition of an undescended testis
cryptodidymus	condition of a being hidden in the body of its twin
cryptococcosis	fungal infection caused by *Cryptococcus neoformans*

Problematica will appropriately conclude this chapter on thinking. It's a useful term for describing something which is of uncertain connection to anything else or cryptogenic, such as the oolite, a rock that might have been carved by natural forces or by human artisans; fossils of uncertain origin; and, by extension, words of uncertain origin.

PART VI: ANATOMY

CHAPTER 19—BODY AND BONES

19.1   The Body
19.2   The Bones
19.3   Out on a Limb

Earliest anatomical drawing in an English book,
from Bartholomaeus Angelicus, *De Proprietatibus rerum*, 1495

The Indo-Europeans knew that the human body contains a heart, and they named that organ, *kerd*, but it's unlikely that they knew of its function as a

233

pump. They knew and named the beech tree, *bhago,* but they knew nothing of photosynthesis.

The ancient Greeks and Romans were more advanced in their knowledge of anatomy, but a literate junior-high school student today knows more about the parts and functions of the human heart than did Hippocrates, the father of medicine. Our teenage hero or heroine knows more about other fields of biology too, from protozoa to genetics, than did all the Greek naturalists put together.

Such a view is not a condemnation of pagan physicians, anatomists, and naturalists. What they began—the investigation of nature—was closed through no fault of theirs for a thousand years and when the investigation opened again in the Renassiance, it did so because what the pagans began was finally revealed. Science could not go much further than they went until experimentation, and that includes the use of instruments.

Paramecium is made up of parts from Greek, *para-* + *mec,* oval + *-ium,* but no pagan had ever seen one. Nobody had before Anton van Leeuwenhoek invented the microscope in the late 17th century. *Paramecium* came into English in the middle of the 18th century.

It was not until a hundred years after the invention of the microscope that the female egg was seen, and not until three hundred years later that the gene responsible for gender was identified. During the Renaissance, biological investigation focused on smaller and smaller things and on increasingly subtler processes of growth and decay. Scientists then and since have applied to Greek and Latin lexical elements to name these things and processes, inventing not only instruments that the Greeks and Romans did not have but also words they did not use.

Anatomical parts will often carry two or three labels, a familiar one coming from OE; a less familiar one from Latin; and a thoroughly unfamiliar technical label from Greek. Of special interest are labels that come from these three languages when the bases in these languages all go back to the same IE root. The words often will be metaphors of some artifact or other item from ancient Greece or Rome.

The following analysis of anatomical terms begins with the largest unit, the body and its bones, and proceeds to its parts: head, skull, and face in Chapter 20; torso, muscles, and viscera in Chapter 21; the integumentary system in Chapter 22. Intermission narratives will be provided for selected items in the inventory.

19.1 The Body

body < OE *bodig*	*bodily*
Greek **som**	*chromosome, somatic, psychosomatic*
acrosome	the body or organelle at the tip of a sperm cell, for penetration of egg
Latin **corp**	*corpse, corpulent, incorporeal*
corpuscle	lit. a little body
corpus callosum	< L. *callous,* hard

a hard body in the brain which connects cerebral hemispheres

For part or segment, the Gk. **mer** is used: e.g., *isomere, merotomy, merismatic, blastomere, Trimerus delphinocephalus* is the name of a trilobite, and *Cryptomeria japonica* of a conifer.

merism	repetition of parts
metamere	a bodily part
polymeric	pert. to many parts
merogenesis	cleavage of an ovum; cp. *dysmerogenesis*
dysmerogenesis	abnormal merogenesis
meroblastic	pert. to partial division in cleavage
meropia	partial blindness

19.2 The Bones

The human body contains 206 bones. The framework for the body is the skeleton. *Skeleton* is a metaphor, from Gk. *skeletos,* dried up.

bone < OE *ban*	*bony, boneless*

L. **os(s)i**	+ *-fy*	*ossify,* make into bone; n., *ossification*
	+ *-ary*	*ossuary,* a receptacle for bones
	+ *-cle*	a little bone
Leipidosteus osseus		a garfish

Gk. **osteo**		*osteopath, osteology, oyster, osprey*
		teleost
	+ *porosis*	condition of porous, weak bones
	+ *malacia*	softening of bone or bone marrow
	+ *phyte*	a growth from a bone
peri-	+ **osteo** + *-ium*	*periosteum,* a membrane on bone surface
hetero-	+ **osteo** + *plasty*	*hetero-osteoplasty,* surgical grafting to achieve a chimera that has bone tissue from a species other than its own
Gasterosteus aculeatus		stickleback

spine < OFr *espine*	

< L. *spina,* thorn	*spiny, spineless*
spinose	bearing spines

L. *vertebra* < L.

Gk. **rachio,** spine < *rhachis*		
	+ *centesis*	surgical puncture of lumbar
	+ *lysis*	therapeutic loosening of curved spine

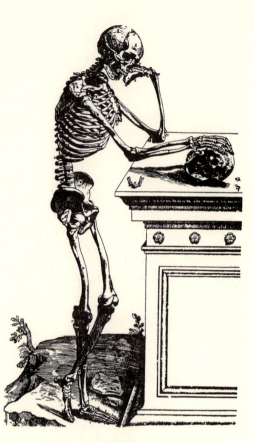

Skeleton from Andreas Vesalius,
De Humani Corporis Fabrica, 1543

+ *myel* + -itis	inflammation of spinal cord
+ *pagus*	twins joined at spines

Gk. **spondylo,** spine < *spondylos,* vertebra

+ *dynia*	pain in the spine
+ *py* + -*osis*	*spondylopyosis,* suppuration of spine

rib < OE   *rib,* to tease, make fun of

L. **costa,** rib, side   *coast, intracostal*
Cinyra costulifera   a beetle

Gk. **pleur,** rib, side
pleura   sacs around lungs
pleurisy   inflammation of pleur
Pleukracanthus dilatatus   an extinct fish

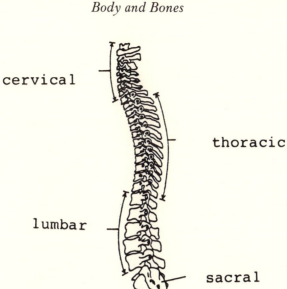

cervical

thoracic

lumbar

sacral

coccyx

The spine

hip < OE *hype*

pelvis < L. *pelvis,* basin

L. **pelvis**	*pelvis, pelvimetry, pelvisection*
Gk. **pyel**	*pyelitis, pyelogram, cystopyelonephritis*
Gk. **ischi**	
ischium	pelvic bone

Gk. *ischion* was translated by L. into *scia,* as in *sciatica.* Homophonic *ischemia,* interruption of blood supply by blockage < *ischein,* to suppress.

Gk. **coccyx** orig. referred to a cuckoo; the resemblance between the bird's beak and a group of fused vertebral bones led to its metaphoric transference to this terminal part of the backbone: the *coccyx,* combining form **coccyg.**

coccyg + *-al*	*coggygeal,* pert. to coccyx
+ *algia*	pain in the coccyx
sacro + **coccygeal**	pert. to sacrum bone and coccyx
tail < OE *taegel*	*to tail,* to follow
L. **caud**	*queue, cue*
+ *-al*	toward the tail

	caudate, caudicle, nudicaudate
Bulimina caudigera	a foraminifer
Gk. **circo**	*circopithecus*
platycercine	flat-tailed
cercaria	tailed trematode larval stage
procercoie	larval stage of fish tapeworms
Cysticercus	genus of tapeworms
cysticercus	tapeworm larva
Cryptocercus punctulatus	a cockroach

19.3 Out on a Limb

As we might expect, the common and simple word *limb* comes from native English, while the uncommon synonym *mel* comes from Greek. *Limb* combines only with *less;* **mel,** meaning limb, however, combines with many other bases and with affixes, as in *melagra, melosalgia, mesomelic, amelia* and *symmelia, nanomelia* and *macromelia, acromelalgia* and *cacomelia.*

IE *ar,* to fit together

Proto-Germanic > OE *earm, arm,* employed in many compounds. *Armpit* is one of these compounds, less medical than its synonym, L. *axilla.* While the speakers of Proto-Germanic directed IE *ar* mostly to refer to upper limbs, the arms fitting onto the body, speakers of emerging Latin used a different metaphor, of body protection and weaponry. L. *arma* went into French with this sense, as seen in *armor* and *armadillo,* little armor. From Latin also *ars, art,* as in *artist* and *inert(ia).* *Ars longa, vita breva,* Art is long, life short.

Armadillo

Although it bears little resemblance to its IE source, L. *ordo,* base **ord** also stems from this source: *order, disorder, coordination, primordial.*

Greek has two relevant bases from IE *ar: artio* and **arthro,** both referring to joint. *Joint* < OFr. < L. *jungere.*

artio   *article, artiodactyl*

Gk. **arthro**

arthropod	*arthritis*	*synarthrosis*
arthropterous	*holarthritis*	*arthropathy*
arthragra	*chirarthritis*	*arthroclasia*
arthralgia	*osteoarthritis*	*arthrocentesis*
arthroncus	*arthroxerosis*	*arthroplastic*
anarthrous	*olecranarthrosis*	

enarthrosis   ball and socket joint, e.g., femur in hip

In biological terminology, the major base for *arm* as upper limb is **brach** (not to be confused with *branch,* gill).

Greek
brach, arm   *brace, brachial, brachioferous*
                             brachiopod

brachiate   swing by the arms, in botany: arm-like leaves
Cactocrinus multibrachiatus   a crinoid

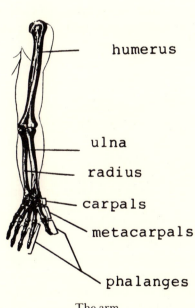

humerus

ulna

radius

carpals

metacarpals

phalanges

The arm

Gibbon, a brachiating ape

The single large bone extending from shoulder to elbow is the L. *humerus;* the two bones of the forearm are the L. *ulna* and L. *radius.* For elbow, the base **cub** may be is used < L. *cubare,* to lie down: *antecubital, brachiocubital, ventricumbent.* Cubit as a measurement orig. referred to the distance from the tip of the middle finger to the elbow, about 18+ inches.

From Gk. *olekranon* the words *olecranon, olecranal, olecranarthritis,* relating to the elbow joint.

From Gk. *ankon,* bent or crooked, come the bases **ancon** and **ankylos.**

ancon, elbow	*anconitis, anconoid*
anconad	toward the elbow
anconagra	seizure, gout, of the elbow
ankylos, looped together,	*ankylosis, ankylodactyly, ankylocheilia*
adhering	*akyloproctia, ankylopoietic, ankylophobia*

wing < ME *wenge* < Scand.

Gk. **pter**	wing, also feather	
pterodactyl	*pteropod*	*pterygoid*
archeopteryx	*malacopterous*	*hyalopterous*
eurypterid		

Pteropus conspicillatus	an extant fruit-bat

L. **al** wing, also structure or process that looks like a wing, e.g., *ala auris, ala sacralis*
alar, alate, aliped

Apteroscirtus inalatus a katydid

hand < OE *hand*

L. *manu* has given many words to the common vocabulary (e.g., *manufacture* and *manure*) but few to the strictly biological vocabulary, and those are rarely used — e.g., *bimana,* the two-handed animal (human beings) and *quadrumana,* an old term for apes, incorrectly signaling that apes have four hands. *Peromyscus maniculatus* is the taxonomic name of the deermouse.

Rare homophonic *mano,* continual, in *sphygmomanometer* (*sphygmos,* pulse).

Almost all the descendants of Gk. **cheir, chir,** hand, are in the biological vocabulary. Most of the following examples will either be familiar (*chiropodist, chiropractor*) or as easy to figure out as *chirospasm, chirology, chiroscope.* **Agra** means seizure of, gout of, as in above *agronagra,* therefore: *chiragra;* and **algia** means pain of, therefore: *chiralgia.* A moment's reflection might indicate that *plasty* means plastic surgery of: *chiroplasty.* *Megaly* means excessively large: *chiromegaly.*

surgeon	< *cheir + ourgia,* lit. someone working with his or her hands
chirognomy	prediction through study of the hands (cp. *chiromancy, palmistry*)
chiropodalgia	pain in the hand and foot
atelocheiria	incomplete fetal development of the hands
Chiroptera	a mammalian order, that of the hand-wing, or bats
Cheiranthus cheiri	taxonomic name of a plant that has a sad metaphoric use: the wallflower

wrist < OE *wrist*

Gk. **carp**

carpus	wrist, adj. *carpal*
carp + *-ectomy*	excision of wrist bones

Another **carp** means fruit, seed; and still another < ON *karpa,* to boast, means to find fault.

A crescent-shaped bone of the wrist is called the *lunate* (or *os lunatum*) < L. *luna,* moon. This bone is subject to *osteochondrosis.*

palm < L. *plano,* flat	*palm tree* and *palmetto,* family Palmae, adj. *palmaceous*
palmar	adj. re. to palm
palmate	palm-shaped
palm	
finger < OE *finger*	*fingernail, fingerling* (a small fish)

L. **digit**	*digit, digital, digitigrade*
digitate	to finger, having finger-like structures
digitalis	a cardiac stimulant, fr. appearance of foxglove leaves

Digitalis laciniata	foxglove
Epidermophyton interdigitate	the fungus responsible for athlete's foot

Gk. **dactyl**	*dactyl, pterodactyl*
dactylogram	fingerprint
dactylology	manual alphabet (also *cheirology*)

dactylorhiza	finger-like roots
dactylosymphysis	fingers (or toes) growing together; also *syndactyly*
hexadactylism	condition of having six fingers on each hand
arachnodactyly	fingers like legs of spiders
Phoenix dactylifera	date-palm
Gk. **phalanx**	a line, as that of finger or toe bones or of soldiers
	phalangeal, phalangectomy, brachyphalangia
	hyperphalangism, symphalangism
phalangi + *grade*	walking on phalanges
Phalangium cinereum	daddylonglegs
L. *pollex*, thumb	*pollical, prepollex*
Pagurus pollicaris	hermit crab
Gk. *kondyl* > **condyl,**	*condyle, condyloma, epicondyle*
joint, esp. knuckle,	*ectocondyle, intercondylar*
knob of bone	
Condylura cristata	star-nosed mole
Gk. *chel,* claw	*chela, cheliferous, cheloid, cheloma*
	chelophores
Chelifer cancroides	book-scorpion
L. *talus,* claw, ankle	
talon	a claw
talus	part of anklebone
tali + *pes*	clubfoot
+ *grade*	walking on claws
talipomanus	clubhand, like clubfoot
talocalcanean	pert. to talus and heelbone
talofibular	pert. to talus and fibula
Campsicnemus brevitalus	a fly

nail < OE *naegel*

Greek **onych,** also for claw and hoof; *onyx.* **Onycho** combines with many of the affixes and bases we have come upon: with *an-,* (*anonychia,* condition of lacking nails), *-osis* and *-itis* (*onychosis, onychitis*), with *platy-, pathy, malacia, lysis, ptosis, clasis, rrhexis, mycosis, schizia* (*schizonychia* or *onychoschizia*), *genic, -tomy* and *-ectomy,*

Onychauxis means excessive growth, thickening, of nails; and *onychocryptosis* means ingrown nail. Of special interest is *onychophage,* one who bites his or her fingernails, and of less interest, *Acinonyx jubatus,* African cheetah.

L. **ungu,** nail, claw, hoof

unguis   nail, or, in Dorland's: "the horny cutaneous plate on
                                 the dorsal surface of the distal end of the terminal

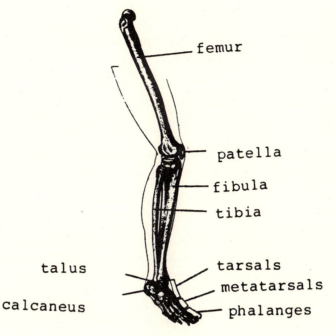

The leg

Greek woman at play:
catching ankle-bones or tali on back of her hand

	phalanx of a finger or toe, made up of flattened epithelial scales developed from the stratum lucidum of the skin"
ungula	a hoof
ungulate	hoofed animal, e.g., horse, cow *multiungulate, polyunguia*
Barbula unguisculata	a moss

Homophonic *ungue* < L. *unguere,* to anoint, means salve or ointment as in *unguent;* from the L. verb also *unction* and *unctuous.*

leg < ON *leggr*	*legless*

L. *femur*	orig. thigh; upper leg bone
L. *tibia*, reedpipe	shinbone
L. *fibula*, buckle	other bone of lower leg

IE *genu*, knee

To OE as *cneo*, Modern E. *knee;* and to OE *cneowlian*, Modern E. *kneel.* To L. as **genu**, knee or bent like a knee, *genuflect, geniculate.*

genucubital	pert. to knees and elbows
genupectoral	pert. to knees and chest

The cognate Gk. **gon**, having the meaning of angle, can refer to the knee, which makes an angle as it bends: *gonalgia, gonatagra, gonitis, gonyoncus, gonyocele,* arthritis of the knee. By extension, it can also refer to angles of the eye chamber: *gonioscope, goniopuncture, goniotomy;* of the skull: *goniocraniometry* means measurement of the angles of the cranium; *intergonial* re. to the mandible. **Gon** further extends to angles that are not necessarily anatomical: *diagonal, pentagon, polygon.*

Polygonatum	plant genus, e.g., Solomon's seal

L. **patell**, kneecap	*patellar, patelliform, infrapatellar*
Gk. **tars**, ankle, flat, foot bones	*tarsier, tarsectomy*
tarsus	instep, pl., *tarsi,* bones at back of foot and ankle; lower segment of insect leg; border of eyelid
metatarsus	pl., *metatarsi,* bones in middle of foot, between tarsi and phalanges
Anopheles albitarsis	a mosquito
L. *hallux*, big toe	*hallucal, prehallux*
L. *plant*, sole of foot	*plantar, plantigrade*
foot < OE *fot*	

One might wonder what lunatic imagination could associate the noble *Oedipus* with the duckbill *platypus.* To the sane mind, it seems the two are worlds apart, *antipodal.* It seems equally unlikely that Oliver North's shredding *peccadillo* had anything, linguistically speaking, to do with Fawn Hall's *fetching* appearance, Admiral Poindexter's *pioneer* efforts at covert activities, with *barefoot* and *talipes, pediculosis, dispatch, impeccable, pajamas,* with *pawn, peon,* and *podiatrist.* Yet all these italicized words, and many more, are offspring of a single IE parent.

The following box differs from the others, in that it will be more comprehensive, specifying non-biological terms as well as biological.

IE *ped*

IE *ped* went into Latin as **ped**, easily recognizable as the base of words having to do with feet or walking, such as *pedal, pedestrian,* etc., with animals that have a hundred (*centi-*), a thousand (*milli-*) or hairlike (*cirri*) feet. That which is in the shape of a foot is *pediform*, and a beautification of toenails is a *pedicure*.

Ped has its metaphoric uses, as in *sesquipedalian*, lit. a foot and a half, a suitable adjective for a very long word, or, as noun, for a person who dotes on words of extraordinarily lengthy construction; *pedigree* < Fr. *pie de grue*, crane's foot, a visual model for a geneological chart; *pedicle*, a little foot, foot-like, stalk, stalk-like.

pediculus	foot-like, a louse
pediculation	formation of stalk or louse
peduncle	a stalk for flower, for connecting parts of the brain, its removal: *pedunculectomy*
pediculous	full of lice
pediculosis	infestation with lice (of family *Pediculidae* — e.g., hair lice)

Pediculus humanus capitis	head louse
Pediculus pubis, (also *Phthirus pubis* and *crabs*), pubic lice
Pediculus humanus	lice responsible for typhus.
Cypripedium	lady's slippers; note eponym from Aphrodite, the Cyprian

This **ped** led to **pet**:

petiole	thin stalk joining leaf to stem
	petiolate, petiolar, petiolule

Several words coming from L. *pedica*, shackle, still have the sense of being fettered: to prevent an action by hobbling the feet is to *impair* or *impede*, noun *impedance*. Another term for trapping someone is *impeach*; this was clipped to *peach* (not the fruit, which comes from *Persia*, but to snitch). To get a foot out of a trap is to *expedite*, and to do that quickly on, say an *expedition*, is to be *expeditious* or even *expedient*. Another word for escaping from fetters is *dispatch*.

L. **pes**

A base parallel to L. **ped** is L. **pes**, as in *talipes, stapes,* and *nudipes*, barefoot;

in disguised forms *trivet*, the Spanish foot soldier *peon*, the French *pioneer*, one who first puts his foot forward, and *pawn*, the expendable footman of chess and political shenanigans. Lusty French lovers rent a *pied a terre*, a temporary lodging permitting a couple to engage in an afternoon's *pas de deux*. Also through French: *piedmont*, foot of a mountain. L. **pes** became Fr. *pie;* that which is before the foot is *avantpie*, which became ME *vampe*, sock, and modern E. *vamp*, sole part of a shoe, also improvisation in music; *revamp*, to redo. *Sisyphus rubripes*, a beetle, dissects into *Sisyphus + rubri*, red + *ped*.

L. *peccare*, to sin, carries the sense of putting the wrong foot forward, stumbling, and it's reasonable that from this verb should come *peccable*, guilty; *peccadillo*, a small stumble, a little sin; *faux pas*, a French false step; *pejoration* and *impeccable*, for one who doesn't stumble.

Gk. *ped* has been less productive than Latin **ped**, supplying among its very few descendants *diapedesis*, emigration of corpuscles (< Gk. *pedan*, to leap); *cheliped*, crustacean appendage.

Gk. *pedon*, rudder > *pilot*.

Gk. **pod** has been moderately fruitful in both the common and biological vocabularies, responsible for *podium*, Frenchified *pew*, surnames *Depew* and *Depuy; antipodes*, the other side of the world.

From Gk. **pod** come many taxonomic names and medical terms: *podiatry*, *podagra, pseudopod, arthropod*.

mono-	+ **pod** + *-ia*		*monopodia*, condition of having one foot
sym-	+		condition of having fused feet
platy-	+		flat feet
chiro	+	+ *-ist*	*chiropodist*
poly-	+	+ *-e*	obsolete name for the squid
diplo-	+		*Diplopoda*, millipede
cephalo	+		*Cephalopoda*
gastro	+		*Gastropodag*
brachio	+		*Brachiopoda*
rhizo	+		*Rhizopod*, subphylum including amebas and foraminifers
branchi	+		*Branchiopoda*
pleuro	+		*Pleuropoda*, like centipedes
uro	+		*uropod*, an insect limb
Pelecy	+		*Pelecypoda*, a mollusk; e.g., clam, oyster; *pelecy* = hatchet
Macropodus opercularis			paradise fish
Isadora antipodea			a snail

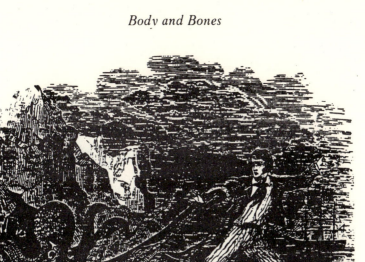

Mr. Beale, an Englishman, tried to catch a squid, here termed *poulpe*, polyp, he encountered on the rocks of Barin Islands. The squid resisted.

Oedipus and the sphinx
from Daphnae

Gk. **pus**	*platypus, Oedipus*
poly- + **pus**	*polypus* > *polyp,* an innocent coelenterate or an obnoxious growth
dasy +	*Dasypus,* lit. hairy foot
trapezoid	in geometry, a quadrilateral with two parallel sides; in anatomy, a small wrist bone; < *tra-,* four +

Platypus
(*Ornithorhynchus anatimus*)

	pus + *-oid*
	trapezoid was clipped to *trapeze*
phalarope	a kind of wading bird < Gk. *phalarus, white spot* +
	pus
Macropus giganteus	a kangaroo

Platypus entered English in 1799, European viewers of the beast thinking it an outrageous fabrication. By 1893 it had achieved commercial value: "Platypus shopping bags and purses are not disdained by the fair who crowd the marts . . . in Melbourne . . . or in Sydney." *Pus* has also been found useful in a small number of medical terms having to do with monstrous births, *sympus, tripus.*

Oedipus continues to have a good deal of trouble. The first part of his name relates to *edema,* both descendants of Gk. *oidein,* to swell. *Oedipus* is the base of a word for the act of putting out or otherwise injuring one's own eyes, *oedipism;* and, worst of all, it's an allusion for an impudent complex.

Persian, one of the descendants of IE, changed IE *ped* to *pai,* leg, which became the second element of *teapoy,* a three-legged table. Knitted with *jamah,* garment, *pai* became the first element for a Persian leg garment, *pajamas.* As *teapoy* is a direct parallel to *tripus,* so *pajamas* is to *podiatry.*

Keeping in mind Proto-Germanic *f* for IE *p,* we can recognize that cousins of *ped, pod, pus,* and Persian *pai* are the Proto-Germanic *foot* and its compounds, *fetter* and *fetch* and *fetlock,* a projection of a horse's foot, a tuft of hair. *Footsy,* archaic slang for a foot through echoism became *tootsy,* which can mean foot or sweetheart.

CHAPTER 20—HEAD, SKULL AND FACE

20.1   The Head
20.2   The Skull
20.3   The Face

20.1 The Head

Head < OE *heafoth* attaches to many native bases and affixes, as in *egghead, behead,* and *heady.*

Grimm's Law would anticipate Proto-Germanic *h* being cognate to a *k* sound in Gk. and L. L. **cap** appears in dozens of English words mostly with that base (e.g., *escape, capitulate*), and in biological terminology, most often metaphorically. *Capuchin* is not only an order of monks, and a hood, but a species of South American monkeys, the kind that accompanies organ grinders. *Caprice* and *capricious* hide a hedgehog. They stem from It. **cap** + *riccio*, bristly. L. *capitellum* retains the meaning of little head in references to the head of a bone; *capital,* head of femur, and *caput medusae* describes the tiny snake-like lines of an umbilical disorder. *Capitation* means physician's fees from medical plans (*decapitation* might then mean the cutting off of such payments). Ornithologists turned to **cap** to name avian genera such as *Capito.*

L. **cep,** a parallel base for head, was metaphorically taken as the head of a muscle, thus *biceps, triceps, quadriceps.* L. *ob-,* against + **cip** > *occipital,* the skull bone at the back of the head. *Precipitation* lit. means the process before being brought to a head.

20.2 The Skull

skull < ME *schull*   *skullcap*

Greek

Cephal, the Gk. base for head, appears almost entirely in words restricted to the medical or anatomical vocabulary. Affixing elements to it creates a long list of terms, such as *microcephalic* and *acrocephalic.* The prefix *en-* renders *enceph* for brain.

From IE *ker,* horn, head, have come *corn* and *horn, reindeer* and *migraine, carrot* and *carat* and *cheer* the perissodactylic *rhinoceros,* the microbial *cornybacterium,* and the dinosaurian *triceratops.*

249

IE *ker,* horn, head:

Proto-Germanic to E.: *horn, hornet.* From Gk. descendants have come bases **ker** and **cer** for something hard, like an animal's horn: *rhinocerous, keratin, carat, corynebacterium,* the first base from a metaphor for a hard instrument, a club. With the sense of head, these bases combined into *carrot, cervix, cervine.* Gk. *karos,* stupor, was used by the Roman physician Galen as the source for his neologism *carotid,* since pressing these neck arteries causes stupor. *Carotid* entered E. in the mid-17th century.

Cran, the Gk. base for skull > *cranium*

crani + *-ate*	having skull; ant., *acraniate*
+ *-otomy*	cutting into the skull
+ *metry*	*craniometry,* phrenological technique of measuring skull to determine intelligence and character
hemi- + *krania*	split head; this evolved into *migraine*

Through French came another variation: *cheer.*

L. translated the Gk. *kranion* into **calv,** as in *calvarium, encalvant,* and *calvary.* One Latin descendant, **cer,** gives us *cervix, cerebrum,* and *cerebellum,* while another L. descendant, **corn,** gives us *corny; cornea;* the musical instrumenta *cornet* and *clavicorn;* the mythical beast *unicorn,* and the Zodiac *Capricorn.*

Lord Byron's "Lines Inscribed upon a Cup Formed from a Skull" praised a human calvarium that had been made into a wine cup. The opening stanza of the skull's monologue sets the theme and mood.

> Start not—nor deem my spirit fled:
> In me behold the only skull
> From which, unlike a living head,
> Whatever flows is never dull.

Bones of the skull

The bones of the skull are conventionally and efficiently categorized as those constituting the cranium and those constituting the face. Eight bones of six types make up the cranium.

The first to be named was the *occiput,* the bone at the back and base of the skull. *Occiput* came into English in 1350, and the more often used *occipital bone* in 1670. The *occipital condyles* were identified even later, in 1855, and the *occipital lobe* in 1885. The combining form is made up of *ob-,* against or back, and *ciput,* head, thus lit. at the back of the head. *Sinciput* refers to the frontal aspect of the cranium.

Two decades after the invention of the term *occipital bone,* that is, in 1695, a pair of bones was identified: the *parietal.* The parietal bones form the sides of the skull, reaching up to the top. *Parietal* is a metaphor, < Gk. *paries,* wall.

The early 18th century saw the identification of other cranial bones. *Sphenoid,* the term for a bone down at the bottom of the skull forming the roof of the pharynx, entered E. in 1725; its root is Gk. *sphen,* wedge. *Frontal,* obviously the term for the bone at the front of the skull, was named in 1735; its root is L. *frontalis,* base **front.** The *frontal lobe* was identified in 1875. 1735 was also the date for the naming of another low bone, at the base of the cranium forming the roof of the nose: the *ethmoid.* Like *sphenoid, ethmoid* is a metaphor, < Gk. *ethmoeides,* like a sieve.

Temporal bone entered E. in 1765, though the *temporal lobes* were named much later, in 1890. One etymology traces *temporal* to L. *tempus,* time, *temporal* an adjective denoting time, as in *temporary* and *contemporary.* This etymology points out that the regular beat of a pulse is a measure of time, so that the place where this beat can be felt, the area by the side of the eye, received its designation of *temple* because it was a sort of clock. But a more economical etymology traces *temporal* as an adjective, not of *tempus,* but of a Latin word referring directly to the skin stretching from the side of the eye back: L. *temple.* This etymology finds *temporal* for time merely a homophone of *temporal* for the bone. To further confuse matters, there is the religious building called a *temple,* which etymologically has nothing to do either with time or with bones. At any rate, for this bone and lobe, the base is **temp.**

The second category of skull bones consists of 14 facial bones of eight types. A chronological survey of facial bones begins in 1375, the year in which the (2) *nasal bones* were named, *nasal* < L. **nas,** nose. 1375 is also the year for the naming of the *mandible* or lower jaw, *mandible* < L. *mandere,* to chew + *bula,* means of, adj. *mandibular,* base **mand.**

Palatine, for the (2) bones of the palate, entered E. in 1650, < L. *palatum,* for roof of the mouth, base **palat** (Gk. *uran*). A few years after that, in 1655, (2) spongy nasal bones were named: *turbinate* < L. *turbinatus,* shaped like a top, also called the *inferior nasal concha. Maxilla,* for the (2) bones making up the upper jawbone, came into E. in 1670, < L. **mala,** upper jaw or cheekbone.

Vomer carries us to the end of the 17th century, entering E. in 1695 as the designation for the single bone that makes up the septum, the division between the two nares. It's a metaphor, < L. *vomer,* plowshare. In 1700, the *zygomatic bone* was named. The (2) zygomatic bones are also called the *malars* and *cheekbones.* The *zygomatic arches* stretch from cheekbones to temporal bones. The source of the term is again a metaphor, < Gk. *zygo.*

Although *lacrimal,* base **lacri,** for tearful entered E. in 1535, it was not until 1790 that the *lacrimal glands* were named, and not until 1850 that the *lacrimal bone* was named. The cognates of **lacri** are *dakryma* and E. *tear,* the lacrimal fluid.

As we saw in the chapter on metaphors, there are many terms that have **sutura** and **sutur** in them for seam, e.g., the *sutura frontoethmoidalis* and the *sutura temporozygomatica.* The *sutura sagittalis* joins the two parietal bones; the *sutura lamboidea* joins the occipital and parietal bones; and the *sutura coronalis* joins the frontal and parietal bones. *Corona* means crown, an apt metaphor for that which lies above these bones.

There exist 200+ terms with *process* < *pro-* + **cess** < L. *cedere,* to yield. The *process* is a projection, as of bone: *processus* is a bony prominence or any similar mass, e.g.,

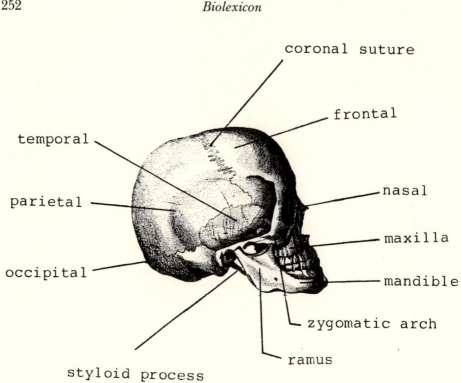

coronal suture

frontal

temporal

nasal

parietal

maxilla

occipital

mandible

zygomatic arch

ramus

styloid process

The skull

mastoid process, coronoid, nasal, palantine, vermiform, processus brevis incudis, processus palatinus maxillae, and *processus vermiformis,* the appendix.

Brain < OE *braegen* attaches to many other parts, giving us *brainy, brainwash,* etc. In anatomical terminology, Gk. **enceph** has been found good for a dozen different combinations, two of which have entered the general vocabulary, *encephalitis* and *anencephaly.*

Gk. has also provided the bases for a number of parts of the brain, such as the *hippocampus,* ridges for the conduct of physiological responses and for the storing of certain memories, from a Gk. word for a fabulous animal with equine forelegs and a dolphin's tail + < **hippo,** horse + *kampos,* monster, entered E. in 1706.

For the major parts of the brain, anatomical terminology turns to L. The word for the upper and largest section of the human brain, *cerebrum* < **cere** + *-brum* is orig. L.; it entered E. 1615: "The cerebrum filleth almost the whole skull." Its outer layer,

Hippocampus

responsible for language and similar high functions is the *cerebral cortex.* Between the cerebral cortex and the skull are the three membrane layers noted as metaphors: *pia mater, arachnoid,* and *dura mater,* and these meninges (*meninges* is Gk. for membrane) extend downwards to sheath the spinal cord.

The middle section of the brain, below the cerebrum, is the *cerebellum* < **cere** + *-bellum,* L. little cerebrum, which controls the muscles which we voluntarily bring into movement.

The third major and lowest section of brain is the *medulla oblongata* which controls basic and involuntary functions such as respiration and circulation of the blood < L. **medulla,** bone marrow, pith. 1876: "those nerves which . . . are formed by late anatomists to proceed from the medulla."

hemisphere
< Gk. *hemi-* + **sphere** < *sphaira,* ball. The cerebrum is divided into two hemispheres, each of which has specialized functions.

corpus callosum
< L. *corp* + *callos,* hard. This structure connects the two hemispheres of the cerebrum.

thalamus, conduit for sensory stimuli, < Gk. *thalamos,* inner chamber

The ancient operation of trephining was to release demonic pressure on the brain. Of more contemporary popularity than trephining is surgical redesign of the brain, cutting out parts to help or allegedly to help effect desirable changes in health or personality.

lobotomy	cutting into frontal lobe
cingulumo + *-tomy* lit. girdle	incision into cingulum, fibers encircling corpus callosum, to relieve pain
amygdal + *-ectomy* lit. almond	*amygdala,* a small complex of nuclei at tip of temporal lobe with responsibility in olfaction

20.3 The Face

face < Fr. < L. *facies*

Face appears in the general vocabulary following adjectives (e.g., *long face*); in the medical vocabulary it follows *adenoid, bovine, dish, cow, frog, hippocratic,* and *moon* in terms descriptive of what the face looks like as a result of various afflictions. Most of the definitions of these and following terms for facial afflictions are taken from *Dorland's Medical Dictionary.* They are creative definitions, reminiscent of what a novelist might write. Genetic or fetal disorders can make many different kinds of faces, base **faci.**

adenoid face	"the dull expression, with open mouth, sometimes seen in children with adenoid growths"; also *adenoid facies*

bovine face	having the placid, heavy-mouthed appearance of a cow; also *facies bovina*
cleft face	also *macrostomia*, defined as "greatly exaggerated width of the mouth, resulting from failure of union of the maxillary and mandibular processes, with extension of the oral orifice toward the ear"
dish face, dished face	"a facial deformity characterized by a prominence of the forehead, a recession of the midface and lower half of the nose, a lengthening of the upper lip, and a prognathic chin"; also *facies scaphoidea*
frog face	"flatness of the face due to intranasal disease"
hippocratic face	also *facies hippocratica*, defined as "a drawn, pinched, and pale appearance of the face, indicative of approaching death"
moon face, moon-shaped face	"the peculiar rounded face observed in various conditions, such as Cushing's syndrome, or following administration of adrenal corticoids"

With *facies:*

facies leontina	"a peculiar, deeply furrowed, lion-like appearance of the face, seen in certain cases of advanced lepromatous leprosy"; also *liontiasis*
facies hepatica	"a thin face with sunken eyeballs, sallow complexion, and yellow conjuctivae, characteristic of certain disorders of the liver"
facies abdominalis	"the expression of the face characteristic of abdominal disease; it is pinched, anxious and furrowed, with the nose and upper lip drawn up"
Marshall Hall's facies	"the facies of hydrocephalus: a triangular face with a broad forehead and prominent frontal bones"
parkinsonian facies	"a stolid mask-like expression of the face, with infrequent blinking"
Hutchinson's facies	"a peculiar appearance in opthalmoplegia externa, the eyeballs being fixed, the eyebrows raised, and the lids drooping"

Facies has an addition reference: to the "face" or front surface (*surface* is also from *facies*) of an organ. Most of the 250+ medical terms from *facies* refer to front surface: e.g., *facies anterior femoris* front surface of thigh bone; and *facies labialis dentis*, front surface of anterior tooth.

Gk. **prosopo,** face	*prosopalgia, prosopodiplegia*
	prosoposchisis, prosopospasm
prosopoagnosia	lit. not knowing or being able to recognize faces

The medical term for a facelift directs attention away from the face to the removal of its wrinkles:

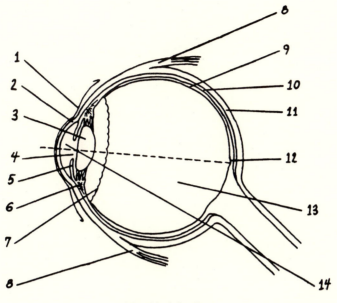

Words of the Eye

Maintaining original meaning: (10) *choroid*, membrane; (11) *sclera*, hard; (14) *aqueous humor*, watery fluid.
Compound: (1) *conjunctiva.*
From mythology: (5) *iris.*
Slight metaphoric value: (2) *cornea*; (6) *ciliary* body; (8) *rectus* muscle.
Strong metaphoric value: (3) *lens;* (4) *pupil;* (7) *serrata;* (8) *retina;* (12) *fovea centralis*, the central pit; (13) *vitreous humor*, glassy fluid.

rhytidectomy   composed from Gk. *rhytis*, wrinkle + *-ectomy* entered
                                   E. in 1930
L. *ruga*, pl. *rugae*, also means wrinkle, as of the palate, adj. *rugate, rugose, rugulose.*

eye < OE *eage* < IE *okw*, eye

IE *okw*

The E. *eye*, its compounds such as *eyelet, ogle* and *daisy* ("day's eye"), and its doublets as in Old Norse *window*, come from this IE source.

Latin and descendants

      oculo
      ocular   *oculomotive*   *pinochle*
      monocle   *oculist*   *inveigle*
      binocular   *inoculate*

oculo + *mycosis*	fungal infection of the eye
+ *nasal*	pert. to eye and nose
+ *plasty*	plastic surgery of the eye
ocellus	invertebrate eye as of locust
	pl. *ocelli*
Oculina	protozoa
Oculospongia	sponge
Oculus	echinoderm

Gk. **op** *optic, optometry, myopia, biopsy*

presbyo	+ **op**	+ -*ia*	*presbyopia,* condition of aged lenses
nyctal	+		condition of not having vision at night
			< Gk. **nyc**, night + *alaos*, blind + **op**
hemeralo +			blindness during daylight
Opsiceros			mammal
opthalm			*opthamologist*
xero	+ **opthalm** + -*ia*		condition of dry eyes
megalo +		+ -*ous*	enlarged eyes
Opthalmomyia			insect genus

The Gk. synonym for **pup**, pupil of the eye, is **cor**, pupil, *corelysis, coreplasy, microcoria, dicoria;* both are metaphors formed on the likeness of the small image in the eye to a doll or child. The color dish of the cornea is named after the goddess of the rainbow, Iris: *iris, irid.*

Gk. **blepharo**, eyelid	*blepharoptosis, blepharoplasty*
anableps	a fish; each eye is divided into two compartments, one for viewing predators above, the other for viewing food below
L. *palpe*, eyelid	*palpebral, palpebrate*
L. *nict,* to wink	*nictinic membrane,* inner eyelid of many animals
ear < OE *eare*	*earful*
Gk. **oto**	*otology, otolith, otitis*
parotid	salivary gland near the ear, entered E. 1680
parotitis	mumps
otolaryngologist	ear-nose-throat physician
L. **mall**, hammer	
mallet	percussion bone of the ear
	cognates: *mallet, massacre, mace*
	? machete
OE *anvil*	platform bone of the ear < OE *anvil*
L. *incus*	the anvil < *in-* + *cus* < *cudere,* to beat

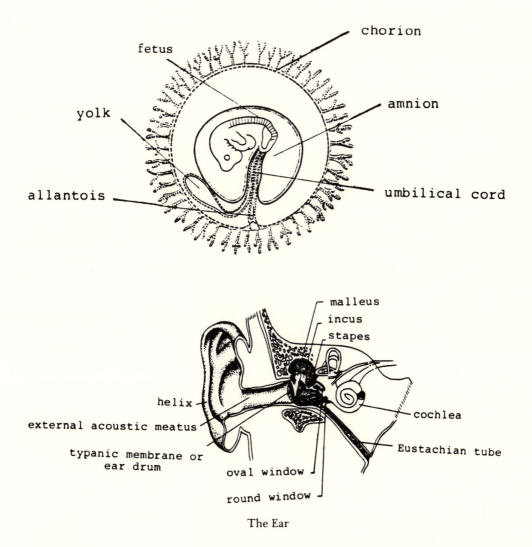

The Ear

L. *stapes*	lit. standing foot < L. *sta* < *stare*, to stand + *pes*, foot
OE *stirrup*	the stapes; also gear for horse < OE *stigrap*

nose < OE *nosu* < IE *nas*

IE *nas*, nose

Proto-Germanic > E.	*nose, nuzzle, nostril*
L. **nas**	*nasal, nasalize, nasturtium,* so-named because its sharp odor could afflict or twist (the *turt* from *tort,* twist) the nose

| **nar** | |
| *nares* | the nostrils |

L. **rostr,** snout, beak	*rostrate, rostral, rostrum*
Aptenodytes longirostris	a penguin
Gk. **rhino**	*rhinoceros, macrorhiny, platyrhiny*
	rhinoplasty
+ *virus*	virus responsible for many colds
+ *scope*	instrument to look into nose
+ *'lalia*	nasal speech

The horn-bill *Rhinocerus*

Gk. **rhynchus,** snout	
Rhynchocoela	phylum of ribbon worms
Rhynchocephalia	a reptilian order consisting only of the *Spenodon punctatum,* the lizard *tuatara* < Maori
Gk. *sim,* pugnosed	*simian, prosimian*
Simocephalus vetulus	a water-flea

Nosology is the study of disease, not of noses, < Gk. **nos** < *nosos,* a disease; *nosocomial,* pert. to developing a disease as a result of hospitalization; *zoonosia,* diseases mostly of non-human animals.

chin < OE *cin*	
L. **ment**	*mental* eminence, *labiomental*
Gk. **geni**	*microgenia, platygenia, genial, genion*

geny, jaw, cheek   *genyantralgia, genychiloplasty*
                         genyoschiza

jaw < ME jowe
L. **mala**   *malar, frontomalar, maloplasty*
also cheekbone and cheek *orbitomalar*
Gk. *gnath*
cheek < OE chece
L. **bucc**   *buccal, buccolabial, cervicobuccal*
                         nasobuccal
                         rebuke, lit. turn one's cheek against
boca   mouth
Perlissus bucculentus an ichneumonid
mouth < OE muth
Gk. **stom**

stomach	*anastomasis*	*xerostomia*
stomatitis	*stomatoschisis*	*macrostomia*

Rhynchostoma cornigerum   a fungus
Cyclostomata   class of agnatha, e.g., lamprey

stomy, putting mouth or   *trachiostomy, pericardiostomy*
opening into   *dacryocystorhinostomy*
                              cholecystogastrostomy

L. **or, os**   *oral, orifice, orator, oracle*
mouth   *orotund*
                           osculum, osculate

lip < OE lippa

L. **labi**   *labial, bilabiate, labiose*
                           labioversion, labium, labia majora
labrum   front part of some (e.g., bee)
                           arthropod mouths

Gk. **cheilo**

acheilia	*brachycheilia*	*cheilosis*
cheilitis	*macrocheilia*	*synchilia*
xerocheilia		

tongue < OE tunge

The two sources of biological terms for tongue have both been subject to metaphoric transference so that they appear in words referring to structures that look like a tongue (that are *linguiform*) and in words relating to language and the study of language. The native E. word *tongue* itself is also used metaphorically in this sense in mother tongue.

Latin **lang** and **ling** are used metaphorically for mother tongue in the words *language, bilingual,* and *linguistics* and their compounds; also in *Linguatula,* tongue-worm parasite. The bases are used literally in *lingualis,* toward the tongue; *linguodental; linguogingival;* and *lingua nigra,* black tongue.

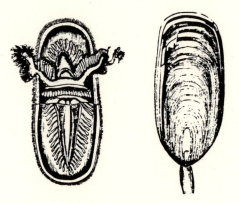

Lingula anatina

Greek **gloss** is metaphoric in the geographer's *isogloss,* and in *glossolalia,* babbling in alien languages. It retains its literal use symbolizing the tongue in *glossitis, glossodynia, glossopexy, schizoglossia, ateleoglossia; glossa,* bee's tongue; *glossotrichia,* hairy tongue; *glossopetrae,* shark's teeth; *Glossina,* a genus including the tsetse fly; and *Tachyglossus,* a genus of echidna.

The parallel base **glot** is metaphoric in *polyglot,* one who knows many languages, and literal in *glottis,* larynx vocal structure.

tooth < OE *toth*	*toothy, toothsome,* etc.

L. dent

dental	*dentifrice*	*denturism*	*indent*
dentistry	*dentilingual*	*dentate*	*indenture*
dentin	*dentoid*		

dandelion	< *dent de lion*
edentate	lacking teeth
Edentata	order of armadillos, sloths, anteaters
Gk. **odonto**	*orthodontist, peridontist, odontology*
+ *nomy*	dental classification
odontoiatrogenic	pert. to trouble caused by dental treatment
+ *clast*	instrument used to break teeth
+ *tripsis*	erosion of the teeth
masto + **odon**	*mastodon*
Odontoglossum pulchellum	an orchid

17th century illustration of fantastic shark's head and realistic shark's teeth, the glossopetrae, from Steno (Neils Stensen), *The Head of a Shark Dissected,* 1667

CHAPTER 21—TORSO, MUSCLES, AND VISCERA

21.1   Torso
21.2   Muscles
21.3   Viscera
21.4   Reproduction
21.5   Excretion

21.1 Torso

Italian anatomists stood out in the Renaissance as the initiators of modern-day anatomy. But since they used Latin in their descriptions, few Italian words have come into the biolexicon. One of these is *torso*, or trunk of the body. It developed from L. *thyrsus*, which came from Gk. *thrysos*, a wand. *Thyrsus* exists as a word for a staff and is used metaphorically in botany for a stem. *Torso* entered E. in 1715.

neck < OE *hnecca*

L. **cerv**, neck	*cervical, costicervical, cervicodorsal cervicoplasty*
cervix	neck; neck, or narrow end, of uterus
cervitis	inflammation of uterine cervix

Homophone *cerv* < L. *cervus*, deer, as in *cervine*, pert. to a deer.

L. *rumen*, throat	
ruminate	which could refer either to a cow's literally chewing its cud or to a person pondering personal destiny
rumen	first stomach of ruminants
ruminant	of the order Ruminantia, e.g., cattle, deer, camels

Gk. **pharynx, pharyng** throat	*pharynx, phargynoscope*
Saccopharynx ampullaceus	a fish

L. **trache**, windpipe	*trachea, tracheole, tracheostomy*
Pseudopeziza tracheiphila	a fungus

Trache traces back to a Gk. word for rough, and retains that meaning for the rough windpipe (as opposed to the smooth artery).

trachycarpous	pert. to fruit with rough skin
trachyspermous	pert. to seed with rough coat
Gk. **larynx, laryng** voice box	*larynx, laryngeal, laryngitis*

Larnacantha bicruciata   a marine protozoan
chest < OE *cest*

Gk. **thorax, thorac** chest   *thorax, thoracic, pneumohydrothorax*
                                  gastrothoracopagus, iliothoracopagus

Thorax, breastplate

Gk. **steth,** chest

stethoscope	*stethomyitis*	*stethoparalysis*
stethometer	*liostethus*	*stethospasm*

L. **pect**   *pectoral, expectorate, subpectoral*
pectoriloquy   speaking through chest
angina pectoris   the pain resulting from cardiac episode

shoulder < OE *sculdors*

Gk. **om**

brachyome	*omitis*	*omagra*
acromiohumeral	*acromiohumeral*	*omodynia*

acromion   high point of shoulder

navel < OE *nafela*

In Greek mythology, the deity Cronus had been alerted to the fact that one of his children would overthrow him. To prevent this tragedy, he ate his children. Rhea, his wife, disgusted with her husband's pedophagy, substituted a stone for one of the children. That child grew up to become Zeus, who overthrew his father. The disgorged stone, or omphalos, was taken and placed in the Delphi temple of Apollo, where it allegedly stood at the center of the earth.

A curious event in intellectual history was the promotion of an idea that a deity had planted dinosaurian and other ancient bones to give the earth the illusion of a history it never had. Philip Gosse was the author of the book, *Omphalos,* and the story is given in another section of this book.

Omphaloskepsis is the practice of looking into one's navel, as Buddha does in his representations, and as the sailors of Melville's *Moby Dick* do when they look at the doubloon fastened to the mast of the *Pequod*. One looks into one's navel to know oneself.

L. **umbili**   *umbilical*
            + *ferous*   bearing a navel
Gk. **omphalo**
omphaloskepsis   navel-gazing
            + *oncus*   tumor of the navel
            + *-tomy*   incision into navel
omphalos   + *-ite*   a fetal monster which, lacking a heart, dies upon
                                             severance of the omphalos
acro-   + **omphalus**   *acromphalus,* extreme height of navel

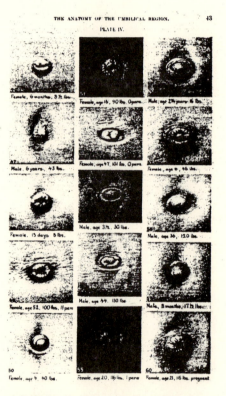

Bellybuttons, from Thomas Cullen
Adenomyoma of the Uterus, 1908

21.2 Muscles

Since the human body has more than 600 muscles, obviously a choice has to be made for selection among them. Many of the muscles have etymologies that satisfy the word-gourmet's palate, as does *sartorius*, a thigh muscle which got its name from the characteristic posture of a tailor, a *sartor*.

IE *mus,* mouse

L. **mus**		*Mus musculus,* taxonomic name of mouse
	+ *-cle*	*muscle, muscular,* etc.
mur		*Muridae,* family of rodents
	+ *-ine*	pert. to rodents
Gk. **myo**		*myocardium, myalgia, myogenic, myology*
	+ *a-* + *sthenia*	*myasthenia,* weakness of myocardium

Myopia is unrelated to **myo**, muscle; it's from Gk. *my* < *myein,* to shut + *ops* eye, the term referring to the nearsighted person squinting to see.

Source of Word	Muscle	Date of Entry	Controls
Metaphor of Appearance	*biceps* two heads	1625	flexion of forearm
	triceps three heads	1570	extension of forearm
	quadriceps four heads		extension of lower leg
	trapezius four feet *tetra-* + *peza,* foot	1685	moves shoulders and head
	deltoid like delta	1675	raises and lowers arms
	serratus like a saw < L. *serra, saw*		brings chest and legs together
	gastrocnemius belly-calf < Gk. *gastro* + *knemia,* calf of leg		extend and flex foot
Position	*pectoral* < L. *pect,* chest	1400	brings arms together
	latissimus < L. *latus,* side		moves shoulder blades, rotates arms
	oblique		rotates upper body, controls

Source of Word	Muscle	Date of Entry	Controls
	< L. *ob-* + *licinus*, bent upward		side flexion
	abdominal < L. *abdomin*		brings chest and legs together

We'll box the largest and most important muscle of the body, the heart, a useful organ, in that it pumps 55 million gallons of blood through 60,000 miles of blood vessels to sustain us during our four score and ten years.

Egyptian amulets representing the heart

IE *kerd*, heart

   Grimm's Law explains the retention of /k/ in Latin and Greek (and Celtic), and its change to /h/ in Proto-Germanic, so that E. *heart* is cognate with Gk. *card*. Indo-European languages look upon the heart muscle as though it can pump sentiments as well as blood—no other organ of the body is featured so heartily in sayings. French *courage* is like E. *strong-hearted*. For purging the heart of fear and pity, which can be overwhelming emotions, we have the useful *catharsis*, an emotional release that's supposed to be caused by seeing a tragedy. *Catharsis* orig. meant purging or purifying of the digestive system.

Gk. *kard*, **cardi**

cardiac	*acephalocardia*	*electrocardiography*
cardiology	*tachycardia*	*cardiolith*
myocardium	*bradycardia*	*cardiohepatomegaly*
endocardium		

cardia   can also refer to the stomach, as in *cardiac sphincter (ostium cardiacum), cardiac glands*

L. *cord*

One of the rare appearances of this base in the biological vocabulary is in *precordium*, the chest wall that lies before, or over, the heart. Most of the words with *cord* in them are metaphors in the general vocabulary, e.g., *cordial, courage, accord, record*, and *quarry* in the sense of prey.

The parts of the heart often receive their names from metaphors, as do *mitral valve* (two metaphors in that phrase: *mitr* orig. a hat and *valve* orig. leaf of a door), *septum* (orig. meaning fence); *ventricle* (belly); *foramen ovale*, oval window; and *auricles* (little ears).

21.3 Viscera

Two general words relevant to this section are *organ* < Gk. *organon*, implement, as in the musical instrument and in *organize;* and *viscera*, internal organs, intestines, < *viscus*, flesh, adj. *visceral*, refers also to a gut reaction. *Gut* < OE gives *gutsy, gut course*. Other synonyms for *viscera* are *pluck, entrails* and *splanchon. Neurosplanchinic* or *neurovisceral* pertains to nerves of brain and spine (cerebrospinal) and of sympathetic nervous system.

belly < OE *belg*
stomach < Gk. *stoma*, mouth, opening

L. abdomen, abdomin   *abdomen, abdominal, thoracico-abdominal*
Tipula abdominalis   a crane-fly

L. venter, ventr   *ventriloquist, ventral, ventricle*
of brain or heart
interventricular, eventration
ventrolateral, ventriculopuncture
Alopecurus ventricosus   a grass

Gk. **gaster**, stomach   *gastrointestinal, gastronomy*
                                      gastrolith, gastropod
Drosophila melanogaster
Chelidon erythrogaster   barn-swallow

Gk. **cel**, abdominal or   *celomic, celiac, celialgia*
other cavity   *celioma, celioscope*
celiotomy   incision of body cavity; also *laparotomy*
coel   *Coelenterata*
acoelomate   lacking abdominal cavity
encephalocoele   hollow cavity in brain

Gk. **enteron**, digestive track

enteritis	*enterocele*	*enterolith*
dysentery	*orthoenteric* ·	*gastroenterologist*

flank, side, between lowest rib and hip < ME < OFr. < Proto-Germanic

L. **lat**   *lateral, ambilateral, bilateral*
                                      collateral, laterigrade

Gk. **pleur**, side
pleurodont   reptile with teeth attached by their sides to the jawbone
pleuron   segment on side of arthropods
Gk. **pleur** more often refers to what is inside the body:
pleura   membranous sces lining lung
pleurisy   inflammation of pleura
Pleurotoma babylonica   a snail

L. **lumb**, area between   *lumbar, dorsolumbar, lumbago*
ribs and hips on side and back
of the body
L. **lumb** > Fr. *loin*, side   *loin, loincloth, sirloin*

Gk. **laparo**, flank
laparocele   ventral hernia
laparorrhaphy   suture of abdominal wall
laparotomy   incision through the flank or abdominal wall

many different kinds, depending on organ targeted, e.g., *laparohepatotomy*, "incision of the liver through the abdominal wall"; *laparoenterotomy; laparohysterosalpingo-oophorectomy*

liver < OE *lifer*   *liver*

Gk. **hepato**   *hepatitis*
          + *megaly*   enlarged liver
heparin   an anticoagulant

From the IE source *speigh* came two bases which look very different but are both equally applicable to the spleen: Gk. **splen,** from which *spleen, splentic, splenculus, splenemia,* and *splenokeratosis,* hardening of the spleen; and L. **lien,** as in *lienorenal.* Most terms from these two bases are entirely interchangeable, e.g., *lienectomy = splenectomy, lienography = splenography, lienopathy = splenopathy.*

kidney < OE

L. **ren**	*renal, reniform, suprarenal, adrenal*
Renicola pinguis	a nematode
Gk. **nephr**	*nephritis, nephropexy, nephrolysis*
+ *lite*	kidney stone
nephridium	invertebrate excretory organ
Nephrolepis exaltata	sword-fern
L. **jejun,** empty of food	*jejune,* empty, trite
+ *-ium*	*jejunum*

The *diaphragm* stretches between chest and lower body. This word comes from a Gk. infinitive, *phrassein,* to block, partition, which appears in four bases: to *phren,* which we've already seen, should be added *phragm, phrac,* and *phrax.*

phragm	*diaphragm, diaphragmodynia, arthrophragm*
phrac	*ethmophract*
phrax	*cataphraxis*
	urethrophraxis

For the membranous sac enclosing the viscera: *peritoneum* < *peri-* + *ton* < *teinein,* to stretch. The *omentum* is a peritoneal fold < L. *omentum,* the greater stretching from stomach to colon, the lesser from stomach and duodenum to liver. *Mesentery* < Gk. *mes-* + *enteron,* membrane composed of peritoneal layers, supports intestines.

The *perineum* < *peri-* + *-ine* < *inan,* to excrete, + *-eum* is the skin between genital and anal areas. Other *peri-* words also relate to covering.

No OE words for veins or arteries have survived. *Vein* was introduced into E. from French in the mid-13th century; its base is **ven,** as in *venous, venipuncture* and *venography.* The Gk. synonym is **phleb:** *phlebotomy* entered E. in the mid-14th century; *phlebitis* in the early 19th century; *phlebothrombosis, phlebosclerosis* and most other terms with **phleb** in them are products of the late 19th and 20th centuries.

Artery, base **arter,** < L. < Gk. entered E. about the same time as *vein;* and most of its combinations, such as *arteriole* and the dreaded *arteriosclerosis* are also products of the 19th and 20th centuries. *Aorta* entered E. about 1570; it comes from a Gk. word that referred to what it refers to today.

marrow < OE *mearg*
pith < OE *pitha*

Gk. **myel**   marrow, esp. of bone, esp. of spinal cord

| *myelocyte* | *myelom* | *myelomalacia* |
| *poliomyelitis* | *osteomyelitis* | *encephalomyelitis* |

hematomyelia	bleeding or hemorrhage into spine marrow
leukomyelitis	inflammation of spinal cord white substance
syringomyelocele	hernia of spinal cord

L. medulla

medullation	*medulla oblongata, medullectomy*
medulloarthritis	formation of a marrow or medullary sheath
medullotherapy	inflammation of marrow spaces
	rabies prophylaxis

gristle < OE *gristle*

L. cartilag   *cartilage, cartilaginous*
Gk. chondr   *chondrocranium, chondroma, chondromalacia mitochondria, chondrichthys*

For bands that connect muscles or bones or other organs, the biological vocabulary has several choices. The discussion could start with two Germanic words: *band* itself, which travelled from Germanic into French before coming back to E. in 1480; and *sinew* < OE *sinu*, which was used early in the history of English. Three bases come from Latin.

tend, tendon   < L. *tendon* < Gk. *tenon*, sinew (the *d* imposed because of association with L. *tendere*, to stretch) entered E. 1535

lig, ligament   < L. *ligare*, to tie + *-ment* entered E. 1375; 500 terms for ligaments

fasc, band
fascia   band of connective tissue for support of organs; < L. *fascia*, band entered E. 1555

Other biological terms with *fascia: fasciate*, an adj. pert. to bundles or bands; *Fasciolopsis*, a genus of parasitic flukes that cause *fasciolopsiasis*, its symptoms severe stomachache and diarrhea.

The Greek base for band is less familiar: *desm*. This combines with a number of suffixes and bases for affliction and repair, such as *-oid* and *-itis* for like a ligament and inflammation of a ligament. In the form *syndesm*, it combines with *-logy*, *-osis*, *-ectomy*, *ectopia*, *graphy*, *pexy*, *plasty*, and *rrhapy*.

| *syndesmophyte* | a bony growth from a ligament |
| *Desmognathus fuscus* | dusky salamander |

From a single IE source (*sneau*, tendon or sinew) come the cognates L. **nerv** and Gk. **neur.**

nerve < L. **nerv**	*nervy, nervous, nerveless*
enervate	to weaken
innervate	to turn a nerve on, activate, stimulate
Gk. **neur**	*neuron, neuralgia, neurotic*
neuroglia	protective nerve cells
astrocyte	supports neurons
oligodendrocyte	supports neurons
microglia	devours invading microbes and debris
neurasthenia	weakened cond. of nerves

Of the 43 pairs of peripheral system nerves, 31 transmit signals between spinal cord and brain. The other 12 connect organ or other part directly to brain; these are called the cranial nerves. An etymological approach would trace these from the dates of their identification, the times the designated words entered English, but an anatomical organization would trace them geographically, from those at the anterior part of the brain (N1) to those at the posterior. For defining the terms, this section will use the geographical approach but will note etymological points of interest, such as that the first cranial nerve to be observed and named was the optic. S = sensory, M = motor, B = both.

N.I   *Olfactory* S
< 1. *ol* + *fact* + *-ory*
The 16th century anatomist Vesalius first identified these, though *olfactory nerve* appeared in 1670.

N.II   *Optic* S
< Gk. *op*
An 1100 Latin document refers to this nerve, the *nervi optici.*

N.III   *Oculomotor* M
L. *ocul* + *motor*
Last of the cranial nerves to be named, *Journal of Microscopic Science,* 1881. Innervates four eye muscles.

N.IV   *Trochlear* M
< Gk. *trokhalia,* pulley, so named because it functions like a pulley in motorizing dorsal eye movement. 16th century anatomist Gabrielle Fallopio first recorded this, *Observationes anatomicae,* 1561. Fallopio also named 5th, 8th, and 9th cranial nerves, and tubes of the female reproductive system. *Trochlear* for the nerve entered E. in 1890. Innervates superior oblique muscles of eye.

N.V   *Trigeminal* or *trifacial* B
< L. *tri-* + *gem,* bud + *-in* + *-al; tri-* + *faci* + *-al*
Innervates scalp and face, with some sensory functions from teeth and skin. Entered E., *Be'clard's Anatomy,* 1830.

N.VI   *Abducens* **M**
< L. *ab-* + *ducens*
Innervates eye muscle—posterior rectus for lateral movement of eyes. *Encylopaedia Britannica,* 1875.

N.VII   *Facial* **B**
< L. *faci*
Mixed motor and sensory, nerve responsible for frowning and other facial expressions, for sense of taste and tear glands. Hooper's *Medical Dictionary,* 1818.

N.VIII   *Auditory* or *vestibulocochlear* **S**
< L. *audit* + *-ory; vest* + *-ibulo* + *cochle* + *-ar*
Receives sensation from inner ear. *Auditory* 1st appeared in 1724; *vestibulocochlear,* 1962.

N.IX   *Glossopharyngeal* **B**
< Gk. *gloss* + *phargyne* + *-al*
Innervates tongue, pharynx, some salivary glands. Receives impulses from pharynx and back of tongue. Entered E., 1823.

N.X   *Vagus* **B**
< L. *vagus,* wandering
As indicated by B, this nerve functions both to sense taste and also to initiate motor functions of organs of the throat and abdomen. *Vagus* entered E. in 1840, the word chosen because the nerve wanders about the body in fulfilling its responsibilities.

N.XI   *Spinal accessory* **M**
> L. *spin* + *-al; accessor,* helper
Innervates soft palate and pharynx. A confusing term, since *spinal accessory* has nothing to do with the spine; it's accessory to vagus nerve. Dunglison's *Dictionary of Medical Science,* 1842.

N.XII   *Hypoglossal* **M**
< Gk. *hypo-* + *gloss* + *-al*
Innervates tongue muscles. Carpenter's *Animal Physiology,* 1848.

Mnemonics are available for help in remembering these 12 cranial nerves. The standard is: "On old Olympus's towering top, a Finn and German viewed a hop." An undergraduate student who researched the etymology of the cranial nerves, Julie Pybas, invented a classier one: "Oh old Octavius, teach them a fantastic and glorious verse about Homer." To remember the functions—S for sensory, M for motor, B for both, one might memorize SSMMBMBSBBMM or "Some say 'marry money,' but my brother say 'bad business marry money.' "

fat < OE *faett*

L. **adeps, adip**   *adiposity, adipofibroma, adipohepatic*
Pholiota adiposa   a mushroom

Gk. **lip(ar)**

1. for genesis	*lipocyte, lipoblast*
2. for fats	*lipid, lipidolysis*
3. for enzymes	*lipase*
4. for diseases	*lipoma, liparomphalus, lipocardiac*
	liposarcoma, lipiduria
liparodyspnea	difficult breathing caused by being fat
Lipotropha microspora	a protozoan

Gk. **stear, steat**

stearic	*stearodermia*	*steatocele*
steatoma	*steatorrhea*	*urostealith*
steatopygia	*steatocele*	

Steatomys pratensis	a rodent

Homophonic **ster** means solid, as in *stereotype, stereophonic, stereoscopic, cholesterol, steroid, asterognosis.*

sterol (< **ster** + *ol* < L. *oleum,* oil (cp. *petroleum*)

stereotropism	turning toward a solid object
stereospondylous	hardening of vertebral column

Gk. **ker,** wax	*ceroplstic, cerotype, kerosene*
myokerosis or *myocerosis*	condition of a muscle becoming waxy
L. **cer,** wax	*cerate, ceraceous, ceriferous*
cerumen	ear wax
Ceroxylon ceriferum	wax-palm

21.4 Reproduction

Males and females share most of the same organs—brains and hearts, kidneys and jejunums and pudenda. *Pudenda,* the external genitalia < L. *pudere,* to be ashamed; the singular, *pudendum,* is applied only to the female external genitalia. *Impudence* orig. meant immodesty < *in-,* not + *pud,* not ashamed; now it denotes impertinence, an attitude stronger than mere immodesty.

breast < OE *breost*

Gk. **mast**	*mastectomy, mastitis, mastopexy*
	mastodon, mastoid
gynecomastia	morbid condition of male having breasts
Mastophora cornigera	a spider
Bumastus globosus	a trilobite
L. **mamma**	*mammal, mammary, mammiferous*
Mammillaria vivipara	a cactus
Cycloclypeus mamillatus	a foraminifer

Mastodon teeth

nipple < OE *neble*, dim. of *neb*, a nib

Gk. **thely** has three meanings: (1) the literal meaning, nipple, as in *thelerethism*, erection of the nipples, and *thelarche*, puberty stage of breast development; (2) female, as in *thelygenic*, birth of females only, also *thelytocia* (cp. *parthenogenesis*); (3) nipple-like. The third meaning accounts for **thel** as a base for skin. orig. for the covering of the tongue, with its bumps like little nipples, *epithelium*, and later that word was used as a model for *mesothelium, endothelium, perithelium. Blastothelia rosea* is the taxonomic name of a medusa.

vagin < L. *vagina*, sheath	*vagina, vaginate, invaginate* *vaginectomy, vaginissmus* *vaginomycosis*
Gk. *kolp* > **colp**	*colpocele, colposcope, colpopexy* *myocolpitis, colpopexy*
pachycolpismus	vaginal wall thickening; also *pachyvaginitis*
womb < OE *wamb*	
L. **uter**	*uterus, uterogestation, postuterine*
Gk. **hyster**	*hysterectomy, hysteria, hysteropexy* *acrohysterosalpingectomy*
Hysteromorpha trilobum	a trematode
Gk. **metr**	*dimetria, metrocele, endometrium*
Cynometra floribunda	a legume

The Gk. word for a bowl to catch the blood of a sacrificed victim was **amnion**; and that word came to denote the sac holding the embryo of reptile, bird, and mammal.

While one might not come across **amnion** itself outside of textbooks, the compound *amniocentesis* does appear in the news, for a procedure that punctures the amnion to test the fetus.

Egg and its parallel bases L. *ov* and Gk. *oo* come from the same IE source.

IE *awi*, bird

Into Proto-Germanic and its descendants as *egg* (Old Norse) and many compounds (*egghead, eggnog*) and *cockney*, a cock's egg, which is absurb. OE *knitu*, the egg of a louse > *nit*, as in *nitpick*

The L. **ov** is easily discernible in *ovum, ova, ovary* and *ovulate*. It went into Fr. to become *l'oeuf*, the egg, or something like an egg, a zero, an *oval*, *l'oeuf* becoming *love* in tennis. *Viola ovata* is the taxonomic name of a violet.

Gk. **oo** is also easily discernible in *oocyte, oogonium, oophyte*, and *ootheca*, an egg case. It is not discernible in *onyx*. *Stereognathus ooliticus* is the taxonomic name of an extinct mammal.

Another base from IE *awi* is L. **avis**, bird, as in *avian, aviary, avifauna*, and disguised in *bustard, ocarina, osprey*, and *ostrich*. *Avis* may be the source of *auspice* and *auspicious*, these words referring to a prophecy, prediction, omen. The etymology of that is: L. *avis* + *spic*, to see. Long ago, one way of predicting was to interpret the flight of birds.

---

yolk < OE *geolu*, yellow

Gk. **lecith**	*alecithal, eutelolecithal, lecithin*
homolechithal	yolk the same throughout
Sterrhurus monolecithus	a trematode
L. *vitell*	*vitellose, vitellicle, vitelline*
Crocus vitellinus	Syrian crocus
testes	
Gk. **orch**	metaphorical: *orchid*
	cryptorchism
Cynorchis villosa	an orchid
Gk. **didym**	*didymalgia, perididymus*

This also means twin attached to another, a fetal monster, as in *somatodidymus, ischiodidymus, cryptodidymus.*

L. **test**, witness	*testify, testes, testicle, testosterone*

Test in *testify* clearly means witness. If this is the source also of *testes*, then the latter term is a metaphor based on function or behavior: witnesses to maleness. *Testes* may, however, come from a homophonic **test** < *testum*, a pot for refining metal. The process is caught in the metaphoric *test*, an examination, and *test tube*, where the examination takes place. *Testes* may stem from this word, in which case its metaphoric sense is that of little pots.

Test < *testa*, L. for shell: *test, testa*, shell or seed coat, *testaceus*, having a shell; *Testacean*, protozoa with shells; *testudinate*, pert. to turtles. A fourth *test* is from Fr. *teste*, head > *testy*, irritable.

The male sexual organ goes under many unprintable terms from Anglo-Saxon. Three bases form words that are permissible in medical and other decent dialogue: L. **pen**, Gk. **phallo**, and Gk. *priap*. The L. base leads to a correction of the easy assumption that *pencil* is a small *pen*. The tale of *pen*, as in fountain pen, stems from L. *penna*, feather. A *pen* is, etymologically, a feather (as it literally was in the times of quill pens). A L. sibling of *pen* is *propitious*. IE *pet*, to which these L. words have been traced, is also the ancestor of Gk. *pter* and *ptosis*, and of OE *feather*.

An entirely different IE root, *pes*, lives on only in Latin **penis**, tail. A metaphoric transference led to a word for a little tail, *penicillus*, which took on the sense of a brush, a painter's brush or *pencil*. *Pencil* entered E. in the second half of the 14th century. Three centuries later, *penis* entered English; other terms with this base are *penile* and *penoscrotal*. In the early 19th century, *pencil* became the model for a much less familiar word, *penicil*, for hairs like a painter's brush, e.g., the hairy coat of a caterpillar. The discovery of microbes that look like tails led to the invention in the 1920s of *penicillium* and its offspring *penicillin*.

Gk **phallo**	*phallic, phallodynia, schistophallus*
	phalloncus, phallicism
Gymnophallus deliciosus	a trematode
Gk. *priap*	*priapitis, Priapulus*
priapism	disordered, chronic erection of penis

21.5 Excretion

In *urinary* and *ureter* is Gk. **uro**, for urine. From the number of medical terms containing **uro**, one would guess that the urinary tract is productive of considerable trouble: *Dorland's* lists over 150, the longest of which are *ureteropelvioplasty, ureterotrigonosigmoidostomy,* and *ureterohemine phrectomy*, and the most exotic *uriposia*, the drinking of urine (practiced by the Indian pacifist Gandhi) and *urolagnia*, sexual excitement from watching someone pee. Taxonomy offers *Uroglena*, a genus of flagellate protozoa. The L. term for urine is *mictur*, as in *micturate*.

Rectum, base **rect**, leads us first to a productive IE root and then to the anus. It seems weird to associate *royalty* and *rectum*, but these words, and perhaps the activities of those bodies, are related.

IE *reg*, to move in a straight line

Straightness is indicated in Proto-Germanic to native English *right* and *reckless*, lit. deprived of rightness. The sense of being right or correct is seen also in words from Fr.: *correct* itself, and *rectitude*.

L. *resurrectus*	*resurrection*
resurrection fern	a remarkable plant that seems to die in drought and revivifies with rain
	taxonomic name: *Polypodium polypodiodes*

A ruler is presumably one who walks a straight line; hence the idea of straightness or rightness appears in many words having to do with ruling such as *reign* and *regimen*, as of a diet.

In biological terminology the base **rect** > *rectipetality*, condition of a plant's having straight petals; *rectus*, straight muscle; *Paltorhynchus rectirostris*, an extinct beetle; and *rectum*.

arrectores pilorum	muscles which raise the hair
rectovesical	pert. to the rectum and urinary bladder
rectocele	a hernia of the rectum

mollusk *Rectogloma*, fish *Regalecus*, Reptile *Regina*, bird *Reguloides*

IE *reg* went into Greek > *orex*, appetite: *anorexia, dysorexia, hyperorexia, orexigenic, oreximania*.

Gk. **procto**, for rectum, has its own words, such as *protology, proctoscope*, and *proctoptosis*, but often is interchangeable with L. **rect**.

proctalgia	*rectalgia*
proctitis	*rectitis*
proctococcypexy	*rectococcypexy*
Gymnoproctus abortivus	a grasshopper

Anus, which like *testes, urinate*, and *rect/proc*, has unspeakable OE synonyms, is from L. *annulus*, ring, source also of *annulus*, ring-like; *annelid*, a worm, such as earthworm and leech, of phylum *Annelida;* and *Chaetogyne analis*, a fly.

This chapter concludes with terms for the bottom. A base that could mean tail, as do L. *caud* and Gk. *circo*, and also backside or bottom is Gk. *(o)ur*.

IE *ors*, backside

From this came the German word for buttocks, *arsch*, and the E. *arse* and *ass*. IE *ors* transformed into Gk. *oura*, tail, from which the bases **(o)ur, ur** before a vowel, and **us**. Homophonic *ur* means urine.

Gk. **ur. us**			*squirrel, cynosure, uropygium* (see below)
uro	+	*pod,* foot	a limb, e.g., on lobsters
	+	*sthenic*	strong-tailed
an-	+ **ur** + *-an*		*anuran,* tailless
platy- +		+ *-ous*	flat-tailed
oxy +		+ *-iasis*	pinworm infection
ourobolos			alchemical symbol of snake eating its tail
uraeus			Egyptian headdress cobra figure
saur + **us**			lizard-tailed
Coryphaena hippurus			dolphin

From another IE base came *buttock,* which once meant a strip of land, and has as its relatives *button, butt, abut, beat, beetle, confute* and *refute.*

Gk. **glut,** buttocks   *gluteua, gluteus minimus, gluteus medius, gluteus maximus*

Homophonic *glut* < L. *gluten,* glue, in *neuroglia, glutinous, glutose;* and < L. *glutire,* to gulp down, *glut, glutton, glutonous, gluttony.*

Gk. **pyg,** buttocks

steato + **pyg**	+ *-ous*	fatty buttocks
calli +	+ *-ean*	beautiful buttocks
uro +	+ *-ium*	bird's bottom, site of tail feathers
di- + **pygus**		double pelvis
pygo + *algia*		pain in the buttocks
+ *melus*		fetal monster, limbs attached to buttocks
+ *pagus*		fetal monster, twins joined back-to-back

Pygal has an unexpected synonym in *natal,* which refers both to birth and buttocks; *nates* means buttocks and the *natal cleft* is the crevice between the buttocks.

Pygmalion was a sculptor who fell in love with a statue he had made, Galatea—an episode brought up-to-date in *My Fair Lady. Pygmalionism* is the morbid condition of falling in love with something one creates.

CHAPTER 22—ROOTS OF HAIR

22.1   Skin
22.2   Baldness
22.3   Hair
22.4   Bristles, spines and thorns
22.5   Scales
22.6   Feathers

*I*ntegumentary < L. **in** + *tegu* < *tegere*, to cover + **ary** refers most generally to a covering, such as a seed's coat. It also refers to skin and hair and scales and feathers.

Flesh is from OE: *flesch.* Its synonyms are Gk. *sarc* and *creas* and L. *carn.*

Gk. **sarc**	*sarcoma, sarcoid, sarcous, sarcophagus*
	sacrolysis

Sarcophaga carnaria	Cyprian sarcophagus
Sarcodina	Protozoa subphylum, e.g., amoebae = *Rhizopoda*
Gk. **creas**	*create, pancreas* (all flesh, no bones or muscles)
L. **carn**	*incarnate, excarnation, carnivorous*
	carnation, carnival
carnal	of fleshly or sexual interest

22.1 Skin

skin < ON *skinne*	*skinny, skinhead*

L. pell
pelisse   fur coat
pellicle   film of skin
  + *agra*   skin disease

L. cori
corium   layer of skin
excoriate   criticize severely, lit., take the hide off

L. cut   *cuticle, subcutaneous*
                 in insects: *epicuticle, exocuticle*

Gk. derm

dermatology	*epidermis*	*dermititis*	*hypodermic*
pachyderm	*echinoderm*	*xerodermia*	*erythrodermia*

transdermal   adj., through-the-skin, for a way of delivering drugs into body
Echinodermata   phylum of spiny-skinned animals, such as starfish and sea urchins
Pachydermata   order of thick-skinned animals, e.g., elephant

The base for the three embryonic germ layers is **derm:** these mature as indicated.

1. *Endoderm*
   sheathing of gut and organs, parts of respiratory, urinary, reproductive tracts, endocrine glands, bladder epithelia

2. *Mesoderm*
   mesodermal somites: skeleton for head and trunk and also muscles
   intermediates or *mesomers:* kidneys, gonads
   lateral plate: coelom lining, muscles

3. *Ectoderm*
   body ectoderm: epidermis, hair, feathers, cutaneous glands and sense organs
   neurectoderm: nervous system, pigment cells, gill arches

All three collaborate in producing the *mesenchyme,* which develops into circulatory system, tissues connecting organs, and smooth muscles.

Turkish contributed *sagri,* leather >

shagreen   rough hide
chagrin   humiliation, shame

Gk. *dipthera,* skin or leather, is the source of *diphtheria,* an infectitious disease caused by *Corynebacterium diptheriae.* The etymological connection may be that a symptom of this disease is the appearance of a skin-like membrane blocking the throat. *Diphtheria* came into E. in 1860.

The term *goose bumps* comes from Old English. The condition of the hair rising to salute cold or fear is called by the French, *chair de poule,* chicken skin. *Horripilation* is the sesquepedalian term for this condition.

For hair of different kinds, the biological vocabulary offers 80+ terms. As usual, the common terms, like *hair,* are from OE, the more technical terms from L. and the most technical from Gk. Most of these terms make a brief appearance, as does *juba,* mane: the species name of the white-haired gnu is *albojubatus.*

We'll procede across this surprisingly large subject from infancy to senility.

22.2 Baldness

The fetus is bald and nude before it sprouts a fine lawn of hair. For smoothness and baldness:

Gk. *leios,* smooth
lei   *leiphemia*
leiodermia   smooth, glossy skin, an abnormal condition
leiomyoma   benign tumor of smooth muscles (e.g., uterus)
leiotrichous   smooth hair
leiorhizae   smooth roots
Telea polyphemus   a moth

L. **glab,** bare, smooth   *glabrous*
glabrificin   an anti-body, renders bacteria smooth
glabella   frontal bone area between eyebrow ridges

L. **nud,** uncovered   *nude, denude,* etc.
nudicaudate   hairless tail
Nudibranchia   a suborder of marine slug-like snails

Doris

Eolis    Tritonia

British nudibranches

L. **calv**, hairless	*calvus, Calvary*
calvities	baldness
calvarium, calvaria	dome-like superior portion of frontal, parietal, and occipital bones

Gk. *psil*, bare, smooth	*epsilon, upsilon*
psilomelane	a manganese ore
psilocybin	a hallucinogenic substance from the mushroom *Psilocybe mexicana*
psilosis	hair falling out
psilanthropism	belief that Jesus was bare of divinity, a man
Psilopa petrolei	a fly; note *lei*, smoothness

More productive has been Gk. **gymn**, naked. *Gymnast* was once a naked athlete practicing in a *gymnasium*.

gymno + *anthous*	
+ *bacterium*	cell lacking flagella
+ *cyte*	cell without cell wall
+ *spore*	without protective envelope
+ *plast*	mass of protoplasm without enclosing wall
+ *scopic*	inclined to or concerned with viewing the naked body; cp. *voyeurism*
+ *sophy*	a rare synonym for nudism
+ *sperm*	plant in which the seeds are not enclosed in ovary

hemi- + **gymno** + *carpous* having the hymenium, or fertile layer, exposed during spore formation, pert. to certain fungi (*carp*, fruit)

22.3 Hair

Words for the structures of hair entered English from the 15th century on.

papillon < L. *papula*, pimple, 1400
follicle < L. *follis*, bellows, 1640
sebaceous < L. *sebum*, sweat, 1720
arrector pili < L. *ad* + *rect* + *-or; pili* < L. *pilosus*, shaggy
pilus, 1955

The hairy story of a human being's rise and decline begins with the down covering the fetus, *lanugo*. *Lanugo*, like *lanolin* and *lanosterol*, *laniferous* and *lana*, is a product of Latin *lana*, wool, Lanugo sheds off to be replaced with *vellus*, fleece, the hair of prepubescence.

While *vellus* is applicable to the hair of prepubescence, the base *vell* in *velvet* and *velour*, **vill**, tuft, usually refers to the *villus* or pl. *villi*, small vascular thread-like projections as lining intestine.

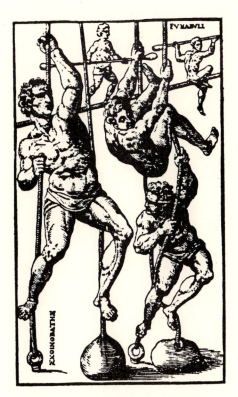

17th century A.D. Italian gymnasts,
from Mercuriale, *De Arte Gymnastica,* 1573

Bull leaper from Cnossos,
15th century B.C.

villosity	the condition of being covered with villa
villositis	a bacterial disease characterized by alternations in the placenta's villi

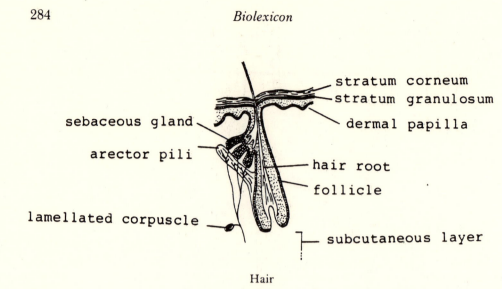

stratum corneum
stratum granulosum
dermal papilla

sebaceous gland

arector pili

hair root
follicle

lamellated corpuscle

subcutaneous layer

Hair

villoma	tumor of the villi, pathological rectal condition
villusectomy	excision of a villus
Ateles vellorosus	a species of spider monkey

Two villi

Innocent babyhood is succeeded by perfidious puberty < L. **pub,** the symptoms of which are breasts for females, an uncertain voice for males, and for both the growth of hair in genital and armpit regions and also, for males, on the face. Hair in the first two regions has the utilitarian function of absorbing and holding moisture and odor; facial hair might be atavistic and vestigial, though in handlebar moustaches and Van dyke beards might also be aesthetic. *Phthirius pubis* is the taxonomic name of the crab louse.

For *comb,* the biological vocabulary has Gk. **cten** and L. **pect.** *Ctenoid* means like a comb or rough-edged; *ctenudium,* structures like the teeth of a comb, or like feathers; and *Ctenophora,* phylum of comb-jellies. A synonym for *ctenoid* is *pectinate,* which refers to structures such as the comb-like teeth of lemurs. **Pect** has been adopted as the base also for *pectineal* and *iliopectineal*, referring to the pubic bone and ilium-pubes.

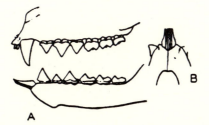

A. Profile View of Ctenoid Lower Teeth of Lemur
B. Dental Comb Seen from below

Through French spelling and semantic transference from comb to dress, *pect* became *peignoir*, a dressing gown. Thus does etymology tempt an association between the toilette of a woman in her boudoir and the dental apparatus of a lemur grooming a significant other in a tree in Madagascar.

Three bases descriptive of hair in general are **pil, cil,** and **trich**; each has specific referents also.

Gk. **pil,** hair

pilose	*piloerectus*	*caterpillar*
depilate	*horripilation*	*plush*

pilifer	carrying hair
mollipilose	adj. for soft hair
pelage	furry hair

L. **cili,** for hair-like process, eyelashes

superciliary	eyebrows
supercilious	adj., haughty, perhaps from image of someone raising eyebrows in disdain
Euciliotia	subclass of protozoa
Gk. **trich**	*trichology, atrichia, pachytrichia schizotrichia, leitrichous*
trichin + *-osis*	not morbid condition of having hair, but an infestation of muscles by the hair-like nematode parasite *Trichinella spiralis*
tricho + *cyte*	protozoan hair-like dart
+ *mono-* + *-iasis*	*trichomoniasis*, genital disease caused by *Trichomonas vaginalis*, parasitic protozoa
trichin + *-iasis*	ingrown hair, as with eyelashes

amphi- + **trich** + *-ia*	condition of a bacterial cell having a flagellum on each end
Trichonympha	protozoa in gut of termites
Trichoptera	order of caddis flies

For hair-like worms, *nemat* and other bases for thread were metaphorized. *Capill* is also used < L. *capill*, hair, nematode taxa *Capillaria, Capillospirura; capill* is the base for a conduit the width of a hair, the *capillary*.

Ciliate protozoa don't wiggle eyebrows a la Groucho Marx, but do wiggle a curly, flexible appendage composed of fused cilia, or *cirrus;* in botany, *cirrus* means tendril. L. *cirrus*, curl, is also used for something high up, the thin and narrow cirrus cloud, and for something low down, *Cirripedia*, the order of barnacles which Charles Darwin studied for eight years. L. **flocc**, lock of wool, tuft

flocculent	adj. for downy or flaky mass
flocculation	a colloid phenomenon, not coagulating
serioflocculation	
floccillation	picking at bedclothes by delirious patient

The distaff sex is called that because Old English women, and young ones too, spun the flax (OE *dis* meant flax). L. *crinis*, hair, renders the relatively unfamiliar biological term *crinite*, having hair-like tufts, and the less unfamiliar *crinoline*, the hoop skirt which Victorian women wore to announce that they lived in houses big enough to accommodate that vast contraption made of horsehair and girders.

Gk. *dasy*, thick-haired, shaggy, bushy

dasyphyllous	full of hairy leaves
dasypygal	hairy rumped
Dasypus	"hairy foot," tropical armadillo
Dasyurus	genus of marsupials, e.g., Tasmanian devil
dasymeter	instrument to measure density of a gas

From densus, thick, the Latin cognate of *dasys*, comes *dense*.

L. *hirsut* means very hairy; *hirsutism* is a disease, its victims looking like furry animals.

L. *barba*, beard, the obvious ancestor of *barber*, may also be the source of *Barbados*. *Barbiturate*, which came to E. from German, might trace back to L. *barba*. Basque *bizar*, which also means beard, took on the sense of bravery in Spanish *bizarro* and now exists in a word that has less to do with beards or bravery than with the federal deficit: *bizarre*.

A Greek word for beard, **pogon**, is used to describe the unwelcome sprouting of a distaff beard, *pogoniasis;* the point of a chin, *pogonion;* a phylum of worms, *Pogonophora;* and an orchid genus, *Pogonia*. An uncle who has a devilishly beautiful beard could be described as being *calopogous* or, if he's given to terrifying his nieces and nephews, as being responsible for inducing *pogonophobia*.

If people live long enough, their hair loses its sheen and its color, becoming *albicomus*. Gk. *kome*, which gave rise to several medical terms with *comus* in them,

Wolfman Family from Munich Petrus Gonsalvus and His Daughters, 16th century

also gave rise to a word describing the astral phenomenon of a spherical object racing through the sky trailing long hair: the *comet*.

In old age, especially for males, hair grows in new places as it retires from old places. L. *vibrissa* means long hair—e.g., that about the muzzle of a dog; *vibrissae* is the term for hair growing in the nasal cavity. Gk. *tragos*, a goat, is applied as *tragus* to the round bump from temple into ear; goat-like strands of hair often decorate this site in the ears of elderly gentlemen.

Gk. *alopekia*, fox-mange = **alopec,** loss of hair, baldness. *Alopecia* is a condition in which the hair falls out as per its genetic programming; also called male pattern baldness. Over 30 kinds plague hairy animals, such as *alopecia areata*, exclamation-point hair, atrophy, attentuation of the bulb. That male pattern baldness symbolizes mange rather than wisdom is one of the sneakier indignities afflicting elderly gentlemen.

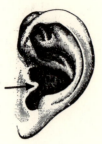

Tragus of ear

22.4 Bristles, spines, and thorns

L. **seta**, bristle	*setaceous, setiferous*
setirostral	hairy beak (*rostr,* beak)

Gk. **chaet**, long hair, bristles	*chaetophorus, achetinous, chaetoplankton*
chaetotaxy	orientation of hair or hair-like structures on an insect's exoskeleton

The application to bristles has led to this base being used for taxa of animals:

Polychaete	class of marine worms
Oligochaeta	class of earthworms
spirochaete, spirochete	an order of microorganisms causing yaws, syphillis, and other disease

Gk. **echin**, hedgehog	*Echinodermata*
echinosis	spiny erythrocyte
echinulate	having small prickles or spines; applicable to bacteria culture
echinopthalmia	spiny-like projection of eyelashes
echinochrome	brown pigment in sea urchins
Echinus	genus of Echinodermata; sea urchin
Echinococcus	genus of tapeworms
Echinostomata	genus of parasitic flukes; the disease: *echinostomiasis*

Echin gave rise to *urchin,* a mischievous street-boy. Slightly homophonic is *echid.*
Echidna is a monotreme, the spiny anteater of Australia.

Gk. **acanth**, thorn, spine	
coele + **acanth**	
coelecanth	a crossopterygian fish; the name of the genus, thought to be extinct, entered E. c. 1610: *Coelecanthus;* a living specimen, was identified in 1938

acantho + *logy*	study of spiny animals
+ *cyte*	a spiny red blood cell
Pyracantha coccinea	firethorn

L. *spina*, thorn = **spin**, spine	*spine, spinal, spinescent*
porcupine	lit., thorny pig < L. *porcus*, pig + *spina;* cp. *porpoise* < L. *porcopiscis*, hog fish; the taxonomic name of the porcupine is *Erethizon dorsatum*, and of porpoise, *Phocoena phocoena; porcupine* entered E. c. 1400, *porpoise*, c. 1300
Penicillium spinulosum	a microbe

22.5 Scales

Although about 30 bases have to do with scales (that word itself from French), only two or three have been productive in the biological vocabulary. L. *scabies* > *scabies*, a mange; and L. *squama*, scale, to *squamate* and *squamous*, scaly—as in *squamous epithelium* and *squamate*, scaly; *desquamate*, to peel off scales; and a few taxonomic names, among them *Macromischa squamifera*, an ant.

A productive base is Gk. **lep(r)**, scale, rind, flake, as in *leprosy, leprology*, and *leprologist. Lepros* means "scaly," **lepido**, flake or scale, **lept**, slender, thin: e.g., *leptodactyly*, very thin fingers.

lepidoma	a tumor from scaly tissue
lepidophobia	morbid dream of contracting leprosy
lepidarium	sanitarium for lepers
Lepidoptera	insect order—butterflies and moths; their study: *lepidopterology*
Lepidosiren	the lungfish

Homophonic *lep* refers to a hare, as in *leporine; leporid* of the family *Leporidae*.

22.6 Feathers

IE *pet*

   IE *pet* meant to fly. The *p* was changed in Proto-Germanic to an *f* sound, *fethro*, which became OE *fether*, modern E. *feather*. Latin retained the *p* sound for words having to do literally or metaphorically with feathers: esp. base **pinna(ti)**, feather.

penna	*pinion*	*panache*
pennant	*pinnacle*	*pen*

pinniger	bearing feathers

Pinnipedia   a mammalian order, of walruses, etc.

IE *pet* also had the sense of to rush, go toward, and that was retained in L. *petere,* from which *petal* as well as *petition, petulant, appetite, compete, impetus, perpetual, repeat;* and from another L. source, *propitious.*

IE *pet* appears in Gk. as **pter** for feather or wing, e.g., *archeopteryx, pterodactyl, pterygoid, coleoptera, pteridology.* Also fr. Gk. *piptein,* to fall: *ptomaine, ptosis, symptom.* Also from Gk. *potamos,* river: *hippopotamus,* lit. the river horse.

L. **pluma,** feather, down > *plume, plumage, nom de plume, Corycaeus deplumatus,* a cyclops, genus of freshwater copepods

Pinnigrade feet of seal

For hard covering of the body, several terms are available:

chitin < Gk. *chiton,* tunic   exoskeleton of insects and crustaceans

test < L. *testa,* shell   shell covering some animals, e.g., tunicates

carapace   structure covering turtles
< Spanish < unknown

CHAPTER 23—AFFLICTION AND REPAIR

23.1 Disease
23.2 Affliction
23.3 Repair

23.1 Disease

Diseases may receive their names from metaphors. Five examples of this linguistic process will suffice here. Gk. *angina*, orig. choking, as from a sore throat, is a metaphor in *angina pectoris*. Gk. *staphylo*, grape, cluster of grapes, and *coccus*, berry, are now in words for microbial agents and infections. Gk. *carcin*, L. *cancer*, Fr. *chancre*, are metaphors based on the manifestation of the disease, remotely similar to the movement of a crab. L. *burs*, purse, became the metaphoric model for a sac of fluid, as in *bursitis*.

The bases which carry the most general sense of disease are *pathy* and *drome*, course. **Pathy** can refer to feeling: *pathos, sympathy;* to disease: *pathology, cholepathia;* and to treatment: *homeopathy, hydropathy. Etiopathology* is the study of the origin of diseases and *idiopathic* is an adjective pert. to that which has no known cause.

Gk. **drome**, course, occurrence	*syndrome,* of which there are about 1000 combinations, most eponymous
	Some of these will be known or easy to define, such as
	acquired immune deficiency syndrome (AIDS)
	anxiety syndrome
	alcoholic withdrawal syndrome
	post-Vietnam syndrome.
	premenstrual syndrome.
bradycardia-tachycardia syndrome	heartbeat alternating between too slow and too fast
Chinese restaurant syndrome (CRS)	caused by ingestion of monosodium glutinate, featuring faintness, fatigue, clenched jaws, backache, and an insane desire to eat some more

Other notable words with **drome:** *hippodrome, palindrome,* a word or phrase meaning the same backward as forward, e.g., "A man, a plan, a canal—Panama!"

orthodromic	correct or right course, as for nerve impulses
prodrome	a foreshadowing of a coming affliction

291

actinodromic	adj., veining of a leaf
photodromy	movement toward or away from light

Disease came into E. in 1300 with a more general meaning than it presently has: *dis-*, reversal + *ease*, thus synonymous with *unease*. In 1760, a word with a parallel etymology joined *disease: malaise*, now having more the sense of a weariness of mind than of body. Some of the many diseases we are heir to, such as the parasitic, are brought on by an alien's invading the body. Others, such as hemophilia, are inherited. Still others, such as cancer, result from bodily mechanisms going awry, often enough provoked to do so by the victim's bad dietary or other habits.

We have seen that *parasite* underwent pejoration in beginning its career as a term for a person who sat at a table and then becoming a term for an agent that exploits and often enough eventually kills its host. Parasites may be classed into those that attack the outside of the body, ectoparasites such as leeches and mites, and endoparasites such as Trypanosoma.

The names of parasitic diseases are often eponyms, such as Salmonella, and toponyms, such as Lyme disease. The nosology of parasitic diseases is cosmopolitan, including terms from Latin or Greek, e.g., *cholera*, and terms from the languages of the countries in which they are virulent, such as the Singhalese *beriberi*, the Tswanian *tsetse*, and the Dravidian + Persian *kala-azar*.

The parasite can be delivered to its human host from contaminated food or water. The microorganism Vibrio in contaminated water is responsible for cholera. *Cholera* < Gk. **chol**, bile, entered E. in 1350; its carrier, *Vibrio cholerae*, a microbe living in contaminated water, was sensationally active in the 19th century, the choleric plague hitting India in 1816, Europe in 1831, and North America shortly thereafter.

Typhus (1635) and *typhoid* (1790) < Gk. *typhos*, vapor. Typhus is an infectious disease communicated by *Rickettsia*, hosted by fleas and lice. Typhoid, however, is caused by the bacterium *Salmonella typhosa* in food; a notorious carrier of this was Mary Mallon, Typhoid Mary. *Typhogenic* can refer either to typhus or typhoid fever.

As illustrated by *Salmonella*, the parasite can be delivered through the mediation of an animal. A snail of the genus *Bulinus* can transmit a blood fluke or trematode parasite that causes schistosomiasis. Mice, sheep, goats and other mammals can be vectors for other schistosomiatic trematodes. The crustacean Cyclops is a carrier of the nematode *Dracunculus medinensis;* the mosquito Anopheles is a carrier of *Plasmodia;* birds can carry the microorganism *Chlamydia*, which causes psittacosis as well as other afflictions.

The rat flea *Xenopsyllo cheopis* may transmit the bacterium *Yersinia pestis*, the etiological agent of bubonic plague. In the 14th century, the bubonic plague or Black Death hit Europe, killing millions of people. Lymphatic reaction to the infection caused the outbreak of rose-like swellings in the groin and armpit. A Greek word for groin, *boubon*, in the form *bubo* is used for such symptoms of this plague. *Plague* (and its cousin *plagarism* < L. *plagi(um)*, kidnapping) stems from L. *plaga*, wound; both *bubo* and *plague* came into E. in the mid-14th century, though the term *bubonic plague* is a late 19th century immigrant.

Among other desperate measures, people tried to clear away the malaise by

Doctor disguised to protect himself from the plague

swinging bouquets; but it didn't help, they wheezed "tisha, tisha" and fell down dead. The progress of the disease is caught in a children's chant.

Ring a ring o'roses,
A pocketful of posies,
Tisha, tisha,
We all fall down.

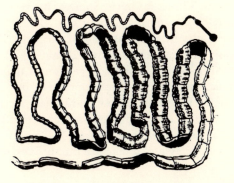

Cestoda, the common tape-worm

The vectors, or carriers, then, can be snails, parrots, goats, fish, insects, acarids. The actual parasites they pass onto human beings are protozoans or helminths. Malaria is caused by the protozoan *Plasmodium;* sleeping sickness by *Trypanosoma;* kala azar by *Leismania.* Millions, sometimes hundreds of millions, of people are afflicted with parasitic diseases. It is estimated that a billion suffer from ascariasis. caused by the worm *Ascaris.* Hookworm infects 750,000,000. Smaller populations. but still impressive, are infected with *schistosomiasis* and *taeniasis,* infestation with tapeworm.

A recent entry into the roster of parasitism is Lyme's disease, a mite on deer infecting its host, which could be a human being, with a treponema.

23.2 Affliction

A bit of preparation will make the coming inventories more accessible. First of all, because we have already come upon most of the bases listed for affliction and repair. examples of combinations will usually be limited to two or three. Secondly, a tightly packed chart could be designed demonstrating that dozens of bases for parts and organs combine with these bases for affliction and repair. This section is a good illustration of the principle that learning a finite number of bases and affixes gives a clue to a googol of combinations.

Here's a vignette of the process:

	Affliction		Repair	
	-itis	megaly enlargement	centesis	pexy fixation
gastro	gastritis	gastromegaly	gastrocentesis	gastropexy
cardio	carditis	cardiomegaly	cardiocentesis	cardiopexy
entero	enteritis	enteromegaly	enterorrhapy	enteropexy
hepato	hepititis	hepatomegaly	hepatocentesis	hepatopexy

We could list 50 terms in the left column for parts of the body. Combing the approximately 75 bases below for afflictions and repairs will give at least 50 that combine with all of the left column's bases for parts. Some of the resulting compounds would not be sensible. *Cardiocentesis* means puncture of the heart, which is a practice followed more meaningfully by assassins than by surgeons (though *pericardiocentesis* is legal). Looking upon the brighter side, the full chart of 50 × 50 yields 2500 words.

Lack of the designation < indicating source signals that the element meant in pagan days what it means today. Where appropriate or of particular interest. boxes will be charted tracing the base to its IE root and indicating cognates in the common as well as biological vocabulary. Knowing familiar cognates might be of help in fixing the unfamiliar bases in one's mind.

As general as the bases *pathy* and *drome* are the suffixes **-osis** and **-itis**.

Gk. **-osis**, morbid condition of
The *sis* will usually be preceded by *o,* but other vowels also precede it: *iasis, asis, esis* — *halitosis, blepharosis.*

exotosis	growth on a bone (as on the *Homo erectus* feumur found in Java by Dubois)
	elephantiasis, podoniasis

In a minority of words, **-osis** means condition of, for example, *symbiosis,* the condition of two organisms of different taxa living together; *anastomosis,* passageway between two organs, which could be a pathological condition or a repair.
Gk. **-itis,** inflammation *otitis, encephalitis*

Urinary discharge caused by schistomiasis,
from ancient Egyptian papyrus depiction

Pain and seizure

Gk. **algia,** pain	*neuralgia, coccygalgia, hysteralgia*
Gk. **dynia,** pain	*odontodynia, proctodynia*
Gk. *spasm,* spasm	*blepharospasm*
Gk. **agra,** seizure	*cardiagra, cheiragra*
podagra	gout
gonalga	gout in the knee

IE (*s*)*lagw,* to seize

   Into Gk. as **lepsy,** seizure.

epilepsy	*narcolepsy*	*catalepsy*
prolepsis	*organoleptic*	*nympholeptic*

Proto-Germanic > English *latch.*

We've come upon the Gk. base *plax* for flat, *plac* in *placenta.* Tracing this back to its IE root exemplifies the Grimm's Law principle that IE *p* became *f* in Proto-Germanic, so that a cognate of *plac* is *fluke,* a flatfish. Several words in the scientific, not just biological, vocabulary also trace back to this IE root.

IE *plak,* flat

   Proto-Germanic to Old Norse to English: *floe, flake, flaw.* Proto-Germanic to OE: *fluke.*

From Latin and French, English has adopted *placate, placid, plea. pleasant. complacent, plank,* and *placebo. Placebo,* important in the testing of drugs. entered E. in the 12th century meaning I shall be pleasing.

From Greek *plessein,* to strike::

plegia, paralysis	*gastroplegia, cystoplegia, paraplegic*
psychoplege	that which paralyzes mental activity
plec	*apoplectic*
plex	*cataplexia*

From Greek *plax,* flat: *placenta;* and from Greek *pelagos,* sea: *pelagic, archipelago.*

Softening and swelling, tumor

Gk. **malacia,** softening   *chondromalacia, myelomalacia*

Gk. **megaly,** enlargement   *acromegaly, cardiomegaly*

Gk. **edema,** swollen   *dactyledema, edematous, pneumonedema*
                                  myxedema

Oedipus   swollen foot
Oedaleonotus enigma   a grasshopper

-Ma could indicate diseased condition of, as in *edema,* but also could merely make nouns, as in *enigma, stigma, aroma.*

Gk. **gangli,** swelling   *ganglion;* 100+ kinds of ganglia

L. **tuber,** swelling, bump   *tuberculosis, tubercle, truffle*
tuberose   a bulbous plant

Gk. **cele,** swelling   *cystocele, encephalocele, omphalocele*

cp. homohonic *cele, coele,* a hollow < Gk. *koilia,* cavity: e.g., *coelom,* a body cavity; *acoelomate,* without cavity; *enterocoele.*

L. *tumor,* swelling   cognate: *thumb*
tumid   swollen
detumescence   a decrease in swelling

Gk. **oma,** tumor   *sarcoma, melanoma, angioma*
In opthalmological terms, **oma** does not refer to a tumor but to some other abnormal condition, e.g., *glaucoma,* abnormal pressure in the eye.

Gk. **onco,** tumor, cancer *oncogenesis, oncology, arthroncus*

Breaking and flowing

Gk. (r)**rhag**, breaking	*hemorrhage, odontorrhagia, gastrorrhagia*
Gk. (r)**rexis**, rupture	*amniorhexis, onychorrhexis*
Diarrhegma modestum	a fly
L. **frag**, break	*fragile, fragment, refrangible, ossifraga*
fract	*fracture, diffraction*
L. **rupt**, break	*rupture, disruptive*
Gk. *emesis*, vomiting	*emetic*
Gk. **rhe**, flow	*diarrhea, pyorrhea dacryorrhea*
catarrh	mucus membrane inflammation
Bostock's catarrh	hay fever
rheuma(to)	*rheumatism, rheum*
Syrrheuma cretata	a moth

IE *bhleu*, to swell, overflow

Bloat, an Old Norse word, comes from this root. Some Greek words may also, but they're contested. Latin is the primary source for descendants of IE *bhleu*.

L. *fluere*, to flow, provides a fine incentive for another look at how affixes work and how resultant combinations are hidden metaphors. Base **flu** operates in the examples of one from whom words just flow out, one who is *fluent* and if they're honied words, then the orator is *mellifluous;* if the orator goes above what is needed, an applicable term is *superfluous.* The act of flowing together is caught in *confluence;* of flowing to something, such as money: *affluence;* of flowing in: *influence* and *influenza.* That which flows out, such as sewerage, is *effluent.* Bones that flow in the sense of losing their hardness, or softening, characterize *ossifluence.*

Another base from L. *fluere* is **fluv**. Nouns corresponding to *effluent* are *effluence* and *effluvium*, pl. *effluvia*, sewerage. There are particular words for the effluvium of the land and of the ocean: *fluvioterrestrial* and *fluviomarine.* That which simply flows, such as a river, is described by *fluvial.* From bases **fluct** and **flux**: *flux, reflux, fluctuate, semi-fluctuation*, like a palpation.

Fluoride is easily misspelled as *flouride*, but it has the base **flu** for flowing in it. So does *fluorine* and the two dozen other words from *fluor(o),* such as *fluorescence, fluoridate,* and *fluorography.* An early *fluor* word to come into E. was *fluorspar* (1785), a mineral now known as *fluorite.* The metaphor here might come from fluorine gas flowing easily into minerals.

IE *gheu,* to pour

Four Proto-Germanic products: *gut, gust, gush, geyser.* Into Gk. as *khein,* to pour.

chy, pouring, mixing together
pyecchysis   pouring out of pus
synchysis   softening of eye's vitreous body

chyl, fluid, juice
chyle   a lacteal fluid
chylemia   this fluid in the blood; for the fluid in other
                                 organs: *chylothorax, chylopericardium,*
                                 chyloperitoneum, etc.

chym
chyme   digested food in stomach
parenchyma   functional aspects of an organ

chlorenchyma   plant tissue that carries chlorphyll
                                 enchym, infusion
mesenchyme   mesodermal cells that mature into connective
                                 tissue, lymphatic vessels, blood and blood vessels

choan, funnel
choana   funnel-shaped cavity
choanocyte   cell of some protozoans and sponges
Choanoflagellida   order of Protozoa

As is regularly the case, the words from the L. descendants of IE *gheu* will be more familiar—e.g., *futile,* the metaphor that of a vessel easily emptied, leaky. L. *fundere,* to pour.

fun(d)   *funnel, refund*
infundibulum   funnel-shaped passage, 15 infundibula in body,
                                 e.g., *infundibulum nasi*
fus   *suffuse, effusion, diffusion, perfusion*

Hardening and other afflictions

Gk. **kerosis,** hardening   *splenokerosis, cardiokerosis*
Gk. **sclero,** hardening   *scleroderma, arteriosclerosis*
                                 rhinoscleroma, sclerotomy
L. **her, hes,** to stick   *adhesion, inherent, cohesive*

	incoherent
L. **string, strict,** draw tight	*astringent, stricture, constrict*
Gk. **sten,** narrow	*stenosis, bronchiostenosis, stenopetalous, stenothermal*
Gk. **schisis,** split	*schistosomiasis*
Gk. **penia,** lack of	*leukopenia*
Gk. **thromb,** blood clot	*thrombus, thrombocyte, thrombogenesis, thrombolysis,* *thrombosis*
Gk. **pto,** drooping, prolapse	*blepharoptosis, omphaloproptosis tarsoptosis, ptomaine,* *symptom*
Gk. *ambly,* blunt, dulled	*amblyopia, amblypod*
Gk. **phthis,** wasting away	*cystophthisis, phthisiogenesis phthisiotherapy*
Gk. **seps, sept,** putrid	*septic, antiseptic, asepsis, septicemia*
Gk. **sapro,** decayed	*saprophyte, sapremia, saprozoic*
Gk. **poikil,** spotted irregular	*poikilodentosis, poikilonymy*
Platypoecilus maculatus	platy fish

Gk. **ankyl, ancyl,** crooked, bent < Gk. *ankon,* bent, elbow, fused	
ankylosis	fusion of joint bones
ankyloglossia	tongue-tied
Anklylosauria	suborder of Cretaceous dinosaurs
Ancylostoma	genus of hookworms; infestation by: *ankylostomiasis*

Gk. **trauma,** wound	*trauma, traumatize, microtrauma* *traumatology*

Terat is a base for monster, specifically for monstrous fetal disorders. The theory of maternal impressions was more popular in the past than today, though some people still believe that a pregnant woman who visits the zoo may give birth to children that look and act like monkeys. The causes of some embryonic defects, such as anencephaly and spina bifida, are not known. Genetic defects account for a quarter of malformations. Other malformations may result from imperfect development of reproductive cells (*teratospermia*), from vitamin A deficiency, from a viral infection. From 1957 to 1961, tens of thousands of pregnant European women took a tranquilizer, thalidomide. This medication was found to be teratogenic, causing at least 10,000 children to be born with imperfect limbs or no limbs at all, a condition termed *phocomelia,* limbs like seal flippers.

Attaching other bases and suffixes to **terat** yields:

teratogen	*teratomorphous*	*teratoma*
teratogenesis	*teratoid*	*teratism*
teratoblastoma	*teratosis*	*teratophobia*

A monstrous lizard goes under the name of *Teratosaurus suevicus* and an extinct bird *Teratornis merriami.*

A survey of three other terms (*monster, pagus,* and *didymus*) for monstrous growths would be suitable here. L. *monstrum* means marvel, as in the word *monster* itself. *Monster* derives from a fairly productive IE root that meant, of all things, to think.

IE *men,* to think

One of the few terms from the Proto-Germanic branch that's relevant is *mind.* Some Sanskrit offspring (*mandarin, mantra*) and Avestan (*Ahura Mazda,* god of light; *Ahriman,* god of darkness).

Many L. offspring, all familiar.

mental	*demented*	*comment*	*mention*	*memento*
money	*monitor*	*monument*	*premonition*	*summon*

Many Greek names for beings in general or specifically: *maenad, Eumendies, Mentor, Muse, Mnemosyne* (and base *mn* as in *amnesia, amnesty, mnemonic*); and from Greek, the bases *mancy,* divination or magic by, and *mania,* condition of being obsessed.

Of these words, the closest parallel to *monster* is *demonstrate. Monster* is a showing, a portent of bad events to come, a warning (cp. *admonition,* a warning). *Monster* entered E. in 1250, *demonstrate* in 1550. *Monster* is used in terms having to do with teratology: *cyclopic monster,* or *cyclops; acraniate monster,* fetus without skull or brain (cp. *anencephalic*); and *sirenoform monster,* like a siren, having fused legs (also *sirenomelus*). Gk. **pagus,** monster

cephalothoracopagus	two torsos with merger of upper bodies
allantoidangiopagus	blood vessels of twins joining
ischiopagus	fusion at the hip
Gk. **didym,** twin	*craniodidymus, gastrodidymus, ichiodidymus, cryptodidymus*
katadidymus or *catadidymus*	separate torsos, fused legs
anadidymus	separate legs, but fused above (*monstra duplicia anadidyma*)

Other bases are also used for descriptions of monsters, for example, *ceph* in *dicephalus,* a two-headed aberration, and **mel,** limb, in *amelia,* no limbs, and *phocomelia.* One agent responsible for phocomelia is the tranquilizer thalidomide. A fetus as thin as paper is called *papyraceus.*

dimeloprosopus	one body and one head with two faces

As a transition to repair, we'll note that several bases can denote either destruction and disorder or repair.

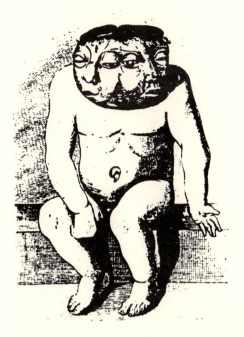

Dicephalic monster, from Samuel Soemmerring,
Abbildungen und Beschreibunger einiger Misgeburten, 1791

Base	Disordered condition	Surgical or therapeutic repair
path	disease in *osteopathy*	treatment of in *homeopathy and heliopathy*
esis	separation of parts in *dieresis*	guided separation in *catheresis*
fistula	duct formed by disease or injury	surgical duct made for draining
lysis	abnormal loosening in *paralysis*	surgical loosening in *tendolysis*
lepsis	seizure in *epilepsy*	*lab,* a handle in *litholabe*

23.3 Repair

For words applicable to repairing a condition, bases can come from many sources in Greek and Latin, for example: *artificial respiration, reanimation, resurrection, resuscitation* (fr. L. *ciere,* to move, with sense of to summon). Some bases have been used a great deal; these are the ones noted.

General repair bases

One of the several IE roots for to make was *kwei.* Its descendants exist in two languages, Sanskrit and Greek.

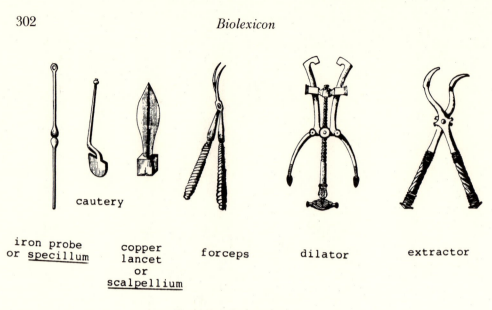

cautery

iron probe
or <u>specillum</u>

copper
lancet
or
<u>scalpellium</u>

forceps

dilator

extractor

Pagan Surgical Instruments

IE *kwei,* to make, build up

One word from the Sanskrit descendant came into English:, *cheetah,* and one base from the Greek: **po(i)e.** One who makes a *poem* is a *poet; mythopoesis* is the process of making myths; *onomatopoeic* is an adjective which pertains to the making of names, or, in its actual more narrow application, to words that echo sounds.

Most of the words with **po(i)e** in them belong to the medical vocabulary. Using the base for flesh in first position and this base in second produces *sarcopoiesis. Erythropoiesis* is the technical term for the production of red blood cells, and *galactopoietic* an adj. pertaining to the production of milk. *Pharmacopeia* is an inventory of pharmacies or drugs.

erythropoietin   hormone governing red blood cell production

Gk. **iatr,** heal
iatr, one or that which heals

iatrogenic	*iatrotechnics*	*podiatry*
psychiatry	*hydriatric*	*pediatry*

cp. **san** < *sanus,* health—*sane, sanity, sanitary*

Gk. **therapy** < *theraps,*   *hydrotherapy, heliotherapy, psychotherapy, therpeutic*
attendant
L. **cult,** tend   *culture, cultivate, acculturate*

Hydrotherapy
19th century

Gk. **phylac,** protect(ion) *prophylactic, anaphylaxis, cryophylactic, phylaxin,*
phylax < *phylassein* to guard *tachyphylaxis*

Gk. alex, protect(ion) *alexocyte, alexipyretic, toxalexin*
L. **stru,** build *instrument, deobstruent*
struct *structure, construct, obstruction*
  reconstructive
strum *antistrumous, strumiferous*

Washing out and dissolving

clysis, washing out, lavage *phlebocylsis, enteroclysis*
clyster, instrument *coloclyster, metroclyst*

A most employable bases, with at least 40 terms to its credit, is **lysis** < Gk. *lyein,* to loosen, break up. On the dark side, one cognate is *forlorn hope.* On the brighter side, another cognate is *resolve.*

IE *leu,* to loosen, take apart

The immediately important cognate for **lysis** is *loose,* into E. from Old Norse; from other Proto-Germanic siblings and from OE itself come *leasing, lose, loss,* the suffix *-less, lorn, forlorn,* and *forlorn hope.* The latter didn't mean what it means today. From Dutch, it meant lost troop, *verloren hoop.*

IE *leu* went into L. and then French to become E. words with the metaphoric sense of loosening to them:

solve	*solution*	*soluble*
absolve	*absolution*	*absolute*

dissolve	*dissolution*	*dissolute*
resolve	*resolution*	*resolute*

Gk. **lysis,** dissolve

lysis	*paralysis > palsy*	*odynolysis*
lysin	*karyolysis*	*steatolysis*
lysogen	*hemolysis*	*chromatolysis*
analysis, analyze	*urinalysis*	*photolytic*
analytic	*dialysis*	*autolytic*

Fastening, suturing

L. **fix,** fasten   *fixation, fixate*
                                 basifixed, dorsifixed, transfixation

Gk. **pexy,** fixation   *nephropexy, pneumopexy, hysteropexy*
                                 chloropexia, colopexostomy

Gk. **rrhaphy,** suturing < Gk.   *myorrhaphy, uranorrhaphy, herniorrhaphy*
rhaptein, to sew

plasty, surgical renovation <
Gk. *plassein,* to flow   *rhinoplasty, blepharoplasty, achondroplasty, uranoplasty*

abdominoplasty   tummy tuck

Shaking, stretching out, drawing

L. **cuss,** shake   *concussion, percussion*
succussion   a violent shaking (*sub-* here means up)

Gk. **ectasis,** stretching   *gastrectasia, papillary ectasis*
dilation
pneumonectasis   emphysema

L. **tract,** draw

traction	*abstract*	*abstraction*
detract	*contract*	*contractile*
protractor	*extract*	*extractor*
retractor		

Intrusive techniques   Gk. *techne,* skill

centesis, puncture of < Gk. *kenteein,* to prick

center	*heliocentric*	*pericardiocentesis*
centric	*geocentric*	*amniocentesis*

| eccentric | egocentric | arthrocentesis |
| | ethnocentric | pleurocentesis |

L. **pung,** puncture
punct

pungent
puncture, punctuate, acupuncture
punctiform, punctum

clasis, breaking

osteoclasis, histoclastic
colloidoclasia

clast, instrument

osteoclast, lithoclast, cranioclast

Other words from *klaein:*

clade, cladocarpous, cladistics, cladoptosis, clon

Gk. **tomy**
tome, segment and
instrument
rachiotome
ectomy, removal of
rhytidectomy

anatomy, phlebotomy, entomology
atom, diatomic, microtome
tomotocia
an instrument to cut into spinal canal
appendectomy
face lift

stomy, opening into
provide with an opening <
Gk. *stomatos,* mouth

gastrostomy, brochostomy

L. **rad, ras,** abrade, scrape

abrade	abradent	erase	raze
abrasion	radula	erosion	razor
abrasive		rasorial	

Ficus radulina

a fig

curettage

L. *cura* > Fr. *curette,* an instrument to scrape a body
cavity, the process: *curettage*

IE *tere,* rub, turn, pierce, grind

For the last in this inventory of repairs, we'll return to IE. Rubbing to remove the husks of grain is indicated in the Proto-Germanic descendants of IE *tere: thresh, threshhold,* and *thrash. Throw, thread, drill,* and *derma,* a Yiddish word for intestinal casing (not the homophonic *derm,* skin) also come from the Proto-Germanic descendants of IE *tere.*

L. *tritus,* base **trit,** meaning rubbing away, appears in words of the general vocabulary. That which has been worn down by overuse is *trite;* the act of wearing down is *attrition;* to be *contrite* is to be ground or worn out; also from this L. source: *detriment* and from that *detritus,* that which is worn off, debris.

Triturate < L. **trit**, means to crush, grind into powder. From a related L. source comes *tribulation*, trouble, its literal sense being thrashed like cereal grain, having one's protective husk ground off.

Triticum turgidum	a wheat
Catostomus teres	sucker, a fish

L. *triturate* is a term in the biological vocabulary, but most terms from IE *tere* came into E. through Gk. *Teredo* is a boring worm, not one whose conversation is uninteresting, but one that bores into wood. From Gk. *trema* and related forms for perforation come *trauma; trepan* and *trephine*, tools for boring into, respectively, rock and skull; and names of living things with base **trem** and **tryp**:

monotreme	a mammal possessing one exit for birth and excretion (e.g., the platypus)
trematode	a parasitic flatworm, class *Trematoda*

Gk. *tribein*, to rub, grind, crush

trip(sy)	*lithotripsy, neurotripsy*
tripsis	
anatripsis	a rubbing away
	entripsis, xerotripsis
Tripsacum dactyloides	a grass
tribe, instrument for crushing	*diatribe*, an attack that wears away one's resistance or patience; a crushing retort
	nototribe, sternotribe
tribo, friction	*tribology, triboelectricity*
	triboluminescence
tribad	lesbian; *tribadism*
triboluminescence	

Gk. *tryein*, to rub down
trype, a hole

trypsin	a pancreatic enzyme; *trypsinogen*
trypan, to bore, a borer	*trypanolysis*
trypanosome	a parasitic protozoa, genus *Trypanosoma*, transmitter of sleeping sickness
trepan or *trephine*	an instrument to cut out bony cores from the skull cap; *trephination*

In the past, long after such events as the 14th century bubonic plague, efforts were made to prevent diseases. One of the most dramatic of these efforts was Jenner's development of a vaccine against smallpox. Though the early experiments in smallpox prevention had their detractors, vaccination was so successful that eventually smallpox was wiped out of existence. Vaccination against poliomyelitis has also been wonderfully successful, though this disease has not yet been obliterated. The history of medicine shows a constant accumulation of knowledge and a constant refinement of techniques so that many of the afflictions of the past no longer exist.

So miraculous has been the success of medical science that we tend to overlook it. While measures could be taken in the past to clean up alleyways, exterminate rats, provide a healthy environment for the body to repair itself, until the 20th century, no physician could cure any disease with a drug. Sulfa and pencillin were harbingers of an extensive pharmacopoiea. Today, few of us have suffered from or know anyone who has suffered from cholera, scarlet fever, smallpox, tuberculosis. Manipulations of genes and instruments and technical advances in surgery collaborate with the pharmacopoeia to save an innumerable host of people who a century ago would have had no chance.

"Dr. Jenner, an excellent portrait, is seen in the exercise of his discovery; a workhouse lad, impressed into the service as his assistant, is holding a milk pail filled with 'vaccine pox hot from the cow.' A second doctor is in attendance, dispensing medicines to promote the effects of the vaccination, which are strongly developed on all sides. Various whimsical results are pictured in the unfortunate subjects with whom the process may be said to have taken. A picture in the background, founded on the worship of the golden calf, represents the adoration of a cow." From a contemporary critique.

PART VII: CONCLUSION

CHAPTER 24—PHIZ

24.1 Physiognomy
24.2 Secretions
24.3 Latry and Mancy

What we look like affects what people think of us. The technical term for interpreting personality from facial or other bodily features is *physiognomy* < Gk. **physio**, nature + **gnom** < *gnomos*, judge + *-y*, a word that was used, with its present sense, in the Periclean Age of ancient Greece. Freud proposed that "anatomy is destiny," by which he meant that a woman's reproductive anatomy programs her to be housewife and mother. Freud's equation, however dubious its scientific merit, reflects popular attitudes towards sex roles. Gk. **hyster** retains its meaning of womb in medical terms, such as *hysterectomy*. It also appears in *hysteria*, a temperamental condition supposedly brought on in (and etymologically only in) a woman because only she possesses a womb.

We all have had experiences testifying to the truth of the observation that our appearance is an important and sometimes critical inspiration of how people respond to us. Rather than address these experiences, which are often intimate and may be embarrassing, we'll turn to the safer terrain of fiction for terms relevant to biological, quasi and pseudo-biological fields.

24.1 Physiognomy

In the physiognomic system, one's *phiz*, or face (*phiz* is a clipping of *physiognomy*) reveals. An antique colleague of physiognomy is *phrenology*, the study of the shape of the head < Gk. **phreno**, skull + *logy*. The notion behind phrenology is that the brain reveals itself in pushing out sections of the skull; a large frontal skull bone indicates that the front of the brain, site of good manners and intelligence, is large, while a large occipital bone indicates criminal aggression. The extrapolation of character from the contour of the skull infuses such metaphors as *highbrow, lowbrow, pinhead, numbskull* and is behind the practice of *craniometry*, measurement of the skull in order to ascertain intelligence and personality.

Interpreting personality from facial or other bodily features has guided human relations from the earliest epics to the latest movies. Directors who want a profitable flick would not cast Woody Allen as Machoman, nor Clint Eastwood as Wimp. We

Lying eyebrows

Stupid eye

Benevolent chin

Selfish chin

Erratic mouth

Desire to love

can tell that Chaucer's Summoner is a villainous character because his face is flush with pimples, and that the Wife of Bath is lecherous because she displays a gap between her upper incisors. The tribulations assailing Dr. Frankenstein's creature began when the eight-foot-tall baby wandered out into the world.

Though he was innately kind-hearted, he looked terrible and people were afraid of him. Their response to his phiz caused him to grow into what they had predicted: a murderer.

People were prepared for interpretating Neanderthal Man half a century before his bones were blasted from a valley's cliff. Throughout the 18th century and into the 19th, phrenological books sold well. They depicted the criminal as having a sloping forehead, prognathous face, a head that seems to rise from the shoulders. When Neanderthal Man was reconstructed from the bones, he fit that outline well and his physique was taken as an index to inner bestiality—the same correspondence between physique and character to be seen in the ape-like Mr. Hyde of Robert Louis Stevenson's *Dr. Jekyll and Mr. Hyde.* Later on in the 19th century and into the 20th, efforts were made to remove Neanderthal from our ancestry because such a hulk was too gross a granddaddy.

Head of an exemplary man,
the Rev. Dr. Tyne

Head of a malefactor,
prototype for Neanderthal

Cesare Lombroso, a late 19th century Italian criminologist, in *The Criminal Man* posited diagnostic features of its subject. The male criminal could be spotted by his ape-like head and posture; some types of criminals could be spotted by the shape of their ears or lips. The female criminal or prostitute could be spotted by her having a large space between first and second toes, the gap revealing a throwback to an ape's foot. Prognathous jaw, large canines, powerful muscles, and a tendency to bite and beat up people were featured in the dentist character of an American naturalist novel by Frank Norris, *McTeague.*

Those who look bad ignite hostile responses, those who look good inspire cordial responses. The Athenian courtesan Phyrne was brought to trial for a crime and was acquitted when she displayed her beautiful body to the judges. The word *beauty* began in IE *deu,* to do, to honor; its many cousins include *bonus, beau, debonair, benign, embellish,* and *beatitude,* a state of blessedness.

One Gk. base for beauty is **aesthe**, as in *aesthetics,* the science of beauty,

A brigand

A trocophale (cone-head) violateur

Faces of criminals, from Caesare Lombroso, *L'homme criminale*, 1880.

and *aesthete*, one who loves beautiful things. **Aesthe** also means feeling, as in *anesthetic*.

Another Gk. base for beauty is **cal(l)i**: *calligraphy. calliope, kaleidoscope* — entered E. in 1817. 1819: "This rainbow look'd like hope — Quite a celestial kaleidoscope." (Byron, *Don Juan*) 1856: "To allow truth and falsehood to be jumbled together in one ever-shifting kaleidoscope of opinions."

calli + *sthen* + *-ics*	athletic exercise, lit. beautiful strength
calli + *pyg* + *-ean*	beautiful buttocks

Entered E. in 1646. 1939: "Young ladies stretching, writhing, callipygously stooping to tie their sandals."

calli + *opsis*	a plant, lit. beautiful eyes
Callimastix	genus of parasitic protozoa
Callichroma moschatum	musk beetle
Calliphora vomitoria	species of bluebottle flies

Vomit < L. *vomere*. Another base for throwing up is *emet* < Gk. *emein: emetic*, that which causes vomiting.

In ancient medical theories, structures could account for behavior. This statement is exemplified by the etymology of *hypochondria*. Gk. *hypo-* means under, as in *hypodermic*, and *chondr* means cartilage and *-ia*, condition of. The word was invented to refer to a site under the cartilage, a site which was imagined as responsible for spouting melancholic feelings. Thus, to be a hypochondriac is to be victim of these feelings, specifically about the prospect of one's health.

The *hypochondrium* or *regio hypochondriaca* refers to the sides of the body from lower rib to hip. One side is designated by *dextra*, right, the other by *sinistra*, left.

24.2 Secretions

Present-day idioms in English attest to the old notion that our personality is influenced or even determined by the action of bodily organs. The alleged temperature of the blood is an index to personality in the terms *hot-blooded* and *cold-blooded*, *fiery nature* and *cold as a fish*. The heart has been given a major role in determining our personality. Aristotle apparently thought that the heart was the seat of the intellect (he also apparently thought that women have more teeth than men do). Today, the heart is alluded to as the organ for emotion, as for example in *hearty*, *heartless*, *cold-hearted*, *heartbroken*, *cordial*.

The term for fluid or moisture was **humor**, used in a general sense in Shakespeare's phrase "humours of the dank morning." *Humor* still retains its old meaning of fluid in *vitreous humor*, the viscous material within the eyeball, and *aqueous humor*, fluid between eye lens and cornea, and its base still means moist in cognates *humid* and Gk. **hygro**, moist, as in *hygrometer*, *hygroma*, *hygrostomia*, *hygrology*, and *Hygrobates galbinus*, a spider.

The theory of humors is based upon the idea that secretions of bodily fluids determine our character and therefore behavior. *Rheumatism* is lit. the condition of having a flow through the body. To be *humorous* was originally to suffer from a swirl of these bodily fluids. *Humor* shifted from meaning fluid or moisture to meaning a sense of fun. There were four major humors: **sangri**, blood; **phlegm**, orig. heat; **chol**, bile; and **melanchol**, black bile; and some minor fluids targeted in the theory.

Base	Biological	Common
L. **sangri** blood	*consanguinity* *exsanguinate* *sanguivorous* *sanguicolous*, living in blood	*sangfroid*, cold-bloodedness *sanguine*, optimistic *sangria*, a Spanish red wine
Gk. **phlegm** heat	*phlegm* *leukophlegmasia* *ureterophlegma*	*phlegmatic*
Gk. **chole** bile	*chole* *cholegogue* *cholelith* *cholangiogastrostomy*	*choleric*
Gk. **melanchol**		*melancholy*
L. **bil**, bile	*atrabilious* *biluria*	*bilious*
L. *splen* spleen	*spleen*	*splenetic*

The nature of the sanguine person was described in a poem of the Italian Renaissance:

Sanguinary

Phlegmatic

Choleric

Melancholic

Complexions cannot virtue breed or vice,
Yet may they unto both give inclination,
The *Sanguine* gamesome is and, nothing nice,
Loves Wine, and Women, and all recreation,
Likes pleasant tales, and news, plays, cards & dice,
Fit for all company, and every fashion:
Though bold, not apt to take offence, not ireful,

But bountiful, and kind, and looking cheerful.
Inclining to be fat, and prone to laughter,
Loves mirth, & Music, cares not what comes after.

Chaucer poetized about a sanguinary physician knowledgeable not only about the humors, but also about astrology, drugs, and finances:

With us ther was a DOCTOUR OF PHYSIK:	
In al this world ne was ther noon hym lik,	
To speke of phisik and of surgerye,	
For he was grounded in astronomye.	astrology
He kepte his pacient a ful greet deal	
In houres by his magyk natureel.	
Wel koude he fortunen the ascendent	
Of his ymages for his pacient.	
He knew the cause of everich maladye,	
Were it of hoot, or coold, or moyste, or drye,	
And where they engendered, and of what humour.	
He was a verray, parfit praktisour:	
The cause yknowwe, and of his harm the roote,	
Anon he yaf the sike man his boote.	remedy
Ful redy hadde he his apothecaries	
To sende him drogges and his letuaries.	syrups
For ech of hem made oother for to wynne	each worked to
Hir frendshipe nas nat newe to begynne.	the other's
Wel knew he the olde Esculapius . . .	profit
Of his diete measurable was he,	
For it was of no superfluites,	
But of greet norissyng and digestible.	
His studie was but litel on the Bible,	
In sangwyn and in per he clad was al,	red and blue silk
Lyned with taffeta and with sendal:	
And yet he was but esy of dispence:	
He kepte that he wan in pestilence.	
For gold in phisik is a cordial,	
Therefore he lovede gold in special.	

Phlegm has a curious etymological history from a stem meaning heat, firey, to a base meaning its opposite. The history of *phlegm* shows that it's a sibling of *phlox*, first cousin to *flame*, second to *blond*, and distantly related to *blue* and *black*. The IE source, *bheu*, meant to burn, to be bright. From this through Germanic came the native E. words *bleach*, *blaze*, *blind*, *blend*, and *black*, that which is burned; and from Old Norse, *bleak*.

From Latin and through French, four bases yielding dozens of words in English, among them *flame* and *flamboyant*. The base **flavo** means yellow as in *flavescent*, *flavin*, *riboflavin*. A base of scientific, though not biological, interest is *fulg*, for lightning, as

Chaucer's Doctour

in *fulgent,* radiant, and *fulminate,* to flash words like lightning. French gave English, again among many other words, *blanch, blank, blemish, blond* and *blue. Gentiana flavida* is the taxonomic name of a gentian.

Phlegm comes from Gk. *phlegein,* to burn. The orig. sense of burning has become metaphoric.

phlox	a plant of bright color
phloxine	a red stain
phlogiston	a mysterious inner quality that supposedly permits things to burn
Phlegethon	the firey river of Hades.
phalarope	a wading bird with bright white spot

The way a word that originally related to burning came to denote thick mucus conducts us to a theory of pagan quasiscience. Some pagan philosophers categorized the world into four basic elements (the fifth was the *quintessential*): air, earth, fire, and water. Each of the four was associated with one of the humors.

air: blood   earth : bile   fire : black bile   water : phlegm

Each of the pairs could be either hot or cold. Phlegm, cold and moist came to be associated with mucus having or supposedly having the qualities of moistness and coldness. A person possessed by those traits was *phlegmatic,* or coldly inactive, listless.

From ancient Greece through Rome and into the Middle Ages, a sane mind in a sane body meant that the humors coursing through the body were in balance, well centered. To stray from this balance or center is, even today, to be unbalanced or eccentric. The fluids were responsible for behavior. The personality resulting from the swirl of the fluids is a *temper*, which entered E. early. before 1000, from L. *tempera*, proper mixture. In 1350, *temper* took on the prefix *dis-* to become *distemper;* and in 1400, a suffix to become *temperament*. *Tempera* (a mixture of oil and egg for painting), an 1825 import from Italian, retains the original neutral meaning; the earlier *temperament* might be neutral, referring to our disposition, or pejorative, so that our disposition becomes a bad disposition; and *temper* in general use is no longer neutral. A person or a climate that is calm and balanced is *temperate*.

Other bases for mixture < L. *miscere*, to mix; L. *turbare*, to stir; and Gk. *krasis*, a mixture. **Mixt** is the base in *mixture* and, from the vocabulary of religion, *commixtus*, putting the surrogate body of Christ into a chalice. **Misc** is the base in *promiscuous*, lit. placing a high priority on (sexual) mixing, *miscegenation*, the act of mixing those of different geneologies or races, and the chemical *immiscible*, not able to be mixed. From L. *miscere* through Fr.: *meddle, medley, melange,* and *pellmell*.

L. *turbare*, **turb**

disturb	turbid	turbine	turbulence
turbocharge	turbojet	turbinate	nasoturbinate
maxilloturbinate		for spongy bones in the face	

Gk. *krasis*, a mixture, > **cras**, which carries the sense of temperament, as in the general *idiosyncrasy*, one's private temperament, and the medical *dyscrasia*, an imbalance in the makeup of blood, and *galactocrasia*, imbalance in milk.

To *humorous, sanguinary, phlegmatic, melancholic, choleric, bilious, splenetic, temper, temperament* and *eccentric*, all reflections of the theory of humors, we can add *gout*, an inflammation of joints. L. *gutta*, a drop, retains the literal sense in the botanical *guttate*, an adjective for something resembling a drop, and *guttation*, the process by which a plant gives off droplets of water. *Guttiform* means like a drop of water, and *gutter* is the place where drops of water accumulate. L. *gutta* > Fr. *goutte*, a condition in which drops of diseased humors fall to the feet, and carrying that sense came into E. in the 13th century.

To turn from this ancient humorous theory to endocrinology is to see intriguing similarities and more important dissimilarities between then and now. *Endocrinology* is the study of secretions. Its origin is IE *krei*.

IE *krei*, to separate

Only one word has come through Proto-Germanic to OE to modern E. from this IE root: *riddle*. From Latin bases **cern** and **cret** we have: *discern, discrete, excrete, excrement* and *secretion*. Also from IE *krei* through Latin and its descendants: *crime, recriminate, discriminate, certain, contain, decree, certitude, secret, secretary,* and *garble*.

From Greek have come **crit, cris,** and **crin,** all carrying the sense of splitting off. A *critic* is one who separates the good from the bad; a *criterion* is a principle we judge by; a *hematocrit* orig. was an instrument to separate erythrocytes but now refers to the constituency of erythrocytes in blood. From **cris:** *crisis, epicrisis, heterocrisis.*

Crin has the sense of that which separates from and has been narrowed to the separation of a secretion from its source. Prefixing **crin** with *endo-* compounds into *endocrine,* that which separates within the gland, and with the suffix *logy,* into *endocrinology.* Other prefixes and bases also compound with **crin.** There are 17 sites in the human body for the production of endocrine secretions.

exo-	+ **crine**	that which separates out, a secretion to the skin, e.g., sweat
apo-	+	the tip of the cell (apical portion) is secreted, e.g., milk
holo-	+	whole separation, the whole of the cell disintegrates to produce the secretion
mero	+	*mer* means part, but no part of the gland's cell separates out; e.g., salivary and pancreatic
chromo	+ **crinia**	a secretion with color
allo	+	another secretion in addition to primary; *heterocrinia*
ec-	+	pert. to sweat cooling off the body
dys-	+	a disordered secretion
hypo-	+ **crin** + *-ism*	deficient secretion
hyper-	+	excessive secretion
	+ **crino** + *genic*	stimulating, causing secretion

Secretions may be to the outside of the body or within the body. Tears are secretions to the outside of the body. In addition to native E. *tears,* the biological vocabulary has Gk. **dacryo** and from that, L. **lacrima,** both referring to the tear ducts.

dacryocyst	*dacryolith*	*lacrimal*	*prelacrimal*
dacryagogue	*dacryopyosis*	*nasolacrimal*	*lacrimination*
dacryorrhea	*chromodacryorrhea*		

Hormone < Gk. *horme,* impulse, > **horm,** entered E. in 1900 and refers to internal secretions that impel or excite organs and tissues. Although most of the terms for hormones apply to those within the human body, as might be expected, some hormones appear in some animals but not others, for example, *juvenile hormone,* which controls the molting of insect larvae. Hormones can influence behavior. Males are usually more aggressive than females; in non-human animals, male aggression is partially due to the flow of testosterone in the male body, and testosterone may also contribute to human male aggression. An excess of thyroxin, the condition called *hyperthyroidism,* induces nervous behavior, and a decrease in thyroxine, *hypothyroidism*, induces phlegmatic behavior. Personality disorders similarly attend over- or under-secretion of other endocrine glands.

50+ terms exist in the medical vocabulary for hormones secreted by organs and endocrine glands. The stomach secretes *gastrin*, stimulus for secretion of gastric juice; the kidney secretes *erythropoietin*, which alerts bone marrow to produce red blood cells; and the duodenum secretes *secretin*, stimulus for the pancreas to secrete its juice, and *cholecystokinin*, stimulus for the gallbladder to secrete bile. Testes secrete *testosterone;* and ovaries, *estrogen* and *progesterone*.

Thyroxin from the thyroid gland regulates metabolism, and *parathormone* from the parathyroid regulates the release of calcium in bones.

adrenal
Located on the kidneys, < L. *ad-* + *ren* + *-al*
Hormones: *cortisone*
inner medulla: *adrenalin* or *epinephrine*, for stress
outer cortex: *adrenocortical*

pancreas < Gk. *pan*, all + *creas*, flesh; cp. *create*
Hormones:
glucogon, increases blood sugar
insulin < L. *insula*, island, for carbohydrate formation and storage

pineal
A small endocrine gland of the brain of interest in the history of philosophy: the French philosopher Rene Descartes thought this was the meeting place between body and soul. *Pineal* < L. *pinea*, pine cone. Synonym for *pineal gland: epiphysis.*
Hormone:
melatonin, causes estrus

pituitary
hypophysis, because it's under the cerebrum
Also in the brain, master endocrine gland for regulation of physiological processes by other glands < L. *pituita*, phlegm—the gland was thought, in the Renaissance, to be responsible for transporting waste products of the brain to the nose, where they were expelled as phlegm. 1615: "it containeth the pituitary or phlegmatic granule"
Hormones:
anterior lobe secretes hormones to stimulate growth (*GSH:* growth-stimulating hormone); the adrenal cortex (*ACTH, adrenocorticotropin*); the thyroid (*TSH,* thyroid-stimulating hormone); gonadal development (*FSH,* follicle-stimulating hormone and *LH,* luteinizing hormone); and milk production (*prolactin*)
posterior lobe, *neurohypophysis*, holds oxytocin and antidiuretic hormone

Anatomical structures of pregnancy release hormones: the *graafian* follicle releases estrogenic hormones and the *placenta* releases *gonadotrophin*, a luteinizing hormone, and *relaxin*, for relaxation of pelvic ligaments. For post-partum nourishment, the anterior pituitary gland produces *prolactin* (also *lactogen, lactogenic hormone,* and *mammalotropic hormone*).

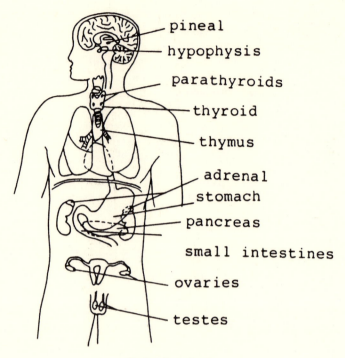

pineal

hypophysis

parathyroids

thyroid

thymus

adrenal

stomach

pancreas

small intestines

ovaries

testes

Endocrine glands

24.3 Latry and Mancy

Latry, worship of, and *mancy,* divination or magic, belong to the occult or pseudo-science rather than to the biological sciences. Anything can be worshipped and just about anything can be used for magic, more specifically for diagnosis and treatment of a condition, such as a locust infestation, and for prognosis, especially for prognosis—analyzing some pattern in stars or in the lines of the palm or whatever. Discussing *latry* and *mancy,* and in the subsequent chapter *phil, mania,* and *phobia* will reveal human desperation and creativity; it will also provide an opportunity to review bases in the biolexicon.

Latry can be attached sensibly to *anthropo, andro,* and *gyn.* for, respectively, worship of people, of men, and of women. The only words common in the general vocabulary with *latry* in them are *idolatry,* the worship of idols, and *bibliolatry,* the worship of (not mere belief in) the bible. *Heliolatry* means worship of the sun as a god and also of sunbathing.

Ophio, snake, is the first element in *ophiolatry,* worship of snakes, widespread in early Greek and Hindu religions, e.g., the snake god of the Delphic temple, Python, had his devotees. Python was killed by a representative of the new Olympic gods, Apollo, though Apollo's priestess was still called by her old name, *pythoness.* An early Christian sect saw Jesus as the incarnation of the Hebraic snake-god who makes an appearance in the stories of Moses and Aaron. In medieval alchemy, the snake is often depicted as being the alpha and omega, the beginning and the end, graphically rendered in the *ourobolos.*

Ophiolatry: Cretan snake goddess of
16th century B.C. Cnossus

Mancy, divination from, prophecy from, working magic with, derives fr. Gk. *mantis,* prophet, the adjective form of which is *mantic.* In the past, as illustrated in the quote from Chaucer, physicians did attempt to prophesize on evidence provided by flying birds, the cast of knucklebones used as dice, the positions of astral objects, and a hundred other procedures. Today, prophecy has become prognosis.

Among the few terms in the biolexicon which have *mancy* in them are *hematomancy,* prognosis by examination of blood, and glosso*mantia,* prognosis by examination of the tongue.

lychnomancy, lychnoscope,	using light for diagnosis and viewing < Gk. *lychn,* lamp; also the species name for an angler fish: *lynchus*

The characteristic posture of an insect gave it the name praying mantis, taxonomic label *Mantis religiosa. Mantis,* prophet, appears in other taxonomic names.

Mantidophaga	an arthropod
Mantisatta	an arachnid
Manteoceras	a mammal

Though the following terms are not in the biolexicon, definitions of them will provide insight into how people attempted to foretell the future and will also serve to remind us of bases in the biolexicon. You will come upon many familiar bases — the process of compounding is as important in the occult as in the real sciences.

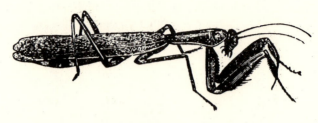

Mantis religiosa

People always want to know what they and other people really are and want to guess the future. Anything that offers a pattern—clouds sailing across the sky, pebbles thrown on the ground, dice, cards, tea leaves, intestines—can be interpreted for the revelation of character and destiny. There could be as many *mancies* as patterns, an awful quantity. *Mancy* is usually employed as the base for this prediction, but other bases also appear—*gnome* in *physiognomy* and *logy* in *astrology, numerology,* and *phrenology*.

Some of the predictive systems must have had very small congregations of believers. *Onychomancy,* for example, interpretation of sun's rays reflected on fingernails, could not have attracted more people than would fit into a psychiatric ward. Others, however, have attracted hundreds of thousands, even millions, of believers and some, *astrology* the outstanding example, hundreds of millions, including a recent president of the United States. Anything can be used to decode the future. But all would fit into three categories: the patterns of inanimate things, the patterns of non-human animate objects or parts, and the patterns of aspects of human beings themselves.

1. the patterns of inanimate things

numerology, astrology, onychomancy
rhabdomancy	using a rod to divine or discover water or oil or hidden term papers
	rhabdopod heterorhabdic
aeromancy	pattern of clouds
lithomancy	of stones
pyromancy	of flame
sideromancy	contortions of straw on red-hot iron
stichomancy	casual coming upon a predictive passage in a book, notably the Bible
	stich, Gk. for row, is in *stichochrome* a chromophilic nerve cell body

2. patterns of non-human animate objects or parts

myomancy	running of mice
ornithomancy	flight of birds; cp. auspice

| *astragalomancy* | knucklebones, usually of sheep |
| *hepatoscopy* | engraved surface of sheep or goat's liver |

3. patterns of aspects of the human self

chiromancy	
oneiromancy	dreams
sciomancy	ghosts, Gk. *scio* in *scioscope*
	the viewing of shadows
graphology	handwriting
moleosophy	moles on the body
metoposcopy	frown lines on forehead

Necromancy, prophecy through examination or interpretation of a corpse; generalized to be syn. with magic; *necromancer* = magician. The necromancer of Gilbert and Sullivan's *The Sorcerer* advertises his trade.

> My name is John Wellington Wells,
> I'm a dealer in magic and spells,
> In blessings and curses and ever-filled purses,
> In prophecies, witches, and knells.

Sanskrit *mantra,* a repeated incantation, comes from the same IE source, *men.*
    The next chapter concludes this text. It examines bases for love and fear.

Hogarth's Bedlam

CHAPTER 25—LOVE AND FEAR

A consensus of any group of people would probably show that most people like other people and dislike snakes. But some misanthropists among us might dislike other people and adore snakes. The several bases of this concluding chapter reflect liking, loving, an extraordinary fondness or obsession for and a morbid dread or loathing of.

A review of history and of the literature of psychiatry, of the occult, of theology shows that people have loved and loathed the most curious things. Some love to be afraid and maybe here and there are people who are afraid to be loved.

English contains hundreds of words formed with the bases **phil, mania, phobia,** *latry* (worship of) and *mancy* (magic with). A long list may be formed inventorying the many actual words in the language, but the important point is that any Gk. base for any thing or event or sentiment adapts to compounding. For example, the base for drooping is *ptos,* from which we can fabricate the following ideas.

ptosophilia	affection for drooping
ptosomania	obsessive need to droop
ptosophobia	morbid dread of drooping
ptosolatry	worship of that which droops
ptosomancy	prophecy through analysis of patterns of drooping

The suffixes for different parts of speech formed with these bases differ.

Adjective: -ic and -ous

scopo	+ **philic**	pert. to an inordinate affection for peeping, voyeuristic
hyphe	+	sexual enjoyment from silken and other fabrics, fetishistic
osphresio	+	obsession with odors
necro	+	affection for the dead, that is, corpses and by metaphoric extension, dead ideas
hydrophilous		living in water

Noun-Condition of: -y and -ia

philanthropy	affection for people
nyctophilia	affection for night

Noun-One Who: -ist -e, -iac

philanthropist	one who loves fellow human beings
algo + **phile**	pain, a masochist
claustro +	being closed in
patho +	being diseased
pharmaco +	medicine or drugs
pedo +	children as sexual targets
misanthrope	one who hates fellow human beings
maniac	

Phil

Phil can range from meaning study of to fondness for, neither of which suggests any abnormality, to a love that seems excessive or has as its target something most of us find unpleasant or disgusting. **Phil** appears in the general vocabulary in several very familiar words: *philosophy, philharmonic, philanthropist, Phillip* (etym., lover of horses), *Philadelphia* (city of brotherly love).

philatry	love of, study of, postage stamps
philology	love of, study of, words and language
philter	a magical love potion
philander	a playboy
philhellene	one who loves Greek culture
Francophile	one who admires French culture
	cp. *Anglophile, Russophile*

Dendro is a combining base for tree: therefore, *dendrophile,* one who loves or lives in trees, arboreal (reversing the bases yields *philodendron*); *dendrophilia* for the condition; and *dendrophilic* for the adjective. Dendrophilia seems a harmless enough interest or even praiseworthy. A similar opinion may be held about parallel compounds with *zoo: zoophilia, geronto: gerontophilia,* and *neo: neophilia,* a mild mental affliction, e.g., a fondness to buy advanced hi-fi equipment.

A symptom mildly abnormal is an affection for night rather than for day: *nycto* + **philia;** and for darkness rather than light: *scotophilia.* And while scarab beetles behave normally in having an affection for feces, human *coprophilists* are in need of counselling (syn. for *coprophilia: scatophilia* and *mysophilia*).

Phil has specialized meanings: (1) easily stainable with; and (2) affinity for, growing well in. We'll add a (3): miscellaneous and taxonomy.

1. easily stainable with

We have taken up bases for colors: *chromato, argyro, cyano, erythro. Chromatophilic* means pertaining to taking color or stains; the other three bases form adjectives meaning pertaining to taking silver, blue dyes, and red dyes. **Bas** means base and *oxy* means acid: *basophilic* and *oxyphilic.* In the development of granulocytes, the hemocytoblast, or stem cell, gives rise to myelocytes, of which there are three kinds: *basophil, neutrophil,* and *eosinophil.*

ampho- + **philic**	easily stainable with base or acid dyes
eosin +	with eosin
safrano +	with safranine
neutro +	with neutral dyes
cyano +	with blue dyes
erythro +	with red dyes
safrano +	with safranine
argyro +	with silver
acromo +	disaffinity for staining
karyochromaticophilic	pert. to stainable nucleus

2. affinity for, growing well in

For this sub-section, we'll first note bases we've taken up: *photo, uro, lipo, organo.* That which is *photophilic* has an affinity for, grows well in light; *urophilic,* in urine; *lipophilic* in fats; and *organophilic* in organs.

thermo + **philic**	pert. to growing well in heat
cry(mo) +	in cold; syn., *psychrophilic*
meso- +	in moderate temperatures
hygro +	in moisture
halo +	in salts
thio +	in sulfur
hapto +	pert. to an antibody that has an affinity for combining with a haptophore; *hapto,* touching, grasping

(3) miscellaneous and taxonomy

Hemophilia doesn't mean an affection for blood but a disease of the blood, failure to clot. *Homophile* has a simiarly restricted meaning: an antibody which has affinity for an antigen.

hydro + **philous**	pert. to capability of absorbing water
glyco + **philia**	tendency toward hyperglycemia
spasmo +	tendency to spasm
calci +	tendency to become calcified
anemophile	flower pollinated through pollen borne by the wind
Philodina	protozoan
Dinophilus	an annelid
Drosophilia melanogaster	fruitfly
Boophilus	cattle tick genus

Mania

English has many native words for being overly fond of, but some very common words turn out to be not from native English. Being fond of runs through a spectrum from appetite to hunger to obsession. *Appetite* < L. *appetitus,* "natural desire"; *hunger* is a native word, while the base *bulim*, for deep hunger, < Gk. *bous*, ox as in *bulimia*, unnaturally constant hunger, a rage for food. Both *rage* and *rabies* < L. *rabere*, to rage.

Gk. **mania** is the condition of having an obsessive love of or need for, a morbid interest in, a craving for. Words in the common as well as psychiatric vocabulary precede **mania** with: *dipso, klepto, ego, megalo, pyro* and *necro*. *Necromania*, like *necrolatry*, could apply to dead bodies or dead traditions. A manic obsession could target an animal. Thus before this base could be set *zoo, cyno, hippo, ophidio, ornitho*, and, perhaps somewhere in the world there are *pachydermomaniacs*.

Sex is a greater interest for human beings than it is for orangutans. Orangutans probably do not enjoy or suffer from

eroto + **mania**	an obsessive need for sex or sexuality
nympho +	on the part of women
hystero +	= *nymphomania*
satyro +	on the part of men
gymno +	for nakedness
gyneco +	for women
grapho +	for writing letters
erotographomania	for writing love letters
mentulomania	for masturbation (*mentu* is a little-used base for penis; *masterbation* < L. *manus*, hand + *sturb* < L. *stuprare*, to rape; therefore, lit., rape by the hand)
habromania	happiness
Trichomanes crispum	a fern

An extravagant indulgence in erotomania could precipitate *hypno* + **mania**, an intense need for sleep, or *clinomania*, for passive lying in bed, or for social and intellectual pursuits.

arithmo + **mania**	an obsessive need for counting
choro +	for dancing
melo +	for music
nosto +	for nostalgia
porio +	to leave home
hedonia +	for pleasure
biblio +	for collecting books
sopho +	for one's own wisdom
mytho +	for lying or exaggerating

Manias can be self-destructive.

ergasio + **mania**	intense desire for work, esp. surgery
asymmetro +	for symmetry, as for example in using both hands to salute
bruxo +	for gnashing teeth

acro	+	an obsessive need for high places
agro	+	for living alone in a rural area
sito	+	for food; cp. *bulimia*
alcoholo	+	for alcohol; syn., *dipsomania*
hiero	+	for religion, sermons
helio	+	for sunbathing
nocti	+	for nighttime activities
noso	+	for disease
narco	+	for drugs
toxico	+	for poisons
pharmaco	+	for medicines
thanato	+	for suicide
necro	+	for death
onychylotillomania		for picking at one's nails
trichotillomania		for pulling one's hair out

Delusions about self:

callo	+ **mania**	delusion that one is beautiful
ego	+	important
megalo	+	great
demono	+	infested with demons
pluto	+	wealthy (*plutomania* is also obsessive need to make money)
bromo	+	insanity brought about by maltreatment in application of bromides
tulipo	+	18th cen. Dutch obsessive need to collect rare tulips
decalo	+	18th cen. English obsessive need to use decals
porio	+	obsessive need to leave home
Leishmania		a genus of parasitic protozoa; *man* < *William B. Leishman*, its discoverer

Two bases of minor employment but related to **mania** are **orex**, appetite or desire for, and **lagnia**, sexual excitement brought on by.

an-	+ **orex** + *-ia*	no appetite, desire to be lethally thin
	orexi + *mania*	mania to eat food
	+ *genic*	that which stimulates appetite
bulim	+ **anorexia**	*bulimarexia*, a mental disorder in which the victim alternately eats heavily and vomits < Gk. *bu.* cow + *lim.* hunger
osmo	+ **lagnia**	sexual excitement brought on by odors
pyro	+	by setting or watching a fire
scopo	+	by peeping
uro	+	by watching someone urinate
psycholagny		by thinking of sex, an inexpensive obsession

3. **lepsy,** seizure by:

narco	+ **lepsy**	seizure by sleep, need to fall asleep as often as possible
nympho +		seizure by nymphs, grand obsession
epi- +		disease of motor dysfunction and convulsions

The Nightmare, by Johann Fuseli, 1781

Phobia doesn't mean merely fear of. A normal reaction to precipitous heights or sharp instruments is to fear them. **Phobia** denotes a morbid fear or dread of, a loathing of. Occasionally, the compound does not mean what its parts mean: *hydro* + **phobia** does not mean fear of water, but rabies, the connection being foaming mouth of a rabid animal. *Xero* + **phobia** does not mean fear of dryness, but having a dry mouth because of anxiety or some similar emotion. Most of the terms, however, do mean what their parts mean, and thus an inventory will serve as a summary of elements already presented. The reader needn't fear having to know all of them, but a comprehensive inventory is given so that the reader can find the word for his or her or friends', relatives', and roommates' peculiarities. *Phil, latry, mania,* and for some bases, *mancy* may be substituted for **phobia.** The inventory is long, but most bases will be acquaintances if not friends.

1. Dread of the heavens and earth

urano	heaven	*uranoplasty*
helio	sun, sunlight	*heliocentric*

nycto	darkness	*nyctambulate*
		pavor nocturus,
scoto	darkness	*scototherapy*
meteoro	meteors	*meteoric*
eo	dawn	*eocene*
geo	earth	*geoid*
baro	gravity	*barometer*
bronto	thunder	*brontosaurus*
kerauno	lightning	*ceraunometer*
aero	air, clouds	*aerodynamics*
hylo	wood, matter	*hylogenesis*
chrono	time	*chronic*
anemo	winds, drafts	*anemometer*
potomo	river	*hippopotamus*
phengo	daylight	
achlu	darkness	
apeiro	infinity	
chiono	snow	
ombro	rain	
homichlo	fog	
thalassa	sea	
cremno	precipice	

2. Of places

topo	place	*topical*
acro	height	*acromegaly*
agora	open places	*panegyric*
ceno	open places	*cenosis*
	emptiness	
dextro	things on the right side	*ambidextrous*
levo	things on the left side	*levocardia*
sinistro	things on left side	*sinister*
oiko	house	*ecocide*
claustro	being enclosed	*cloister*
domato	house	*domestic*
stygio	hell	*stygian*
clithro	being enclosed	
bato	high objects	
bathmo	steep places	

3. Of living things

micro	small things, germs	*microbe*
zoo	animals	*zoographia*

bacterio	bacteria	*bacteriophage*
helmintho	worms	*platyhelminth*
vermi	worms	*vermiculite*
teaeno	tapeworms	*Taeniidae*
entomo	arthropods	*entomology*
acaro	insects	*acarus*
arachneo	spiders	*arachnoid*
parasito	parasites	*parasitology*
pediculo	lice infestation	*pediculosis*
apio	bees	*apiculture*
melissa	bees, wasps	*Melissa*
ichthyo	fish	*ichthyology*
ornitho	birds	*ornithology*
cyno	dogs	*cynodont*
muso	mice	*muscle*
anthropo	human society	*anthropoid*
demo	people	*endemic*
andro	men	*androecium*
gyno	women	*gynoecium*
partheno	virgins	*parthenogenesis*
	young girls	
gymno	naked people	*gymnospore*
xeno	strangers	*xenogamy*
tricho	hair	*trichinosis*
hemo	blood	*hemostat*
ptero	feathers	*archeopteryx*
blenno	slime	*blenny*
batracho	frogs	*batrachian*
pogon	beard	*pogoniasis*
ailuro, gato, geleo	cats	*ailurophile*
ochlo	crowds	*ochlocracy*
euroto	female genitals	
harpaxo	robbers	
dora	fur	
sclero	bad men	*arterosclerosis*

4. Of Things

pharmaco	medicine	*pharmacology*
hyelo	glass	*hyaline*
spectro	mirrors	*spectroscope*
hydro	water	*hydrocephaly*
pedio	dolls	*pedagogue*
copro	feces	*coprolite*
megalo	large things	*megalomania*

ballisto	missiles	*ballistics*
toxico and *io*	poison	*toxin*
belono	needles	*belonoid*
cibo	food	*cibarian*
metallo	metal	*metal*
mechano	machinery	*mechanic*
aichmo	sharp instruments	
amaxo	vehicles	
amatho	dust	
myso, rhypo, rupo	dirt	
chremato	money	

5. Of Diseases

noso	disease	*nosology*
patho	disease	*pathogenic*
monopatho	any specific disease	
algo	pain	*analgesic*
lysso	rabies	*alyssum*
cardio	heart disease	*cardiac*
cyprido or *venero*	venereal diseases	*Cyprus, Venus*
or *syphilo*		*syphilophyma*
meningito	"brain disease"	*meningitis*
dermato	skin disease	*scleroderma*
dysmorpho	being deformed	*morphology*
nanoco	being dwarfed	*nanosecond*
terato	bearing a monster	*teratospermia*

6. Of Events

acara	itching	*Acarina*
angio	choking	*angitis*
avio	flying	*aviation*
batho	falling	*bathysphere*
emeto	vomiting	*emetic*
dromo	running	*dromedary*
aqua	water	*aquarium*
ankyl	joint adhesion	*ankylocheilia*
astheno	weakness	*neurasthenic*
auto	self, loneliness	*autonomous*
coito	sexual intercourse	*coition*
geno, eroto	sex	*genital*
		erogenous
electro	electricity	*electric*
odonto	dentistry	*orthodontist*

Luposlipaphobia: The fear of being pursued by timber wolves around a kitchen table while wearing socks on a newly waxed floor.

chrom(at)o	colors	*chromocyte*
carno	eating meat	*chile con carne*
toco	childbirth	*tocology*
scopo	being seen	*scope*
hiero	of hearing or giving sermons	*hierarchy*
penia	of poverty	*erythropenia*
neo	new things	*neoteny*
thanato	death	*euthanasia*
triskadeca	13	*decade*
ataxo	disorder	*ataxocephalus*
pano	everything	*pandemic*
panta	nothing	
eremio	being alone	*hermit*
pluto	wealth	*plutocrat*
mytho	lying	*mythopoeia*
erasto	kissing	
basi	walking	
climacto	climbing stairs	
chero	gaiety	
amycho	being scratched	
catagelo	being ridiculed	
pelado	baldness	
bromidrosi	bodily odors	

kathisophobia, akathisia inability to sit still
This last condition might be curable by an *ataractic* drug, to lessen nervousness and bring about *ataraxia,* tranquility, calmness. These two words < Gk. *ataraktos,* calm.
    In biochemistry, **phobia** indicates resistance:

osmiophobic	resistant to being stained with osmium
halophobic	resistance to salt

    Your guide concludes with the hope that our survey of the biolexicon has excited lexicophilia rather than a morbid dread of words.

German gnomes excavating remains of ichthyosaurus

APPENDICES

APPENDIX A: GRIMM'S LAW

Grimm's Law is a complicated affair. The relationships between *t* and *d* or *f* and *p* and the other pairs are not haphazard. Though at first consideration, it may not be apparent, the members of each pair have in common features of pronunciation. Most IE languages retained the consonants of their parents, but the Proto-Germanic languages, among which is English, changed these sounds. This Appendix discusses the most important of these changes, but not all of them.

Voiced to Unvoiced

The word for the number 10 is *ten*. December was once the 10th month of the year, and a period of ten years may be called a *decade*. *December* and *decade* do not look or sound like *ten*, but the *d* sound is related to the *t*. Another example of the relationship is seen in the *d* to *dent* and the *t* of *tooth*. *Ten* and *tooth* are native English words, while *December*, *decade*, *dentist* and *orthodontist* are words from Latin and Greek. This is not much evidence that *ten* and *decade* are cognates, evolving from the one prehistoric source, or that *tooth*, *dent*, and *odont* are also cognates, evolving from a different but still single prehistoric source. Scrutinizing these words, we can hypothesize that there is a relationship between the English *t*, a voiced sound, and the unvoiced Latin and Greek *d*.

English *t* = L. and Gk. *d*

If we search through our vocabulary, common as well as biological, we can come up with other examples that exemplify a relationship between English *t* and Latin and Greek *d*. For example, English *tree* has a cognate synonym in Gk. *dendron* as in *philodendron* and *dendrite*, tree-like, a term for a mineral and for a nerve cell.

English *t*	Latin and Greek *d*
ten	L. *decade*
tooth	L. *dental*
	Gk. *odontology*
teach	L. *edict*
two	L. *duplicate*

English *p* = L. and Gk. *b*

337

English *p*	Latin and Greek *b*
lip	L. *labial*
slip	L. *lubricate*
puff	L. *boil*
	Gk. *bubo,* a swelling
hip	L. *cubitus*
	Gk. *kybos*

English *k* = L. and Gk. *g*

In addition to the relationships between *t* and *d* and between *p* and *b,* Grimm also uncovered a relationship between E. *k* and L. and Gk. *g:*

English *k*	Latin and Greek *g*
kin	Gk. *geneology*
know	Gk. *diagnosis*
knee	L. *genuflect*
corn	L. *grain*
queen, qu = k	Gk. *gynecology*
yoke	L. *jugular*

The parallel extends to Sanskrit, E. *k* in *yoke* rendered by *g* in Sanskrit *yoga* and *yogi.*

Grimm concluded that the relationships are systematic. What happened is that most of the descendants of IE—Latin and Greek, Sanskrit and Iranian, Lithuanian and Russian, Irish and Welsh—pronounced *d, b,* and *g* the way their parents had. But the group that became the Germanic people, for some unknown reason, changed these sounds from voiced to unvoiced: *d > t, b > p,* and *g > k.*

Plosive to Aspirated

A second cluster accounts for other English-Latin/Greek cognates.

F and *p* are alike, in that both are made by the lips and in that both are voiceless, the vocal cords kept still in their production. They differ in that labial *p* is a stop or plosive—the sound explodes and cannot be continued, while labial *f* is an aspirate—the sound can be continued. The evolution of IE *p* into Germanic and therefore English *f* accounts for a number of cognates in the biological and common vocabularies.

English *f* = Gk. and L. *p*

The type specimens of this change are *pisces/fish, ped/foot* and *pater/father* (Iranian *pidar* and Sanskrit *pitar*). Many other pairs of words illustrate *p* to *f,* so many that an inventory can be designed. Several of these cognates have been the subjects of our etymologizing.

IE	Greek	Latin	English
pag, to fasten	*craniopagus*	*propagate*	*fang*
pei, to be fat	*proprionic*	*pituitary*	*fat*
pek, to comb		*pectinate*	*fight*
pel, skin	*erysipelas*	*pellagra*	*film*
per, to lead		*portal*	*ford*
pet, to fly	*pteryoid*	*centripetal*	*feather*
pete, to spread	*paten*	*patella*	*fathom*
plak, to be flat	*placenta*	*placebo*	*flake*
plak, to strike	*apoplexy*	*plague*	*fling*
plek, to fold	*diplocardiac*	*simplex*	*flax*
pleu, to flow	*pneumonia*	*pulmonary*	*flood*
pol, to touch		*palpate*	*feel*
pu, to rot	*pyorrhea*	*purulent*	*foul*
penkwe, five	*pentadactyl*		*fist*

Penkwe went into Sanskrit as *panca*, which became English *punch*, a drink originally of five ingredients—water, tea, sugar, lemon, and arrack, an alcoholic distillation of molasses which empowered the drink with the other kind of punch.

English *h* = L. and Gk. *k*

English *h*	Latin and Greek *k*
horn	L. *cornea*
	Gk. *keratin*
hide (skin)	L. *cuticle*
head	L. *decapitate*
hell	L. *cell*
hound	L. *canine*
	Gk. *cynic*
	Welsh *corgi*
heart	L. *cord*
	Gk. *card*
	Irish *cridhe*
haven	Gk. *cope*
	L. *cap*, seize

English *th* = L. and Gk. *t*

The third and last subdivision of plosive to aspirated is Indo-European *t* to English *th*.

English *th*	Latin and Greek *t*
toothsome	L. *dental*
	Gk. *periodontal*
three	L. *triceps*

	Gk. *tripod*
thread	Gk. *trypanosome*
	L. *triturate*
thumb	L. *tumor*
thrust	L. *intrude*
thin	L. *attenuate*

Subsequent linguists have worked out laws analyzing other systematic changes to account for differences among cognates of IE families and within a family—for example, Latin *s* and Gk. *h: serpent — herpes, sept* as in September; *hept* in *heptagon;* E. *father* but German *vater,* E. *ten* but German *Zehn.*

APPENDIX B: ALPHABET

Several combinations of Gk. letters have no counterpart in Latin or Proto-Germanic.

bd (bdellium)	*cn (cnidophore)*
ct (ctenophore)	*mn (mnemonic)*
pn (pneumonia)	*ps (psychology)*
pt (ptomaine)	

When a word begins with one of these, the first letter is not pronounced. Speakers of English would naturally not pronounce the *p* of *pneumonia, psychology, ptomaine* any more than they would pronounce the *k* of *knee*. When, however, the combination is preceded by a vowel, then the first letter is pronounced: no pronunciation of *p* in *ptosis*, drooping, but it is pronounced in *proptosis*. Cp. *symptom*, where the *p* is pronounced, though preceded by a consonant. *Mnemonic* is pronounced "nemonic"; but cp. *amnesia, amnesty*.

ph	*diphtheria*
th	*asthma*

With these combinations, one or both of the letters are suppressed: "diphtheria," "asma."

Greek diphthongs:

ai	Gk. *aither*, upper air	*ether*
	aitia, cause	*etiology*
		aetiogenous
oi	*amoibe*, change	*ameba*
	oidema, swelling	*edema*
	oisophagos, gullet	*esophagus*
ei	*eidos*, form	*oid: ameboid*
	eikon, image	*iconoclastic*
		eikonogen
	cheir, hand	*chiropodist*
		cheiromegaly
oe	*hyoeides*, like a U	*hyoid*
ou	*oura*, tail	*saurus*
	ouron, urine	*diuretic*

Gk. **paid** means child. This became *paed* in British English: *paederastry*, but *ped* in American English: *pederastry*, whereby the *ped* is homophonic with *ped* for foot.

341

British English employs other diphthongs where American English substitutes a single vowel: *haemorrhage/hemorrhage, aesthetic/esthetic.*

The Greek alphabet has the letter *k* but lacks the letter *c*. It also lacks the letters *f, j, g, u, v,* and *w*. The Latin alphabet lacks the letters *k, w, x, y,* and *z*. The Latin alphabet incorporated much of the Greek, using its *c* to take the place of Gk. *k*. English thus has words from Latin beginning with *c* but having a *k* sound, such as *cranial, excavation, cuspid*. It also has letters that begin with *c* but have an *s* sound, such as *cell, cirrus, cerebrum*. Sometimes a pair of doublets will have both *k* and *s* sounds: *kinetic* and *cinema*. The *s* sound is generally used when the *c* precedes *e, i,* and *y*.

The 7th letter of the Gk. alphabet is *eta*, corresponding to Hebrew *heth* and our *h*. In derivations, the *h* of (*h*)*eta* may appear or not. For example, Gk. *haima*, blood, retains the *h* in *acardiohemia* but loses it in *anemia*. *Glycemia* and *glycohemia* are both acceptable. Gk. *hidros* > base *hidr*, sweat, is in *anhidrosis* and *cyanephidrosis*, but lacks the *h* in *osmidrosis* and the smellier *bromidrosis*. *Chromhidrosis* and *chromidrosis* are both acceptable.

The 17th letter of the Gk. alphabet, *rho*, may appear as *r* or as *rr*.

macrorhiny
amniorhexis
raphiferous
notorhizal

platyrrhine
karyorrhexis
uranorrhapy
Glycyrrhiza
diarrhea
hemorrhage

APPENDIX C: COMBINATION WITH AFFIXES

This appendix will address combinations between initial and central elements. In most cases, the prefix undergoes no change when it attaches to the central element: thus, *trans-*, through, stays as that when it combines with *fix: transfix: pre-* remains unchanged: *prefix*.

But some prefixes undergo assimilation: the last letter of the prefix changes to be the same as the consonant of the base, assimilates with that consonant. The process, undergone by six prefixes, is called assimilation.

ad- to, toward	assimilates with *f, g, l, n, p, s, t*
	ad- + *fix* > *affix*
	ad- + *glutinate* > *agglutinate*
	ad- + *lude* > *allude*
	ad- + *notate* > *annotate*
	ad- + *pend* > *append*
	ad- + *sist* > *assist*
	becomes *a* before *sp*
	ad- + *spire* > *aspire*
con-, against	assimilates with *l* and *r*
	con- + *lude* > *collude*
	con- + *rode* > *corrode*
	becomes *com-* before *f, m, p*
	con- + *fort* > *comfort*
	con- + *ment* > *comment*
	con- + *press* > *compress*
	becomes *co-* before *h*
	con- + *here* > *cohere*
dis-, apart, reversed	assimilates with *f*
	dis- + *fer* > *differ*
	becomes *di-* before *g, l, v*
	dis- + *gress* > *digress*
	dis- + *late* > *dilate*
	dis- + *vest* > *divest*
ex-, out	assimilates with *f*
	ex- + *fect* > *effect*
	becomes *e-* before *l* and *s*

ex-	+ *lude*	> *elude*
ex-	+ *sud*	> *exude*

in-, in, not   assimilates with *l* and *r*

in-	+ *lusion*	> *illusion*
in-	+ *rigate*	> *irrigate*

becomes **im** before *b, m, p*

in-	+ *bed*	> *imbed*
in-	+ *press*	> *impress*

ob-, against   assimilates with *c* and *p*

ob-	+ *clusion*	> *occlusion*
ob-	+ *press*	> *oppress*

sub-, under   assimilates with *f* and *p*

sub-	+ *fauces*	> *suffocate*
sub-	+ *puration*	> *suppuration*

becomes *sus-* before *c, p, t*

sub-	+ *ceptible*	> *susceptible*
sub-	+ *pend*	> *suspend*
sub-	+ *tain*	> *sustain*

If a prefix ending with a vowel joins up with a base beginning with a vowel, the prefix's vowel is usually retained:

peri- + *odont* + *-ist*	*periodontist*
micro + *anatom* + *-y*	*microanatomy*

Or the prefix's vowel may be lost to the base's initial vowel, a process called elision:

para- + *osm* + *-ia*	*parosmia,* disordered sense of smell
magni- + *anim* + *-ous*	*magnanimous*

Turning from prefix to first base combining with second base, we can first note that most Gk. bases ending in consonants take on a combining *o* when they join with other bases:

gastro + *enter* + *-itis*	*gastroenteritis*
odonto + *-logy*	*odontology*
narco + *lepsy*	*narcolepsy*

Most L. bases ending in consonants take on a combining *i* when they join with other bases:

denti + *frice*	*dentifrice*
reni + *form*	*reniform*

A Gk. or L. base ending in a vowel will usually keep it; if the final letter of the base is a vowel like that of a combining suffix, only one of the two identical vowels is kept:

Gk. *cardi* + *o* + *-logy*	*cardiology*
Gk. *pachy* + *derm*	*pachyderm*
Gk. *gyneco* + *-oid*	*gynecoid*
L. *cori* + *-ium*	*corium*

There are exceptions to these principles, e.g., Gk. *glossa* becomes **glosso** in combinations: *glossodynia.* Sometimes the same prefix or base will take on two different vowels, and both will be acceptable: *septavalent, septivalent; gynephobia, gynophobia, venepuncture, venipuncture; muscacide, muscicide.*

BIBLIOGRAPHY

General Sources

The Oxford English Dictionary. Oxford: Oxford University Press, 1971.
The Random House Dictionary of the English Language, 2nd ed. New York: Random House, 1987.
Buck, Carl Darling. *A Dictionary of Selected Synonyms in the Principal Indo-European Languages.* Chicago: University of Chicago Press, 1949.
Giangrande, Lawrence. *Greek in English.* Ottawa: University Press of Canada, 1987.
. . . *Latin in the Service of English.* Baltimore: University Press of America, 1987.
Pei, Mario. *The Families of Words.* New York: Harper & Row, 1962.
Shipley, Joseph T. *The Origins of English Words: A Discursive Dictionary of Indo-European Roots.* Baltimore: Johns Hopkins, 1984.
Watkins, Calvin, ed. *The American Heritage Dictionary of Indo-European Roots.* Boston: Houghton Mifflin, 1985.

Specialized Sources

Andrews, Edmund. *A History of Scientific English.* New York: Richard R. Smith, 1947.
Bettmann, Otto. *Pictorial History of Medicine.* Springfield, Ill.: Charles C Thomas, 1970.
Brown, R. W. *Composition of Scientific Words.* Washington, D.C.: Smithsonian Institution Press 1956.
Dobson, Jessie. *Anatomical Eponyms.* London: Baillière, Tindall & Cox, 1946.
Dorland's Illustrated Medical Dictionary, 26th ed. Philadelphia: W. B. Saunders, 1985.
Dunmore, Charles W. and Rita M. Fleischer. *Medical Terminology: Exercises in Etymology,* 2nd ed. Philadelphia: F.A. Davis, 1985.
Gledhill, D. *The Names of Plants.* London: Cambridge University Press, 1985.
Haggard, Howrd W. *Devils, Drugs, and Doctors.* New York: Harper and Row, 1929.
Jaeger, Edmund G. *A Source-Book of Biological Names and Terms.* 3rd ed. Springfield Ill: Charles C Thomas, 1978.
Jaeger, Edmund C. *A Source-Book of Medical Terms.* Springfield, Ill: Charles C Thomas, 1978.
Leonard, Peggy G. *Building a Medical Vocabulary.* Philadelphia: W. B. Saunders, 1988.
Nickon, Alex and Earnest F. Silversmith, *Organic Chemistry: The Name Game.* New York: Pergamon Press.
Nybakken, Oscar E. *Greek and Latin in Scientific Terminology.* Ames, Iowa: Iowa State University Press, 1959.
Pepper, O.H. Perry. *Medical Etymology.* Philadelphia: W. B. Saunders, 1949.
Singer, Charles. *The Evolution of Anatomy.* New York: Alfred A. Knopf, 1926.
Walton, John, Beeson, Paul, and Scott, Ronald, eds. *Oxford Companion to Medicine,* 2 vols. New York: Oxford University Press, 1986.

ILLUSTRATIONS AND PERMISSIONS

Some scenes and figures from pagan times have been widely reproduced, for example: the Cretan snake-goddess, Hercules fighting the Hydra, Atlas holding up the world, the sirens luring sailors, women at play with tali, Medusa, Aesculapius, and saltatio. Sources used for such pictures are Catherine E. Avery, *The New Century Classical Handbook* (New York: Appleton-Century-Crofts, Inc., 1962); G. E. Marindin, *Classical Dictionary of Greek and Roman Biography* (London: John Murray, 1909); William Smith, *A Dictionary of Greek and Roman Antiquities* (London: John Murray, 1973); and, especially, H. T. Peck, *Harper's Dictionary of Classical Literature and Antiquities* (New York: American Book Co., 1896).

Four of the natural history pictures reproduced from 16th–18th century books are identified in their captions. The Latifau and Muenster pictures are reprinted with permission by The Huntington Library. The picture of lemur teeth (p. 285), from W. E. LeGros Clark, *History of the Primates*, 1940, is reproduced by permission, University of Chicago Press. The pictures of Professor Beringer's lügensteine (p. 155) are from Jahn and Wolf, *Lying Stones of Johann Bartholomew Adam Beringer*, and are reproduced by permission of the University of California Press. Useful for its detailed discussions of anatomies as well as for its abundance of illustrations by Brian Price Thomas is Diana R. Kershaw, *Animal Diverssity* (London: University Tutorial Press, 1983).

Sources for most of the natural history pictures are 19th century natural history books:

William Buckland, *Geology and Mineralogy Considered with Reference to Natural Theology* (London: George Routledge and Co., 1858): Plesiosaurus colichodeirus, Plesiosaurus macrocephalus, phosphatic coprolites, crinoid.

Robert Chambers, *Vestiges of the Natural History of Creation* (London: W. & R. Chambers, 1884): labyrinthrodont teeth, Lingula anatina.

S. G. Goodrich, *Johnson's Natural History*, 2 vols. (New York: A. J. Johnson Publishers, 1874): Chiropteran (bat), sea cucumber, tarantula, Venus' girdle, Hercules beetle, sea cat Chimaera, tunicate, kangaroo marsupium, tapeworm Cestoda, sea anemone, Sagitta, earthworm clitellum.

P. H. Gosse, *Life in Its Lower, Intermediate, and Higher Forms* (New York: Robert Carter and Brothers, 1857): hydrozoan, freshwater copepod.

Howard L. Haggard, *Devils, Drugs, and Doctors* (New York: Harper and Brothers, Publishers, 1929): Gillray caricature of Jenner, Hogarth's Bedlam, plague doctor.

349

J. G. Heck, *Iconographic Encyclopaedia of Science, Literature and Art* (New York: D. Appleton and Co., n. d.): ammonites, also source for pagan artifacts.

Worthington Hooker, *Natural History for the Use of Schools and Families* (New York: Harper and Brothers, 1873): Flying dragon, Nereis, Coleopteran tiger beetles and ladybug, orang-utan, armadillo, Mr. Beale and the polyp, platypus, rhinoceros hookbill, Mantis religiosa.

Huxley, T. H., *A Manual of the Anatomy of Invertebrated Animals.* (New York: D. Appleton, 1878): fasciculi of striated muscle, sacculus.

Kinns, Rev. Samuel, *Moses and Geology* (London: Cassell and Co., Ltd., 1895: fight between iguanadon and megalosaurus.

Sebastian Kneipp, *My Water-Cure* (Kempten, Bavaria: Jos. Koesel Publisher, 1897): shower-bath therapy.

E. Ray Lankester, *Extinct Animals* (London: Archibald Constable & Co., Ltd., 1905): belemnites, marsupial skull, mastodon teeth, Cro-Magnon drawing.

Hugh Miller, *The Testimony of the Rocks* (Boston: Gould and Lincoln, 1858): Cyclophthalmus bucklandi, fossil footprint of dinosaur, trilobite, Silurian crinoid.

Richard Owen, *The Anatomy of Vertebrates*, 2 vols. (London: Longmans, Green, and Co., 1866): condor cloaca, artiodactyla and perissodactyla toes, pinnigrade feet.

F. A. Poucet, *The Architecture of God* (Portland, Me.: H. Hallett & Co., n.d.): stamen and pistil, head and proboscis of butterfly, nidus, ichneumon larvae, gnomes and ichthyosaurus.

Tenney, Sanborn and Abby, *Natural History of Animals* (N. Y.: Charles Scribner's Sons, 1866): argonaut, Amphioxus, jellyfish medusa, dextral and sinistral openings, garden snail Helix, ichneumon wasp, British nudibranches.

Rudolph Wagner, *Icones Zootomicae. Handatlas zur Vergleichchenden Anatomie* (Leipsig: Leopold Voss, 1841): African chaemeleon, acetabulum of pelvis.

Chaucer's doctour reproduced with permission by Huntington Library. Those medical books for which captions do not indicate sources are:

T. H. Huxley, *Lessons in Elementary Physiology* (London: Macmillan and Co., 1881): labyrinth of ear, spinal cord neuroglia cell, chiasma, diastole and systole, villi.

Johannes Ranke, *Der Mensch* (Leipzig: Verlag des Bibliographischen Institus, 1887): Darwin's tubercle, clavicle of ape, uterine structures, fibula and tibia of ape leg, zygomatic arch of gorilla, cochlea, sacral bone, helix of ear, brachiating ape, arm, leg, skull, hirsute family, tragus of ear.

Robert Todd, *The Cyclopaedia of Anatomy and Physiology*, 4 vols. (London: Longman, 1835–52): atlas first cervical vertebra, Gorgonia, hyoid bone, calculi.

These works supplied illustrations on physiognomy and phrenology:

O. S. and L. N. Fowler, *New Illustrated Self-Instructor in Phrenology and Physiology* (New York: Fowler and Wells), 1859: phrenological signs (e.g., malefactor).

Annie Oppenheim, *The Face and How to Read It* (London: F. L. Ballin, n. d.): physiognomic signs (e.g., stupid eye).

Cesaere Lombroso, *L'homme criminale* (Paris: Bailliere, 1887) and *Atlas* (Rome: Bocca, 1888): criminal faces.

Ford Mathis drew these pictures for *Biolexicon:* Atlas bone, sea mouse Aphrodite, Priapulus, nymphon, caduceus, mudfish Lepidosiren, miter and mitral valve, tunica layers, Euglena, Leewenhoek's microscope, bones of inner ear, Trypanosoma, membranes of brain, aneurysm, planes, Peripatus, double helix, coeloms, the cell, spine, eye, ear, hair follicle, endocrine glands.

The two cartoons by Gary Larson are "Hey, what's this Drosophila melanogaster doing in my soup?" (p. 132) from *The Far Side* (Copyright 1985, Universal Press Syndicate. Reprinted by permission. All rights reserved); and "Lupislidophobia" (p. 333) (Copyright Chronicle Features, San Francisco, Ca. Reprinted by permission).

Passages from *Dorland's Medical Dictionary* are quoted by permission, W. B. Saunders Co., Philadelphia, Pa.

INDEX

Asterisk indicates that prefix undergoes assimilation.

A

a(n)-, not, lacking 60, 110
ab-, a-, abs-, away from 116
abdomin, stomach 267
ac(m), tip 116
acanth, thorn, hook 97, 288
acar, mite 55
acetabul, hipbone socket 71
acou, to hear 212
acr, tip, top, extremity 116
actin, ray, radiation 88
acu, needle, sharp 75
ad-*, toward 116
-ad, toward 144
aden, gland 112
adip, fat 272
ager, agr, field, land 93
agog, leading to, producing 220
agra, pain, seizure 241, 295
-al, pertaining to 143
al, wing 240
al, to nourish 207
albi, white 129
alg, pain 241, 295
all, other, foreign 190
alopec, mange, baldness 287
alpha, Gk. letter, first 103
alveol, cavity, sac 94
ambi-, both, around 116
ambul, to walk 122
amni, embryonic membrane 70, 275
amphi-, both, around 116
ampulli, flask, dilation 70
amygdal, almond, tonsil, brain area 97, 253
an(n), ring, anus 82
ana-, up, again, throughout, intensively 111

-ance, action 142
ancyl, ankyl, adhering, stiff, elbow 240, 299
andr, male, stamen 9
-aneus, of, pertaining to 143
angi, blood vessel 77
anima, spirit, life, animal 173
ante-, before 107, 116
antho, flower 96
anthrop, human being 22
anti-, anth-, against 60, 110
antr, cave, cavity, sinus 94
apex, apic, tip, extremity 117
(h)aph, ap, to touch, fasten, grasp 215
aphrodisi, sexual desire 41
apo-, aph-, away from 111
-ar, pertaining to 143
arachn, spider, web 58, 140
arche, archi, early, first, primitive 107
argenti, silver 129
-arium, -ary, place for 142
arteri, artery 269
arthr, joint 239
-ase, an enzyme 144
aster, astr, star 139
atax, incoordination 167
-ate, function as, do 144
-ate, a salt 144
atelo, incomplete development 120
ater, atr, black 131
ather, fatty deposit, plaque 72
atri, auricle 65
audi, aus, to listen to, hearing 212
aur, ear 212
aur, gold 130, 212
aux, to increase 205
avi, bird 50, 182, 275

B

bac, rod-shaped bacteria 85
bas, base 325
bathy-, deep 119
bene-, good, well 108
beta, Gk. letter, second 103
bi-, bin-, bis-, two, twice 133
bi, life 201
bili, bile 313
blast, bud, embryonic cell 96, 197
-ble, able to 143
blephar, eyelid 256
bol, throwing, growth 113
brachi, upper arm 239
brachy-, short 109
brady-, slow 107
branchi, gill 177
brevi-, short 109
bry, to swell 206
bucc, cheek, mouth 259
-bulum, instrument 142
burs, sac 77

C

cac-, bad, disordered 109
cade, cas, cid, to fall 125, 226
caec, cec, blind tube 56
calc, stone, calcium 162
calli, beautiful 312
calv, skull, bald 250, 282
calyx, cup 71
Cambrian, first Paleozoic period 158
can, dog 99
cancer, crab, cancer 99
cap(it), head 101, 249
carcin, crab, cancer 98
cardi, heart 267
carni, meat, flesh 279
carp, wrist 241
carp, fruit, seed 241
cartilag, cartilage 270
cas, to fall, see **cade**
cata-, cath-, down, disordered 111
caud, tail 237
ced, cess, to go, movement 125, 251
cele, swelling, hernia 296
cell, cell 73

cen, caen, recent 160
cen, empty 160
cenosis, an emptying 160
centesis, puncture of 304
cent, one hundred 134
cep, head, see **cap(it)**
cephal, head 113, 249
cept, to seize 216
cer, wax 273
cer(at), horn, cornea 250
cere, brain 252
cern, to separate, secretion 317
cervix, cervic, neck 262
cess, to go, see **ced**
ceta, whale 183
chaet, chet, hair 288
che, chy, chym, chyl, to pour, juice 298
cheil, chil, lip 259
cheir, chir, hand 241
chel, claw 177
chi, Greek letter X 103
chiasma, chiast, crossed, decussation 103
chimera, hybrid 47
chit, tunic 80
chlor, green 131
choan, funnel, collar 72, 298
chol(e), bile, anger 313
chondr, cartilage 181, 270
chord, sinew, cord 74, 180
chroia, skin color 133
chrom(at), color, pigment 128
chron, time 106
chrysa, gold 129
chyl, to pour, juice, see **che**
cid, cis, to cut, kill 125, 226
cid, to fall, see **cade**
cili, eyelid, hairlike 285
cip, head, see **cap(it)**
cine, to move 218
cing, band, girdle 82, 253
circ, tail 238
circum-, around 117
cirrh, orange 130
clad, clon, twig 97, 171
clasis, breaking 305
class, class 166
clast, instrument for breaking 305
cl(a)ud, claus, clus, to shut, a closing 66, 222
clavi, collarbone 66, 222

-cle, small 141

clei(st), to close, sheathe 221

clin, to bend, lie down 125

cloaca, excretory and reproductive duct 66

clon, replication, see **clad**

clysis, to wash, wash out 303

clyster, instrument for washing out 303

cocc, berry, berry-shaped bacterium 97

coccyx, coccyg, tail bone 98

cochlea, spiral 98

coct, to cook 69

coel(om), cel, cavity, gut, hollow 176, 268

cole, living in 65

colp, vagina 274

con-*, with, intensively 108

condyl, knuckle, knob, joint 101, 242

coni, dust 164

contra-, against 111

copr, feces 141

corac, raven 99

cori, skin 280

corn, horn, hardened 250

coron, coroll, crown 83

corp, body 234

cortex, cortic, outer layer 96

costa, rib 101, 236

cotyl, socket, cup 70

crani, skull 250

cras, temperament 317

creat, flesh 279

cresc, cre(t), increase, grow 204

cret, separate, see **cern**

crin, separate, see **cern**

crust, shell 177

cry(m), ice-cold 219

crypt, hidden 232

cten, comb 82, 284

cuba(t), cumb, cubit, to lie down, elbow 124

-cule, -culus, small, see **cle**

cult, culture, cultivate 65, 302

cusp(id), point, bump 75

cuss, shake 304

cut, skin 193, 280

cy, be pregnant 206

cyan, blue 131

cyesis, pregnancy 206

cycl, circle, cycle 57

cyst, sac, bladder 207

cyt, cell 76, 133, 197

D

dacry, tear 318

dactyl, fingers, toes, digits 241

de-, down, off, away from 117

deca-, ten 134

delta, Gk. letter D, delta-shaped 103

demon, devilish spirit 48

dendr, tree, tree-like 97, 325

dent, tooth 260

derma(t), skin 133, 280

dextr-, right side 117

di-, two 133

dia-, through, across, separate 117

didym, twin, testis, fetal monster 275, 300

digit, finger, toe, number 241

dilat, dilate 110

diplo-, double 192

dis-, dif-, di-, separation, apart, removed from 111

dist, far from 117

dolich-, long 109

dorm, sleep 45

drom, a course 291

duc(t), to lead, a conduit 123

duo-, two 137

dys-, difficult, disordered 109

E

(h)e(n), to send, release 217

ech, to sound, an echo 60

echin, hedgehog, spiny 48, 288

ec(t), ex-, out from, outside 117

ec, ecium, site of 64

ectasis, stretching, dilation 217, 304

-ectomy, excision of 60, 226

ed, es, to eat, corpulence 213, 296

edema(t), swelling 296

(h)em, blood 133

emesis, emptying, vomiting 297

en-*, in, very 118

end-, ent-, in, within 118

-ence, action 142

encephal, brain 114

end-, ent-, within 118

enter, digestive tract 220

eo, dawn, rosy 40, 160

epi-, eph-, on, upon 118, 120

equi-, equal 108
-er, operator, one who 142
erg, energy, work 221
eros, erot, love, sexual desire 41
erythr, red, red blood cell 130
-escence, -escent, beginning, act and state of
        132
es-, in, within 118
esthe(s), feeling, sense 209, 311
estr, receptive sexual period 98
ethm, sieve 72
eti, source of, origin 27
eu-, good, well, normal 108
eury-, wide 109
ex-, e-, ef-, out of 118

F

faci, fici, face, surface 253
fasci, band 76, 270
fauna, animal population 50
fenestra, opening 63
fer, carry 205
ferous, bearing 205
fibr, fiber 74
fibula, a leg bone 82
fige, fix, to fasten 304
fil, thread, filament 74
fiss, fid, to cleave, a splitting 226
fistul, duct 66
flagell, whip, appendage 84
flav, yellow 130, 315
flecte, flex, to bend, a turning 148
flocc, tuft 286
flor(a), flos, flower 50
flu, fluct, flux, to flow, a flowing 297
foramen, window, opening 66
form, ant 131
fossa, cavity, ditch 92, 153
frag, fract, to break, a breaking 297
frons, front, front 118, 251
fug, to flee 122
fund, fus, to pour, a melding 298
furc, fork, separate, branch out 96
fusc, dark, dusky 131
-fy, to carry, do 205

G

gala(ct), milk, galaxy 102
gam, marriage, union 190
gamet, germ cell 190
gamma, 3rd letter of Gk. alphabet 103
gangli, mass of nerve tissue or hard swelling
        296
gastr, belly 268
ge, earth 161
gemma, bud 96
gen, kind, family, birth 187
gen, geny, jaw, cheek 259
geni, chin 258
genesis, birth, origin of, see gen
genu, knee, kneelike 244
genic, producing, produced by, see gen
germ, sprout, seed, see gen
ger, gest, to bear, a carrying 206
giga, billionth 137
glabr, smooth, bald 281
glauc, bluish-green to gray 131
glc, gli, glu, glue 75
glob, glom, globe, mass 75
gloss, glott, tongue, language 260
glut, buttock 75, 278
glyc, sugar 133
gn, birth, see gen
gnath, jaw 113
gno(s), to know 231
gnom, to judge 230, 309
gon, generation, seed, see gen
gon, angle, knee, joint, see genu
gonium, place for birth, see gen
grad, gress, to walk, go 171
graph, gram, to write, a record 230
gusta(t), to taste 213
gymn, naked 282
gyn(ec), woman, pistil 10
gyr, spiral, ring 82

H

hal, salt 214
hect-, hundred 134
heli, sun 40
helix, helic, spiral 146
helmint(h), intestinal worm 176
hem(at), em, blood 133

hemer, day 106
hemi-, half, partially 134
hepat, liver 268
hepta-, six 134
her, hes, to adhere, an adhesion 298
heter-, other 111
hexa-, seven 134
hier, sacrum 102
hipp, horse 99, 252
hist(i), tissue, see sta
hol, whole 160
homo-, same 13, 108
homo, homin, human being 13
humor, bodily fluid 313
horm, hormone 318
hydr, water 161
hydra, hydra 48
hygr, moist 313
hyl, wood, matter 152
hymen, hymen, membrane 43
hyoid, like Gk. letter upsilon, U-shaped 103
hyper-, over, above, excessive 60, 110
hypn, sleep, hypnotize 45
hyp-, under, below, deficiency in 60, 110
hyster, womb, hysteria 274, 309

I

iatr, to heal, healer 302
-ia, condition 61, 143
-iac, -ian, one who 142
-iasis, morbid condition 60, 132
-ic, pertaining to, state of, that which 61, 142
-ics, science of 139
ichn, footprint 141
ichthy, fish 140
-id, of the family of 54, 142
-id, place for, state of 142
-id(e), a compound 144
ide(a), idea 212
ide, idi, self 212
-il, -illa, small 141
-ile, able to 143
ile, ileum, part of small intestine 56
ili, ilium, flank 56
in-*, in, into, not, very 111, 118
-in, a substance 144
incus, incud, anvil, bone of ear 87
-ine, pertaining to, like, belonging to 142

infra-, beneath 118
inter-, between 118
intra-, intro-, within 118
intus-, within 118
-ion, action 142
iris, irid, iris 40
is, equal, same 108
-ism, belief in, condition of 61, 143
-ist, one who 142
i(t), to go 122
-ite, belonging to 142
-ite, a salt 144
-itis, inflammation of 61, 295
-ity, condition of 143
-ium, place for, instrument, small 140
-ive, pertaining to, tendency 144
-ize, to make into, impose quality of, practice, become 144

J

jejun, section of digestive tract 56, 269
jug, to join, a yoke or juncture 191
juxta-, beside, near to 118

K

kary, cary, nucleus 96, 195
ken, cen, empty 160
ker, cer, horn, cornea 250, 298
ker, cer, wax 273
kerosis, hardening 298
kil, thousand 134
kinesi, cine, to move, movement 218

L

labi, labr, lip 259
lact, milk 101
lacr, tear 251, 318
lag, rabbit 99
lagn, sexual excitement 328
lal, to talk, babble 28
lambda, shaped like Gk. L 103
lamin, lamell, layer, plate 70
lang, lingu, language, tongue 260
lapar, flank, abdomen 268
lapis, stone 162
larynx, laryng, voice organ 262

lat, carry, bear, see fer
lat, wide, broad 110
lati, side 118, 268
lecith, egg yolk 275
lei, smooth 281
lens, lent, bean, lens 95
-lent, full of, pertaining to 143
lep, lepsy, to seize, seizure 61, 329
lepid, lepr, scale 289
lept-, thin, narrow 110, 289
leth, drowsy, fatal 44
leuc, leuk, white, white blood cell 129
lev, left 118
lex, to speak, word, reading 229
lien, spleen 269
lig(at), to tie, bind 270
limb, border 66
lip(ar), fat 273
lith, stone 163
littor, sea shore 161
log, logy, word, study of 60, 139, 229
long-, long 110
lumb, lower back 268
lumen, lumin, opening, light 66
lute, yellow 130
ly, lysis, to break up, a loosening 304
lymph, a body fluid 53

M

-m(a), action 143
macr-, large, long 110
macul, stain 132
magni-, great 110
mal-, bad, diseased 108
mal, upper jaw, cheek 251, 259
malac, soft 296
mall, hammer 87, 256
mamma, breast 182, 273
mand, lower jaw bone 251
man, obsession, madness 60, 327
mar, sea 161
marsup, pouch 77
mast, breast 101, 273
mastig, whiplike appendage 84
meat, opening, passage 66
med, healing 57
medulla, marrow 253, 270
medusa, jellyfish 48

mega(l)-, very large, very long 110, 296
mei-, mio-, less 110
mel, limb 300
melan, black 131, 313
mens, month 223
mens, ment, mind 223
ment, chin 258
-ment, action, agent, instrument 142
mer, segment, part 235
mes-, middle, moderate 107, 118
meta-, meth-, above, change, after 118
metr, womb 274
micr-, small 110
mill-, one thousand 134
mit, thread, thread-like 74
miss, sending 217
mne, to remember, memory 39
moll, soft 179
mon-, single 134
morph, form, shape 44
mort, death 46
mot, to move 121
multi-, many 110
musca, fly 98
mus, mur, mouse, muscle 98, 265
muta(t), change 148, 201
my(s), mouse, muscle 98, 265
myc(et), fungus 127
myel, marrow 269
myria, a great many 137
myx, slime, mold, mucus 127

N

nan, dwarf, billionth 137
nar, nas, nose 251, 257
narc, drug, stupor 45
nat(i), to be born, see gen
necr, death 46
nemat, thread, worm 74
nephr, kidney 269
nerv, nerve 271
neur, nerve 271
nid, nest 99
niger, nigr, black 131
no, nous, mind, mental activity 223
noct, night 107
nom, law, arrangement of 167
nom, name 168

non-, not 111
non-, nine 134
nos, disease 189, 258
nuc, nucleus 96, 195
nud, nude 281
nulli, nothing 137
nutri, sustenance 207
nyc(t), night 106
nym, name 168
nymph, pupa, labial tissue 52

O

ob-*, against, back 111, 118
oct-, eight 134
ocul, eye 255
od, way 91
odont, teeth 260
odyn, pain 213
-oid, like 143
-ol, alcohol, phenol 144
ol, emit a smell 218
-ole, -olus, small 142
olig-, few 110
om, shoulder 263
oma, growth, tumor 133, 296
omal, even, level 108
omega, end, last letter of Gk. alphabet 103
omni-, all 110
omphal, navel 264
onc, tumor 296
onych, nail 242
oo, egg 275
op, ops, opt, to see, vision 256
ophid, ophiuro, snake 180
ophthalm, eye 256
opistho-, behind 118
-or, one who, that which 142
or, os, mouth 259
orch(e), orchi, testes, orchid 101, 275
ord, order, arrangement 172, 238
orex, appetite 328
organ, instrument, organ 87, 221
orig, ort, origin 200
-orium, -ory, place for 142
ornith, bird 140
orth, straight, normal 108
-ose, full of, relating to 143
-ose, a sugar 144

-osis, abnormal condition of 60, 132, 294
osm, impulse 219
osm, sense of smell 218
oss, bone 235
ost, orifice 66
oste, bone 235
ot, ear 256
our, tail 277
-ous, full of, pertaining to 143
ov, egg 101
oxy, sharp, pointed, acid 325

P

pachy-, thick 110
pagus, fetal monster 300
palat, palate 251
pale, old 140
palp, to touch, feel 215
pan(t), all 51, 110, 118
para-, near, beyond, resembling, disordered 109, 111
par(t), to give birth 6
parie, wall 66
patell, kneecap 70, 244
path, feeling, disease, treatment 209, 291
pecten, pectin, comb 82, 284
pector, chest 263
ped, paid, child 42, 341
ped, pet, pus, pod, foot 245
pedicul, louse, stem 245
pel, to push, throbe, a pulsing 217
pelag, deep sea 161
pell, skin 280
pelv, pelvis 71, 237
pen, penis 276
pen, deficiency in 133, 299
penta-, five 134
pep, pept, to digest, digestion 69
per-, pel-, through, thoroughly 111, 118, 120
peri-, around 118
peron, fibula 82
pes, foot, see **ped**
pet, stalk, see **ped**
petri, stone 164
pexy, surgical fixation, attachment 304
pha, to speak, speech 227
pha, phan, phen, to appear, appearance 160
phac, phak, lens 95

phag, to eat, swallow 213
phalanx, phalang, finger, toe bone 91, 242
phall, penis 42, 276
pharmac, drug, medicine 141
pharynx, pharyng, throat 262
phas, phem, speech, see **pha**
pher, phor, to carry, a transporting 206
phil, love of, affinity for 324
phlac, protection 303
phleb, vein 269
phlegm, to burn, phlegm 313, 316
phob, abnormal fear of 60, 329
phac, lens 95
phon, voice, speech 227
phos, phot, light 160
phrag(m), phrac, enclose, block up 269
phron, phren, to think, the mind, diaphragm
    224, 309
phthis, wasting away 299
phyl, ancestry, race, tribe 172
phylax, phylac, to protect, protection 303
phym, phyma(t), growth, swelling see **phyl**
phys(i), nature, growth, see **phyl**
phyt, growth, plant, see **phyl**
pil, hair 285
pinna(ti), feather 289
pin(e), pine, pineal 97
pith, ape 184
plac, flat 72
plan-, flat, level 108
plant, sole of foot ((22-5))
plas, plast, to form, formed 196
plasty, surgical renovation of 196, 304
platy-, flat 108
plec, pleg, plex, to strike, stroke 296
plegia, paralysis 296
pleur, rib, side 236, 268
pli-, ple(i)-, pleo-, more 110
plica(t), ple, to fold 192
-ploid, folded 192
pluma, feather 290
pnea, breathing 29
pneum(at), air, gas 29
pneumon, lung 29
pod, foot, see **ped**
poie, to make, produce 302
poiesis, production of 302
pogon, beard 286
poikil, mottled, irregular 132, 299

poli, gray 131
poly-, many 110
pons, bridge 94
por, pore 174
porphyr, purple 130
porta(t), to carry, passageway 65
pos(it), to put, position 123
post-, after, behind 107, 118
pre-, before, in front of 118
preme, press, to press 217
primi-, first 134, 135
pro-, before, forward 107, 118
proct, anus 277
pros(th), in addition to, substitute for 110
prosop, face 254
prot-, first 134
proxim-, nearest 118
pruri, itch 217
pseud-, false 60, 109
psor, itch 217
psych, mind 53
pter, wing, feather 178, 240, 290
ptos, fall, droop 299
pub, pubic 284
pulm(on), lung 30
puls, throb, see **pel**
punge, punct, to puncture 305
pup, pupil, insect stage 101
pus, foot, see **ped**
pyel, basin, pelvis of kidney 71, 237
pyg, buttocks 278
pyle, gate, opening, passageway 65

Q

quadr-, quart-, four 134
quinque-, quint-, five 134

R

rachi, spine 235
rad, ras, to scrape, a scraping 305
ram, branch 96
rana, frog 99
re(d), back, again 111, 118
reg, rect, straight, rectum 277
ren, kidney 269
retro-, back, backward 118
rhin, nose 258

rhod, red 130
rhynch, snout 258
rose, rose 130
rostr, beak 258
rot, wheel 87
(r)rhag, abnormal discharge, rupture 297
(r)rhaph, suture, sew 75, 144, 304
(r)rhea, rheuma(t), to flow, stream 297
(r)rhex, rupture 297
(r)rhiza, root 96
ruber, rubr, red 130
rupt, break 297

S

sac(c), sac, pouch 78
sacch, sweet, sugar 214
sacr, vertebral section 102
sagitta, arrow 91
sal(t), to leap, a jump 152
salpinx, salping, anatomical duct 83
san, health 302
sangui(n), sangri, blood 313
sapr, putrid, decayed 299
sarc, flesh 279
satyr, male sexual obsession 51
saur, lizard 164
sax, rock 164
sci, to cut, know 225
scinde, sciss, to cut, split 225
schisis, to split, a cleft 224, 299
schiz, schist, to split, a cleft 224
scler, hard 298
scop, to look at 211
scrotum, sac holding testes 77
seb, grease, fat 72
sect, seg, to cut, a part 226
se(d)-, apart, away from 111
sed, sess, to sit, a settling 126
semi-, half, partially 134
sent, sent, to sense, a feeling 209
seps, sept, putrid, decayed, infection, see **sapr**
sept, partition 65
sept-, seven 134, 137
seta, bristle 288
sext, six 134
sicc, dry 220
sider, iron 164
sigma, Gk. letter, S- or C-shaped 103

sin, hollow, sinus 94
sinistr, left 118
siren, amphibian, marine mammal 57
sol, sun 40
soma(t), body 234
somni, sleep 45
spasm, spasm 295
spec, spic, look at, an examination 211
sperm(at), sperm 189
spher, sphere 253
sphinct, tight, muscular ring 215
spin, spine 97, 209
spir, to breathe, spirit 223
splen, spleen 269
spondyl, spine 236
spor, spore, seed 96
sta, ste, to stand, stop 169
stal, stol, to send, a constriction, see **sta**
stamen, stamin, thread, male organ of flower 74
staphyl, grape, uvula 97
stasis, a stoppage, control, see **sta**
stat, stand, stop, see **sta**
stear, steat, fat 273
sten, narrow 110, 299
stere, solid 273
steth, chest 263
stimul, goad, arouse 84
stom(at), mouth 259
-stomy, make an opening into 61, 259, 305
streph, stroph, strept, streps, strabs, strobe, strabo, to turn, a twisting 149
stria, groove, layer 93
string, strict, to draw tight 299
stru, struct, strum, to build, built up 303
styl, pillar, a support 65, see **sta**
sub-*, under 118
sulc, furrow, groove 93
super-, supra-, sur-, over, above, excessive 112, 118
sutur, seam 75, 251
syn-*, with, together, joined 108
syrinx, syring, cavity, duct 84

T

tabul, table 69
tachy-, fast 107
tact, tag, tang, to touch 215

tal, claw, ankle-bone 242
tars, flat, foot bone, eyelid tissue 79, 244
taut-, same 108
tax, order, arrangement, coordination 167
tel(e), completion, purpose 120
tele, at a distance 119
temp, time, skullbone 251
tend, tent, tens, to stretch, tendon 216, 270
terat, monster 299
terr, earth 161
terti-, third 134
test, shell 276
testi, male reproductive organ 100, 275
tetart-, fourth 134
tetra-, four 134
thalam, area of brain stem 73
than(at), death 46
theca, case 78
thel(e), nipple 274
thely, female 274
ther, beast 182
therap(eu), to treat, a healing 66, 100, 302
therm, heat, temperature 219
thesis, place, put 123
thorax, thorac, chest 263
thromb, blood clot 299
thym, gland in neck, mind, spirit 97, 101, 223
tibia, flute, shinbone 84
toc, childbirth 207
tom, tome, -tomy, cut, instrument for cutting, excision 60, 226, 305
ton, tone, stretching, tension 216
torque, tort, tors, to turn, a twisting 148
tox(i), poison 91
trach(e), windpipe 262
tract, to draw 304
trans-, tra-, across 119
trauma, injury, wound 299
trema(t), to bore, perforated, see trit
trep, trop, to turn, affinity for 149
tri-, three 134
trib, trips, to rub, grind, crush, see trit
tribe, instrument for crushing 306
trich, hair 285
tripsy, surgical crushing, see trit
trit, to abrade, rubbing away 305
troph, nourishment 206
trypan, a borer, hole, see trit

tuber, swelling 296
-tude, action 142
tum, to swell 205
tunic, covering of vessel or organism 80
turb, to stir 317
tympan, ear-drum 83

U

-ula, -ule, -ulus, -um, small 142
ultra-, above, excessive 112
umbil, navel ((217))
umbra, shadow 91
un-, one 133
-unc, hook, hookworm 89
ungu, nail, claw, hoof 242
upsilon, Gk. letter U, see hyoid
ur, urine, ureter 133, 276
ur, us, tail 277
uran, heavens, palate 38
-ure, action 143
uter, womb 274
uv, grape, palate lobe 97

V

vag, wander, vagus nerve 122
vagin, sheath 274
valv, valve 66
vas, vessel 77
ven, vein 269
vener, love, genital disease 40
ven(t), to come 121
ventr, belly 267
verb, foliage, see vert
verg, to bend, turn, see vert
vert, vers, to turn, a rolling out 146
vir(u), poison, virus ((161))
virid, green 131
vitr, glass 201
viv, vit, life 200
volv, volut, to roll, turn, see vert
vora, eat, consume 214
vors, vort, turn, see vert

X

xanth, yellow 129
xen, stranger 189

xer, dry 220
xyl, wood 153

Y

-y, condition of 61, 143

Z

zo, animal 201
zyg, yoke 93, 191
zym, enzyme, fermentation 69